ALEXANDER III

KING OF SCOTS

ALEXANDER III

King of Scots

MARION CAMPBELL

Acknowledgements

Plates
Plate I. Copyright: Dean and Chapter of Westminster.
Plates II, III, IX and X. Copyright: Royal Commisssion on the Ancient and
   Historical Monuments of Scotland.
Plates V, VI, VII and VIII. National Museum of Scotland

Other illustrations
1. Exers. of late F.S. MacKenna.
2. Bibliothèque Nationale de France
3, 4, 5, 8, 9, 10 and 11. British Library.
6. Crown Copyright: Royal Commisssion on the Ancient and Historical
   Monuments of Scotland.

British Library Cataloguing in Publication Data
A catalogue record of this book is available from the British Library

ISBN 1 899863 55 9

First published 1999
by House of Lochar

© Marion Campbell 1999

Typeset by XL Publishing Services, Tiverton
Printed in Great Britain
by SRP Ltd, Exeter
for House of Lochar
Isle of Colonsay, Argyll PA61 7YR

A.M.D.G.

ET

IN PIAM MEMORIAM

ALEXANDRI III[ii]

REGIS SCOTTORUM

ISTE QUI A SUIS

DICTUS ERAT

PACIS ZELATOR

To the greater glory of God

&

in pious memory of Alexander III

King of Scots

He who was called by his own people

the Zealot for Peace

ORKNEYS
(NORWEGIAN)
Durness
CAITHNESS
Stornoway
THE LONG ISLAND
SUTHERLAND
ROSS
SKYE
THE ROUGH BOUNDS
THE ISLES
BUCHAN
NORDREYS
SUDREYS
MAR
ATHOLL
ANGUS
MULL
Oban
IONA
STRATHEARN
Scone
Perth
ARGYLL
LENNOX
COLONSAY
FIFE
MENTEITH
THE
JURA
ISLAY
Kinghorn
Largs
DUNBAR
AND
KINTYRE
ARRAN
Ayr
RATHLIN
CARRICK
Annandale
THE GLENS
OF ANTRIM
SCOTLAND
ENGLAND
GALLOWAY
Alston
IRELAND
MAN
Stainmore
ISLE
OF
MAN

Map I Man and the Isles, showing Scotland's earldoms

CONTENTS

Genealogical Tables

Maps

Plates (between pages 146 and 147)

Illustrations in text

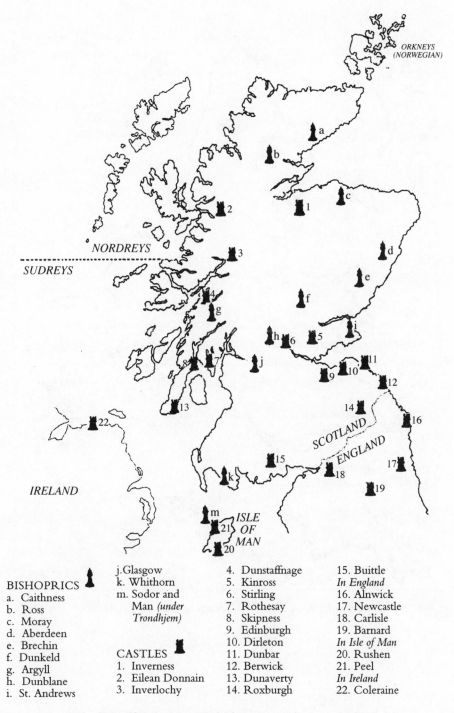

ORKNEYS
(NORWEGIAN)

NORDREYS

SUDREYS

SCOTLAND

ENGLAND

IRELAND

ISLE
OF
MAN

BISHOPRICS
a. Caithness
b. Ross
c. Moray
d. Aberdeen
e. Brechin
f. Dunkeld
g. Argyll
h. Dunblane
i. St. Andrews

j. Glasgow
k. Whithorn
m. Sodor and
   Man (under
   Trondhjem)

CASTLES
1. Inverness
2. Eilean Donnain
3. Inverlochy

4. Dunstaffnage
5. Kinross
6. Stirling
7. Rothesay
8. Skipness
9. Edinburgh
10. Dirleton
11. Dunbar
12. Berwick
13. Dunaverty
14. Roxburgh

15. Buittle
In England
16. Alnwick
17. Newcastle
18. Carlisle
19. Barnard
In Isle of Man
20. Rushen
21. Peel
In Ireland
22. Coleraine

Map II Scotland, showing bishoprics and some castles

Map III Alexander's holdings of land in England

INTRODUCTION

IN THIS AGE of specialisation it is a monstrous impertinence for an amateur to embark on historical biography. My excuse must be threefold, that there has been no recent study of King Alexander, that I have taken an interest in his life and times for forty and more years, and that I am writing, not for the professionals but for people like me who were taught little or nothing of their country's history in their schooldays.

I grew up between two sorts of history. There was the schoolbook kind, lists of the kings and queens of England and events from Magna Carta to the Corn Laws, into which intruded such irrelevancies as the battle of Flodden, the execution of Mary Queen of Scots, and the doings of a romantic incompetent called Bonnie Prince Charlie. Against that there was kitchen-history, for ever associated with the scent of baking, with Somerled landing his salmon before tackling the Norsemen, the Good Sir James Douglas, and the Prince (it was long before I connected him with the shortbread-tin 'Charlie'). From these ravelled materials I assembled an outline-notion of Scotland's past, always with the belief that before 'Bruce-and-Wallace' there was little besides Shakespeare's Macbeth.

In 1947 I began drafting a first children's novel about castles and ships; the plot called for a sea-fight, and hadn't there been something at Largs? I was quickly so horrified at my own ignorance that I got down to reading anything and everything about the thirteenth century; luckily that led me to Sir James Fergusson's *Alexander the Third*, a work of profound scholarship lightly handled.

For years I followed the trail, visiting surviving buildings, assembling family-trees. I began to hope, as the children's books mounted up, that some day I might produce a fuller study. When the first volume of *Regesta Regum Scottorum* appeared in 1960 I told myself it would be madness to proceed without the volumes for Alexander II and his son; in 1991 it became clear that I would not be around to write at all if I delayed much longer, so here I am.

Of course new material turns up all the time; of course the trained eye will readily detect my blunders; but at least I have carried Sir James's work a little forward (one of the last letters he wrote was to urge me to tackle the job). His *Alexander* is long out of print now, and there are reasons for a new study.

One reason is that most people know nothing of this medieval King of Scots, beyond the belief that 'he galloped over a cliff and broke his neck'.

Many who know that much would have to think hard to work out if he came before or after 'Bruce-and-Wallace'. Yet no other medieval reign is described as The Time of Peace, and it was Alexander's peace that laid the foundations of a national consciousness which upheld Sir William Wallace and the Wars of Independence. The thirteenth century throughout Europe was a turning-point in political and social development. What emerged as I wrote was a general study of a period but also a family history, in a time when a tiff between queens or a disputed legacy could affect the fate of nations; a time also when European nations took on recognisable characters and became more significant than their rulers of the hour.

Now that I have come to work up the notes of many years' gathering I find some references lacking, some sources forgotten; nor can I adequately thank all who have helped me. I can no longer reach the research libraries where a few hours' work would eliminate mistakes; I have used some 'popular' editions not because I am ignorant of better ones but because they are on a shelf within reach. I have resisted the temptation to turn the whole thing into a novel with imagined dialogue, but I have applied a novelist's reasoning to disentangle some puzzles (Chapter 9, for instance). I have tried to give fair weight to all possibilities and to mark where I have speculated beyond verifiable fact. For ease of reading I have used the modern forms of such names as *de Brus* and *de Moravia*, to the extent of emending some quotations. Different chanceries started their year at different points (at Christmas or the Feast of the Annunciation, at a king's accession-date or a legal term), and for convenience I have converted these, too, to modern usage.

Something must be said about primary sources. Most monastic houses kept an annual record of feast-days (especially the great Moveable Feasts, hinging upon Easter, but also those of particular interest to their own community), and where space allowed, might add a few words about last year's chief events. If the record lapsed it might be renewed by borrowing a neighbour-house's book. Our best contemporary Scottish source is the *Chronicle of Melrose* (1136–1264), superbly translated and edited (Bibliography, p.235). John of Fordun wrote his great *History* a century later, and was the first to travel widely in search of materials; his work was enlarged and revised soon afterwards by Walter Bower. The *Chronicle of Pluscarden* is later again, but contains a few nuggets which might derive from lost sources. Outside Scotland, the inspired observer was Dom Matthew Paris OSB, of St Albans Abbey, a chronicler, artist, goldsmith, and friend of Henry III (to the point that he was sometimes invited to sit on the steps of the throne to get an accurate report). His work was so popular that notables called at the abbey to discover what he was saying about them, so that he wisely kept more than one version of his text. When he died in 1259 he left an unfillable gap.

Very different is the *Chronicle of Lanercost*, a Franciscan compilation whose house of origin is debated, but must have been somewhere about Carlisle. It extends to the mid-fourteenth century, is careless about dates and sometimes wildly inaccurate, and collects moral anecdotes suitable for sermons; but one of several compilers had personal knowledge of Alexander's court.

I have drawn shamelessly on the goodwill and knowledge of many kind friends, to all of whom I am more grateful than I can express. Some, sadly, are no longer here to be thanked – Sir James Fergusson of Kilkerran, Bart., Professor J.D.Mackie, Dr J.S.Richardson, formerly HM Inspector of Ancient Monuments, Scotland, and R.B.K.Stevenson; all were generous with their knowledge. Mrs M.O. Anderson, Professor G.W.S. Barrow, Mr Stewart Cruden, Professor A.A.M.Duncan, Dr G.G.A. Simpson, are all due my sincerest thanks. I owe a special debt of gratitude to the staff of Argyll and Bute District Library Service, who have achieved wonders. All these did their best to educate me, and I can only hope they are not too ashamed of the errors remaining.

My thanks are due to Nicholas Holmes, both for Appendix E and for his help with illustrations; to Fionna Ashmore, Director of the Society of Antiquaries of Scotland, Neil Cameron, Gavin Atchison, and their colleagues in RCAHMS and the National Monuments Record of Scotland for choice of subjects and supply of photographs; to the National Museum of Scotland for photographs of coins and seals;to the Bibliothèque Nationale, the British Library, and English Heritage for other illustrations; to Dr Warwick Edwards and John Purser for guidance on the 1281 Marriage Hymn and to Joanna Gordon for research. Thanks also to my agent, Giles Gordon, to Richard Drew, and to all at House of Lochar, especially Georgina Hobhouse and Dilly Emslie.

If, despite the best efforts of all these kind people, blunders have slipped by, they are indeed all my own work.

Kilberry
May 1999

I

1249: In Western Seas

ON 8 JULY 1249 a concourse of little ships sailed up the west coast of Argyll. They were single-masted craft with a square sail, a tall stem- and stern-post, and from eight to twenty oars on either side. Some had a tiny cabin aft, most were open boats. A very few might have the newfangled stern rudder, far more used the traditional steering-oar on the starboard side. Normally they carried tradegoods and castle stores about the Clyde or to Ireland, under sail with a minimal crew; on the present voyage they were well manned, two at least to each oar, amid a crowd of landlubbers encumbered with heraldic finery. Some might be King's ships out of Ayr; most were provided by coastal landowners to carry the King of Scots to the fringes of his realm.[1]

Alexander II was making a sweep along his western frontier, the first in almost thirty years. In the 1220s he had marched overland into Argyll to overawe potential troublemakers and to reward loyal subjects. This time he came by sea, to meet his principal vassal, to take a closer look at islands he hoped to acquire, possibly to make pilgrimage to Iona if time and weather allowed.

Alexander had ruled Scotland since his sixteenth year. In youth he had been red-haired, like all his house. John of England called him a little fox-cub. Now, at fifty-one, he was growing grey and formidable. He had completed his father's work of welding Galloway and the far north into the fabric of Scotland, and now only two problems remained. One was the perennial minor friction with England (yet another joint commission on Border Law had just broken up); the other was this chain of islands among which he now sailed, islands his father's great-uncle Edgar had been forced to cede to Norway in a time of dynastic upheaval. The Kingdom of the Isles, indifferently controlled by Norway through sub-kings, was a haven for rebels, a seedbed for piracy. The obvious solution was to reclaim them, and Alexander had offered to buy rather than conquer; Haakon IV rejected his overtures with fury, and before another embassy could be sent, local events had turned tricky.

Firstly, the bishopric of Argyll had been vacant for seven years, since the last incumbent had accidentally drowned. The Norwegian Bishop of Sodor and Man, appointed by Pope Gregory IX to administer the see, had resigned

Table 1. Man and the Isles

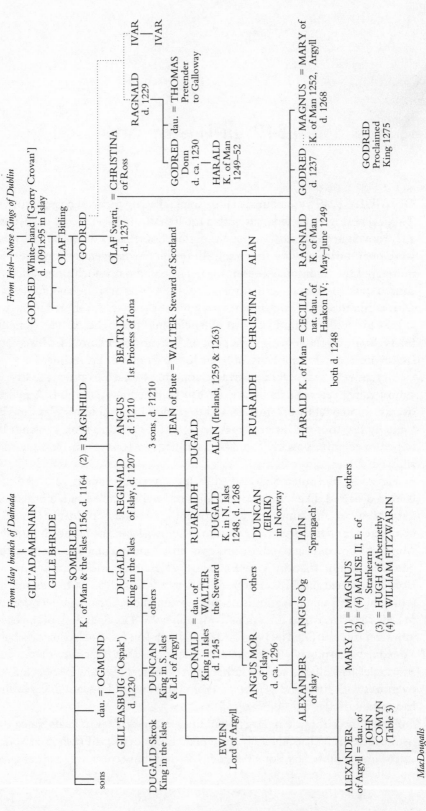

From Islay branch of Dalriada

From Irish–Norse Kings of Dublin

MacDougalls

the task and died, and Innocent IV then appointed the Scots bishop of Dunblane, an energetic Dominican with first-hand knowledge of the troubles attending long vacancies. Bishop Clement had at last found a suitable candidate; along the way he must have had useful contacts with the lay overlord, Ewen of Argyll, and so knew more than most royal counsellors about affairs in the west.[2]

Ewen – or, to give him his correct name for once, Eòghann mac Dhonnchaidh mhic Dhugaill – was himself the key to many problems. He was born to difficulties, for his father Duncan was both feudal Lord of Argyll under the Scots and *Regulus,* Sub-king, of part of the South Isles under Norway. He lived by balancing duties and administered a mixed population of conflicting loyalties.

Ewen succeeded his father between 1240 and 1248. In 1248 he learned that his cousins, Harald, King of Man, and Dugald, King of the North Isles, were going to Norway to do homage and obtain King Haakon's endorsement of their titles. Harald was fourteen when he came to his throne, twenty-five before he felt secure enough to visit Norway. Dugald was around Ewen's age and without ties to Scotland. There was intense rivalry between the descendants of Ewen's great-grandfather Somerled, and with the Kings of Man (whom Somerled had briefly dispossessed). It was advisable for Ewen to join the gathering, but before he could leave his mainland fief he needed Alexander's permission; probably he obtained it in person, early in 1248.[3]

Perhaps we should remind ourselves what feudal tenure involved. It had grown from ancient tribal custom, in essence a personal bargain between a warlord and his supporters, whereby they got a share of conquered territory in return for promising a quota of fighting-men in future. By the thirteenth century feudalism was a code covering every aspect of land-holding in many countries, all with local variations but maintaining the basis of an individual bargain, cancelled by the death of either party.

It could happen that a man might inherit or marry into lands beyond the original bargain. In that case the land his forbears had held longest had first claim on him. If he gave homage, his formal oath of contract, to a second lord, he should add 'Saving my duty to So-and-so'. Kings grew wary of accepting such qualified homage and tried to ensure their subjects were also their liegemen. Where loyalties conflicted, either lord or vassal might cancel their mutual oath by a declaration of 'defiance', literally 'un-faithing', and must do so before any overt breach.

To return to Ewen; he and the Scots would agree that his primary loyalty was to Alexander, for his ancestors were of the old Dalriadic line and had made their landfall on Islay when the King's ancestors founded their kingdom of Dalriada-in-Alba in the fifth century. Norsemen first settled the Isles some centuries later, while Dalriada was expanding eastward into Pictland. Kings of Norway had sent governors and tax-gatherers into the Isles with varying success since the days of Harald Fairhair, but from Somerled's time the islanders had managed their own affairs with little outside interference.

Whether Alexander bought the Isles or invaded them, he would have little joy of them without support from the 'Sons of Somerled'. Ewen may well have undertaken to see what he could do to persuade King Haakon to accept Alexander's offer, may even have proposed himself as future administrator of lands he already ruled.

Among the mass of archives removed by Edward I during the succession dispute and listed in a vast indenture of 1292, was

> a letter from the earls M of Fife, W of Mar, M of Asteles and ... others named, by which they bound themselves as sureties for *dominus* Eugenius of Argyll for the annual payment to the lord King of 320 marks for a certain *firma* of lands.[4]

Apart from a small tear after 'and' the document is clearly legible. The mark was a unit of account, not then a coin, and equalled two-thirds of £1, or 13/4d; the sum promised is £213 per annum. It has been called a 'heavy fine' for Ewen to 'buy his peace', perhaps for failure to come to the King; but *firma*, 'farm', is the sum due from an authorised collector, a business transaction outside the feudal system; the 'farmer' paid the agreed figure and kept any surplus for his trouble.

Ewen may well have backed a bid for office with an estimate of likely profits. His offer may have covered only his own islands – Mull, Coll, Tiree, Scarba and the northern half of Jura – or he may have proposed that with Scots backing he could take his cousin Angus's lands of Islay, Colonsay and south Jura. In later times the 'Old Extent' valuation of Islay and Colonsay amounted to 325 marks.

The guarantors have been identified as Malcolm of Fife (earl 1230–66), William of Mar (1243–81) and probably Malise II of Strathearn (1244–70), a known friend of Ewen's. 'M de Asteles' is impossible; between 1244 and 1266, the dates set by the other names, the earls of Atholl were John and David. A foreign clerk may be excused for omitting one alien earldom and one name. Norway knew that 'four jarls of Scotland' guaranteed Ewen's safety when summoned to meet the King of Scots.[5]

But if Ewen was bidding for office in 1248, next year he had graver preoccupations. It appeared to the Scots that he was getting out of hand. If the little fleet was not actually going to war, neither was it going to help Ewen. It probably mustered at Rothesay, under the rosy walls of the Steward's castle, the royal party joining from Dunbarton and the ships working through the Kyles of Bute to Tarbert. Here Magnus II of Norway had made his treaty with King Edgar's emissaries and had his longship dragged overland to demonstrate that Kintyre was an 'island', and here a permanent slideway across the isthmus allowed ships to avoid the dangerous passage round the Mull of Kintyre.[6]

Tarbert Castle was held of the crown by Dugald MacGilchrist, whose kinsmen – Lamonts, MacSweens, MacLachlans and others – held much of the surrounding countryside, tracing their descent from an eleventh-century prince of the Northern Úi Néill who settled in Knapdale and Cowal with Scots approval. He had been a welcome counterweight to Norse and Islesmen then, and his descendants were equally ready to help the Scots.[7]

The slideway between the lochs would be busy for some days. It is tempting to wonder if Alexander rode across, after a stay in the castle, or whether instead he sailed to Loch Gilp and rode to Crinan to rejoin the fleet, passing the rock of Dunadd where his remote ancestors had been enthroned. At all events by 7 July the ships were well to the northward. We may even catch a glimpse of them in *graffiti* at Kilchattan church on Luing, overlooking a sheltered anchorage. These show slender craft with figureheads of hounds or deer, lying at anchor or beached with a gangplank at the bows. Very probably the last night of the outward voyage was passed here in Shuna Sound, the King perhaps ashore in little Torsa, one of Ewen's many castles.[8]

A strong floodtide early next forenoon would carry them into the strait between Kerrera and the mainland. Here they landed again – perhaps only to prepare food, send messages ahead to the cathedral clergy in Lismore, take a look at an excellent anchorage and a potential site for a new cathedral (the Pope wanted it moved somewhere more accessible than Lismore). Or they expected to find Ewen waiting for them, almost on neutral ground – an island, but within a mainland parish.

At the bay called the Great Horseshoe the passengers landed and reached the field still called *Dail Righ*, King's Meadow. They looked around, glad to stretch their legs, turning from the red mainland bluffs to the brilliant greens of the island, the huge sweep of Oban bay and the old castle of Dunollie perched above the northern entrance. Dunollie was Ewen's too, but where was Ewen? His main centre, his *caput*, was Dunstaffnage, a few miles up the coast, but surely he would have had people on the lookout for the fleet which must have been heralded all up the seaboard?

This strolling about was pleasant enough, but they wanted to see a ship come driving through the farther narrows, or a troop of horse under the Macdougall banner cantering down the bay. They were anxious to get on to Lismore – Clement especially so – and besides, the King was far from well. The year before, the Queen and his physicians had persuaded him to ask the Pope for a dispensation from eating fish, which always made him ill, and the case they submitted was strong enough to earn him exemption even for Lent, when he might eat eggs and cheese instead. But what had he been offered at every halt on this voyage? Ask any Argyll housekeeper to plan a summer feast and she starts with salmon, lobster, trout, shellfish; and important visitors give mortal offence if they reject what is set before them.[9]

His companions were his closest associates; they could try to divert his mind, but they could not get away from the sticking-point. Where the devil was the wretched young man they'd come so far to meet?

Of course he was back from Norway, they knew that; he'd sent a request for military aid to hold his Argyll lands while he set off on some obscure sea venture. The King had replied briskly, mentioning the difficulty of serving two masters. The question of two masters was much in the thoughts of Scots lords with English connections; some of them had a burning interest in what happened to Ewen.

Besides Bishop Clement (traveller, linguist, graduate of Paris), there was Alexander the Steward of Scotland, Alan of Lundie the Doorward (Usher of the King's Chamber), the husband of the King's natural daughter, and old David Lindsay the Justiciar of Lothian. There were Robert Meyners and Walter Murray of Petty, Walter Bisset, the son of the King's half-sister, and William of Brechin whose father was the King's first cousin.

Clement's concern was with the bishopric. His own see had lain vacant for nearly ten years before he came to it, to find its revenues gone astray and the cathedral itself ready to collapse. He had at last got a bishop-elect ready to swear fealty and to be installed in the King's presence. He may well have wanted to arrive with a sign of royal favour in his hands; it would be he who suggested granting *ad mensam*, for the new bishop's household expenses, the church and parish of St. Brigid in Lorn which included Kerrera. It was a parish in Ewen's gift, and for his overlord to grant it away might threaten more loss to come. The idea pleased King Alexander, let clerks be summoned.[10]

They stand around the makeshift table, watching the clerk's pen fill up the strip of parchment with elegant script. All their names go down as witnesses, there is a bustle to heat wax and produce seals. The King turns away, sighs... and is suddenly on the ground at their feet.

While people call for a chair, a cushion, a cup of wine, young William of Brechin kneels to lift the grizzled head into his lap. Beside him Clement goes down on the thyme-scented turf; as he raises his crucifix he thinks fleetingly of a distant street, and a scuffling crowd parting before two young Dominicans to leave a man lying in the dust. The cross he holds now is not the plain cross of those days, but the words are the same for a groom knifed in a brawl or a king in a sunny meadow – and the look is the same, the profound astonishment fading into peace.

In the moment before Clement rises, while they stare and bless themselves and say 'Amen', they have moved into unprecedented crisis. Not since Malcolm III was killed in Northumberland a century and a half before has

Table 2. Scotland
From Dalriadic Kings of ca. 500 AD

Succ. 1043, d. 1040 DUNCAN = [? ETHELREDA] of Northumberland

INGIBORG = (1) MALCOLM III Ceann Mór (2) = MARGARET d. 1093   DONALD III Bán d. 1097   MAELMOIRE
of Orkney   Succ. 1058, d. 1093

BETHOC/BEATRIX = UCHTRED   MADADH, E. of ATHOLL

DUNCAN II d. 1094   MALCOLM   DONALD d. 1085

RICHARD = (1) HEXTILDA (2) = MALCOLM E. of ATHOLL
(Table 3)   of Allerdale

WILLIAM

MACWILLIAM CLAIMANTS

EDWARD d. 1093   EDMUND d. in religion   AETHELRED E. of FIFE d. post-1100   EDGAR d. 1107   ALEXANDER I d. 1124 = SIBYLLA Nat dau. of Henry I   DAVID I b. 1084, d. 1153 = (2) 1113 MAUD of Northumberland   EDITH (MATILDA) d. 1118 = Henry I of England (Table 5)   MARY = EUSTACE of Boulogne

CLARICE   HODIERNA   MALCOLM   Earl HENRY d. 1152 = ADA de Warenne d. 1178

CECILE = E. of Albemarle   Others

WILLIAM of Egremont d. 1156

MALCOLM IV The Maiden b. 1141, d. 1165   WILLIAM the Lion b. 1143, d. 1214 = 1186 ERMENGARDE de Beaumont d. 1233   DAVID E. of Huntingdon d. 1219 = MAUD of Chester   MARGARET d. 1201 = (1) CONAN IV of Brittany, (Table 4) (2) HUMPHREY de Bohun   MAUD

MALCOLM

ADA = PATRICK E. of Dunbar   ISABELLA = (1) ROBERT III Bruce (2) ROBERT   MARGARET = AUFRICA = Wm De Saye = EUSTACE de Vesei   ISABELLA = ROBERT II Bruce   MARGARET = ALAN of Galloway   ADA = HENRY HENRY of Hastngs Stirling   HENRY = yr. son of E. of Streathearn

ALEXANDER II b. 1198, d. 1249 = (1) 1221 JOANNA of England d. 1238 (2) 1239 MARIE de Coucy d. 1284   MARJORY 1235 = GILBERT Marshal E. of Pembroke   ? ALBINUS Bp. of Brechin   WILLIAM of Brechin

sons, d. in infancy   JOHN E. of Chester d. 1238

ROBERT HENRY WALTER de Ros

AGNES = JOHN Bisset

HUBERT 1221 = MARGARET de Burgh d. 1259 E. of Kent

ISABELLA 1223 = ROGER Bigod, E. of Norfolk

MEGGOTIA b. 1222, d. 1238

ALAN = MARJORY of Lundie   3 daughters

ERMENGARDE b. 1240?, ?1243

JOLETA de Dreux (2) = ALEXANDER III = (1) 1251 MARGARET of England d. 1275 = (2) ARTUS II (Table 4)   (2) JOHN de Brienne (Table 4)   b. 1241, d. 1286

MARGARET b. 1261, d. 1283 = (1) ERIK II of Norway   ALEXANDER b. 1264, d. 1284 = (1) 1282 MARGHERITAIN of Flanders (Table 6)   DAVID b. 1273, d. 1281

MARGARET 'Maid of Norway', Queen of Scots b. 1283, d. 1290

(2) RENAUD de Gueldres

a King of Scots died so far from the centres of power. The eight councillors scarcely know how to send news from here, only David Lindsay remembers much about the death of old King William and the accession of the man now lying where he fell. They know who his heir is, and it is small comfort, for never has a seven-year-old been the sole heir; seldom if ever has there been no choice for the Seven Earls to make. It is very much the way of this feudal kingdom to look back to pre-feudal custom, and by ancient custom a king's successor was chosen, by seven rulers of provinces (or so they all believe), from the unblemished adult males of the royal house, lawfully descended from a former king out to the fourth generation. This time there are no candidates, bastardy is as rigid a bar as the loss of hand or eye. Brechin has no thoughts of glory, nor any of the children of King William's plentiful love-children.[11]

They have lost a revered and beloved ruler, and with the throne vacant all laws are suspended, all lesser titles invalid. They must get back into Scotland as fast as possible, bring the new King to Scone – fetch the regalia – break the news to Queen Marie (dear saints, whose task is that?) – assemble bishops and earls and all the rest.... the Isles, the bishopric, the Lord of Argyll no longer matter.

The short summer night passes in grief and frantic planning. Ships are victualled and despatched as the tides serve, up Loch Linnhe to summon northern lords, back towards Tarbert. Messengers are landed to commandeer horses and ride to Loch Awe, there to be ferried onward. Forlorn groups meet around campfires, but neither then nor later is one question raised. When every lingering illness and most sudden deaths were confidently attributed to witchcraft or poison (or both), nobody suggests Alexander died from either. Chronicles mention 'a sudden fever', and a warning dream in which the King was threatened by three saints – Olaf of Norway, Magnus of Orkney, and Columba – against dealing unjustly, but nobody trots out the usual formula.

The King's grave is waiting at Melrose, where he enjoyed hearing the monks sing. Burial elsewhere is not an option, not even in Iona where so many kings lie, for Iona is in Ewen's realm.[12] The first plan is to escort the body reverently by ship to Ayr, but someone points out that all seas are perilous and where would they be if they lost his late majesty overboard? No, it must be by land, starting at first light; all the best horses are away, the corpse is too long for a single horseload, rigor has not passed off. Desperation sets in; when in the twentieth century the grave was opened, archaeologists found the bones in decent order but the femurs hacked through. They were practical men at Kerrera, and doubtless restored the decencies before they got to Melrose.[13]

Even as they set off, Ewen was hurrying homeward. Probably someone intercepted him in the Sound of Mull; ill news always travels fast.

At Bergen the year before, he had witnessed the marriage of Harald of Man to Haakon's daughter Cecilia, a wedding beset by ill omens. Matthew Paris, the chronicler of St. Albans abbey, making an official visit to Norwegian Benedictines, gives a graphic account of a thunderstorm in which the quayside palace, and the ship from which he himself had just disembarked, were destroyed by lightning; his first sight of King Haakon was as leader of the firefighters. That autumn the whole wedding-party were lost in Sumburgh Roost.[14]

Ewen and Dugald, new-made *reguli* (sub-kings) of the South and North Isles, were to attend Haakon to a confrontation with Sweden. When the Shetland tragedy became known Haakon appointed Ewen his viceroy in all the Isles including Man, promising ships when he could spare them. Ewen set off in the first ship of spring (ocean-going ships were all laid up before his voyage could be arranged), and sailed straight to Man, sending word to Alexander as he went. In Man he saw to the enthronement of Harald's brother Ragnald and, being a prudent man, took the youngest brother Magnus home with him. Magnus was still a boy, and after him Ewen himself was next heir to Man by descent from a Manx princess. He sped back hoping Alexander understood the situation.

The Manx coronation was on 6 May; on 30 May King Ragnald was murdered and a bastard cousin took over. The news did not reach Ewen for a month, and by then he knew his plea for support had failed. In theory, a feudal tenant could call on his overlord to help defend his lands, but it was doubtful that he could expect help if he intended to operate outside his overlord's territory. Perhaps in face-to-face consultations something could be arranged, but the immediate need was to get Magnus to safety. Ewen took the child out to Lewis, where the Manx house had many supporters, and himself hurried back.

Distant chroniclers understandably found all this confusing. The Haakon's Saga says:

> King Alexander was very covetous of dominion in the Hebrides and summoned King Jon [Ewen] to meet him, but he would not until four jarls pledged their faith that he should go in truce from that meeting. The Scots king required King Jon to surrender Biarnaborg and three other castles held from King Haakon, and all his lands, promising him a much larger dominion within Scotland and his friendship. All pressed Jon to agree, but he would not break his oaths to King Haakon, and he went away and did not stop until he reached Lewis.

(Alexander's dream is then recounted):

> The King told his dream, and men begged him to turn back but he would

not, and later he fell ill and died. Then the Scots broke up the levy and conveyed the king's body up into Scotland.

From nearer the action the *Chronicle of Man* reports that, after the island *coup d'état*,

> Alexander King of Scots collected a numerous host of ships, wishing to make the kingdom of all the isles subject to himself. And when he arrived at the island called Kjarbarey he was seized with a fever and died.

At Melrose the abbey chronicler had spoken to those who brought the body:

> Alexander the renowned King was attacked by a serious infirmity while on his way to pacify the districts of Argyll, and he was conveyed to the islands [*sic*] of Kerrera, where after receiving the sacraments his happy soul was taken from this light.

Matthew Paris, keenly interested because he knew Alexander and had met Ewen in Norway, displays his considerable talents:

> Alexander King of Scots, a man wise and modest, after living many years in justice and peace, is said in his last years to have swerved from the path of justice, prompted by greed. Seeking an opportunity of oppression he laid a charge of treason against one of the noblest of his realm, Oenus of Argyll, a vigorous and very handsome knight, because he had done homage to the King of Norway for an island which his father had held of the same king and which lies between Scotland and Orkney. Oenus, fearing his threats, wrote that he would render all service due both to him and to the King of Norway. The King of Scots, still enraged, replied that no man could serve two masters, and having received the answer that one could well do so if the masters were not enemies, he prepared an army ... Oenus begged for a truce so that he could resign his Norwegian homage ... When the King refused, his perversity was apparent and he incurred the hostility of St Columba, who lies in these parts and is greatly honoured there, and of many nobles.
>
> The King therefore declared Oenus unfaithful and pursued him by ship to near Argyll, urged, as is said, by the vehement promptings of a certain indiscreet bishop of Strathearn, a friar of the Order of Preachers. Leaving his ship, before he could mount his horse, as if in retribution he was stricken by a sudden and mortal disease. And while wishing to disinherit an innocent man he unexpectedly breathed out with that ambition the breath of life, in the hands of his nobles.[15]

As soon as he learned of Alexander's death, Ewen knew he had lost all hope of Scots backing. True, he had not been deprived of his four best castles, but if he had surrendered them he might by now have four Scottish garrisons within call. One thing was sure, whoever else might hasten to Scone for the enthronement, Ewen could not leave his kingdom and viceregality to their own devices.

Chapter 1 Notes

1   The tides have been ascertained from local tidetables by reckoning the state of the moon from the Easter full moon (found by reversing the equation for 'determining the date of Easter' provided in *ES I*). A new moon and minor spring tides on 6/7 July gives a north-flowing stream off Luing by 0700 on 8th, failing around noon, but tides in the area are notoriously unpredictable under the influence of the Corryvreckan whirlpool.

2   The 'fox-cub' gibe was widely reported (M.Paris, *Chronica Majora* II, 641, qu. in SA, 332). Sodor = Sudreyar = South Isles, the Hebrides south of a line due west from Ardnamurchan, Nordreyar, North Isles, lies above this line to the Butt of Lewis. The use of 'Northern Isles' to mean Orkney and Shetland is recent; these formed no part of the Kingdom of Man and the Isles. Bishop William of Argyll was drowned in 1241; his 1249 successor was Bp Alan (? of Carrick), Watt, *Biog*, 4 . Bp.Clement, OP, *ibid*.99. He was probably the first Dominican to attain a bishopric anywhere in Europe.

3   For relationships of Kings of Man and Isles leaders see p.2

4   *APS* I; *NMssS*, I, LXXIV (facsimile), the tear cannot account for more than two letters.

5   I am aware of my temerity in proposing a different interpretation from Duncan & Brown, 'Argyll & the Isles in the Early Middle Ages', *PSAS XC* 192 *inf*. (where the earls are identified). The valuation figures come from a transcript of the 1751 Argyll Valuation Roll. 'Old Extent' is usually taken to refer to the reign of William the Lion, perhaps to a taxation for his ransom, (*RRS II*, 15); figures for the Isles must have been compiled after 1266 (see Chapter 16).

6   Tarbert (and Tarbat, Tarbet) denotes an isthmus where boats can be portaged. The Tarbert Lochfyne/West Loch crossing was routinely used before the Crinan Canal opened, and is still occasionally followed; cf *ES II*, 113, for Norse usage.

7   11th-c.Irish settlement, D.H.Sellar, 'Family Origins in Cowal and Knapdale', *Sc.Studies* 15, 121 *inf*. Tarbert Castle, RCAHMS *Argyll 1*, no. 316.

8   Kilchattan, RCAHMS, *Argyll 2*, no. 256; Torsa, *ib*. no.280.

9   *ES II*, 558, cites Theiner, *Vetera Monumenta* (1864), 49, no. 131, and Bliss, *Cal. Papal Regs*. (1893), i.243; 'constant eating of fish was so distasteful to him that he was ill almost the whole of Lent'.

10   The Kilbride (Lerags) charter is calendared, with witnesses, in *RMS* 1424–1513, no. 3136. Walter Bisset, whose mother was one of King William's bastards, had lately returned from exile to make his home in Arran, and died there in 1251; *CDS* I, *1836*.

11   See p.7.

12   Dalriadic and Scots kings to Duncan I, and also Duncan II, were buried in Iona. Malcolm III, while piously restoring a chapel ('St.Oran's') near these graves, prepared his own tomb in Dunfermline and the custom lapsed.

13   Personal information from the excavator, the late Dr.J.S. Richardson, HM Insp. of Ancient Mons. (Scotland). The page of the Melrose Chronicle which probably described the funeral is illegible (A.O. & M.O.Anderson, *CM* introduction).

14   Matthew Paris induced Henry III to send English masons to help rebuild the Haakonshalle, now restored again after the Norwegian Resistance blew up an ammunition ship at its quay. Cecilia was Haakon's natural daughter by Konga the Young. For M. Paris in Norway see *Chronicles of Matthew Paris*, tr. & ed. R. Vaughan (Alan Sutton, 1984), pp.125, 128 *inf*.

15   *ESII*, 555 *inf*, citing the Saga, *Chron.Man* and *CM*; SA 360, citing *Chr.Maj*.V.88–9. 'Jon'

for Gaelic Eòghann (now usually translated 'Hugh'). 'Biarnaborg' is probably Cairnburgh
Mor; the others might be Dun Chonnaill in the Garvellochs, Duart and/or Dunara on
Mull, and/or the lost 'Islaborg' perhaps in Tiree (see Fordun, *Annals*, X, 'the island Tyree,
where there is a very strong tower'); RCAHMS *Argyll 3*, nos. 335, 339, 340, 355 (but
cf. *ib*. p.189); and *Argyll 5*, no. 402 (Dun Chonnaill).Matthew Paris appears to mean
Stroma (*SA* 360), but perhaps intended Lismore – within the Isles but the see of a Scots
bishop. His grasp of Scots geography is shown by his map (*NMssS II*, Va) showing Arbroath
in Sutherland and Dingwall on the Clyde. At least he tried.

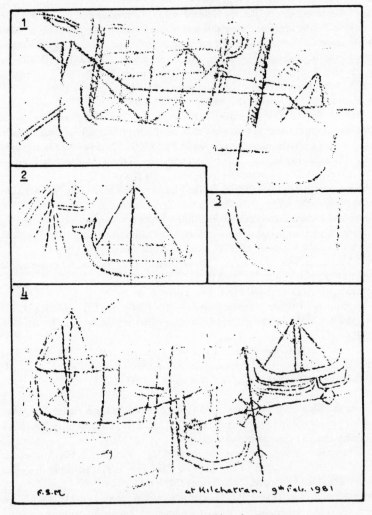

Graffiti at Kilchattan Church, Luing

2

1249: Vivat Rex!

THE LATE KING was twice married. He was betrothed in childhood to King John of England's eldest daughter, as part of a treaty which involved his two older sisters becoming hostages in England, supposedly as brides for John's (much younger) sons. The treaty failed to avert a savage invasion of Lothian in 1216, countered by Alexander capturing Carlisle and marching through England to join the Dauphin at Dover. Despite this contretemps he eventually married Joanna in 1221 in York Minster. She was then aged eleven, and had to be fetched from Gascony where she had lived from babyhood, betrothed to Hugh X de la Marche who held her hostage for an unpaid dowry; her mother Queen Isabella consoled the bridegroom by marrying him herself. (From that marriage sprang the tribe of Lusignans who exerted such influence on their half-brother Henry III from 1247).

Joanna was childless and unhappy; in 1235 she visited England with Alexander and remained there. Some contemporaries said she was forcibly detained, others that she chose to desert her duties. In 1238 she died in a Dorset nunnery, on which Henry lavished gifts, causing 'the effigy of a queen' to be carved for her tomb.

In May 1239 Alexander married Marie de Coucy, a French lady of royal descent whose father Enguerrand had briefly governed southern England for the Dauphin (and presumably met his future son-in-law at that time). Enguerrand was later invited to lead a revolt against the child Louis IX and his Spanish mother, but declined with the couplet:

> *Je suis ni roy, ni prince aussi,*
> *Je suis le Seigneur de Coucy !*

Henry III was paying him an annual fee up to 1230 (when finances permitted), in compensation for abandoning larger claims. It can hardly have pleased Henry to find his pensioner's daughter made Queen of Scots.[1]

There were at least two children, a short-lived girl named Ermengarde after her father's mother, and the boy, born in 1241. There is no record of where the Prince and his mother stayed while Alexander travelled westward; Kinghorn and Haddington were among the Queen's manors, Roxburgh a favourite royal castle, but Roxburgh is fully a hundred miles from Scone, and the astonishing thing is that news could reach the royal household, and the boy (and the regalia) could be got to Scone, within five days of that death on Kerrera. Carrier pigeons were used by the Saracens, but were notoriously vulnerable to falcons (and falconry was a widespread activity); moreover there is no evidence of their use in Scotland at the time. There must have been some very hard riding.[2]

Scone Abbey is neither the oldest nor the largest of Scottish religious houses. David I founded a priory there, replacing an older community in decay, and Malcolm IV made it an abbey. Its importance lay in a large flat-topped mound in its grounds, and a lump of rock in its guardianship.

The mound remains, labelled 'Moot Hill' on maps, or 'Boot Hill' from an absurd story that 'all the nobles of Scotland' came 'with their boots full of their own earth' to build it. In the earliest references it is *Collis Credulitatis*, the 'Hill of Trust'; the name may hide a reference to Credhé, an Irish spring-goddess ' for whom the cuckoo calls'.

In Irish, and thence Scotic, tradition the notional centre of a kingdom was fixed at some venerated spot close to the physical centre; Tara, with its prehistoric graves, is an example, Dunadd another, a prominent crag inhabited from earliest times which became a head-place for the Scots of Dalriada. As their realm spread, the *caput* moved until it reached Forteviot, a few miles southwest of Perth. The final move to Scone was involved with the delicately balanced accord between Scots and Picts, part treaty after conquest, part acknowledgement of an inherited claim to kingship. To hold ceremonies at a place already hallowed in Pictish tradition was a means of enforcing the accord (it leaves one wondering why an Irish goddess was venerated at a Pictish site in Christian times, but such oddities are often potent symbols).

Irish kings were elected by the leaders of their tribe from the unblemished adults of a royal kinship-group, the *rigdomna*, of males within four generations of any previous king. If the procedure caused a fairly high turnover in the job, and a tendency to lop the odd toe or finger off a rival, it also allowed the choice of a man fit to lead, in war or peace as need be. The Pictish system was more complicated; it was apparently confined to the sons of royal women. The 'Seven Earls of Scotland', whose task it was to elect the kings of the combined kingdom, derived from Pictish provincial governors, *Mormaers* descended from seven sons of Cruithne (the Gaelic word for 'Pict') named Fib, Fidach, Fodla, Fortren, Cait, Ce and Ciric – whence Fife, Moray, Atholl (Athfodla), Strathearn, Caithness, Mar and Angus (earlier Mearns, *Maghcircinn*).[3]

By the eleventh century the function of the Seven Earls was largely ritual, Malcolm II (died 1034) having declared that 'the child of one day' of the direct line was to take precedence. His ruling ensured the accession of his daughter's son Duncan I. In the confusion after the death of Duncan's son

Malcolm III, the earls distributed their support among the sons of Malcolm's two marriages and his own brother, during four years of civil war. Through the next century revolts flickered in Moray and Galloway in support of rejected branches of the *rigdomna*. When William the Lion died there were ten earls in Scotland, seven of whom attended his son's enthronement – a remarkably high count, given that the ceremony took place within forty-eight hours of the death, and in mid-winter. Alexander II created three more earldoms, Ross, Sutherland and Carrick, in areas where he had quenched insurrections. The author of *Haakon's Saga* may even have been correct in suggesting Ewen might have become Earl of Argyll.[4]

Only three earls are recorded at Alexander III's inauguration (others may have been there, of course). Whether the three could constitute a quorum, or indeed if they held a formal meeting, is not recorded. In any case there was no choice within the kinship. Irish tradition allowed a reserve category a step farther out, in necessity; but even that added no claimant. If female descent was accepted, as it had been for Duncan I, two foreigners and one native son were eligible; they were the earls of Brittany and Hereford, and Robert Bruce of Annandale.

Robert's mother was the daughter of King William's brother David, the Earl of Huntingdon. David was believed to have declined to challenge his nephew's accession; he was old and ill and his only lawful son was heir to a great English earldom. Fordun reports him meeting William's cortège at the bridge of Perth and briefly helping carry the bier, 'though not active in mind nor alert in body'. In 1291 Bruce would claim that Alexander II, 'despairing of an heir of his body', had nominated his cousin and caused the other magnates to swear fealty to him, duly enrolled 'in the state records'. The royal archives were catalogued towards the end of Alexander III's reign, but no such document was recorded. The nomination would anyway lapse at the birth of a prince, and there is no suggestion of a Bruce claim in 1249.[5]

The Melrose chronicler says the child was

> ... bequeathed the kingdom by his father, chosen by the magnates, placed upon his ancestral throne and honoured by all as rightful heir;

as precise a statement as one could wish, in the absence of 'Our Man in the Abbey' touches by a Matthew Paris. Malcolm IV, the youngest king hitherto, had been eleven and had already toured Scotland as his grandfather's chosen heir; but strangely enough, several thirteenth-century kings began their reigns very young – Louis IX and Haakon IV at twelve, Henry III at nine, the Emperor Frederick at three. Civil wars attended all these accessions; nobody could forget the text *Woe to the land whose king is a child*.[6]

On Tuesday 13 July the Prince has arrived, so have some nobles and bishops; others are coming in fast. Early sunlight draws mist from the meadows; the broad Tay slides past the abbey gardens. The air is full of the scent of mown grass and campfires, there are tents and horse-lines everywhere. A deep riding-ford and a ferryboat mark the meeting of Roman roads at the vanished grain-port of *Bertha*; along the ghosts of these roads, horsemen come cantering. Two miles downstream Perth has opened its gates and sent a stream of burgesses and indwellers pouring out, with foreign merchants, seamen, food-sellers, jugglers, cutpurses, all out to enjoy themselves. Some old people can recall the last enthronement, a cold Friday in December thirty-five years back. Him that's away, he was just a laddie of sixteen, and came from his father's wake; and a good king he proved to be. He was born so late in his father's life that they kept his birthday like a saint's feast, regarding him as a miraculous gift. The chroniclers catch the mood of the nation (seldom given to hero worship, perennially critical of any ruler) and record that he was *rex mitissimus*, the most good-natured king, who hated iniquity and loved righteousness; very just, longsuffering, kindly, who

> was a most gentle prince towards his people, comforter of the needy, helper of the fatherless, pitiful hearer and most righteous judge of the widow and all who had suffered wrong.[7]

These are more than conventional tributes. One acidulated scribe later digs out a nasty little tale of an Edinburgh burgess's widow, brought to penury by the castle victuallers and clinging to the King's rein as she entreats him to make them pay at least for her very last hen; he 'spurs away in shame', and she cries after him, 'May you have as much joy of your only son as I had of my poor bird with her neck thrawn yesterday!' (this to explain that son's death forty years later). It fits the narrator's world-view but runs counter to much evidence of thoughtful and modernising legislation (and strict oversight of royal officials). Among Alexander II's Acts were the abolition of trial by ordeal and the phasing out of trial by combat.[8]

Trade is flourishing, new markets have opened in the north, any English interference with shipping leads to swift protest and recovery. Everyone along the roads has something to praise. The nearer the Abbey, the greater the babel of tongues – Flemish, Gaelic, German, English, French, Scots. A group of young clerks crack jokes in Latin; there are the robes of every Order from Templars to Franciscans. Some pack into the church; those in the know make their way towards the great mound, and sit on the grass.

All our sources are at least a century late. Fordun lists three earls, the bishops of St Andrews and Dunkeld, Alan the Doorward 'and many other magnates' among those present. One might expect that those who had hastened to attend would hasten to complete the business, but instead, (according to Fordun), Alan himself made determined efforts to halt the whole ceremony.

He raised three objections; taken singly, each sounds like a frantic improvisation, together they amounted to something serious. He had been thinking
hard along the way from Kerrera. Firstly, he said, there had been no time to
invite English representatives, and such unseemly haste must displease King
Henry; secondly, the child was not yet a knight; thirdly, this was an unlucky
day.

His first point got short shrift. Everyone knew how long and carefully
English kings had sought to establish sovereignty over Scotland, and how
skilfully Alexander II had parried their claims; deferment now would virtually
admit English rights.

The knighthood question was important because Alan raised it. He was
himself reputed the best knight in Scotland, the Flower of Chivalry, and he
knew more of such matters than many of his hearers; maybe they should not
offer homage to an un-knighted king. Two answers were found; one from
a schoolman, that the greater must comprehend the less and so kingship
comprehends knighthood. While the audience worked that out, the Earl of
Menteith thumped down a more decisive response.

He had often heard, said Earl Walter (according to Fordun) of kings
enthroned before knighting, indeed 'he had himself seen a king consecrated
who was not yet a knight' (this cannot have been Henry III, who had two
coronations, in 1216 and 1220, but was knighted by the Old Marshal before
the first one). Louis IX perhaps? Or perhaps Fordun misread his source,
whatever it was, and Menteith had spoken of Malcolm IV nearly a century
back, whose fervent desire for knighthood led him to follow Henry II to
France, without his earls' approval, and brought him home to face rebellion.
Menteith may have known that William II of England had come to his throne
whilst still, notoriously, a squire at thirty-one; not the precedent one would
choose. Anyway, did the Flower of Chivalry propose to give himself the
honour of knighting this child – eh?

Someone hastily said the Archbishop of Canterbury had knighted William
Rufus during the ceremony, and might not the Bishop of St Andrews do
the same today? It was possible, though in recent times only kings had
knighted kings; Bower says this solution was adopted but he is probably
wrong, for Henry III was to knight Alexander two years later, and knighthood, like baptism, is not normally repeated.

That left the date. 13 July, St Silas's day, appears in some lists of the 'black'
or 'Egyptian' days on which the prudent avoid important business, but the
thirteenth of a month was not held unlucky – whatever one might think of
thirteen at table. The clearest objection is that it was the sixty-fifth anniversary of the capture of King William at Alnwick, an event which led to national
humiliation and the king's enforced homage to Henry II.

Alan might well reckon that any anti-English lord would accept delay sooner than proceed on such a day. But Menteith was ready:

> No day can be unlucky for deeds that depend on the free arbitrament of men;
> it would be base superstition to think so. It is otherwise in matters that depend
> on celestial influences, as sowing of seeds, taking physic, felling trees or blood-
> letting; then it is no superstition but wisdom and prudence.
>
> But a realm without a ruler is a ship without a helmsman. I greatly loved
> our king who is dead, and so shall I love his son, not only for his father's sake
> but because he is our natural and rightful lord. Let us therefore advance him
> to be our king as quickly as we may, for to delay what is ready always does
> harm.[9]

Fordun says the bishops, the Abbot of Scone, and all the clergy and people
with one voice gave assent and consent (he sees the whole edifying debate
taking place among the crowd). Nobody mentioned a point that would
weigh most with the majority of that crowd, that by Gaelic custom a Tuesday
is the best day to start anything.

Finally, the great men enter the church and the others settle down to wait.
They hear the chanting, they follow the order of the Mass, then there is a
sudden hush. Those nearest the doors can hear the Bishop of St Andrews
administer the accession oath, and a small voice following through the phrases.
The words are lost and there are disagreements as to whether it was taken
in Latin or in French. Bower says in both; but he may mean there was a
simultaneous translation for the benefit of the laity, or even for the oath-
taker whose Latin may not have been fluent.

After the oath came ordination, a laying-on of hands following the rite
used by St Columba at Aidan mac Gabhrain's enthronement in 572 AD. It
replaced unction in the Scottish ritual (although Alexander II had sought
papal approval for unction, later on).[10]

The chanting grew stronger, candles flickered in the doorway, out into
the sunshine came clergy and bishops, behind them a blaze of armorial
surcoats, and between the two, a space in which walked the small boy in his
white robe. The procession moved towards the mound, eastward of the
church, on which stood – a throne? Yes, possibly a throne, one with carrying-
staves, and under its seat a low roughly-shaped boulder. Or possibly there
was no throne, simply the boulder itself, shrouded in cloth-of-gold until the
moment when the procession reached it.

Fordun calls it a 'marble chair' and tells of its origin in Egypt, and how it
was lost, off Ireland, and miraculously recovered by an ancestor of the
Dalriadic kings; later legend makes it Jacob's pillow, later still it was reputed
to be Babylonian basalt. It was blessed in Ireland, by 'soothsayers' or by St
Patrick, with the promise that wherever it rested the race of Fergus would
reign. Accordingly they brought it to Scotland and bore it forward as the

kingdom advanced. Edward I, slightly mistaking the promise, had it carted to London in 1296 under the impression that he was subjugating the kingdom thereby. He had a new chair made to hold it – he wanted bronze, though after a glance at the estimates he settled for gilded wood – but he also sent troops to tear Scone Abbey apart, as if the trophy had not been quite what he expected. Doubts have continued ever since, but the prophecy remains, and from 1603 to the present, descendants of Fergus Mor mac Eirc have been enthroned upon the Stone.

The Earl of Fife took the child in his arms and seated him on the throne, or the Stone, whichever it was. The physical installation of a new king was Fife's hereditary duty, in right of which, in the absence both of the Stone and of a later pro-English Earl, his sister the Countess of Buchan would crown Robert I at this place in 1306, and pay dearly for it.

Now visibly King of Scots, the child received 'tokens of sovereignty'. These are not detailed; perhaps there were six, for the other senior earls. Seals and coins show a jewelled crown of four upright leaves, a sceptre with a leafy head, an orb with a tall cross, and a sword (possibly two swords; in the illuminated initial of Kelso Abbey's founding charter, David I has a huge sharp sword and Malcolm IV what might be the short sword of mercy called *curtana*). Almost certainly there was a mantle of royal purple, perhaps a ring or armlet.

Enthroned and endowed with emblems, the King must have his title proclaimed. A 'venerable highlander' came forward to bend his knee before the Stone and recite (Fordun says 'read') the royal pedigree, thus:

> *Beannaichte thu, Alasdair, mac Alasdair, mhic Uilleim, mhic Eanruig, mhic Dhaibhidh,*
> *mhic Mhaelcoluim, mhic Dhonnchaidh, mhic Beitris, nic Mhaelcoluim*

and so back to Fergus Mor and beyond him into the mists; 'blessed be thou, Alexander, son of Alexander son of William', and so forth. This was the Celtic side; the laying-on of hands, the Stone, and now the recital by the *Seannchaidh*, keeper of tribal memory, heir of Druids. He would have his hereditary holding nearby, where in each generation a son learned the lengthening catalogue of names; but after this day it would be heard no more.[11]

Most of the watching nobles could get the gist of the words, all knew they were necessary, but when the old man wrapped his red cloak around him and made 'a kind of grudging obeisance' (druids ranked above kings of old), it was time for more modern rituals.

The bishops got themselves into line and came to give fealty, touching the crown and vowing faithful council.[12] After them came earls, heads of royal religious foundations, and those barons who 'held of the Lion'. The laymen gave homage as well as fealty, kneeling to put their joined hands between the child's hands and swearing to be his men 'in life and limb and earthly service against all men'. Their lands were granted for that service, and with their oath they were safe in their possessions.

The line moved up the slope, stooping, kneeling, murmuring, moving down. The grass grew slippery, dust rose, background talk blotted out the voices of birds flighting to roost. Three days of feasting lay ahead, during which latecomers would turn up hoping for a quick word on some private matter; thereafter the King would ride into the south country to attend his father's funeral.

In the last couple of days he had seen his mother's grief and had been told, and gradually understood, that his father was dead. He had been rushed across country by grave elders whom he knew at most by sight, and who loaded him with advice and instructions as they rode. Now there was this endless line of bobbing heads, and what would happen next? Were we ever going to have supper? The women in the crowd, hushing fretful toddlers, whispered that it was high time the wee soul was away to his bed. The dignitaries, of whichever faction or alliance, asked themselves what on earth they had undertaken.

Chapter 2 Notes

1 Grant of Alexander's marriage to K. John, *CDS I, 508*('1211x12'). Marriage, *ib. 761–2, 786 inf.*; grants to Q. Joanna on return to England *ib. 1245, 1258, 1292, 1308–9*; to Tarrant (O.Cist.) and mortuary offerings, *ib. 1399, 1401, 1405* (6 March 1238, tombstone), to 1422 &c. Coucy family, p.33; Enguerrand's 'fee', *CDS I, 1072* (17 Jan. 1230, writ for £40). *ES II*, 417n(*Anns. Dunstable*).

2 The only trace of Ermengarde's short life is a gift of ¹/₂ stone of wax for a perpetual candle for her soul and those of the kindred of Alexander of Stirling, Constable of Roxburgh, d. 1244 (a nat. grandson of E. David); *Reg. Arbroath*,268, no. 309.In 1242 the Bp. of St Andrews authorised prayers for 'the K. and Q. and their children', *Stat.Sc.Ch.* 61.

3 Scone, OSA, App.C. 'Collis', *Chronicles of the Picts & Scots*, ed. W.F. Skene (Edinburgh 1867) 91, and *ES II* 224n (giving Reeves' proposed etymology). A private chapel now caps the mound. *Rigdomna* &c., J. Cameron, *Celtic Law* (Hodge, 1937). Pictish succession, M.O. Anderson, *Kings & Kingship in Early Scotland* (Sc.Acad.Press, 1973)164–8, 203, *Chron.P-S* ciii and no.XVII (*De Situ Albanie*). Mrs Anderson shows six of the seven provinces are cited by their Gaelic (not Pictish) names.

4 Scots royal line, p.7. Alexander II's new earls were Ross ca. 1225, Carrick 1225x30, Sutherland ca. 1235. Ewen's 'larger dominion', see p.9 above.

5 E. David's son John succ. his maternal uncle, the great Ranulf, as E. of Chester 1232, and died 1238. K. William's funeral, *Fordun* XXIX.Bruce claim; Barrow, *Bruce*, 57, (and *SHR LXIX*, 120)and Stones & Simpson, *Gt.Cause*, 144 *inf.* Grant alleged ca.1233 'when the K. was about to go to war in the Isles' (? the first Argyll expedition, ca.1221); i.e. while Q. Joanna was still in Scotland.

6 *CM* 108. Text, *Ecclesiastes* X,16.

7 Alex.II's birth, 24 Aug.1198, *Fordun Annales* XXIII. Obituaries, *ib.*XLVI, *Chron.Pluscarden* VII, XII. *APS I*, 1292 Indenture, cites an obligation by Coupar Abbey to erect and maintain a chapel on Kerrera, with three monks, using funds from Alexander II 'by the hands of …' No such building survives. The money was presumably for use wherever he

died.

8 *Chron.Lanercost* 49. Castle victuallers taking burgess goods without payment were brought before the burgh court (*BL I*,ch.102). For *Lanercost*, see p.xi above. A statute of ca.1230 substitutes jury trial for ordeal (condemned by the Fourth Lateran Council, 1215) and abolishes combat except as an option for knights brought before their overlord's court. Combat survived in the 1249 Laws of the March, where mutually acceptable juries were unlikely; *APS I*, and *cf* Ld. Cooper's Introduction to *Reg.Majestatem*.

9 *Fordun*, XLVII; *Chr. Bower*, II,81. 13 July is 'Egyptian' (accursed from the Plagues of Egypt) in the Holyrood Calendar, *PSAS LXIX*, 476 ('addition in 15th-c. hand'). William was captured in Northumberland on the day of Henry II's penance at Becket's tomb. (Note the Arbroath dedication to S. Thomas Becket, App.C).

10 For the whole ceremony, M.D. Legge, *PSAS LXXX*, 73 *inf.* See also Adomnan, *Columba*, 107–8 (tr. & ed. A.O. & M.O. Anderson, Nelson, 1961).

11 The Stone of Destiny is sometimes called 'Lia Fail' by confusion with the stone at Tara which 'cried out under a true king'. W. F. Skene, *PSAS VIII*, 68; Cruden, *Sc. Churches*, 91–2. An important article on Scottish thrones 1107–1296, by Dr.J.S. Richardson, appeared in *The Scotsman* of 17 Feb. 1951 (during the Stone's first absence from Westminster). Edward's chair cost £5; it remains at Westminster but the Stone is now back in Scotland. An imaginative drawing of the 'genealogist', from *Fordun* is reproduced in *PSAS LXXIX*, pl.14. Fordun extends the pedigree, in Gaelic and Latin, to Iber Scot, grandson of Pharaoh's daughter Scota.

12 Scottish royal grants to the Church were free of feudal obligation apart from *servicium scoticanum*, the general muster for defence. Bishops-elect gave fealty before their enthronement (cf. Chapter 1).

3

1250: The Sainted Ancestress

IT WAS customary for the chief clergy and the earls to meet in the King's presence three times a year, together with those lesser barons who held directly of the Crown. These meetings took place around Michaelmas in September, about Candlemas in February, and between Easter and Whitsunday; they were called *colloquia* (Latin) or *parlements* (French – the court speech, as Latin was that of official business). Throughout the year the King had an informal 'inner council', chosen from those who could readily attend him. Routine government lay with the Chancellor (whose writing-office, the *capella*, evolved from the royal chaplainry), with the Chamberlain, and one or more Justiciars.[1]

Those who got to Scone for the enthronement presumably held an emergency meeting if only to continue the existing administration. A new coinage and Great Seal must await the autumn *colloquium*. The child could remain with his mother for now; King Louis of France had lived under Queen Blanche's firm hand into his thirteenth year.

English archives preserve no intimation of Alexander II's death; it would have been interesting to know who signed the letter. Possibly, as in 1286, it was the Bishop of St Andrews.[2]

After the funeral the earls of Menteith and Buchan travelled westward. In late July they looked in at Bruce's baron-court before continuing into Galloway where Scots overlordship was a recent and uncertain thing. Both earls had held responsibilities there at times; Buchan's wife was a daughter of the Earl of Winchester, Constable of Scotland by marriage and nominal overlord of much of the province.[3]

Menteith and Buchan were half-brothers, sons of a former Justiciar made Earl of Buchan through his second marriage. The Comyn family had enjoyed royal favour for four generations, a little eclipsed recently by the Doorward. Menteith was the elder; he had been witnessing documents as far back as 1213. His inheritance was Badenoch, the mountainous area between Atholl and the Great Glen, his two elder brothers had died, and his earldom came, like his father's, by marriage. His sister was Countess of Ross.

Buchan was made earl on his mother's death. In 1249 he was around thirty. On the Annandale journey the earls were accompanied by Menteith's

Table 3. The Comyns

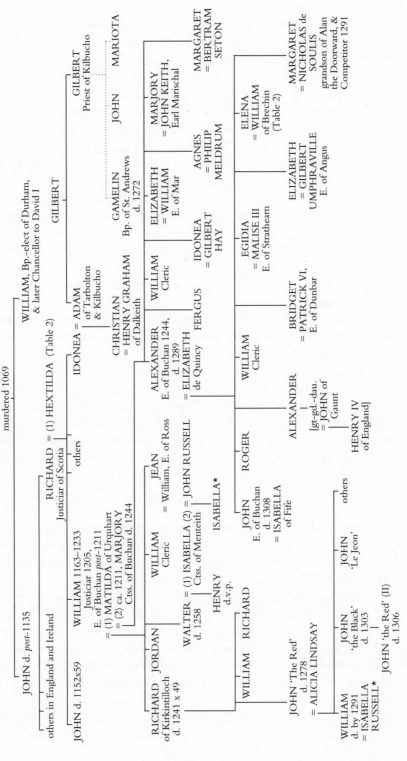

nephew John, the first 'Red Comyn', who held lands around Kirkintilloch and large estates in Tynedale in Northumberland. These came from the family's most important alliance, the marriage of the earls' grandfather to the grand-daughter of King Donald III Bàn. This brought them, like Bruce, into the reserve category of Celtic kingship (John was outside it).[4]

While they and others checked the mood of the country, Alexander was doing lessons. Many great men sent their sons to other noble households at the age of seven or eight; a parallel Celtic custom of fosterage established bonds stronger than blood. Scots royal children were more often trained at home, or so it seems. Alexander II's plans for his only son's upbringing probably involved the 'Flower of Chivalry', Alan the Doorward, with riding-masters and tutors under him. A boy must ride well by seven or he would never make a horseman, so the young prince had begun under his father's eye. A 'governor' for day-to-day supervision was needful – Alan could not be there all the time – and in 1255 one William of Cadzow is named among the household; nothing is known of him, but Cadzow was an ancient royal residence and he might be one more of old King William's brood, an acknowledged kinsman without expectations. It looks as if Alexander of Stirling, or his wife, had care of the baby Ermengarde, and William's position might be similar.[5]

A King of Scots needed several languages – Latin for business, French for courtly conversation, Flemish for the body of merchants and traders in the south – a large immigration of Flemish knights, wool-merchants, and craftsmen had arrived as refugees after Stephen of England's death, and launched the Border cloth-trade. Gaelic was essential if he was to deal with the bulk of his subjects; tradition was strong that old King David spoke all his country's languages and would dismount to talk with anyone he met along the road. And besides all that, he must know his history, and a smattering of arithmetic.

The choice of tutor was important, a man of wide education, able to interest the boy and hold his attention without undue severity (learning was literally hammered home by most masters). The clever young men of the *capella* offered a field of choice. Among them was one Gamelin, a priest's son from the Borders, with an M.A. degree from the University of Paris (and possibly another from Toulouse, where at that date the works of Aristotle were studied while Paris banned them). When he got home he became a canon of Glasgow cathedral and thence entered royal service while Bishop William Bondington of Glasgow was Chancellor. In 1245 Mr Gamelin undertook a mission to the papal curia at Lyons, but from 1248 he is not named among the *capella* staff. He shot into prominence in 1252 as a candidate for election to St Andrews, the chief episcopal see of the country, no less, and though passed over that time, he was made a papal chaplain *in absentia* and became chancellor of the diocese of Moray. He was carving a career, not without patrons. Research has shown that Gamelin's uncle had married Idonea Comyn, an aunt of the two earls, and that Idonea's daughter acknowledged her cousin the priest's children. Possibly the late King had provided a counter-influence to Alan in the person of the quiet young man who kept a child's attention on the making of pothooks on wax tablets and the decipherment of crabbed scripts.[6]

Around the King's eighth birthday his *colloquium* approved a new coinage and Great Seal together with a lesser 'seal of the minority'. The mint-masters went to work calling in old coins and melting them down, while the seals were entrusted to the Chancellor, Abbot Robert of Dunfermline.[7]

That winter a crisis developed from small beginnings. The Augustinian prior of St Andrews cathedral died, and the royal councillors impounded his worldly goods, the 'temporalities of his office', to guard them until a successor was chosen. The priory had been founded and endowed by the bishops, so it was for the bishop to have custody; besides, though the Crown routinely held the temporalities of vacant bishoprics (a case could be made for equating them with lay fiefs, since bishops swore fealty), it was not the custom in lesser positions. Much clerical wrath was directed at the Chamberlain, Mr Richard of Inverkeithing, himself bishop-elect of Dunkeld, and at the Chancellor. The first administered Crown property, the second authorised the seizure. Both churchmen owed a prime duty to the Church.[8]

Matters came to a head in June 1250 at the summer *colloquium*. Abbot Robert was much occupied with Dunfermline arrangements, but managed to attend both the *colloquium* and the concurrent General Council of the Scottish Church. That Council was a curiosity to the rest of Christendom and an abiding affront to successive archbishops of York. The fourth Lateran Council had instructed the clergy of every country to hold annual councils under their respective archbishops, but every time Rome was asked to make St Andrews an archbishopric, York protested with English royal backing. Three popes declared Scotland subject only to Rome, *Filia Specialis*, and in 1225 Honorius III ordered the Scots to hold their own Council. He may have hoped they would meet only to arrange a submission to York, but his letter was taken as authority for a permanent convention.[9]

It consisted of ten of the eleven bishops (Whithorn adhering to York for historic reasons), together with heads of religious houses, deans and archdeacons, and such other clergy as they might summon. They met annually under an elected Conservator of the Privileges of the Scottish Church, whose duties resembled those of a present-day Moderator of the General Assembly of the Church of Scotland: he convened the meeting, he preached the opening sermon, he supervised the election of his successor, and during his year of office he was the Council's spokesman. Much of its work consisted in reviewing decisions made elsewhere and deciding their applicability to Scotland; if Grosseteste had to forbid his Lincolnshire painters to mix their colours on altarstones, we had better beware of that sacrilege ourselves. But in 1250 they tackled the affair of the prior's temporalities, drew up a mandate which they presented to the *colloquium*, and published it for good measure in the form of a general letter in the names of the bishops of St Andrews and Brechin and the archdeacon of St Andrews. The mandate, signed by seven bishops, opens with due salutations to their most excellent lord Alexander, by God's grace illustrious King of Scots, and proceeds:

> although the rules ordained in the last council of the kingdom held at Edinburgh
> in your presence and that of your magnates have scarcely (*minime*) been reduced
> to writing, we cannot believe that they have escaped the memory of your
> councillors; namely that churches and their prelates should enjoy peaceful
> possession of all those rights and liberties which they received in the time of
> King Alexander your father of happy memory, your right and possession being
> in all cases reserved. Yet now something new and unheard-of has been brought
> in by your councillors; that ecclesiastics should, without any judicial cognition
> by their prelates, be despoiled by laymen of possessions bestowed on their
> churches in alms, as we understand has lately happened in the case of the Prior
> of St Andrews. Now, since such attempts against God and the freedom of the
> Church ought not to be allowed ... we humbly and devotedly petition your
> Excellency to revoke whatever has irreverently and inconsiderately been done
> and not to permit such deeds in future. Otherwise we shall, at whatever risk
> to ourselves, rather denounce than endure such incalculable injury to the
> Church. May your Excellency ever prosper in the Lord![10]

Unfortunately there would be graver injuries before long, but for the moment a report went to Rome while the churchmen prepared themselves to meet foes and friends alike at a grand ceremony in Dunfermline a fortnight later.

Dunfermline Abbey stood beside an ancient palace and on the site of the chapel where Malcolm III had married his second queen in 1070. Legend has gathered so thickly around this queen, a princess of the Saxon line of England, that we need some facts.

Margaret was the elder daughter of Edward the Exile, one of two sons of Edmund Ironside who fled into Europe on their father's death. Margaret's mother was Agatha, a kinswoman both of King Stephen I of Hungary and of the Emperor Henry II. Edward spent forty years in central Europe until invited home in 1056 by his father's half-brother Edward the Confessor, to whom he was nearest heir. He accepted with deep reluctance, but eventually brought his wife, two daughters and his son Edgar to England. He brought also considerable wealth and a large collection of holy relics, some given him by the Emperor, others rescued from the general recrudescence of heathendom which followed the death of St Stephen. They included a fragment of the True Cross in an ebony and gold box, later to be known as the Black Rood.

The Exile did not long survive his move, but his family remained at court, where they overlapped briefly with Malcolm, a refugee in England from 1040 until 1058 when he set off to reclaim his throne from Macbeth's stepson Lulach. When the Confessor died, at Christmas 1065, the Londoners proclaimed young Edgar king, but he was swept aside by Harold Godwinsson. After the Conquest Edgar and Agatha quickly made their peace with William of Normandy and settled comfortably on lands near Romsey, where Christina, the younger sister, entered religion. In 1069 Edgar unwisely joined the northern rebellion, and on its collapse he fled with his supporters to their Scottish allies, with Agatha and Margaret in tow. Both Malcolm III and Edgar soon renewed peace with William, and a year or so later Malcolm, now a widower with three young sons, married Margaret.

The new Queen's background was intensely devout; to the childhood influences of a newly christianised homeland she added the piety of the Confessor's household. Her family tree blossomed with Saxon and European saints, she had been steeped in doctrinal learning from infancy. Much that she met in England she thought heretical, in Scotland she found even more shocking irregularities. She threw herself into the task of reform.[11]

Christianity had reached Hungary only in her mother's lifetime, and had struggled to survive, anchored in monasteries and bishoprics. Scotland had been evangelised from the fifth century onward and its Church combined Irish, Pictish, Anglian and European elements. There were few bishops, of vague jurisdiction, and many monasteries now had secular 'Abs', often descendants of saintly founders, and holding large estates called 'Abthens'. Some establishments housed fellowships of priests who preached around the countryside from their community; they called themselves *Célé Dé*, 'servants of God', and are loosely called 'Culdees' in modern usage. They originated in an Irish reform movement around the time of the Viking raids, though the name was later attached to religious centres in Pictland. (Margaret's son David would later persuade some 'Culdee' houses to adopt the Augustinian rule, while others continued their own course into the thirteenth century). Margaret made gifts to some 'Culdees'; her sole move towards monastic reform was to bring Benedictines from Canterbury to Dunfermline.[11]

Her debates with churchmen were prolonged, her husband interpreting and enforcing most of her wishes. He was probably quite as well informed as she on points of doctrine, and the tales of the 'hairy Celt' falling on his knees to kiss the wonderful books he could not read are fairy-stories; no prince grew up illiterate through eighteen years at Edward's court. The arguments ranged over Sabbath observance, the obligation of frequent communion, and a 'barbarous rite' which was probably the old Irish order of the Mass. Her confessor and biographer Turgot, Prior of Durham, saw her as a ray of light in alien darkness; the people of Scotland cared little for theological niceties but a great deal for a merciful queen who fed the poor and tended the sick.[13]

They revered her in life, they prayed at her tomb, they claimed miracles from her intercession. Her youngest son rebuilt her new priory into an abbey, bringing Durham masons to rear the pillars which still rise like beech trees in its nave. It was he who erected bishoprics throughout his realm and encouraged his bishops to establish a parochial framework countrywide, and he who brought monks of many orders to Scotland.[14]

As the centenary of David's Dunfermline approached, Alexander II obtained a papal grant of the mitre and ring for its abbot and asked the Pope to consider canonising his ancestress. Two committees studied her life and the reported miracles, and just in time for the ceremony the late king's desire was granted.[15]

Of Margaret's eight children, only David and the two daughters left descendants. From these came, by 1250, the Kings of Scotland, England, France, Castile and Portugal, the Duke of Austria, the Earls of Cornwall and Hereford and the Counts of Brittany, Holland, Poitou and Anjou, the Queen-Mother of France and the Queens of Aragon, Castile and Hungary, the Countesses of Cleves, Flanders, Kent, Leicester and Norfolk, and the nominal Emperor Baldwin II, forlornly touring Europe in search of someone to restore him to his throne. There were the Bruces, and Devorguilla Balliol (whose children were perhaps too young to attend the ceremony), while from the wrong side of several royal blankets came the Earl of Dunbar and the Bissets, Brechins, Lindsays, de Ros, de Saye and Stirlings, among others. The two elderly princesses, Margaret of Kent and Isabella of Norfolk, did not undertake the northward journey, and the foreign families may not have been represented, but even without them the church would be full for the service on 19 June. The King and his mother, bishops and earls, abbots and nobles, children of the abbey school, burgesses and craftsmen, packed the nave and aisles like brilliant flowers on a forest floor. Plainsong with cascades of ornament filled the air like birdsong, the bells clashed and pealed.

The abbey authorities had already opened the queen's tomb and gathered her bones, encountering 'a most sweet scent as if all were strewn with flowers and spicy balms'. The relics had been placed in a new shrine of pinewood encased in silver and set with gold and jewels, which was borne to the nave altar by a procession of bishops and abbots. After dedicating the shrine they moved towards the arch into the choir-aisle, and in so doing passed Malcolm's tomb. Here the shrine became so heavy that they had to set it down and could not lift it again, although the congregation gathered to help. At last 'a voice inspired by the Lord thundered forth from a bystander', telling everyone that the queen refused to be parted from her husband.

Immediately they saw the answer. The king's tomb was opened, his bones were carried ahead of the shrine, round to the prepared place at the east end of the church.[16]

This would have been a tricky improvisation; perhaps the abbot had foreseen a possibility of saintly intervention. His fellow Benedictines of Tynemouth, where Malcolm's body and his eldest son's had been buried in 1093, were claiming to have found a very large skeleton with a smaller one beside it, and expressing fears that bodies of 'rustics' had been returned by mistake when Alexander I claimed his dead. Abbot Robert had no patience with such notions and may have decided to quash them conclusively. At the same time he could quash any murmurs that the new saint had been a contentious and obstinate female; the little hitch at the graveside proved her to be the model of a respectful and loving wife.

The small drama became the highlight of the day. The shrine has gone, we know its materials but not its form. A gabled box, like a miniature church, was a long-established design, but later references to 'St Margaret's Head' suggest that a golden bust encased the skull and crowned the casket of bones.[17]

Once the ceremony ended and the congregation flowed out into the sunshine, the waiting crowds could press in, shuffling along the new circuit beyond the monks' choir to venerate the earthly tokens of a queen already enshrined in their affection.

The palace, the abbey guest-house and the town would be thronged that night with laity and clergy, tired, happy and exalted. If anyone was slightly less delighted it might be the Doorward's wife. Marjory's position at court had always been ambiguous, although as she named her eldest daughter after old Queen Ermengarde she may well have had kindness from her grandmother. Perhaps it was easier in former days when there were tribes of young red-heads underfoot, but she was the nearest relative to her nephew (if you left out the two old countesses, as you clearly could), and it was irksome to be placed among the wives of Officers of State, behind such as Madame de Balliol.

If only Alan was an earl; she felt sure her father would have found him an earldom before long. He had held one in right of his first wife until his stepson came of age, then held it again after the young man's untimely death; Marjory's marriage had been a kind of compensation for losing Atholl when Isabella died. Why, she demanded, did Alan not press his claims to Mar? His father had claimed that earldom as daughter's son of Earl Gilchrist, but the title went instead to Gilchrist's half-brother Duncan, whose son William succeeded him around the time of Isabella's death. That was when Alan should have moved, but now that he and his friends were in power surely something could still be done. And another thing; she was persuaded that there had been a secret marriage between her own parents, proof must exist somewhere, what was the good of being Justiciar of Scotland if you could not look into your own wife's rights?

Marjory's age is unknown; she had married Alan between 1245 and 1249. Her insistence on legitimacy raised horrifying possibilities, for no bastard could rule Scotland, and from 1221 to 1238 Alexander II was the husband of Joan of England; in 1239 he married the present Queen; if Marjory was right, the second marriage was bigamous. One might hesitate to raise such questions, but Alan was ambitious, he had enjoyed being Earl of Atholl, and he disliked young William of Mar who seemed to lean towards the Comyns. He took his problems to Abbot Robert, a good lawman as a Chancellor must be.

Robert felt Mar was difficult, not to be hurried; but precedents existed for royal daughters to be legitimated by papal decree. Twenty-five years earlier Henry III had obtained the legitimation of his half-sister Joan, wife of Llywelyn Fawr of Wales. The object had been to promote Joan's son Dafydd as legal heir to Wales, in the hope that his English blood would make him less intransigent than his elder half-brother Gruffydd. Marjory's case was not strictly comparable, but it was a constant anxiety that only an eight-year-old stood between Scotland and anarchy There could be little harm in sending to Rome such evidence as Marjory could assemble, no need to publicise anything until guidance was obtained. He would entrust the drafting of the letter to a reliable clerk and – since everyone knew that delays could occur – a royal seal would ensure that the letter was read before too long. No file copy has survived; the reply was to receive full publicity.[18]

Chapter 3 Notes

1   See Chapter 11.
2   The earliest surviving reference is dated 16 April 1251, *CDS I, 1799*, Sheriff of Cumberland to account for lands held by late K. of Scots, from 20 July 1249 (probably when news arrived).
3   All three witness a grant in Bruce's court, 29 July (*CDS I, 1763*). Roger de Quincy, E. of Winchester, married Ela/Elena dau. of Alan of Galloway and became Constable in her right. Buchan married their daughter Elizabeth, and became Constable on Roger's death (1264).
4   Comyn family tree, p.23. Celtic succession, and Bruce's claim, p.15 above. John Comyn was outwith even the reserve group.
5   William of Cadzow, p.72 below; Ermengarde, p.13 above. See p.7.
6   Mr Gamelin, Watt, *Biog*.209–214 and Barrow, 'Problems'; they deduce the kinship (Comyn, p.23) from a grant 1242x49 by Christian Graham, endowing prayers for kinsfolk including Gamelin and his sister Mariota.
7   Mints and coinage, Apps. B and E, pp.116, 225 below and pls.6, 7.

8 Episcopal temporalities were troublesome everywhere, echoing the supremacy contest between Pope and Emperor. The St Andrews Priory case produced a fulminating Bull of Innocent IV, 31 May 1251; *St. Sc. Ch.*, 212–17.

9 For origin and proceedings of the General Council see *St. Sc.Ch.*, xxxiii *inf.*

10 *St. Sc. Ch.*, 211; *APS I*, appendix to *Acta Alex.III*. Letter by Bp. David de Bernham of St Andrews, Bp. Albinus of Brechin, and Mr Abel of Golin (Gullane), archdeacon of St Andrews; mandate by Bernham, Albinus, William Bondington of Glasgow, Peter Ramsay of Aberdeen, Clement of Dunblane, Robert of Ross and William of Caithness.

11 Ritchie, *The Normans in Scotland* (Edin.U.P. 1954), 9–10, discusses the relics, and events (*passim*). For the Black Rood (and others possibly from the collection) App.D, p.253.

12 *Abthen* = Appin in modern placenames. Much ink has been spilt over the 'Culdees'. By mid-13th .c. communities remained at Abernethy, Brechin, Muthill and St. Mary of the Rock at St Andrews.

13 G. Donaldson, *Scottish Church & Nation* (Sc.Acad.Pr.1972), 17–18, summarises her demands :- Lent to begin on Ash Wednesday, not the following Monday; marriage with stepmother or brother's widow to be banned; refusal to take Communion on grounds of unworthiness to be overcome; Sunday to be a day of prayer only (she may thus have invented the 'Scottish Sabbath'). Donaldson attributes her partial success to her husband's strong arm as much as to her urging, and notes relapses after 1093.

14 For David I's foundations., App.C; Dunfermline building sequence, Cruden, *Churches*, 22.

15 Canonisation could be initiated by relatives, and always required their consent – D. Attwater, *Penguin Dictionary of Saints* (1965), 10. Innocent IV authorised enquiries July 1245 and August 1246, approved decision Sept. 16 and pronounced her *sancta* 21 Sept. 1249; *ES II*. Her feastdays are 19 June (birth) and 16 Nov. (death).

16 *Fordun* XLIX, briefly; *Chron.Pluscarden* enlarges, *Wyntoun* (Laing, ii, 266) moralises on wifely devotion. The church was extended beyond the choir to give lay access to the shrine, whose base now lies outside the east end of the present church; *PSAS II*, 81 *inf.*; Cruden, *Churches, loc.cit.*n.14 above.

17 *PSAS II.* (which gives the Tynemouth story) cites a note in an edition of Turgot for 'Q. Margaret's Head' being taken to Edinburgh for the birth of James VI (1566). The shrine went for safety to Antwerp, 1597, and to the Scots College at Douai, 1627, only to vanish in the French Revolution. Other relics, of Margaret and of Malcolm, were acquired by Philip II of Spain and may still exist in the Escorial. For 'head' shrines see Labarge, *St.L*, pl.15.

18 For Mar, Skene, *PSAS XII*, 603 *inf.*, also *RRS II*, 200–1; Thomas of Lundie's claim impugned the legitimacy of his grandfather's half-brother; he lost his case but received a barony in compensation. Alan's first wife was Isabella of Atholl, widow of Thomas of Galloway. Patrick, her son by that first marriage, became earl when of age, but died in a fire at Haddington after a tourney in which he had unhorsed one of the Bissets, who were exiled on suspicion of his murder. Walter Bisset, their head, had married the sister of E. Thomas and was restored to favour by 1249 (see p.6 above). Alan resumed the earldom until Isabella died in 1244, when the title passed to her sister's husband David Hastings. For the result of the Chancellor's letter to Rome, see p.42.

4

1251: Royal Wedding

WE MISLEAD ourselves if we imagine thirteenth-century people were sedentary. From market-women through pilgrims to grandees, there was constant movement. In 1248 the old Earl of Dunbar rode through France to join Louis IX's Crusade, and died at Marseilles while waiting to embark; the Steward's brother died next year on an Egyptian beachhead. Neither man travelled alone, followers of both doubtless suffered capture, the lucky were ransomed and got home. It was the best-planned, best-equipped Crusade ever launched, and it ended in disaster; the news only reached France in August 1250.[1]

Among the many casualties was Raoul de Coucy. Perhaps her brother's death, coming soon after her husband's, drew Queen Marie homeward. Around her son's ninth birthday his Council sent envoys to England, on business of great interest to her; she summoned kinsmen to escort her and set out with the Earl of Strathearn and the delegation. Fordun explains their mission:

> The magnates of Scotia, perceiving danger to the realm under the rule of a boy (whose councillors, perhaps the greatest in the land, were swayed by their own advantage), with consent of the clergy sent envoys to King Henry to renew the treaty between him and the late King Alexander and to secure it by the marriage arranged between the young King Alexander and King Henry's daughter.

The 1244 Treaty of Ponteland had closed a period of tension. For Henry, the attraction of the betrothal was that he could raise an Aid for his eldest daughter's marriage, one of three allowable feudal taxes (the others were for a personal ransom and for an eldest son's knighthood). He could only collect nearer the event, but the prospect cheered his creditors.[2]

The Princess Margaret was a year older than her bridegroom. There is no surviving record of Queen Marie visiting the English court on this journey, but Henry's deep interest in ceremonial would make him as eager to question her as she was to meet the child. One matter surely concerned him; his Eleanor had been crowned at their marriage, but he could recall nothing about Joanna's coronation. Marie was obliged to say that, alas, Scots queens were not

Table 4. France–Dreux–Coucy–Montfort

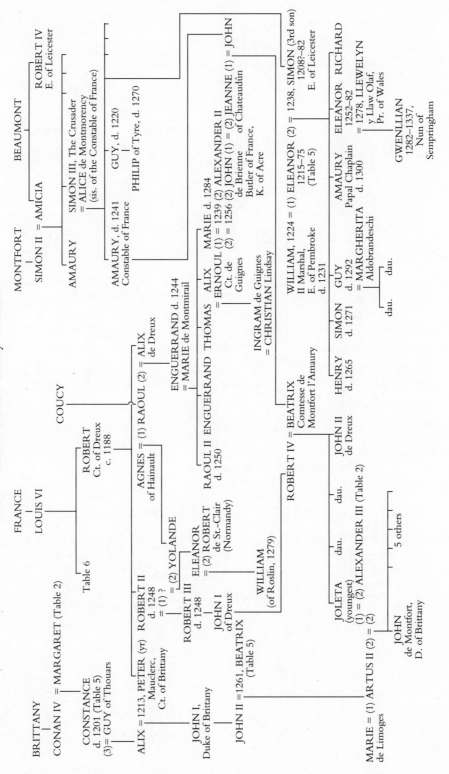

Table 5. England

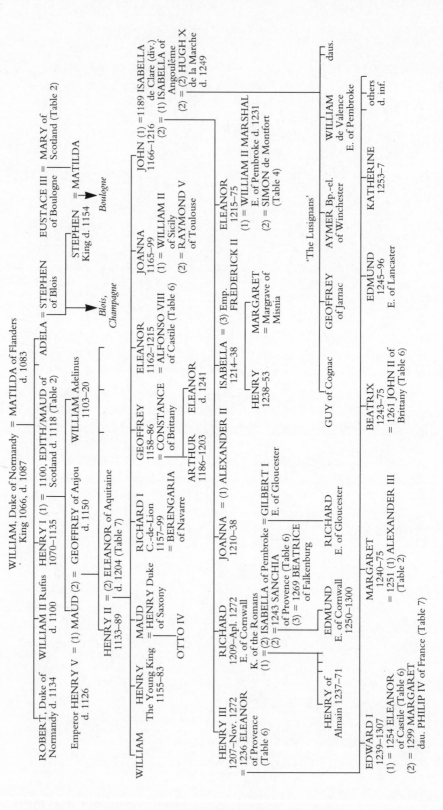

crowned; crowning was a minor ritual even for kings, nor were they anointed with holy oil like her own French relatives and indeed the English; but she must avoid reminding her host of his furious opposition to her late husband's hopes of obtaining a new rite of unction from the Holy Father.

She went on to stay in the royal apartments at Rochester, and to have her progress to Dover smoothed by the Sheriff of Kent; but she had stirred Henry's memory, for some unwary approach brought him a crushing rebuke from Innocent IV:

> It has been strongly represented to us on your behalf that we should grant you that our beloved son in Christ, the illustrious King of Scotland, may not be anointed or crowned without your consent, since he is your liegeman and has done you homage. The Apostolic See is little accustomed to admit requests of this kind, as tending to prejudice the royal dignity. Concerning your request for the grant of a tenth part of ecclesiastical revenues in that kingdom, we have not granted it (be not distressed) because it is altogether unheard-of that any ruler should be given this privilege in another sovereign's kingdom.[3]

Henry, or his envoys, had overcalled his hand. Alexander had not been asked for homage; as for a tithe of church revenues, Scotland was guarded by many papal immunities. Henry, who had taken the Cross during 1250 and would talk of making his Crusade all his life, had been allotted a tenth of English church revenues for three years from the time his departure-date was fixed, but his bishops were already mustering opposition.

Still, he was an incurable optimist, never happier than when planning some great occasion. He was a good-looking man of middle height, then aged forty-five, with light brown hair, a short curled beard, and a drooping left eyelid which gave him a whimsical air. He had fancied himself in love with one of Alexander II's sisters (either Margaret, fourteen years his senior, or her youngest sister Marjory), but married Eleanor of Provence when he was twenty-nine and she was twelve. Their daughter Margaret was born in 1240, a year after her brother Edward. Her first recorded public appearance was in 1243, when the citizens of London provided both children with 'robes of scarlet, delicate and well-dyed, and hoods trimmed with miniver'. 'Scarlet' was a fine woollen, invented in Flanders and copied in Lincoln and Norwich, often (not always) dyed red; miniver is ermine. Edward was 'fair as flax' in childhood; two miniature blond Santa Claus figures move hand-in-hand across the mind's eye.[4]

In August 1251 Queen Marie applied for return safe-conducts through England; soon after, Henry set off on a hunting-tour which would deliver him to York for Christmas; in October the time-honoured machinery of a Scots state visit creaked into action.

Modern Heads of State may approve banquet-menus; Henry ran the show.

From Reading he ordered vestments and church plate for Margaret's chapel; near Marlborough he despatched his own wine-steward to York, to start preparing cordials from the castle cellars – clove-scented *gariofilatum*, *claret* a sweetened blend of white and red. (Ugh; but all wine was drawn from the wood, and last season's was almost undrinkable unless doctored). A little silver pan for hot drinks, a sword for the bridegroom, a surcoat of violet samite with golden leopards (for himself), and cloth-of-gold for Edward, came to mind between Hales and Derby. From Nottingham, in the intervals of hunting in Sherwood, he ordered a large fur bedspread and a scarlet jupon; winter was coming. On 1 December he required '200 marks from the treasurer of the New Temple and all the money in the Exchequer' to be sent to him, while issuing more instructions to his tailor:

> See that Edward the King's son has, in the church where the nuptials are to be, four tabards with the King's arms, in cloth-of-gold if possible or else in scarlet, with leopards of golden skin, one for him and the others for his knights, Edward's furred with miniver and the others with vair; another set in cloth-of-gold with another colour, and a third entirely of richer cloth-of-gold; and shirts, striped or of taffeta. The tabards at least must be made in London; if there is no time to make the rest, send the materials.

With the wedding three weeks away, the royal almoner in York must provide cloth and boots for the poor (boots at 4½d, 5d and 5½d); Margaret must have 'divers jewels' to the value of 200 marks, and lengths of cloth-of-gold, to take as presents. Scarlet saddlecloths and reins, green dresses for her attendants, furred surcoats for royal marshals, were last-minute needs. Let Alexander hunt at will, and keep the game, as he comes, but send a galloper to Langwath for 'all the roes they can take by Christmas, with hounds, bows, nets and all other engines', never mind sporting niceties. The supplies ordered from the sheriffs of Cumberland, Lancaster, Lincoln and Northumberland, from the Mayor of York and the bailiffs of Lincoln, Scarborough and Newcastle, are tabulated opposite.

Alexander set out in mid-November on a route governed by protocol older than the Normans and redefined in 1194. There were ten stages between Berwick and York; the escorting sheriffs paid a corrody (travelling-allowance) of £5 daily, and once arrived at court, the King should receive thirty shillings a day and wine, bread, spices and candles as issued to the English household. At Berwick Bridge the Bishop of Durham and the Sheriff and barons of Northumberland mustered, at the Tees they handed over to the Archbishop and Sheriff of York; had they been going farther south, the Lincolnshire authorities would have received them at the Humber.

Alexander's companions had much to tell him. Here, before Alnwick, Malcolm III died; over there, William the Lion was captured (in a fog, by

York, Christmas 1251: Provisions

Brawns (bacon pigs) with heads	70	
Bucks (Fallow)	27	
Cod	1,000	
Congers	500	
Does (Fallow)	200	
Freshwater fish from York vivary – no quantity given		
Haddock	10,000	
Hens	1,992	
Herring	5 lasts	(= approx 60,000)
Hinds (Red)	500	(50 cancelled, one forest 'took none')
Partridges	1,600+	(1 amount not stated)
Peacocks	120	
Pheasants	290	
Rabbits	300	
Roe Deer	100	(50 cancelled)
Salmon 'calivered in pane'	280	(dried, sealed in baked crust)
Swans	125	
Swine (domestic)	400	
Wild boars and sows	200	

Wines
Bought 'by the hand of Robert Dacre at York', 132 casks from 11 named merchants, at an average price of £1.13.6d per cask, four French merchants receiving less per cask than Henry's Bordeaux merchants (*CDS 1, 1859*, 5 Jan. 1252 at York.)

The other orders are *ibid, passim* from 28 October onward.

the Balliols). At Thirsk they recalled his father's refusal to proceed until he knew Henry was at York, lest he be found waiting like a vassal. Alan the Doorward, and the young Earl of Dunbar, and the Chancellor, were in the party, so were Menteith and Mar. Some hoped King Henry would prove a benign father-figure (Dunbar was famously pro-English), while others were determined to resist any encroachment. It cannot have been a relaxed journey, given the need to project harmony for the escort's benefit.[6]

They reached York on Christmas Eve. The city was packed:

> The archbishop's men provided accommodation sufficient, considering the season, for all, though they exceeded number, lest a scarcity of lodgings should provoke strife[7]★

Matthew Paris, ensconced in the Benedictine abbey and resolutely painting a glowing picture, was forced by his instincts for a story to note a brawl between some English lords' marshals which began as fisticuffs and ended with one dead and several seriously injured. An entire street had been reserved for the Scots, but home supporters were less easily segregated.

Queen Eleanor and the bride were at the castle, with Henry and the boy Edward, Richard of Cornwall the King's brother and his wife Sanchia, the Queen's sister, and the King's only surviving sister Eleanor with her husband, Simon Earl of Leicester. The Leicesters had come from Gascony hoping for a quiet consultation about the problems of that troubled overseas possession. De Montfort was its viceroy, but Henry was far too busy to talk about all that; he did however find time to hear the complaints of some Bordeaux wine merchants delivering supplies.[8]

Alexander's aunt, old Margaret of Kent, gamely travelled up from her Surrey manor, to be joined by the Earl of Gloucester whose boyhood had passed in her household and who had a tragic childhood romance with her daughter Megotta. Gloucester was displeased to find he had no lodgings prepared, his servants having been arrested for poaching in Rockingham Forest – with his hounds.[9]

Then there was the bridegroom's mother:

> Many nobles accompanied her, not of Scotland only but also of France, whence she took her origin. For she had obtained, as is the custom with widows, the third part of the revenues of the kingdom of Scotland, 4,000 marks and more, besides the possessions received from her father Engelram. And she proceeded exceedingly loftily with a magnificent and numerous retinue.★

Matthew really could not be impartial about a Coucy.

The meeting of the kings was tinged with sentiment for Henry. He had been just Alexander's age when the Old Marshal promised to carry him on his shoulders, 'one leg here, the other there', until he could establish him on his father's throne.[10]

Next day was Christmas, a Sunday. Henry knighted Alexander and twenty others, giving them all 'choice robes' and Alexander the sword, swordbelt and spurs his goldsmiths had prepared. Custom required aspirants to pass a night's vigil after ritual baths and moral lectures from their sponsors, but after the long journey there was none of that; homage, which should have followed immediately, was also deferred. Henry was finding everything was taking too long, and he had discovered another snag.

Almost every European cathedral had builders at work, pulling down old-fashioned round arches, putting up soaring columns. Thirty years back, when Joanna married Alexander II, in York, a new south transept was rising outside the old one; it was now complete with its rose window glazed, but the masons were in the northern arm. The Five Sisters window was empty, wheel-cranes and dressed stones were everywhere, the floor was permanently gritty past sweeping, the north porch (where bridal parties traditionally entered) was blocked. The Dean said the nave itself was unsafe, and he was proved right within years.[11]

Archbishop Walter de Gray would conduct the service at the high altar, but the choir stalls could not hold the guests (never mind displacing the singers). There was only one solution:

> Because the people hurrying in troops crushed one another that they might see the celebration of such nuptials, the marriage was performed in the earliest morning, secretly and before the expected time.*

That must have ensured cordiality. Matthew rushes on with a background piece:

> There were so many diversities of people, such hosts of English, French and Scots nobles, so many large troops of knights in wanton robes, vain in their silks and changing adornments, that if their profane and wanton vanity were fully described it would provoke wonder and disgust ... The English king had over a thousand knights clothed in silk and, to use the vulgar term, *cointises*. Each day they threw these aside and presented themselves in new robes. On the King of Scotland's side sixty and more knights, and many the equivalent of knights, adorned with sufficient appropriateness ... And if I should expound further the abounding diversity of banquets, the applause for jesters, the numbers at table, it would arouse derision ... But that the rest may be under-stood from one thing, by the archbishop's gift more than sixty pasture cows provided one first and universal course.
>
> They feasted in turn now with this, now the other king, who emulously prepared voluptuous repasts, that the world's vanity might offer mortals whatever it could of brief and transient happiness ... all dined several days with

the archbishop, who as a northern prince and cheerful host ... in that Lord's
Advent sowed on a barren shore in gifts of gold and silver and silk 4,000 marks
he never reaped.★

Most people everywhere lived outside cities and clothed themselves in
homegrown, homespun, homewoven woollen or linen. On an occasion of
conspicuous consumption those who could afford better showed it. The finer
the shirt, the lower the neck of the *jupon*, a knee-length (or longer) tunic;
over the *jupon* was the *cointise*, sleeveless or wide-sleeved to show the gold
sleeve-buttons of the *jupon*. Women wore a fine shift, a fitted gown, an open
overgown; both men and women might add a padded silk coat called a *peliçon*,
derived from Persia, and top the whole outfit with a fur-lined circular mantle,
valuable enough to be an heirloom.

The *cointise* became an embroidered *cyclas* with bullion fringe, and Queen
Eleanor usurped that male fashion, turning it into an overgown with a train;
her hair was caught in a golden net topped by a circlet of jewelled flowers;
let others continue to wear real flowers if they could get them in this dreadful
climate.

Married ladies generally wore a small round cap of pleated cambric with
a neck-veil and a band, called the *barbette*, which did wonders for a double
chin. Men also wore caps, shaped like babies' bonnets, tied under the chin
with hair curling out; these began as old men's comfort but were taken up
by all ages, even boys, indoors or out, and worn under hoods or hats
(sometimes all three together).

Breeches and boots were for riding (and for either sex, the ladies with a
long gown slit fore and aft). Men wore linen drawers under *braies*, leggings
with feet, tied up to the waist with strings to the shirt and laced to fit at ankle
and knee (whence later 'clocks' on stockings). Women's hose laced at the
ankle and were kept up by garters. (If their bodies needed support they
resorted to bandages). Shoes, leather or cloth, fastened with a button or
buckle and might be furlined. Gloves ranged from hawking gauntlets to
embroidered silk knitting.

Fabrics were dazzling – taffeta and newly-invented velvet from Italy, silk
from Sicily, Spain, India, even Cathay if the Mongol terror did not interrupt
the caravans; Persian brocades, muslin and dimity from Mosul and Damietta,
were traded alongside the finest Flanders cloth. No crusading zeal could deter
the Italian merchants, who also imported spices and sugar, and jewels –
sapphires, opals and emeralds from Sri Lanka or Burma, lapis, turquoise and
rubies from Afghanistan, orient pearls. The stones had mystic 'virtues';
sapphires promoted truth, amethyst averted drunkenness. Classical cameos
were re-set and treasured, with whatever curious interpretation.

In their bright layers the ladies moved slowly, leaning back from the waist
(it was perhaps desirable to appear pregnant), and trailing their long gowns:

If the feet be not small and delicate, let the robe fall on the pavement; those whose feet are beautiful may lift the robe under pretence of stepping briskly.[12]

When the wedding-feast ended, when knives were wiped and sheathed and tables taken down, and before the entertainers ran in, Henry invited Alexander to give his homage.

The Scots kings held half Tynedale in heritage; Alexander II had accepted six Cumberland manors in partial compensation for abandoning claims to the earldoms of Northumbria and Cumbria. The Earldom and Honour of Huntingdon, with lands across eleven counties, were held by David I and his successors, but Henry would not re-grant Huntingdon yet. The boy knelt to put his hands between Henry's and promise faith and service for his English lands; but Henry was waiting, and the Scots held their breath:

> And when in addition the King of Scotland was required to do homage and fealty with allegiance to his lord the King of the English by reason of the kingdom of Scotland, as his predecessors had done and as is clearly written in the chronicles, the King of Scotland answered that he had come in peace and for the honour of the King of England, to be allied with him in matrimony, not to reply to so difficult a question. For he had not held full deliberation or suitable council with his chief men, as such a matter demanded. And when the lord King heard this, he refused to becloud with any commotion so placid a festival ... passing it over for the time in silence.*

Things were not to remain placid. The Earl Marshal, Alexander's uncle by marriage, demanded to be given his horse (claiming, rightly, to be upholding tradition). Marshals of old had re-horsed new knights, taking their lighter mounts into reserve, but it was absurd for Norfolk to claim a boy's hack. The English court had many such archaisms; Simon de Montfort, officiating as High Steward at Henry's own wedding, had found himself obliged to give his robes to the chief cook.[13]

Alexander replied with dignity that

> The King of Scotland lay under no such obligation, for if it pleased him he could receive knighthood from any Catholic prince or any of his own nobles, but had chosen to be knighted by the King through reverence and honour for so great a prince, his neighbour and father-in-law. And thus all strife disappeared entirely from that feast.*

Or perhaps Matthew got the flu. He is sorely missed for the next couple of days.

There was a family tiff. Eleanor de Montfort perhaps hoped aloud that her niece would be luckier with dowries than she had been; Henry had never backed her claim to a third of the Pembroke estates from her first marriage, he even accepted a measly cash payment in lieu. It was a tangled inheritance, all five sons of the Old Marshal inheriting in turn, three leaving widows. Eleanor and Simon, with a growing family, managed on his limited resources. He had arrived in England as a penniless younger son and successfully claimed the earldom of Leicester, but much of its wealth had been stripped long before. As Viceroy of Gascony he sorely needed funds for castles and merce- naries to fight off rebels who had foreign backers. Henry flew into a passion, raking up every fault he had observed in Simon in the thirteen years since the young Frenchman had first dazzled him. It took all Richard of Cornwall's diplomacy to effect a truce, and despite his efforts, commissioners soon went to Gascony to gather evidence against Simon.[14]

A second explosion followed. The earls of Menteith and Mar had discov- ered the Chancellor's overture to the Pope on the Doorward's behalf. Possibly the messenger returning from Rome, unable to locate the Chancellor's secretary in the throng, handed his missive to the first Scot he could find and went off to join the party. The earls brought the matter before the whole company:

> Alan, *Hostiarius* of Scotland and then Justiciar also, was said to have sent messen- gers with gifts to the lord Pope to obtain the legitimation of his daughters by the King's sister, so that in the event of accident to [Alexander] these daughters would be his lawful heirs. Had he obtained this, none doubted that he would have turned traitor to the King and Queen.

Fordun, while echoing Melrose, changes the emphasis:

> Robert, Abbot of Dunfermline, the King's Chancellor, was accused that he had proposed legitimating under the Great Seal the [late] King's illegitimate daughter, wife of Alan the Doorward, that she might be the heiress to the King in succession to the kingdom.[15]

Both chroniclers report some of the accused fleeing from York (*clamdes- tine et turpiter repatriarunt*, says Fordun). Abbot Robert bolted to Newbattle, whose abbot was his ally, and there transferred himself from the Benedictine to the Cistercian Order.

Fordun continues:

> All the King's first councillors were removed and new ones appointed, namely Walter Comyn Earl of Menteith, Alexander Comyn Earl of Buchan, William Earl of Mar, Robert de Ros kinsman of the King; but as many consuls, so many kings. [Alexander] with advice of the King and nobles of England, having arranged everything with moderation, returned to his country with his wife and awaited better times to correct such excesses.

All this happened on the wedding day, for on 27 December Henry issued a general letter, narrating that after the 'solemnly celebrated marriage',

the said king of Scotland's *ballivi* there present, at his own instance, sponta-
neously restored their balliaries to their said lord. And lest from such an example
[that they resigned their posts outside the kingdom] prejudice might arise to
the king and kingdom of Scotland, [Henry] has caused these letters to be
fortified with his seal.[16]

The same day he sealed the marriage contract, promising to give Margaret
5,000 marks of silver 'when required' within the next four years, in *maritagium*
(the sum was agreed in 1244). Alexander presumably assigned lands of at least
equal value for her support; his grant has not survived, but if the dower lands
of other queens are any guide, the lands extended through southern Scotland.
The manor of Haddington is almost certain; Crail, Kinghorn, Lanark and
estates in Stirlingshire are strong probabilities (but some would still be Queen
Marie's). In later years Jedburgh had a 'Queen's stud-farm'. From his new
Cumberland holdings Alexander gave Margaret Sowerby.[17]

Henry was sending representatives to watch over his daughter and, in some
eyes, to manage Scotland too. Robert de Noreis, his guest-marshal, and
Stephen Bauzan, were soon recalled for the Gascony enquiry; Mathilda de
Cantilupe, widow of a Steward of the Household, was Margaret's chief lady.[18]

On the eve of departure Alexander exercised his right under the old
arrangements to present a fugitive seeking pardon. He produced Philip Lovel,
a chancery official lately dismissed. Matthew Paris, restored to duty, gives a
vivid account of bystanders reduced to tears by Alexander kneeling, 'as a
child without age or knowledge', turning to Henry as to his only friend ('My
mother has left me in my tender age'):

> 'Therefore from this time forward I adopt you as my father ... that you may
> supply the loss of both father and mother'.

Having got Henry 'checking a sob',

> the child speaking not childishly added, 'In this I shall test and know that you
> have hearkened to me, if you give effect to my desire and remit all offence to
> Philip Lovel ... for I have learned from men worthy of trust that he has been
> unjustly accused ... '
>
> Now in this affair John Mansel was an efficient helper and chief preceptor.*

Lovel was Henry's Treasurer within weeks. Of John Mansel we shall learn
more.

At the end of the month the Scottish party set off homeward, Henry
sending messages to the Sheriff of Newcastle about New Year gifts and entertainment. He was left with the matter of Gascony and the bills for bacon,
bedspreads and Bordeaux. Queen Eleanor, hating the chills of York, grieving
for her little girl exiled to still bleaker lands, would not see her again for four
years.[19]

Chapter 4 Notes

1 St Louis' first Crusade is fully described in Runciman, *Crs. III*, and by Joinville (participant). Young, *R of C*, 162, quotes M.Paris, *Chr.Maj.V*, 147,165–9 for the letter read to Queen Blanche and reported to London by Richard's man in Paris.

2 Safe-conducts for Mary Q. (-Mother) of Scotland and retinue, to France and return to 24 June 1251; *CDS I, 1785* (13 Sept.), and for Thomas de Coucy and others, to 11 Nov. 1250, *ib., 1786*. Strathearn's presence in the embassy is deduced from his presence with Henry on 30 Oct., giving homage for lands newly inherited by his young daughters; *CDS I, 1792* (and *cf.ib., 1798–99*, division between numerous heiresses 'from the coalshed to the garden-door ... half the third of the garden'). *Fordun* XLIX ('perhaps' is a nice touch). The Treaty of Ponteland (*CDS I, 1631–1654*) is discussed by Powicke, *H.III*, App.B 740 *inf.*, suggesting dispute arose over possible Scots harbourage of Geoffrey de Marisco, whose mother was an Irish Comyn and whose son had been executed in England for piracy and treason.

3 Q.Marie's journey, *CDS I, 1791, 1795* (outlays by sheriff). For Henry's opposition to Alexander II's hope of unction, in 1233, *CDS I, 1181*. Innocent IV's letter, Stones, *Docs*. 29 (and calendared in *CDS I 1798*). Alexander III had not yet been asked for homage. Henry's crusading plans never developed; Powicke, 231, starting-date of June 1256 announced in 1252. Bishops' objections, *ib*. 367–8; they had not been consulted, and proceeds were to go to the King, not to papal funding of the Crusade. Papal immunities to Scotland (*Filia Specialis*), pp.25, 86.

4 Henry's appearance, cf. his tomb-effigy in Westminster Abbey (pl.1). Edward was born 16 or 17 June 1239, Margaret 1 or 2 Oct. 1240. Robes, *CDS I, 1600*.

5 S/cs for Q.Marie, Thomas and retinue, to Candlemas 1252, *CDS I, 1804* (5 August), replaced *ib. 1807* (24 Sept) by another to include (her nephew) Gilles and endure to Easter. S/c for Alexander and retinue, *ib. 1812* (18 Oct). The hail of instructions begins *ib. 1815* (to *1846*).

6 Corrody, Stones *Docs*. 9 (1194), cal. *CDS I, 226*; Ritchie, *Normans in Scotland* (EUP 1954), App.B; *SA* 311–2; and cf. *CDS I, 1–6* (temp.Henry I). For Alexander II at Thirsk, 1221, *CDS I, 805–6*.

7 This, and subsequent extracts marked ★, are from M. Paris. *Chr. Maj.V*, in *SA* 363–7. The *SA* report of the brawl is amended in *ES II*, 570n.

8 Powicke (esp.227–9) treats fully of de Montfort in Gascony.

9 Margaret of Scotland, b.1191, was taken hostage with her next sister Isabella, half-promised a royal husband but eventually married in disparagement to Hubert de Burgh, E. of Kent. (Isabella was married to the young Norfolk). Richard de Clare, E. Gloucester (1222–62) was de Burgh's ward; in 1232 Margaret asserted that he and her (even younger) daughter had married; Powicke, App. C. The poaching marshal, cook and clerk are in Labarge, *Bar.Hsehd.*,67.

10 M. Paris is consistently hostile to the Coucy, reporting Enguerrand's death (1244) with gusto (see fig.4, p.85). For the Old Marshal, (William I,E.Pembroke) Powicke, 5 *inf* (see fig.5, p.105).

11 Lacking *RCHM (Engl) York VI*, I have followed the York Minster *Handbook* (1983) for the state of the building in 1251.

12 Ritchie, *Normans*, 56 & n., 269; M.F. Moore, *Lands of the Sc. Kings in England* (Allen & Unwin, 1915), *passim*. North Tynedale was heritage from David I's queen. Manors granted, 1237, assigned 1242 (*CDS I, 1358, 1575*). Order to give seizin to Alexander III, *ib. 1857* (2 Jan 1252). The manors were Salkeld, Langwathby, Scotby, Carlatton, Sowerby and part of Penrith. Like North Tynedale, these lie across a route often followed by English

armies and Scottish raiders. C.McNamee, *The Wars of the Bruces*, Tuckwell, 1997, maps 4 & 5. See map 1, p.xiv.

13. Edward I would order a frantic and vain search for chronicle evidence of Scots liege-homage in 1291; of Stones & Simpson, *The Great Cause*. E of Norfolk, *SA* 366; for E. Simon in 1237, Labarge, *Bar.Hsehd.*, 13.

14 Eleanor (1215–75) m.William II of Pembroke in 1224; he d. 1231. In Jan 1238 she m. Simon privately but with Henry's consent. Simon came to England 1230 to pursue claims to the vacant earldom of Leicester as grandson of the last earl's sister (p.33). He became an immediate favourite with Henry but only obtained the title in 1237. Richard of Cornwall's first wife was a sister of William II; she d. 1240 leaving a son Henry, later 'of Almain'. Young Henry's rights were involved in the Pembroke dispute; the wrangle over Eleanor's claim affected the Treaty of Paris (p.112). See Powicke, and Labarge *S. de M.* and *Bar. Hsehd.* For later action on Gascony, p.58.

15 See p.30; the letters have not been traced. *CM* 109–110; *Fordun*, L.

16 *CDS I, 1848*, by K. and Council, 27 Dec.

17 There were three elements in a marriage contract; *dos* or *maritagium* (Scots tocher) provided by the bride's father; *donatio propter nuptias*, a matching fund provided by the bridegroom to support the household, and terce, 'a reasonable third' of his estate with which he endowed the bride at the church door (if he omitted to do so, the law did it for him). Terce became the widow's portion if she outlived her husband, reverting to his family if she had no children. *Sel. Cases* 2–3 reports a 13th-c. judge reproving sloppy confusion between terce and tocher, with *dos* used for both.

'Haddingtonshire' was dower by David I's time (1139). Q. Ermengarde held Crail and Kinghorn in terce. Q. Joanna had £1,000 in land, including Jedburgh, Hassendean, and St Boswell's with 'Kinghorn and Crail if Q. Ermengarde will surrender them', or an equiv-alent; Barrow *A/N Era*, 63. Jedburgh farm, *ER I*, 43 (there assoc. with Q.Joleta, 1288, she probably received most of Margaret's lands). In 1257 Henry allows Margaret to enclose land at Sowerby, *CDS I, 2051*.

18 Representatives named, M. Paris, *Chr. Maj. V* 272 in *SA* 368.

19 *CDS I, 1851* (30 Dec. 1251) sheriff to provide 2 casks wine, meat, fish and other gifts as befits Henry's honour and in his name.

5

1252: Castle, Burgh and Croft

IT IS NOT hard to imagine the counsels of fortitude showered upon Margaret as she left her mother. Eleanor had come from Provence to northern barbarism, and beyond England lay misty lands where minstrels set tales of ogres. The long train rode under January skies between grey sea and dark moorland where peasants vanished like rabbits at the approach of horsemen.

At last there was a long timber bridge over a river, a substantial castle above it and a snug town behind a forest of masts. Here at Berwick the English escort left; in a few days the royal party followed the north bank of the Tweed to Roxburgh.

If any place was home to Alexander it was here in Marchmont Castle where he was born and spent much of his early childhood. The castle crowned a ridge; below its southern curtain the slope fell eighty feet to the Teviot. On the north side it was slightly less steep above burgh farmland beside the Tweed; westward a deep fosse divided castle from burgh, and from the eastern tip of the triangle the wall overlooked the meeting of the waters with Kelso Abbey beyond, its bells sweetening the air. The town stretched upward from the first bridge since Berwick.

Within the massive curtain wall was a stone keep on a mound and a multitude of timber houses, stables and barns. The officers of state had lodgings appointed; the Chancellor's and Doorward's houses stood empty.[1]

One of the wedding guests must surely have been Devorguilla Balliol, last surviving daughter of the last Lord of Galloway. She and her husband very probably entertained the bridal party in Barnard Castle on their homeward journey; though she often came to her south-west Scottish lands (which she managed independently of her husband's Durham estates) she is unlikely to have travelled in winter, especially when the royal party was taking up all victual and accommodation. Still, she had some contact with Margaret, for the new Queen's first letter home asked a favour for a Galloway kinsman she cannot have met.

Devorguilla's father Alan had ruled a wide tract of country but only a fragment of his ancestral lands; his forebears were kings whose realms extended from Loch Lomond to Windermere. Alan's grandfather Fergus married a daughter of Henry I of England and challenged Scots sovereignty.

The Galloway lands had been pared down ever since, David I establishing the Bruces on the eastern flank, Alexander II carving the earldom of Carrick along the Ayrshire coast for a cousin of Alan's. Despite such changes Alan was a loyal supporter of the Crown, Constable of Scotland (by inheritance from his mother's family, the Morvilles) and lord of a fleet and army. With the fleet he routed a Norse invasion in 1230 (remarking airily that 'it was as easy to go to Norway as to come into Scotland'); with the army he helped subdue Moray, and provided mercenaries for King John's Irish wars. He was at Runnymede, as a great baron of England, and his Irish service was rewarded with lands on the Antrim coast. His brother Thomas received interlocking grants inland to Lough Neagh, and built Coleraine Castle.[2]

Alan's first wife, a daughter of Reginald of Islay, gave him two daughters; the elder died a hostage in English hands, the younger married the Earl of Winchester (who became Constable on Alan's death). Alan's second wife was Margaret of Huntingdon; again there were two daughters, Christina, Countess of Albemarle, and Devorguilla, married to her north-country baron just before her father's death. There was no lawful son, but Galloway resented alien rule and revolted in support of a natural son named Thomas. The King suppressed the revolt and put Thomas in Balliol keeping; he spent fifty years in Barnard Castle with his family (his wife was a Manx princess), acknowledged and mistrusted.[3]

When Christina died childless and de Quincy and Balliol moved in to possess their inheritance, revolt flared again. The Constable was put to flight:

> [finding himself] besieged and choosing to die by the sword rather than starve, he mounted his horse and opening the gates cut a way for himself ... he cleft and scattered the whole army and ceased not to ride until he came to the King of Scotland, who punished the rebels and established the earl peacefully in his possession.[4]

New stone castles replaced a multitude of little mottes, but Galloway kept its own laws, guaranteed by King William and probably by King David before him (though offenders might opt for jury-trial). The older laws settled all offences, civil or criminal, by fines reckoned in cattle and graded to the status of both parties. They reflected the survival of Celtic tradition in a mixed population which gave the land their name, *Gall-Gaidhil*, 'Stranger-Gaels'. The laws' survival ensured the survival of a class of native judges, until Edward I abolished the whole system as 'laws too barbarous to be called Law'.[5]

Alan's brother Thomas became Earl of Atholl by marriage, leaving a lawful son Patrick and (in Ireland) another son named Alan. Patrick was killed in 1242 after a tourney; the Bisset family were accused and fled to England, whence many of them went to serve in Irish wars. Henry's Irish administration rewarded them with vacant lands around Larne, and thus unwittingly

brought them into range of Patrick's half-brother who undertook the oblig-
ation of the blood-feud, since no compensation had been paid for Patrick.
This is where Devorguilla sought Queen Margaret's help; at the end of
January, in one of her first letters home, Margaret sought pardon for

> Alan son of Thomas Earl of Atholl in Scotland, for transgressions charged
> against him in slaying some men of John Bisset in Ireland in conflict, and taking
> six casks of wine and some corn from Irish merchants at the siege and storming
> of the castle of Dunaverdin.

'Dunaverdin' has been explained as Dunaverty, on the southern tip of
Kintyre, but Henry could not pardon offences against a Scottish castle, and
there would have been considerable reaction from those newly in office if
their Queen had made any such plea at her first arrival. It seems probable
that 'Dunaverdin' was the Irish name of some Antrim stronghold now
disguised, like so many, under an Anglicised gloss. Wherever his offence
took place, Alan was pardoned and next appears in the 1270s, in Man, as a
servant of the Scottish crown. In 1285 he bequeathed a handsome gift of
Galloway cattle to Devorguilla's hostel for poor students in Oxford.[7]

There was much else to engage the Queen's interest. In April the Court
was at Linlithgow, in the old keep above the loch; a day or two later they
were in Edinburgh. There, high on its rock, with its burgh clustering along
the ridge and Holyrood abbey a mile away under Arthur's Seat, was a castle
so old that it incorporated buildings the earlier Queen Margaret had known.
Her tiny oratory, rebuilt by her son, stood on a crest, and nearby was a
treasury called 'Holy Cross dormitory', probably because it had housed the
monks who came to build Holyrood. From the castle walls one could look
across the Forth to distant blue hills.[8]

She was revising her ideas; this was not entirely the savage country of
minstrels' tales. There were rich abbeys, flourishing towns, good farmland,
and the court ladies were quite as well-dressed as those at home. She missed
her sister Beatrix and her brothers, and any companions of her own age, for
her attendants were married women; no responsible mother would let a
young daughter go off to attend a queen too young to protect her from inel-
igible courtiers.

If it was dull at times, there was little risk of real boredom. Alexander was
back at his lessons and Margaret had plenty to learn too; if anything, she was
starting late. Many little girls, betrothed in infancy like herself, were transferred to their future homes to be reared by aunts and mother-in-law by the
age of six, to learn the basics of life in that family and those castles. In a society
geared for war it was the women who planned and provided. Some, like a
bygone Countess of Leicester, rode with their husband's army, *ipsa etiam
loricata* ('herself also in armour'), but that did not prevent them running a

household and rearing children.[9]

It was unnecessary for a woman to be educated beyond reading her psalter; some clerics actively disapproved of females learning to write. Whatever their walk in life, they must be numerate, to count threads on a loom, eggs at market, castle stores. A woman who desired education faced a struggle; she might attain her desire in the cloister, perhaps too late to learn. Most upper-class families throughout Europe saw girls as bargaining-counters in alliances, and begrudged dowries taken into nunneries and alienated from family funds.

At least the child-brides had prospects of a managerial career. A castle required careful organisation. The building cannot be considered in isolation; it lay amid farmland from which came its food and its manpower. Produce came in for storage, medical help was provided for dependants and livestock; clothes, bedding and entertainment for travellers must be ready. The smallest motte-and-bailey carried such responsibilities.

For great landholders the problems multiplied. Their lands might be scattered far and wide, and as rents paid in kind could not readily be transported, households went where the food was. All sorts of equipment from beds to glass window-panels must be loaded into carts or on pack-horses while messengers galloped to alert the next lodging. The ladies rode apart from the wagon-dust but with ever-present thoughts of something left behind, a quarrel between cooks, an axle breaking at a ford. Certainly there were officials – a Steward, a Clerk of the Pantry – but also, inevitably, demarcation disputes.

A wife must know how things were done, what customs prevailed, which stores got damp in winter. She must cater for wildly changing numbers, always with enough fresh bread and new ale while avoiding waste. Even a queen, if she were not to be disastrously swindled, must know how many loaves a boll of meal should yield, how much wine should have been issued for nine men yesterday, seventeen on Tuesday; and though she might never dress a wound or nurse a fever she must supervise and prepare.[10]

It has been customary to dismiss all medieval houses as bleak and dirty and their food as coarse and nasty, but this is to carry our notions into the past. We see fire-less ruins, rain and jackdaws; given window-shutters, wall-hangings, scented herbs underfoot, hearths heaped with logs, peat or seacoal, they were not half so grim. Nor are gibes of 'a thousand years without a bath' justified; everyone, peasant or king, got into a tub of hot water by the fire whenever they had the tub and fuel to heat a cauldron.[11]

Food was mainly home-grown, but often elaborately prepared. There were seasons of glut and shortage, and problems of preservation; sea-salt hardens meat, rock-salt was rarely available. No farm could over-winter its whole stock, so culling and salting was autumn routine. The long weeks of Lent in early spring came as a relief to the thrifty housewife if her stores of dried and salted fish lasted. All food was as spicy as possible, using native herbs or imported spices; rich households bought rice, raisins, almonds and dates from Spanish suppliers.

Every castle and most small houses had gardens. Fordun says that David I took up gardening in his old age, specialising in grafting fruit trees; with his son's wife Ada de Warenne he made a memorable orchard at Haddington (King John felled it in the 1216 war). David had another garden below Edinburgh Castle, by the Nor' Loch (where Princes Street Gardens now lie), and Alexander III employed gardeners at Forfar and Menmuir. Such gardens were often in three parts – a vegetable plot, a herb close, and a lawn with flowerbeds where castle ladies might sit on turf benches or even have their baths prepared in warm weather. Apples, pears and cherries were grown, and on a few well-tended lawns the game of bowls began.[12]

As she travelled through Lothian Margaret might well envy the *bourgeoises*, the merchants' wives who never had to pack and move, living secure within their burgh bounds. Their houses were often more comfortable than castles, so that nobles preferred a *hostilegium* or *hôtel* within a burgh to their official quarters in its castle. Margaret may have seen inside such houses before long; on his last day of life Alexander would be invited to stay in one, in terms that imply it was a commonplace proposal.[13]

In such a house the heir was entitled to inherit

> the best table, tablecloth, hand-towel, basin, laver; the principal bed with linen sheets and other bedding, the best featherbed (or wool or flock mattress if there be no featherbed); a brewing-sink, mash-vat, cask and barrel; a cauldron, kettle, tripod, porringer, hearth-hood, pitcher and pot-crook. Also a chest, a churn, a plough, a wain, a cart; a brass pot, saucepan, iron cauldron, [baking-] girdle, mortar and pestle; a mazer [maplewood cup], a double trencher, a goblet, twelve spoons; a bench, a form, a stool; a balance and weights; a spade, an axe … Of all these the best pertains to the heir.[14]

The house to hold these possessions was usually of timber on stone foundations, standing gable-end to the street with a narrow entry between it and the next, and a long yard behind, in which might be stores and workshops as well as a byre and a detached kitchen-house. The ground floor of the dwelling-house was often an open booth, for the owner's goods or rented to another burgess if the householder was a sea-captain or long-range merchant. From the yard an outside stair led up to the main room overlooking the street, a bedroom behind it (with that featherbed) and a garret above for the apprentice or stores or both. In huts down the yard might be journeymen or other indwellers. Whatever their social standing they enjoyed the privileges of burgh life; the runaway serf from a country estate was safe within the palisade if he could survive undetected for a year; he might even buy himself into the burgess-roll through time, if he worked at his trade. The tall houses were for the master tradesmen, rulers of the town, who between them made up the Merchant Guild and elected their governing body from among themselves. Their towns were tiny by modern standards, two streets and a marketplace inside a ditch or a stockade, but they knew their rights.

David I began chartering royal burghs, on the pattern of Newcastle-upon-Tyne which he ruled at one time. He took Newcastle's laws as the basis for his burgh laws, which were thereafter altered or extended by an annual convention of representatives from Berwick, Roxburgh, Edinburgh and Stirling, meeting at Haddington. Every royal burgh had a castle alongside but always outside its precincts; the burgh supplied the castle's needs on a strictly commercial basis and expected its protection in time of danger. At other times the burgh mounted its own night-watch by rota, passing a staff of office from house to house. A tolbooth by the marketplace displayed official weights and measures; there dues were collected from foreign merchants and country-people coming to market. It became the place for meetings on town business, sales of land within the bounds, civil and criminal cases. Only the four Pleas of the Crown – rape, arson, murder and treason – went to the Justiciar on his twice-yearly visit to the castle. Nobody from the castle could interfere in burgh affairs without a request from the burgesses; a burgess who fell foul of the law elsewhere could claim trial in his home burgh.[15]

Most royal burghs were ports of entry by sea or land. All began as trading-posts, some (like Inverness) on the edge of newly subdued country. Their charters bade them elect their own *prepositus* and *ballivi* (whence the later Provost and Bailies); by the end of Alexander III's reign they began consolidating their citizens' dues into a block payment to the Crown, nominating one burgess to collect and account. Before the end of Robert I's reign there were customars in every royal burgh, with an official seal for stamping manifests when import duty was paid; the system may have begun under Alexander.

It was not a Scottish idea to overtax foreign trade; most imports were subject to a small levy, exports were taxed only in times of scarcity. The burghs protected their own trade by taking market-dues from outside merchants, obtaining royal bans on rival markets in the countryside, and maintaining standards by licences and inspections. Annual returns existed in 1291 (all lost soon after) but clearly trade was growing fast; Berwick was said to handle an annual volume equal to any two of the Cinque Ports. The royal initiative in founding burghs was followed by bishops and nobles erecting chartered 'burghs of barony', mostly for internal trade (the bishop's burgh of St Andrews being a notable exception).

Outside the towns life might be less comfortable. A fourteenth-century bishop of Moray's rules for equipping his canons' manses required

> a hall, kitchen and brew-house, with a trestle table, a basin and ewer, table-cloth and hand-towel; a brass jug, saucepan, tripod and chain, and a pestle and mortar; a brewing-sink, vat, dish and barrel.[16]

How the working population lived is more obscure. Their possessions are seldom recorded, their houses were built and rebuilt by the neighbours. In the north and west the design of recent houses goes back into prehistory, for rounded ends and thick walls are best for exposed sites. In Lothian, where repeated invasions wrought havoc, homes were of wattle, or clatt-and-clay, readily repaired. Down to recent times in some parts, turf was stripped in wide ribbons from fields and laid in layers against a wicker lining; the resulting house, with a good central hearth, was warm and windproof. The small wooden ploughs, lacking a knife ahead of the share, could not break dense turf, so the stripping was not quite as catastrophic as it seems.[17]

Picts, Gaels, Anglians, Norsemen and Danes had mingled their genes and customs and begun to call themselves Scots. David I's knights brought followers from the Danelaw and Brittany, and there were the Flemish colonists mentioned earlier, some of whom may have found their new upland peasants speaking a Cumbric Welsh not unlike the speech of Pembrokeshire.[18]

Bosses came and went but the people on the ground changed seldom. In feudal terms they were villeins, *nativi*, 'neyfs' unable to move without orders, but in their own eyes they were perpetual tenants living where their forebears lived and running their communities in ancient ways. Actual serfdom, familiar in much of Europe, was rare in Scotland except for the few who sold themselves for debt or to acquire a strong protector. Malcolm III is accused of bringing slaves back from raids into England:

> therefore Scotland was filled with slaves and handmaids of English race, so that to this day cannot be found, I say not a hamlet, but even a hut without them.[19]

A grain of salt needed, perhaps, and by the thirteenth century the descendants of such unfortunates would have blended into the general population. William the Lion made laws for the liberation of serfs, restricting the right to reclaim runaways to those who applied for a royal brieve, to be granted only after examination of the reasons for flight. A serf must be freed by the courts if his master wounded him, refused to stand surety for him on a criminal charge on which he was subsequently acquitted, or committed adultery with his wife (the *droit de seigneur*). There is a series of deeds of sale of named serfs and their families to Coldingham Priory in 1242, in the seller's 'great necessity'. Such sales raised money, or sometimes released a man of uncertain status into monastic service, enabling his son to enter the priesthood.[20]

Some landlords clearly thought they owned their workers; what is not so clear is whether the workers thought they were owned. Much arable land was worked by groups of smallholders, under larger tenants or holding directly of the Crown. There were also large farms on which monastic houses pioneered advances in crop and stock management, and others held on the ancient system called *métayage* or steelbow elsewhere, 'bowing' in Scotland. This looked back to Celtic tenures and involved the landlord providing the initial seed and livestock, drawing a percentage of the yield, and receiving an equivalent in stock and seed at the term, seven or nine years later. As well, there were special tenures by 'sergeanty', for some special service (an annual stock of peats, a pair of spurs or a snowball on demand) – oddities delightful to antiquarians and provoking much speculation as to origins.[21]

Perhaps the greatest difference between England and Scotland was hard for Margaret to grasp. It was less than two hundred years since the Norman conquest, less than one hundred since her own Angevin family took power; they and their followers were well entrenched but few felt a need to learn the vulgar tongue. Her uncle Richard spoke English, her brothers could do so at need, but these exceptions were not entirely approved. A deep gulf divided 'Norman' from 'Saxon', increasingly mythical but no less powerful. In Scotland a contrasting myth prevailed, that all Scots were kinsmen of their kings, that kings were elected, not imposed, and the state itself (insofar as anyone perceived such a thing) was an extension of the extended family. It was this conviction that gave the poorest dignity and confidence, producing a jocular familiarity between self-styled master and so-called man that troubled foreign observers. *Lanercost* preserves a glimpse of the Doorward's baron-court on Deeside (after mentioning, and misdating, his death) :

> Alan ... of whom for fleeting worldly faith I produce a tale both grave and funny. The agricultural lands of Scotland are not, as elsewhere, given on perpetual location, but the leases are renewed annually or else the rents are raised. A certain countryman having been summoned to say whether he would pay more or remove, and not wanting to tackle a new holding, agreed with his lord and sought security. To whom the knight, in the custom of the country, offered his right hand in guarantee. Much good it did the countryman, for next year the same question arose ... After six years he sought a fixed bargain once and for all and, many being there present, his lord said 'Here's my hand'. The simple man turned to him and 'Nay, sir,' says he, 'give me the other hand for I have found that one very shaky'. Everyone burst out laughing, and the knight, abashed, said 'Away with you, rustic, and keep all you have in perpetual peace for that faith'.[22]

It is tempting to replace the Latin phrases with colloquial Scots. The

Queen's attendants would have been scandalised, and waited to hear what befell the wretched peasant; it was disturbing that the Scottish ladies found the story amusing. Madame de Cantilupe could only sigh, and yearn to get back where jokes were jokes and property was sacred.

Chapter 5 Notes

1   Roxburgh, *RCAHMS Roxburgh I*, no.521 (burgh); no.905 (castle). The sites are some 3 km NE of the modern town.

2   *ES II*, 464–8, 471–8 (various sources), for the invasion &c. (see p.79) *ib.* 393–5, *Annals of Ulster* 1212–14, Alan and Thomas in Ulster; land grants to them calendared in *CDS I*, 573 (1213) and 625–6 (1215). Galloway history, Barrow *K& U*, *passim*.

3   Thomas the bastard m.a dau. of Ragnald Godfredsson, K. Man (he d.1229; p.2). They had at least one son. See pp.227, 235.

4   M. Paris, *Chr. Maj.IV*, 653 (1247), in *SA* 359.

5   For *Leges inter Britos et Scotos*, see *APS I* and *Regiam Maj.*, IV, 36–40; *APS I, Ass. Wi.*, for option of jury and fines in cattle. Edward's abolition, in line with his 1284 Statute of Rhuddlan for Wales, Barrow, *Bruce*, 192.

6   For the Haddington tourney see p.31. Pardon for Alan, *CDS I 1865* (20 Jan. 1252, Woodstock). Although Latin renderings of Gaelic are often arbitrary, the altered stress between Dun-*av*-erty and (presumed) Duna-*verd*-in (?for *Dun a' bhairdein*, 'Fort of the small fence or garrison') imperils the identification, as does 'in Ireland'; but see Barrow, *Bruce*, 209 *inf*.

7   *Chron.Lanercost*, 64, lists 'Alan fitzcount' among Scots bailiffs of Man post-1264; see also p.220 (1284 oath). Barrow, *A-N Era*, 3n, qu. Balliol College records for the legacy (120 cows).

8   For the early buildings, *PSAS XXI*, 291 *inf.* (restoration of chapel after use as gunpowder store); *dormitorio S. Crucis*, see App.D, list of valuables removed 1291 from chests there.

9   The lady 'herself also in a hauberk' was Petronilla de Grantosnil, coming to England 1172 with her husband Earl Robert III; the phrase is Fordun's.

10 There were relatively few religious houses for women in Scotland; App.C. An excellent study of housekeeping and journeys is in Labarge, *Bar. Hsehd.*, using Eleanor de Montfort's household books.

11 Cf. *ER I*, 27 (1266), 5 chalders of sea-coal for Berwick castle, with carriage, 15/- (10 chalders salt, £5.4.4d).

12 Harvey, *Gardens*, is a splendid general guide, with plant-lists; *ib.* fig. 7, bowls (c.1280). *ER I*, 8 (Sheriff of Forfar, 1263–4), gardener's wages at Forfar, 5 mks.; at Menmuir, 1 mk.

13 Owning a *hostilegium* did not necessarily convey burgess-rights; it was usually let to a burgess or indweller who kept it ready. For the Inverkeithing burgess, 1286, see p.229.

14 *BL I*, no.116.

15 *BL I* is the main source for these remarks; see also J.G. Dunbar, *The Historic Architecture of Scotland* (Batsford 1966), and the ongoing Scottish Burgh Survey (Soc. Ant. Scot., *PSAS 113* onward, and monographs). List of burghs at 1286, App.B.

16 *BL I* lists tolls beginning *temp.* David I; wain with 4 oxen, bringing non-burgess goods, 4d; horseload of fish, outward for resale in countryside, 1d. Imports (e.g. pepper, ginger, almonds, rice) entered free but paid 4d per bale if taken out in bulk. Visiting traders must not break cargo until offered to burgesses. Burgh courts licensed bakers and alewives, inspecting premises and fixing prices, fining sellers of substandard goods (e.g. re-heated pies). The manse rules, *Moray Reg.*, CCLXXXIV (ca.1350).

17 *Glasgow Archaeol. Journal*, 10, (Miss D.N. Marshall), MacEwan's Castle excavation; *Folklife* 22, 68 *inf.*, (J. Ross Noble) reconstruction of a turf-walled house at Kingussie Folk Museum.

18 The best analysis of these interlocked populations is W F H Nicholaisen, *Scottish Placenames*. (Batsford 1976). Flemings, p.24.

19 Symeon of Durham (1070) in *SA* 93.

20 *Regiam Maj.* II, 12 & 13. Under Canon Law a bondman could not become a priest, but could obtain personal freedom by becoming a monk or lay-brother. *QA* 56, form of writ, grounds, and procedures for reclaiming neyfs; *ib.* 70 (*Ass. David*, 9) voluntary renunciation of liberty. *NMssS I*, LIV, LVII, LIX, sales of serfs to Coldingham.

21 *ER I*; the fragmentary accounts for 1262–3 show many small rents paid in grain and cheese at Forfar, Forres and elsewhere. *Ib.*, 1ii, n2, Tyrebeg and 'Balmoschenore' held for obligation to furnish 300 cartloads of peat when the King came to Forfar (*ib.*76 bolls barley paid for this cartage, 1266). Ritchie, *Normans*, 221, for sergeanty.

22 Matthew Paris says Richard's ability to speak English endeared him to the German Electors of the Empire (Young, *R of C*, 86–7). Edward I could at least curse in English. *Chron. Lanercost*, 85, '1267' (Alan died 1275).

6

1252–1255: The Comyn Years

BEFORE THEY lit their fuse at York, Menteith and Mar must have formed some plan for clearing the wreckage, but having forced the resignation of the Chancellor and Justiciar they could do little until they returned home. *Parlement* was due to meet in February; then or earlier the Great Seal was broken and the lesser 'seal of the minority' entrusted to Mr Gamelin. Mar became Chamberlain; the office of Chancellor was left vacant. Anyone could foresee a flurry of appeals against the ex-Justiciar's verdicts, and accordingly two knights shared that post.[1]

No further action was taken against the Doorward, who still had many friends. It was more important to ensure general backing for the Comyn faction, ruling in the King's name. Never before had there been a King of Scots too young to select his advisers. Malcolm IV had inherited his grandfather's councillors, and as chance befell none of them died or retired for six years. The men Alexander II favoured kept power until the York crisis. The Comyn earls – Mar's wife was Buchan's sister – found themselves in the position of a long-standing opposition brought suddenly to office, without an established civil service to ensure continuity. Their acts would set the pattern for a graver situation which only Buchan would live to see.[2]

They relied first on kinsmen, with the support of the Bishop of St Andrews, a former Chamberlain, and his colleague of Glasgow, a former Chancellor. Some chroniclers paint the years of Comyn dominance as a time of unparalleled tyranny, but it is difficult to substantiate their case.

Three events offered scope for abuses which surely would have attracted notice. These were vacancies in the sees of Moray, Whithorn and St Andrews itself. Selection of a new bishop lay with the diocesan or cathedral clergy (procedures varying from bishopric to bishopric), although the king normally suggested a preferred candidate (not always accepted). Great temporal possessions were involved, and reverted to Crown custody until a new officebearer gave his fealty for them.

In 1252 the Bishop-elect of Moray died before consecration. Next year the dean was elected, approved by the Pope, and enthroned; he was Archibald, a Douglas or a Murray, of the Doorward party. In 1253 the Bishop of Whithorn died in Melrose, to which he had retired some years earlier; he

was a Cistercian, formerly abbot of Glenluce. Undeterred by their experience of a Regular as bishop, the Whithorn canons elected the Augustinian
abbot of Holyrood, but their choice was opposed by John Balliol as a principal
layman of the diocese. He had influence at York, to which Whithorn was
subject for historical reasons, so that Bishop Henry was not installed until
late in 1255. Despite the long interval (and appeals went to Rome about
delays), nobody alleged plunder of temporalities.[3]

Bishop David de Bernham,
from his Pontifical. (The leaf
has been cropped at some time,
removing the peaks of the mitre.)

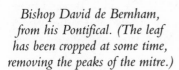

The third death was a loss to the whole country. David de Bernham,
Bishop of St Andrews since 1239, was renowned for hard work in his diocese
and as a royal servant. St Andrews was the premier see; it had an Augustinian
cathedral-priory, and nearby stood the Culdee house of St Mary of the Rock,
entitled to participate in electing bishops. Most Celtic monasteries had faded
away or been replaced, but Bernham befriended the clifftop community. It
had been agreed that the Culdee prebends should pass to the cathedral at
their incumbents' death; in practice, these livings were filled by Crown
nominees (the community was on the way to become a chapel-royal), often
graduate clerks, retired from royal service, and they formed a resolute fellowship. They were already at law with the priory over a disputed living when
Bernham died.

The canons met secretly, without Culdee representatives, and in such haste
that they excluded the Archdeacon, Mr Abel of Golin, whose right to take
part was unarguable. They chose the Dean of Dunkeld, Mr Robert Stuteville,
a former royal clerk but not a royal nominee. When their proctors left to
obtain papal approval, they were followed hotfoot to Rome by Mr Abel, by
Mr William Wishart for the Culdees, and by royal letters of protest. Innocent

IV took time to consider; in February 1254 he annulled Stuteville's election and himself appointed Mr Abel. Abel came home in June for enthronement, but died within months. Much would happen in Scotland and Europe before a successor was chosen.[4]

One might have expected Henry III to exert influence at a time of such uncertainty, but he was engaged elsewhere. The judicial enquiry into Simon de Montfort's administration of Gascony lasted five summer weeks, conducted in the refectory of Westminster Abbey (which cannot have been convenient for the monks). Cleared on all counts, to Henry's fury, Simon returned to Gascony for a last campaign and then withdrew to France. The Gascon rebels were greatly heartened by his going and by the accession of an energetic young king in Castile. Alfonso X showed signs of reviving ancestral claims to Gascony and Navarre, as well as intensifying the war to dislodge the remaining Moors from southern Spain. Gaston de Béarn, Queen Eleanor's uncle and an old enemy of Simon's, promptly offered homage to Alfonso. Eleanor was outraged, but Henry found Gaston one of those witty foreigners he greatly preferred to self-righteous earls.[5]

In summer 1252 Henry had a visit from another amusing foreigner, Alan the Doorward, who went home in autumn just ahead of Henry's new guardian for Margaret. Geoffrey de Langley was not a good choice; as justiciar of the northern forests he had been renowned for rapacity. The Scots refused to accept him; instead, Henry nominated John Balliol and Robert de Ros.

Matthew Paris believed Ros to be the principal guardian:

> So the Queen of Scots was entrusted to the guardianship of Robert, also the kingdom and the king, by council of the magnates of either realm, because he was held to be of blameless repute. And he was bidden not to let the king and queen of Scotland sleep together, because of their tender youth.[6]

De Ros was another of William the Lion's grandsons. His mother had first married a Bruce, great-uncle of the Lord of Annandale; her second, de Ros, marriage was in 1191, and although Robert was her second son he must have been well into middle age by 1253. His appointment conformed to the Scots custom of placing half-royal kinsmen around the throne. His home castle was Wark, on the English bank of the Tweed, and he was already in dispute with Henry over it.

For the next two years Henry had little leisure to consider his daughter's affairs. Eleanor kept in touch, with messages carried by William her butler or Walter, the Queen of Scots' tailor, and by gifts of the latest fashions. In June 1253, Henry summoned Margaret to come and keep her mother company while he sailed for Gascony. A fortnight later, on the eve of embarkation, he ordered Eleanor and his brother Richard, his regents, to dismiss Anketille Malore from Margaret's service and replace him with a fit

Table 6. Castile/Provence

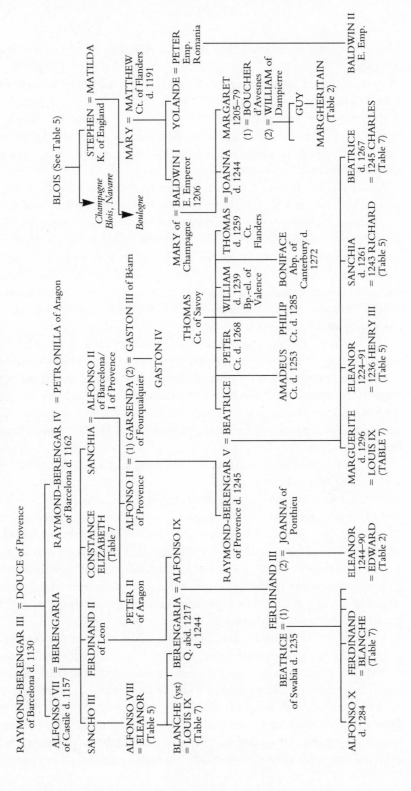

person; presumably Anketille had delivered the news that Margaret was not to come.[7]

Nothing could persuade Henry that his family's military genius had passed him by. He set off from Portsmouth with an army, to settle Gascony for ever and secure it for young Edward who had been promised it in 1243. The prince, aged fourteen and eager for action, had expected to lead the force himself; he was left 'lamenting' according to contemporary reports, but more probably in a bawling Angevin rage.

Henry still dreamed of a crusade, but first he must leave his realm in order and provide for his sons. The Queen-Regent of France, Blanche of Castile, had died in November 1252 and her son Louis was expected home at any time; French opinion favoured throwing the English out of their last continental foothold, and with Louis to lead them they would probably succeed. The troubadour-king of Navarre, widely believed to have been Blanche's lover, died soon after her, leaving a boy as heir; it seemed likely that Castile would intervene during the minority. All this made an end to the Gascon revolt imperative.

As he left, Henry sent letters to Norway, Scotland and Wales, 'commanding' their rulers to prevent raids on the Isle of Man whose king was absent 'by my leave'. Young Magnus of Man had at last earned his subjects' acceptance and was off to give homage to Haakon IV of Norway; he had safe-conducts across England, but he was not Henry's subject. The grandiloquent letters served to remind the world of Henry's wide influence; and they encouraged Henry too.[8]

The Queen Mother of Scotland passed almost unnoticed through England on her usual visit to France, and the Steward of Scotland also left the country, making his way to St James of Compostela. He could hardly hope for safe-conduct through England to the realm of one of Henry's suspected enemies, so probably he sailed all the way. Spain and Scotland had seaborne trade links, and Scots volunteers fought against the Moors. The Steward had no active part in government for the time, but he would never have gone overseas if things were unsettled at home. Buchan was now Justiciar, and Mr Gamelin began to be called Chancellor in papal letters (perhaps because he was already *cancellarius* of the see of Moray).[9]

In October 1253 Earl Simon rejoined Henry, his reputation greatly enhanced by his generous lack of resentment at bygone wild accusations. In November Queen Eleanor, still joint-regent, gave birth to her third daughter, a delicate child named Katherine. (She died before her fourth birthday, never having learned to speak, probably profoundly deaf). By early December Henry was calling for more men, and especially more money, and the regents wrote to remind Alexander of 'the link and league between us' which required 'interchange of all matters affecting our kingdoms'. They asked him to assemble his magnates in February to hear envoys from Gascony who would report 'most difficult and urgent matters wherein it is needful that you and your lieges afford aid and council'.[10]

At the same time Eleanor well knew peace was coming; she began planning Edward's marriage, and sent two knights and a lady, Margery de Creke, to Margaret, possibly with secret assurances. The official line was still of looming crisis; the English *parlement* met, to hear that

> The King of Castile, with a large army of Christians and Saracens, will attack our land of Gascony a fortnight after Easter, to devastate and occupy it; and if he succeeds, he aims to invade England and Ireland.[11]

This was sheer fiction, but it induced the baronage to summon the feudal host. They also decided to call two knights from each shire to the next meeting, in May, to discuss ways of raising money in addition to the scutage (the payment by feudal tenants who chose to commute their personal service and fund the hire of mercenary replacements). The tentative step towards 'knights of the shire' has long overshadowed the dubious manoeuvres which prompted it.[12]

On 14 February Henry invested Edward with a noble appanage – the county of Chester, Bristol and other castles, most of Wales, all Ireland except the counties of Dublin and Limerick, and all Gascony. If these yielded less than 15,000 marks a year, the shortfall was to be made up 'from elsewhere'. Geoffrey de Langley was sent to Wales, to insure those lands produced their full value; within eighteen months he produced a full-scale revolt instead.

The English *parlement* still had to find means to meet their king's needs in face of the reported dangers and his generosity to Edward, but their anxieties were dispelled by Earl Simon, who came to the May meeting with a cheerful and realistic assessment of the true situation (Henry and Alfonso were holding 'secret' peace talks). The shire representatives saw the Earl as their deliverer, and would not forget. As for Henry, he had a new and glittering idea.[13]

The Norman kingdom of Sicily, including much of southern Italy, had passed a generation earlier to the German-based Holy Roman Emperor. The grandson of Barbarossa and son of the last Norman Queen of Sicily was the Emperor Frederick II, physically insignificant, intellectually *Stupor Mundi*, the Wonder of the World. He survived a miserable childhood mainly through the kindness of his Saracen guards, who fed him and taught him Arabic. Among other achievements he negotiated truces with Arab rulers which opened access to the Holy Places (but earned him papal condemnation). A mortal feud with Innocent IV saw the Pope driven into exile at Lyons, from which he returned with loud rejoicing at the Emperor's death in 1250, only to encounter inter-city warfare in northern Italy, nominally between Guelf (pro-papal) and Ghibelline (pro-imperial) factions, but based on ancient rivalries. Two of Frederick's sons were also at war, and Rome, with several Sicilian cities, seized the chance to declare themselves self-governing communes.

Frederick had married three times, and also maintained a harem. His first Empress was an Aragonese princess, whose son died young; the second was nominal Queen of Jerusalem, whose son Conrad was proclaimed King at a week old, his mother having died; the third was Henry's sister Isabella, who left a son and daughter. None of his legitimate children gained Frederick's love; that was reserved for Manfred, his son by Bianca Lancia, though he bequeathed his realm to Conrad. The Pope, insisting that Sicily was a papal fief, not to be held by an excommunicated heretic like Frederick, rejected Conrad and, during one week in 1252, offered Sicily to King Louis' youngest brother Charles of Anjou, and to Richard of Cornwall who declined on the grounds that one might as well offer to sell the moon (he had visited his sister on his way home from his own crusade). Charles was forbidden to accept by Louis, who felt strongly about royal bequests.[14]

Innocent then considered young Henry, Isabella's son, but the boy died in December 1253 (naturally both Manfred and Conrad were accused of poisoning him). A month later Conrad accused the Pope of heresy and found himself excommunicated in turn. Manfred and the Saracen guards held most of southern Italy; in May 1254 Conrad died, worn out by campaigning; and King Henry had his brainwave. Nobody had done much for Henry's younger son Edmund, a good-natured boy who lived in Edward's shadow and endured a spinal deformity with patience (they called him 'Crookback', but affectionately). He was now nine, and must wait many years before England could afford to provide him with a fitting establishment; and there was a faint idea that he could be considered a possible heir to young Henry of Sicily.

Innocent liked the scheme and offered the kingdom. In his joy, Henry quite failed to grasp that there were conditions attached; he, or rather England, was to have the honour of financing not merely the conquest of Sicily but the whole accumulated papal debt, past and future. Henry did appreciate that he could not make his own crusade until Edmund was established, and he set about commuting his vows; unfortunately he had already led his new friend Alfonso to believe that English forces would help expel the Moors and pursue them through North Africa.[15]

The extent of the Sicily commitment was hidden from Henry's *parlement*. The knight-service set out for Gascony, Alan the Doorward volunteering to meet Strathearn's obligations for his Northumberland holdings. Alan spent summer 1254 abroad; he was present when Eleanor and Edward landed in Bordeaux, and expected to attend them into Spain – for in August a treaty was signed, and in October the whole royal party crossed the Pyrenees to Burgos, for the marriage of Edward to Alfonso's young half-sister Eleanor.[16]

Around the time of the treaty, Simon de Montfort came to Scotland, charged with 'secrets causing the King anxiety', and perhaps authorised to hint that Alexander might soon receive Huntingdon if Henry's worries were assuaged. These worries are not instantly obvious; he had his peace with Castile, the matter of Sicily was not yet made public. Perhaps France was the main problem. Louis had landed at last, and was slowly moving towards Paris. Henry had a truce with Louis's brothers, the prudent Alphonse of Poitiers and the ruthless Charles of Anjou; they had been sent ahead to take joint charge after their mother's death. (Charles was proving a ferociously efficient administrator of his wife's Provence. Her sister Eleanor disliked him, the eldest sister Marguerite of France loathed him). The background of Earl Simon's mission was probably the usual English fear that Scotland might prove pro-French, forgetting its prime obligation to support England.

Henry left Burgos in a glow of triumph and set forth on his first visit to France, both summit-meeting and sightseeing tour. He went first to Fontévrault where his Angevin forebears were buried, and arranged for his mother's body to be moved from the churchyard to the royal aisle. Then he met Louis at Chartres, and together they saw the glorious rebuilding works. The two kings entered Paris together on 9 December and Henry could inspect the Sainte Chapelle, which he admired so greatly that he 'wished he could put it on a cart and take it home'.

For the first time in seven years Louis would celebrate Christmas in his capital. To add to the splendour, the four Provençal sisters and their mother were re-united for the first time since their marriages. Old Beatrice of Savoy had around her Marguerite, her crusading ordeals behind her and her children beside her; Eleanor of England; Sanchia of Cornwall, thought the most beautiful, and Beatrice of Anjou, the youngest and richest (for her father bequeathed her Provence, endowing the older girls cautiously). Henry went home after the feast; Eleanor, convalescing from a stillbirth in November, remained a little longer in Paris.[17]

Far away from the family gathering, Margaret had lost her old duenna Madame de Cantilupe, who had gone to help a widowed daughter-in-law rear the heir to large estates. There is no word of a replacement, unless Margery de Creke filled the gap; by midsummer Margaret would be complaining about her attendants.

The Scottish administration was concerned with another election for St Andrews. This time proceedings were correct, the Culdees took part, the country's governors proposed a candidate. On 14 February 1255 Mr Gamelin was duly elected, and proctors set off for Rome to obtain not only approval but a dispensation for illegitimacy which would let him become a priest. (His colleagues of Brechin and Aberdeen had needed the same). The Bishop of Moray replaced him as Chancellor, an appointment approved by the Pope in June; Gamelin's dispensation took a month longer.[18]

Back in England, Eleanor sent a physician to enquire into her daughter's health. Mr Reginald of Bath found her pale and depressed, complaining of neglect and loneliness. He blamed her guardians, whom he 'severely reproved', and 'after disputes and bitter altercations and even threats', wound up roundly accusing 'all the nobles' of treason against both King and Queen. He then fell ill, and hastened to Oxford where on his deathbed he put his allegations into writing:

> he had come thither under an inauspicious star, for he had seen that [Margaret] was unfaithfully and inhumanly treated by those unworthy Scots, and because he had blamed them the Northerners had prepared snares of death for him. And when the king heard this he was much enraged, and silently planned vengeance for so great an offence.[19]

Henry was a genuinely affectionate father, and rushed to the rescue. First he despatched the earls of Gloucester and Albemarle, with John Mansel and Robert Walerand, his Seneschal, accrediting them to the bishops, earls, barons and other lieges of Scotland 'for the special benefit of Alexander King of Scots'. The same day he wrote, from the archbishop's manor of Cawood near York, to the earls of Dunbar, Strathearn and Carrick, twelve named barons, and:

> all others who shall adhere to [Henry] in opposition to those Scots who have caused or shall presume to cause damage to Alexander King of Scots or [Henry's] friends and adherents, or shall be gainsayers of his dearest daughter Margaret, Queen of Scotland, whose condition he intends to redress in good faith. He gives full power to his envoys, or any two of them, to provide full security for the said friends and adherents in the business, in all convenient modes, promising to hold their acts firm and sure.

He followed with letters of protection to the same named group, declaring that

> he has no design against the person or dignity of the King of Scotland, will not procure the dissolution of his marriage, and will make no peace with the said gainsayers and *malefici* without [these adherents]. These letters to endure until the King of Scots completes his twenty-first year.[20]

On 13 August in York he penalised John Balliol over a dispute with the Bishop of Durham. Three days later, when his envoys can scarcely have had time to report back, he ordered the sheriffs to mobilise the feudal army ('all holding of the King in chief, and all other vavassours and knights not holding in chief') in these terms:

The King to —. Having lately sent Richard Earl of Gloucester and John Mansel, Provost of Beverley, to Scotland, for the reformation and amelioration of the condition of its king and Margaret his queen, [Henry's] dearest daughter, and having heard from them that his presence is necessary, the King requires — to join him with his whole power, night and day with horses and arms to set forth to Scotland, desiring nothing but the good of the said king and queen.

He also, a little belatedly, sent for his own armour from the Tower of London.

Moving on to Durham, he deprived Balliol of the custody of Carlisle castle and entrusted it to Robert Bruce. He commanded the northern sheriffs to close all markets and tell those with victuals to sell to bring them to the army, 'and they shall be paid'. On 25 August at Newcastle he issued another proclamation:

> Understanding that some fear he proposes to weaken the state of Scotland and its liberties, whereas he is under many bonds to maintain the King of Scots' honour and the liberties of his kingdom unharmed, the King declares that nothing was done [at the York wedding] concerning the state of his councillors and their bailliaries calculated to injure [Alexander's] kingdom or its liberties. He is about to approach the Scottish frontier to see the said King and his daughter according to the great desire of his heart, and will neither do nor permit to be done anything prejudicial to that King or his kingdom, but rather, as bound by the link of parental affection, will give all his power and influence if need be to preserve the same.

He then commandeered Wark-on-Tweed, and sent a marshal to get the castle ready for royal guests.[21]

His envoys had reached Edinburgh just as a meeting of the governors ended with agreements to reconvene at Stirling and continue trying to heal the rifts with the Doorward and his friends. The Earl of Dunbar was still in the city, and with his help the envoys entered the castle. Matthew Paris reports them slipping past the gatekeepers one by one, posing as 'humble knights of Robert de Ros'. It is difficult to picture Mansel slipping past unobserved, even on horseback, for he had a grotesquely crippled leg (smashed by a stone during the siege of a Gascon monastery in 1243). Still, by dusk they held the castle, and with it both Alexander and Margaret.

The Queen, overcome by their sudden appearance, poured out her sorrows. She was 'unfitly guarded or rather imprisoned in that castle, a dreary and solitary place wholly lacking wholesome air and verdure, being near the sea'. (Maybe a summer haar enveloped the Castle Rock, helping the entry of the intruders). She was not allowed to go about her realm, or have her own household, or even choose her ladies. She and Alexander were kept apart and 'forbidden the comfort of mutual embraces'. That much the ambassadors could remedy; they saw the young couple bedded together that very night.[22]

So much for de Ros's instructions on appointment. He was to be the scapegoat; Balliol (according to the Melrose chronicler) soon made his peace 'with money whereof he had abundance', but de Ros was not a rich man. In vain did he plead that he had obeyed orders; his charges were fully old enough by contemporary standards to begin married life. Henry was not to be appeased; he pursued de Ros for exemplary damages of 100,000 marks (£66,000) until 1259, when his own barons made him admit de Ros's innocence.

But for the moment Henry only wanted to see Margaret. He had her and Alexander brought to Roxburgh, and on 7 September to Wark. The Comyns were calling out forces to attempt a rescue; it was perhaps Alexander himself who checked that lurch towards war. A distinguished company escorted the King and Queen into England – two of Henry's Lusignan half-brothers and four earls. They issued their own guarantee that neither King nor Queen nor any retainer should be kept in England except by consent of the Scots magnates, and that they personally would not permit any act prejudicial to Alexander or to his kingdom. They could do no more, and they rode in some apprehension alongside a simmering volcano of suppressed fury. We hear no details of the kings' meeting; Alexander appears to have gone back to Roxburgh the same day. He had things to arrange.[23]

Chapter 6 Notes

1   D.E.R. Watt, 'The Minority of Alexander III' (*TRHS*,1970), qu.M.Paris, *Chr.Maj*.V,501. The joint Justiciars were Michael de Montealto/Mowat and Philip Meldrum. Mowat's father had followed old William Comyn the Justiciar, Buchan's father, Meldrum married Buchan's sister Agnes. 'Seal of the Minority', pl.5.

2   Cf. the Guardians of Scotland from 1286 (p.235), of whom Buchan was one until his death in 1289.

3   Whithorn was different from the other Scottish bishoprics because it had been established during the early period of Anglian/Danish control (and because it claimed a pre-Columban origin from the days of St. Ninian, who died in 421).

4   Bernham's career, Watt, *Biog*.41–4; as Paris-trained musician, *Purser* 52–3 (& ill.); as diocesan, *PSAS XX*, 195 *inf.*, *ES II*, 520. Abel, Watt,*Biog*.225–7; William (I) Wishart,*ib*.590–4. In 1252 the 'Culdees' included Mr Adam of Makarstoun their provost, Mr Richard Vairement and Mr Wishart, all in Watt. Prebend dispute, *Sel.Cases* no. 43. Bp.Abel died 31 Aug.(*CM*) or 1 Dec. (*Chron.Bower*).

5   Powicke, 228–230.

6   Alan, s/c, *CDS I, 1888* (17 July 1252); Langley, M.Paris, *Chr.Maj*.V.340, in *SA* 369, and *CDS I, 1899* (2.Nov.) & *1900*. De Ros appt., M.Paris *H.A*, iii, 118, in *SA* 368 n.2.

7   Eleanor/Margaret, *CDS I, 1897, 1898, 1903, 1928–30, 1932*; Margaret summoned to England, *ib.1935* (2 July 1253); Anketille Malore, *ib.1936* (25 July).

8   Q.Blanche's funeral was 29 Nov.1252; Thibault IV of Champagne (I of Navarre) d, June 1253 (Powicke, 235n). Letters to Wales, Norway, Scotland, *CDS I, 1917* (4 Apl.1253); the Welsh princes addressed are Owain Goch and Llywelyn y Llew Olaf.

9   S/c for 'Queen M.' (wrongly extended 'Margaret'), to own country and ret., *CDS I*,

1916 (2 Apl). I cannot retrace my source for the Steward's pilgrimage; St. James the Great was joint-patron of Paisley abbey, App.C. The Steward's heir (b. 1243) was James.

10 Eng. Regents to Alexr., *CDS I, 1974* (misdated 27 Dec '1254').

11 Powicke 234–5 for 'threat' and Q. Eleanor's plans. *CDS I, 1949* (15 Jan. 1254, by the Queen), 40 mks. expenses for Matthew de la Mare, Wm. de Chaveringworth and Margery de Creke, going to Scotland. Margery's late husband had served Eleanor de Montfort's first husband; Labarge, *Bar. Hshd.,* 49.

12 Powicke 234 and n.

13 Grants to Edward, Powicke 233; E.Simon, *ib.*235.

14 Runciman *SV,* passim, for the Hohenstaufens and the Papacy. Richard visited Sicily 1241, returning from Crusade.

15 'The Sicilian Business', Powicke 236–9; Runciman *SV,* 73; Young, *R. of C,* 83.

16 Alan to Gascony, *CDS I, 1956, 1984–5*; Eleanor of Castile, b. 1244, was the only child of Ferdinand III's 2nd.m., to Joan of Ponthieu (to whom Henry III was betrothed before he m.Eleanor of Provence).

17 Simon's embassy (from Bordeaux) *CDS I, 1966* (25 Aug.1253); Charles of Anjou, Runciman *SV.passim.* Henry in France, Powicke 240–1 (Louis gave him an elephant for his Tower menagerie; it arrived Feb. 1255 and was drawn by M.Paris); Labarge, *St.L,* pl.16c.

18 William III de Cantilupe d. 1254; his widow Eva de Braose was a co-heiress of the Old Marshal. Wm's bro. was St. Thomas C.,Bp. of Hereford, and Simon de Montfort's friend Bp. William C. of Worcester was an uncle. Gamelin's election, Watt *Biog.* 209–214, & see p.23. Innocent IV d.7 Dec.1254, succ. within a week by Alexander IV.

19 M.Paris, *Chr.Maj.*V, 502–2, in *SA* 370–1.

20 *CDS I, 1986–8* (all 10 Aug.1255,Cawood). Full list of addressees, p.72. NB the ref. to Alexr's 21st year (p.70).

21 Dispute (Longnewton Ch) *CDS I, 1989*; form of summons, and armour, *ib.1990* (16 Aug., York); Carlisle, *ib, 1991* (18 Aug., Newburgh), *1993* (22 Aug., Durham). Markets, *ib. 1992* (21 Aug.); proclamation *ib. 1995* (25 Aug.); Wark, *ib. 1998* (28 Aug.; all Newcastle).

22 M.Paris, *Chr.Maj.V,* 504–6, in *SA* 371, with Burton and Dunstable annals, *ib.,* fns. *CM* 111–12 (opposite view) in *ES II,* 581–2. Mansel, Powicke 294 & n., Young, *R of C,* 48.

23 De Ros case closed, *CDS I, 2168* (1259). S/cs for Alexr. and Margaret, *ib.1997* (to Gloucester and Mansel, 28 Aug., Newcastle), and *ib.2001* (2 Sept., Alnwick) to Geoffrey de Lusignan, William de Valence, and Es. of Norfolk, Surrey, Albemarle and Lincoln. Guarantees by these, *ib.2002* (4 Sept., Chillingham). 4 Sept. was Alexander's fourteenth birthday.

1255: The Faithful Father

ON 8 SEPTEMBER the two kings met in Kelso Abbey church for mutual declarations of friendship, and rode together to feast in Roxburgh. No details are recorded of others present; Menteith, Mar and de Ros had safe-conducts from Gloucester and Mansel permitting them to 'come to the King' with retinues, and presumably they escorted Alexander home. Bishop Bondington of Glasgow, and Mr Gamelin as Chancellor, were probably at Roxburgh, and Bondington may already have received the papal mandate for Gamelin's consecration, sealed in Rome on 7 July. If so, it may be that he enabled Gamelin to swear fealty immediately, before sending him into cover, to his stall in Glasgow Cathedral or, even more probably, to his childhood haunts above Ettrick. In either place he would be safe, whatever powers were deployed against the Comyn faction.[1]

There were discussions of a sort, prolonged over two weeks even though all decisions had been made elsewhere. There was some slight easing of tension; Henry dismissed a team of miners from Alston, called up in case siegeworks were necessary, and showed his gratitude with a gift of £1 (between them). The feudal army remained, spread from Wark to Chillingham. The queens moved south to Morpeth, with Margaret's sister Beatrix. Eleanor (pregnant again, and none the better of her journeyings) had points to make about wifely duties which Margaret might justifiably resent, given her recent regime. Meanwhile, Margaret exerted herself to win privileges and pardons from her father, sometimes with Beatrix's help, for Berwick merchants and others. It was as if she wanted to stress her loyalty to her husband's country, and to make good use of the indulgent climate while it lasted. Each small gain might ease her return to a resentful kingdom.[2]

By 20 September both kings issued declarations, Alexander from Roxburgh, Henry from Sprouston (which he may have believed was English ground, being south of the Tweed, though in fact within the big southward bend of the Border). It was a grim test for Alexander, for he was required to dismiss all his recent advisers and even members of his household, down to his personal chaplain, declaring that they should not serve him for seven years, until his twenty-first birthday. To give a gloss of normality the outgoing Council were invited to affix their seals; Henry 'took it ill' that Gamelin and the earls refused. A century later, Fordun saw the change as happy:

> Judgment and justice being asleep in Scotia, for goodwill to his son the king
> and his nobles Henry King of England came, like a faithful father, at their
> request to the castle of Wark, where the kings and their councillors went busily
> to work to discuss the state of the kingdom of Scotia; immediately all the King
> of Scotland's councillors were dismissed from their offices. Appointed were
> Richard, Bishop of Dunkeld, as Chancellor, David Lindsay as Chamberlain,
> and Alan Dorwart as chief Justiciar, for seven years.

Among those thronging Roxburgh appeared Ewen of Argyll (obviously
not alone; one would like to know how many came with him). Though the
Manx had rejected his authority he had set young Magnus safely on his
throne, and thereafter divided his time between Norway and his own Isles.
Someone had called on him for military aid; now he needed safeguards,
fearing the new masters who were, after all, the men who had inflamed the
old king against him. He got help first from Mansel ('and if he incur forfei-
ture, the King will see it amended') and later from Henry himself; and rode
homeward.[3]

The Sprouston document opens resoundingly and is of uncommon length,
incorporating the whole of Alexander's letter:

> Henry, by God's grace King of England, Lord of Ireland, Duke of Normandy
> and Aquitaine, Count of Anjou, to all to whom the present letter shall reach,
> greeting. Know that we have received letters from our beloved son and faithful,
> Alexander by the grace of God illustrious King of Scots, in these terms ...

Alexander's text is in a painfully convoluted style (with two exceptions) and
in terms which neatly echo expressions in Henry's usual forms. Addressed
not to Henry, but to 'all the faithful in Christ to whom this writing shall
come', it opens with a narrative; Henry the illustrious King, Alexander's
dearest father and lord, has graciously come in person to the Border, for the
honour and advancement of Alexander and his kingdom. At his insistence
and with the advice of his own (named) magnates, Alexander has removed
from office a number of former councillors (also named, and including some
of the first list) 'because their faults require it, as is said', (*ut dicitur*). They and
their accomplices will not be admitted to affairs of state, to favour or to
friendship, until they have atoned 'by concord or by judgment' to King
Henry and to himself for 'faults imputed or to be imputed'; if need be,
Alexander will compel amendment by all just means.

The first of the concise clauses follows; if a foreign power should invade
Scotland 'it shall be permitted' (*liceat*) to call upon the services of those
removed, as on all others.

'To this end' (we are back with the purge) a new group of advisers has been appointed by advice of King Henry and of the 'aforesaid magnates', to 'our council, to govern our realm and to have custody of our person and that of our queen'. They shall not be removed from office until seven complete years 'from the feast of St Cuthbert just passed' (4 September, Alexander's fourteenth birthday) or a briefer period agreed between Henry or his heirs and Alexander, except for unworthy conduct; vacancies are to be filled by advice of the survivors. Nothing may be done concerning wardships or escheats (forfeitures) without the councillors' consent; they shall replace sheriffs and lesser officials who offend; royal castellans may not be changed without common counsel of the advisers. (There are no signs of escheats or wardships being abused; established procedures existed for appointing sheriffs, but all these matters had been fruitful sources of trouble during Henry's own long minority).

Alexander promises to treat Margaret 'with matrimonial affection and every consideration befitting our queen and the daughter of so great a prince', causing due and proper honour to be shown her. He ratifies the 'reasonable undertakings and concessions' made to Henry by the bishops and magnates, 'as representing our own command and desire'. The Earl of Dunbar has sworn on the King's soul that Alexander will faithfully keep all these provisions (this was customary; it was beneath royal dignity to make oath in person). He submits himself to the Pope, so that if he offends, which God forbid, he may be compelled by ecclesiastical censure to keep his undertakings without recourse to law; and (the second sharp clause), when seven years are up, the document is to be returned and thereafter held of no account:

> in evidence whereof we have caused our seal to be affixed to the present writing. *Teste meipso apud Rokesburg.*

Henry concludes his own proclamation by declaring that he has granted in good faith to the King of Scots that at the end of the seven years no prejudice shall be caused to him or to his heirs, his realm or his royal liberties, by this writing which shall then be held of no effect but which, nevertheless, shall be restored as void.

The whole document was then enrolled on the Charter Roll of England and the Patent Roll as well, for greater security, under the title *De Facto Scocie*. A note is attached:

> *Memorandum*, that letter was made and granted to the King of Scotland by command of the King of England at Carham, by the advice and at the sight of Richard Earl of Gloucester, Geoffrey de Lusignan and William de Valence the King's brothers, John Mansel Provost of Beverley, Roger Bigod Earl of Norfolk and Marshal of England, John de Warenne Earl of Surrey, William de Forz Earl of Albemarle, Edmund de Lacy, John du Plessis Earl of Warwick,

Hugh Bigod, Roger of Mold Steward of Chester, Elias de Rabbayne, John de Grey, Robert Walerand, William de Clere and many other barons and counsellors of the King then and there present.[4]

This then is what Fordun considered the act of a faithful father. On internal evidence it was prepared in advance, with only the reference to invasion, and the provision for return and annulment, inserted during the fortnight's conference. The plan may well have begun with Mr Reginald of Bath's visit.

The Scots involved are shown overleaf. Some (not all) addressed in August took office in September, among them at least four who witnessed Alexander II's death. Others had not been approached beforehand, notably the Earl of Fife. Among those removed the most remarkable must be Mary Maxwell, sitting in council with her husband and unique as a woman in public life. The abstention of the Crawford brothers is also noteworthy; though closely linked to the Lindsays, their lands covered the road from Carlisle to the passes into Clydesdale. They were not collaborators.

Only an absolute necessity to avert invasion and civil war could have induced Alexander to seal such a humiliating parchment. He may well have been advised to do so by Bondington or Gamelin, firstly because the reference to the Pope would ensure a copy being sent to Rome and closely scrutinised when it arrived, and secondly because that scrutiny would show that the sole signatory was a minor (*teste meipso* ...). Minors could not make contracts without the endorsement of guardians; which is probably why Henry was so angry about the refusals to seal.

The dismissed councillors' faults are never specified; 'imputed or to be imputed' invites a witch-hunt. And what were those 'undertakings and concessions' made to Henry by bishops and magnates? Can they have had to do with the twentieth of Scottish church revenues he was hoping to receive for his Sicilian enterprise, a year later?

In adult life Alexander was adept at simulating anger when he did not feel it, concealing it when he did; maybe he had learned the art from his red-haired father; September 1255 was a time to develop such skills, not least in preparing for Margaret's return.

Henry's barons had witnessed some devious procedures and maybe misliked them, however willing they were to consider Scotland a tiresome province which, like Wales, would be none the worse of a good mauling. They or their fathers had protested at York in 1244 at Henry's plan to hire Flemish mercenaries for the war that never happened; they felt then, and they said now, that they were quite capable of doing the business themselves. Henry and Norfolk had had one of their frequent rows at Newcastle on the way north, with Henry calling Norfolk 'traitor' and threatening to 'reap his corn', and Bigod replying that in that case he would reap the harvesters' heads.[5]

ADVISERS

Bp.Glasgow (Wm.Bondington)
Bp.Dunkeld (Rd.Inverkeithing)
Bp.-el.St.Andrews (Mr Gamelin)
Abbot of Dunfermline (John)
A. Kelso (Robert of Smailholm)
A. Jedburgh (Nicholas)
A.Newbattle (Roger)
Earl of Fife (Malcolm II)
† Earl of Dunbar (Patrick III)
† Earl of Strathearn (Malise II)
† Earl of Carrick (Neil)
† Robert Bruce (*le Noble*)
† ★Alexander the Steward
† ★Alan the Doorward
★Walter Murray (of Petty)
† ★Robert Meyners
Gilbert Hay (Sheriff of Perth)
Roger Mowbray
William Douglas
John de Vaux (Castellan of Dirleton)
'& others'

REMOVED

Bp.Glasgow
★Bp.Dunblane (Mr Clement OP)
Bp.-el.St. Andrews
E.of Menteith (Walter Comyn)
E.Buchan (Alexr.Comyn)
E.Mar (William)
John Balliol
Robert de R.os
Aymer de Maxwell
Mary de Maxwell (1)
Nicholas de Soulis
Thomas Normanville
Alexr.Uviet (Sher.Selkirk)
John of Dundemore
David Graham (2)
John le Blund
Thomas son of Ranulf (3)
Hugh Gurle (4)
William Hugh's brother
Mr.Wm.Wishart,A/deac.St.As.
Brother Richard, O.T. (5)
David of Lochore
John Wishart (6)
William of Cadzow (7)
William, the King's Chaplain

NEW COUNCIL

Bp.Dunkeld; Chancellor
Bp.Aberdeen (Mr Patrick Ramsay)
Earl of Fife
Earl of Dunbar
Earl of Strathearn
Robert Bruce
Alexr.the Steward
Alan the Doorward
David Lindsay (8)
★Walter Murray
★William of Brechin
★Robert Meyners
Hugh Giffard
Gilbert Hay

Addressed on 10 Aug. but not named as new Councillors

William Murray (9)
John Crawford
Hugh Crawford (his brother)
William Kalebraz (=Galbraith)
'& many others'

★ Kerrera, July 1249
† Addressed, letter of 10 Aug. p.64

1 neé ?MacGeachan; heiress of the Renfrew Mearns
2 Of Mellerstain; feudal tenant of Earl Patrick of Dunbar
3 Grandfather of Robert I's Thomas Randolph, Earl of Moray

4 Formerly a page to Q.Joanna (name=Gourlay)
5 Almoner of the Order of Templars in Scotland
6 Elder bro. of Mr. William; lands at Conveth, Laurencekirk
7 See p.24
8 David L. of the Byres, son of ★David (who died 1249)
9 Possibly scribal error for Walter,*q.v.* (s. of William who died about 1250)

However shocked or delighted the great men might be, the country at large is unlikely to have known the extent of English intervention. Men had marched away, women and grandfathers finished the harvest, the men returned unscathed. If someone saw the knight riding by, and a gey sour face on him, there was no knowing what put him in bad trim. When the pedlar came by, they might learn more.

Pedlars who had passed through Dumfries had a juicy tale, of murder on the king's highway. A soldier from the castle had killed the town's miller; well, the miller was dead, but seemingly the soldier was not to blame. There had been an inquest before the coroner – terms that fall oddly on a modern ear, where we would expect a fatal accident enquiry before the sheriff. The jury-list supplies a handful of local worthies; Adam Long, Adam Mills, Hugh Shearer, Roger Whitewell, Richard Haket, Walter Faccinger, Thomas Scot, Robert Muner, Bald Thomas, Robert Boys, Willy Scut, William Tanner, Henry Dyer. The soldier was Richard, son of Robert, son of Elias (perhaps a local man, his folk were known). He fell out with Adam the Miller in the kirkyard after service; Adam called Richard *Galuvet*, and said he'd run him out of town. (*Galuvet* is not explained; it might mean 'outsider from Galloway', or 'hired fighter', like the Galloway men who served in Ireland. It was evidently insulting). That was on a Sunday; the next Wednesday Adam was standing at his door when a woman cried to him, 'Away in! Here's Richard!' Adam went indoors for a knife; 'Never you pull me away, mine's as sharp as his.' He ran out at Richard, 'seeking to disembowel him'; Richard parried the blow with the flat of his short sword. Adam threw his arm round the sword and fell bleeding; Richard said to him, 'I have not killed you, you have killed yourself'.

If the jury had brought in a verdict of murder, Richard would have gone into ward in the castle until the justiciar came to try crown pleas; as it was, a jury of knights was empanelled to join the townsmen, and all agreed that 'Richard was in all respects a faithful man, but Adam a known thief and defamer'.

Richard was cleared on previous good repute; moreover Adam had fetched the knife, Richard only defended himself. His sword marks him as a cross-bowman, one of a trained élite; put bluntly he was too valuable to lose. Millers by contrast were always reviled. They leased their mills from lairds or burghs, they took a grinding-fee in grain, everyone was thirled to that mill and could use no other. Inevitably they were seen as rogues in league with authority. (Just before someone assumes the coroner's court was a recent imposition, it should be said that it was well-established; the two legal systems had not then grown apart, in the areas once settled by Danes and Anglians). '

Across Scotland, at Dryburgh, ambitious building-projects had brought the Abbey into financial trouble with creditors in Glasgow, St Andrews, and

London, and eventually into receivership, with the Pope appointing the Bishop of St Andrews (Gamelin) and the Abbot of Jedburgh to receive all revenues and apply them to clearing the debts, assigning enough to keep the community in being. These are the oldest recorded bankruptcy proceedings in Scotland.

If the Abbot of Dryburgh was embarrassed, so was the Earl of Dunbar, three of whose knights were awaiting trial for nothing less than highway robbery. John of Pitcox, his brother Patrick and their uncle Nigel of Whittingehame had held up a Dunbar merchant named Roger le Perour, and had so bungled the affair as to be caught. They were cooling their heels in Edinburgh Castle because nobody (including their Earl) would stand bail for them, and because they insisted on their knightly privilege of defending themselves by combat. Trial by combat had been removed from the statute-book by Alexander II, and that these hooligans demanded it gives reason for its abolition. Eventually the Queen and Bishop Bondington induced them to accept a jury trial; an indignant group of knights found them guilty. John was fined 100 marks and forfeited all the goods found in his house at the time of arrest; Patrick was despatched to the Holy Land, never to return without the King's leave; what became of the uncle is not recorded. Earl Patrick had evidently been too busy to keep his followers in order.[6]

The new rulers were resolved to prevent Gamelin's elevation, seeing him as the Comyns' best ally. They despatched allegations to Rome that he had abused his position as Chancellor, both in undue influence to obtain election, and in misappropriation of the temporalities of the see. While their envoys set off, they forbade Bondington to execute the mandate, and they set about impounding the remaining assets (justifiably, if the intention was to assess how much had already disappeared).

Bondington was too old a hand and too loyal a churchman to let laymen come between him and his obedience. On 26 December he installed Gamelin as the premier bishop in Scotland. Ritual required three bishops to be present; Clement of Dunblane must be a strong probability, Albinus of Brechin seems likely. (A close kinsman of William of Brechin, now in power, Albinus was not a whole-hearted supporter of the new régime, and indeed William himself may have served as a moderating influence).

The climate of Scotland would not be healthy for the new Bishop. The Melrose chronicler asserts that he was 'outlawed',

> because he refused to acquiesce in their abominable plans, and because he scorned to give a certain sum of money, as if for the purchase of his bishopric. And since Scotland cast him out, and England refused him passage, he followed Neptune and went to France, and boldly approached the Roman court in opposition to his adversaries. After his departure the King's councillors

plundered the goods of his bishopric, and consumed it at their leisure.[7]

It cannot have been a comfortable voyage, in midwinter, to a French or Flemish port; the wonder is that there was a ship to undertake it. Gamelin knew his way around Europe, of course, but this journey was to be different. He had not acquired an episcopal entourage, but he did have the company of his Archdeacon, Mr William Wishart, concerned to see the Bishop received everywhere with fitting state. Once in Paris, they could find plenty of distinguished Scots, many of them old friends, but first they had to reach land and set out through mud and snow. In summer conditions, the round trip to Rome and back could be done inside six weeks, but the well-worn Alpine routes were closed in winter, and inter-city wars flickered across northern Italy; most probably the travellers went down the Rhône and thence took ship for Genoa or Pisa.

Wishart's own university was Bologna, though he had taught in Paris. Paris was of the northern type, founded and controlled by the Church, and its lecturers would be scandalised by Gamelin's misfortunes. Bologna was among the oldest of the southern universities, run by its students who hired and fired their professors; Bologna would whoop out along its pillared arcades if Wishart arrived.

There was just one drawback to Mr Wishart as travelling companion. Lanercost, which has much to say about him and little to praise, throws in a 'notable saying' of the time. There were three remarkable men at King Alexander's court; one who always quarrelled but was never angry, and that was Mr Nicholas of Moffat; one who preached piety but did not practise it (John of Cheam, a later Bishop of Glasgow); and one who always laughed and was never joyful, Mr William Wishart. We know that laugh; it brays across the centuries.[8]

While bishop and archdeacon toiled towards Rome, there was plenty for loyal diocesan clergy to do at home. With Bondington's support they dug in for a long siege. An early sign of their resolve was a firm accord with the Culdees, that reservoir of legal talent. From the clifftop they watched the little ship lurch away, then they girded their gowns and went to work. Parishioners must be encouraged to squirrel away the bishop's share of teindcorn and livestock (no great persuasion needed), while they themselves buried the palace plate and put the fine vestments into safe-keeping, a jewelled mitre in one monastic sacristy, a gold-laden cope in another. Some chests may have gone back with Bondington to Glasgow; it would be a bold layman who inspected his storerooms.[9]

There were also letters to write, to old college friends now at Cologne or Toledo or Oxford, wherever a leader of opinion could be stirred into protests against lay oppression. They knew already that under the present Pope decisions did not come quickly.

Chapter 7 Notes

1 S/cs by Gloucester and Mansel to Menteith, Mar and de Ros, *CDS I, 2003* (Chillingham). The papal mandate, and dispensation for illegitimacy, were dated 7th July and addressed to Bp. Bondington; Watt, *Biog.*,210. Gamelin's father's parish was Kilbucho, in a high valley within the Lamington/Biggar/Broughton triangle, on the watershed between Clyde and Tweed. See Comyns, p.25.

2 Alston miners, *CDS I, 2007* (7 Sept., Wark). See p.210. Between 15 and 24 Sept., Margaret obtained pardons and reliefs for sundry petitioners, sometimes with Beatrix (*CDS I, 2009, 2011,2020, 2032*). Lindsay became Chamberlain on the death of Bishop Ramsay of Aberdeen, December 1255.

3 Fordun, LI. S/c for Ewen, *CDS I, 2014* (Mansel) and *2018* (Henry, 23 Sept., Alnwick). See also Ch. 1.

4 The Sprouston/Roxburgh declaration is given in full by Stones, *Docs.* 30–34 (I have extended the opening titles as directed) and calendared in *CDS I,2013.*

5 English barons' protest against mercenaries, 1244, Barrow, *K & U*, 150. The Bigod quarrel, (over Henry's treatment of de Ros), Powicke, 342.

6 *Sel.Cases,* no.42 (Dumfries), no.48 (Dryburgh); papal mandate, 13 Jan.1256, placing revenues in receivership. Pitcox case, *CDS I,2673* (Addenda, 'ca.1254').

7 *CM* 113; *ES II*, 585. (Albinus was perhaps William's natural brother).

8 *Chron.Lanercost,* 53; for Wishart's career, Watt, *Biog.* 590.

9 It was Mr William's relative, Bp. Robert Wishart of Glasgow, who produced robes for Robert I's enthronement in 1306; Barrow, *Bruce*, 210.

A raider threshing corn-sheaves so as to carry off the grain.

8

1256–1257: The Doorward Years

THE IMPULSE to project twentieth-century political ideas back into earlier times must be resisted. The Council installed under Henry III's guidance in 1255 was not a political party but a gathering of powerful individuals. If anything united them, it was a dislike of the Comyn group that they replaced. Little more can be deduced about them, except that Alan the Doorward was both able and ambitious, and that the young Earl of Dunbar was reported to be fervently pro-English. (The Lanercost chronicler claimed personal knowledge of the Dunbar household, and to have witnessed the Dowager Countess's death-bed forgiveness of her son for 'his long absence in England'. This seems doubtful; the Earl was active in Scotland up to and beyond his mother's death in 1267.)

The Countess Euphemia was the eldest sister of Alexander the Steward; her sisters were the Countesses of Carrick and Lennox, and the wife of King Donald of the Isles (who died in 1245). The Steward, Alexander of Dundonald, is the one councillor who may have developed a new government initiative.

The office of state called the Stewardship had humble beginnings; a steward was originally a kind of major-domo. The first hereditary Steward of Scotland, Walter son of Alan, was appointed under Malcolm IV, having arrived in Scotland around 1136 from Shropshire, where his father was sheriff. The FitzAlans were a Breton family, with a strong crusading tradition; in every generation the eldest Breton son was named Jordan. Alexander's brother John died on the Egyptian beach-head in Louis IX's 1249 Crusade. There were two other brothers, Walter called *Ballach* ('Freckled') and Robert of Tarbolton. Their lands extended far beyond the ancestral fief of Renfrew, where the first Steward had founded a Cluniac priory with monks brought from Much Wenlock; this was later moved to Paisley and enlarged into an abbey, preserving its Shropshire dedication to St Milburga and adding St James the Great and a locally venerated St Mirinus.

Some time after the death of Somerled the Great near Renfrew in 1164, the Stewards obtained custody of the Isle of Bute and built a splendid moated castle at Rothesay. Alexander's mother was the heiress of the former Lord of Bute, a kinsman of Somerled. Heredity and practical considerations combined to make seamen of the brothers; Walter *Ballach* would eventually have charge of the 'King's ships', and Alexander needed his own small fleet to keep him in touch with his mainland and island holdings along the Clyde coast.

There had been a gap in western defences since the death of Alan of Galloway and the division of his lands. No particular danger threatened in the 1250s, but petty raiding and escapes from justice were reminders that the coasts lay open to trouble. Ewen of Argyll, the bishops of both Argyll and Sodor, and Earl Nigel of Carrick, were all concerned to see peace kept. The Earl of Carrick was dying, leaving only a baby daughter and a kinsman appointed *Ceann-cinneil* ('Head of the kinship' or in later terms 'Tutor of the clan'. There can be no clearer proof that Carrick, carved out of Galloway in the previous reign, was Gaelic-speaking and Celtic-minded). Alexander of Dundonald would have to concern himself with the earldom when his brother-in-law died. He might also have a better grasp than his east-coast colleagues of the complexities of the island kingships, their relation with Man and Norway, their internal tensions. Earl Nigel had a useful link with Argyll in the person of its bishop, variously called Alan 'de Carrick' or '*Carricensis*'. The first form indicates close kinship with Nigel, the second merely locates his origin; either way, Bishop Alan hailed from the Clyde shore. The Bishop of Sodor and Man, whose allegiance was to Norway, was a canon of St Andrews named Richard. The Scots Council might hope he would exert his influence to keep the peace; on the other hand he might share his associates' quarrel with the Doorward supporters. At all events, the Steward appears to have tried to settle at least some of the uncertainties of the western seaboard.[2]

It can be hard to convey to landward-oriented outsiders the importance of seaborne communications. Until the mid-twentieth century passengers and goods of all kinds moved routinely by sea between Ayrshire, Kintyre, the Clyde and the Western Isles. Man is within sight of Galloway, Islay of Ireland, Antrim of the Kintyre and Knapdale coasts. The roots of the Kingdom of the Scots grew on the southern shore of the 'Dalriadic Sea'. The 1098 treaty of Tarbert gave Kintyre and all circumnavigable islands to Norway, and though Arran, Bute and the Cumbraes had drifted back into Scottish control, Angus of Islay and his kinsmen still held much of Kintyre.

In 1263 Angus would excuse himself to King Haakon of Norway for uncertain support with the claim that he had been compelled to do homage to Scotland seven years earlier, despite fleeing to Ireland. There is no sign of a massive seaborne attack, such as might 'compel' submission, but presumably the Steward visited his nephew in sufficient state to make co-operation seem advisable. In 1256 King Henry instructed his Irish officials not to receive Angus 'or other malefactors of the King of Scotland' whose names were to follow; like the Sprouston declaration, the order was to last seven years. The

1282 list of Scottish archives included:

> a letter of the barons of Argyll, that they would faithfully serve the King under pain of disinheritance and that they would all rise against Angus son of Donald if he did not do the King's will.

This, presumably, was the Steward's strongest weapon.[3]

Magnus of Man had visited the English court at Easter 1256, on his way home from Norway. Henry knighted him and granted him letters of protection 'for as long as he is faithful'. Henry also warned his lieges in Ireland and Wales not to shelter Harald Godredsson (the 1249 Manx usurper), Ivar (the probable murderer), or their accomplices who 'wickedly slew the late King Ragnald, the King of Man's brother'; the King of Scots was asked to observe the same sanctions. Belated though they were, they signalled a new English interest in Man.[4]

Angus might be attached, Man might be neutralised, but the Norwegian problem was unresolved. The last major attack took place in 1230 in the Steward's youth, when seaborne raids by Alan of Galloway had been reported to Bergen. A daughter's son of old Somerled, known in Norway as Uspak Ogmundsson, was despatched with a small fleet which he augmented in Orkney, the Nordreys and Man so that he led about eighty sail when he reached Islay. There he fell foul of his home-bred kinsmen, but continued into the Clyde and captured Rothesay, 'hewing through the wall with axes'. (This feat was long dismissed as 'a typical saga exaggeration', until renovations recently disclosed the patched-up breach). Sailing away triumphantly, Uspak encountered Alan 'lying south upon the headlands' with a larger fleet. A running fight through Kilbrannan Sound, between Arran and Kintyre, cost Uspak his life and shattered his expedition, though the survivors were hailed as victors in Norway.[5]

A hostile reception in Islay for any future invasion was obviously desirable. The Council could not rely on Henry to avert Manx raids; in 1244 he had summoned Irish chiefs to join his projected attack on Scotland, and the possibility remained of a joint Manx-Irish assault on the western seaboard if the Council strayed out of line with English policy. They had no intention of straying but English intentions were not always discernible.

By the year's end the Earl of Carrick was dead. The infant Marjory was left in her mother's care. It may have been about then that another document was sealed, eventually to be indexed immediately after the Argyll parchment:

> letter of the captains and lieutenants of Carrick obliging themselves to serve the King against all men while they live and to death.[6]

Elsewhere, in Scotland and England alike, a late spring and a wet summer led towards a disastrous harvest. There was such corruption of the air and inundation of rain that both hay and corn were almost totally lost and grain rotted in the fields; some, shaken by the wind, sprang again under the husk ... the sickle was first put in about St Martin's Day or later ...[7]

Despite the weather a State visit was in prospect. A minor set-back was the theft of a waggon-load of London fashions for Queen Margaret, waylaid in Northumberland; six local men and a Suffolk waggoner were outlawed at Newcastle (but not caught). Presumably they had hoped for a load of food and were sadly disappointed. The visit was planned with unusual care. The Lord Edward came north in July to lead the escort – his first sight of Scotland – bringing an elaborate missive:

> Alexander King of Scots and his Queen have safe-conduct for themselves and their retinue to come to the King. The King of Scots and his friends are not to be addressed on any matters touching himself or his kingdom without his will, and should he be prevented, by war in Scotland or any other reasonable cause, from coming to England, [Henry] takes the Queen and her retinue, excepting outlaws, under his protection.[8]

Such caution suggests that Henry had been warned not to expect submission. Alexander was not his Council's puppet, and the Council itself, after a year in office, was showing internal stresses. For the Queen, however, to see Edward again was joyful. They held considerable influence over each other; while Margaret lived, Edward's relations with Alexander were cordial. At seventeen, Edward had taken long strides into manhood; he had spent a year in Castile, returning just in time for his brother's investiture with Sicily. He had grown immensely tall and now stood head and shoulders above his company. His lint-white hair had darkened, though hardly to the reported 'raven's wing' (unless he was dyeing it). In Spain he had lived among men who fought the infidel on their home ground, men for whom tournaments were essential battle-training, and he had shared in the life of the most civilised Court in Christendom, where Jewish scholars mingled with Muslim artists under the protection of Alfonso, 'the King of the Three Religions'. Alfonso had written the definitive manual of chess, and Edward had taken up the game; but that was not his only new hobby.

An action-hungry boy, released from over-protection, Edward had formed his own team of tourney-fighters. His father was appalled; a modern equivalent might be for the heir to a throne to become a Formula One racing-driver. Tournaments were not yet affairs of protective barriers and cushion-headed lances, but remained very near lethal combat. Teams charged each other, breaking into duels with the sole aim of forcing the opponent to buy his life with arms, horse or money. Young men made perilous livings on the circuit, picking rich targets and hoping to catch the eye of some elder lord who maintained a stable of hungry young fighters. The heir of England was a prime target; if he won, he took prizes others needed to stay in the game, if he lost he could always find new arms or mounts. To the eve of his own coronation he would go anywhere for a good contest, in the teeth of entreaties (Henry envisaged him scarred for life or trampled under the hooves, and constantly inveighed against dissolute companions).[9]

There was time to hear of Edward's adventures as the cavalcade wound through the sodden countryside towards Woodstock. Henry awaited its arrival amid elaborate preparations, ordering

> All the King's curtains, two dozen cloths of gold and four dozen of Arras, the greater and lesser carpets, the great couch given by the Countess of Provence, … two *bulla* of almonds, two hundreds of raisins, four loaves of sugar, fifteen pounds of saffron, half a hundred of pepper, one quarter of cumin, half a hundred of zingiber, half a hundred of cinnamon, four pounds of cloves, two pounds each of nutmeg, mace and galingale, two *milliares* of wax …

and with these his Treasurer was to send

> the long coffer with the King's short mantle, the two coffers with silver vases and the two with silver horses, the great cup of York, the bowl with pendant shields, the enamelled bowl, and the other things the King uses on solemn feasts, if there are any that presently escape his recollection.[10]

Henry was often accused of developing a bureaucracy 'worse than the Saxons'', but it had not quite reached the stage of being able to order List A Equipment. At least the requirements were less exacting than those for York, but a good many laden carts would creak out of London through the mud.

Woodstock had been a favourite summer palace since Norman times. Henry I enclosed its park and stocked it with exotic beasts. Henry II began adorning 'the spring called Everswell'; Henry III himself, with his wife's Provençal gardeners, built a loggia around the main pool and designed a smaller one with seats at its edge. He erected an iron trellis for roses, made a new garden by the Queen's chapel and one each side of his own lodging, and walled the Queen's main garden for greater privacy. A new lawn was laid in 'the great herber', and the fishpond was hedged about. A few years later he would set a hundred pear trees around Everswell, for fruit and for massed blossom.

The many separate gardens were bordered with hedges of flowering trees, quartered by gravel-paths leading to a central fountain or summer-house, banked with flowerbeds. They were linked by covered alleys on which grew vines, roses and honeysuckle, with openings to vistas of peonies, lilies, or the many-petalled white rose. There were herb-plots, and beds of the newest novelty lavender (rosemary was still not acclimatised). There were orchards where strollers could pick peaches, plums, cherries, gooseberries and straw-berries, and turf-benches where they could eat them, places for flirtations and laughter, shelter from summer showers, and glimpses of the park through gateways and windows.[11]

Alexander and his train of three hundred horsemen passed from Lincoln onwards through lands formerly held by his father or his great-uncle David, parts of the Honour of Huntingdon whose fiefs extended through eleven counties. Many of the local escort and of his own entourage were keenly interested in the possibility that King Henry might intend granting the Honour, with or without the Earldom, as Simon de Montfort had hinted on his Scottish visit.

The Earldom of Huntingdon had been held by the Kings of Scots ever since the future King David received it while he was merely 'the Queen's brother', the youngest of the Scots royal princes. His son Earl Henry held it with his mother's Northumberland; Earl Henry's third son took his title from it. Alexander II had to exert long pressure to obtain it after his uncle's death, only succeeding under the 1237 accord. Huntingdon was desirable not only because of its value but because it clarified the feudal relationship between the crowns. North Tynedale and the handful of Cumberland manors were minor by comparison; a great earldom was enough to ensure any man's loyalty without insistence on homage for his kingdom. It was desirable also from the English side because many of its manors had long been assigned to families whose liege-homage lay with Scotland and whose good behaviour was best assured by securing the allegiance of their own overlord.[12]

After a holiday-time at Woodstock the whole court removed to London, where they found the city adorned and John Mansel awaiting them with a banquet. The Honour of Huntingdon included two manors at Twickenham and a soke (ward) within the city, and it was probably at one of these locations that Henry invested Alexander on 2 September

> with both the Earldom and the Honour pertaining thereto, to hold and to
> have as some of his ancestors had and held it. And so the King decreed, although
> daily impoverished.[13]

Then it was time to take leave of Henry, and of the old Countess of Kent. Presumably the homeward journey halted at Brackley, for Alexander to take seizin at the *caput* of his Earldom. It had been a fruitful visit; much had been accomplished. Alexander had 500 marks 'by the King's gift', a belated first instalment of Margaret's marriage-settlement. The Sheriff of Cumberland was to give Margaret 'all the amercements of the last eyre' (the fines levied for faults or for absence from visitations of the justices) exacted from her holdings. The fines levied from Sowerby cannot have been immense, but it was a gesture of goodwill. The Doorward, for his part, obtained payment of his annual fee of £50, a handsome retainer for a principal officer of another country.[14]

The Doorward rode home nursing some anxieties; he and his colleagues were uneasy at what might have happened during their absence. Henry wrote to his northern sheriffs on 1 September, warning them to be ready to help Alexander against unspecified 'enemies'. On 12 September Mansel was despatched 'in the King's own place, to arrange the King of Scots' affairs as best befits his dignity and advantage', and northern barons were put on standby in case Mansel needed help to deal with Alexander's 'gainsayers'. Despite the terms of the safe-conduct there had been some discussion of problems.[15]

The day after Mansel's orders, Henry issued a safe-conduct for Queen Marie to 'pass to her own country', valid to the next Whitsunday. The Queen Mother had delayed her customary visit to France while her son was out of his realm, which might suggest she had some unacknowledged part in affairs of state. Marie was then in her thirties, if we assume she was around seventeen at her marriage in 1239. She may well have felt the lack of a man's support in recent turbulent times, but it was not easy for a widowed queen to find a second husband of fitting status. Feudal law was usually punctilious about 'disparagement', marriage between persons of unequal social class (there had been strong resentment when the princesses Margaret and Isabella, held hostage in England as possible brides for the much younger English princes, were instead belatedly matched with Hubert de Burgh and the child Roger Bigod). Widows had more freedom than young girls, but if Queen Marie should choose a nobody the affront would be deep. Once her wishes were known, within her family and to her kinsman King Louis, matters resolved themselves smoothly, with an impeccable choice. Somewhere between autumn 1256 and summer 1257 she married John de Brienne, the Butler of France.

John was more than an important French functionary; he was the King of Acre, a prestigious if empty title. His father 'Old John' had been a famous crusader who lived to the age of eighty-seven (a triumph in itself). Young John was the eldest son of his father's first marriage; his second made him King of Jerusalem, with a daughter who married the Emperor Frederick; after the third, to an Armenian princess, his fourth was to a Castilian aunt of Alfonso X. From that final alliance came another daughter, married to the luckless 'Eastern emperor' Baldwin II; Old John was notional co-emperor of Byzantium with his son-in-law during his last years. Young John and his brothers had no part in their father's adventures; they grew up under the stern eye of the Queen Mother of France, older playmates for Louis IX and his brothers.

Young John was a widower when he married Marie. His half-sister the Eastern Empress had arranged his first marriage to Jeanne of Chateaudûn, widow of the crusading John de Montfort (Earl Simon's nephew, son of the Constable of France). All in all it would have been difficult to find a more suitable bridegroom for the Queen; the only problem was that Henry III might imagine some risk of increased French influence over Scotland.[16]

John hardly stirs a ripple in Scottish affairs. The couple seem soon to have gone their own ways, John mainly in France, Marie active in both her countries. After passing the winter at Coucy, and marrying at an unknown time and place, she brought John back through England in June 1257. A lot of water had flowed under Berwick Bridge by then.

Chapter 8 Notes

1   *Chron.Lanercost.*, 82–3

2   The Stewardship, *RRS I*, 31–3; Paisley Abbey, App.C; Barrow, *A-N Era*, 47 and 67; Bute, *ib*. 68. Rothesay, Cruden,*Castle*, 29 (and *Sc.Cas.*, 7–8). Jean of Bute (p.2) is shown as Alexander's wife in some sources, but dates and daughters' marriages make Walter II more likely. For Bp. Alan, and 'Alan the Earl's son'; Watt, *Biog*. 4; *ib*.91, Mr Robert 'of Carrick'. The Bp. of Sodor & Man, replacing Bp. Laurence (drowned with K.Harald, 1249, see Ch.1), was Richard (1253–75); *ES II*, 573n. E. Nigel's charter to Roland *de Carrik*, appointing him and his heirs *capites tocius progenies sue*, conf.1276 (?on succ.of Roland's son), *Hdlist A.III*, No. 98.

3   Treaty of Tarbert, p.4 above. For Angus in 1263 see Ch. 14. Henry's instructions and request, *CDS I,2046* (21 April 1256). Argyll barons' letter in 1282 Archives list, *APS I*.

4   Protection for K.Magnus, *CDS I,2046*, as cited above. For the 1249 regicide, see Ch. 1.

5   *Chron.Man* in *ES II*,472–8; 'Uspak' = Gaelic *Gilleasbuig* (Gillespie), Barrow, *K & U*, 110. Rothesay, see n2 above.

6   For Marjory, Ctss of Carrick, p.189, Carrick letter, *APS I*.

7   *Chron. Lanercost* 64; St Martin's Day is 11 Nov.

8   Waggon robbed, *CDS I, 2047* (Apl.1256); S/cs, *CDS I, 2053* (29 June, Winchester). The ref. to 'outlaws' was because only the King of Scots, in person, could present fugitives for pardon.

9   Tournaments, Powicke 20–23 and 414. Edward's Eleanor, aged 11 at marriage, remained in Castile for some years. For Alfonso's court, see G. Jackson, *The Making of Medieval Spain*, Thames & Hudson 1972.

10 *CDS I, 2055* (30 July, Hereford). The 'carpets' perhaps came from Spain; they were virtually unknown in northern Europe. The list also includes counterpanes, table linen &c.

11 For the account of Woodstock I am greatly indebted to John Harvey, *Medieval Gardens*, (Batsford 1981), *passim*.

12 Moore, *Lands*; Barrow *K & U*, 37, 47, 147, 150. Simon de Montfort's visit, p.63 above.

13 M.Paris, *Chr.Maj. V*,576, in *SA* 375. For the lands, see map 3.

14 Princess Margaret, Countess of Kent, died early the next year. *CDS I, 2057* (23 Aug., for Alan); *2059* (Ctss of Kent buys a writ); *2060* (6 Sept., Merton), Tr. to pay Alexander ('postponing all other payments authorised'); *2061* (12 Sept.) Sher. of Cumberland for Q.Margaret (and cf.*ib.*, *2069*, payment to her *vallet* Adam de Forde of £300 given her by K. Alexr. 'out of the arrears due' for marriage-sett.). The court-seat of the Honour

was at Brackley, its former castle of Fotheringhay having been destroyed by Henry II (so Mary Q. of Scots died in a later building).

15 *CDS I, 2058*, (1 Sept.) *2062, 2063* (12 Sept., Westminster).

16 S/c for Q. Marie, *CDS I, 2064* (13 Sept., Westminster). Brienne family, mainly from Runciman, *Crs.III* and Labarge, *St. Louis*. Joinville records Young John with the Crusade 1248–50 and leaving Acre with his half-sister. By his first marriage he acquired a step-daughter, Beatrice de Montfort-l'Amauri, later the mother of Q. Joleta; p.33.

Death of Enguerrand de Coucy

9

1257: Kinross

WHEN POPE INNOCENT IV died at Naples on 7 December 1254 his war was almost lost. Manfred had routed the papal army and captured the imperial treasure-house of Lucera with the help of its Saracen guards, and with Lucera went the last hope of paying the Pope's soldiers. Innocent had broken the Hohenstaufen Empire but had discredited his own office in the process. The cardinals chose a successor within seven days, fearing external pressures, and Rinaldo Conti, Cardinal-archbishop of Ostia, was enthroned as Alexander IV.

Rinaldo was greatly respected for his piety and kindliness. Most of Innocent's policies continued; the plan to instal a vassal-king in Sicily particularly appealed to the new Pope. In autumn 1255 he sent a nuncio to invest young Edmund of England. This delay, however necessary while financial implications were assessed, was to prove sadly typical. Gentle and fatherly as Pope Alexander was, he also proved to be fair-minded to the point of inertia.

Bishop Gamelin and his companions reached Rome in the spring of 1256. Their story shocked the Pope. Hard on their heels came the Scottish government emissaries; the first ones died (this seems rather drastic, even for Mr Wishart, so natural causes must be assumed), and there were further delays while the resident proctors awaited instructions. It was December before the Pope wrote to Henry III:

> We have heard with grief that some of the King of Scotland's so-called counsellors, who might rather be termed flatterers, have turned his tender mind by crafty and evil advice, and that G., Bishop of St Andrews, is spoiled of his goods and driven into exile from his church to the no light injury and contempt of the Holy Name and His apostle. We beseech King Henry to use his influence to right these wrongs.[1]

Henry was unlikely to obey. The numerous Scots clerics assembled at the Curia had united to explain the impossibility of assigning a twentieth, or any proportion, of Scottish church revenues for Henry's use without overturning the privileges granted by former popes. Despite this, in September Pope Alexander instructed his nuncio Rostand Masson (fast becoming Henry's friend) to

enjoin the bishops and other chief clergy of Scotland to afford liberal aid to
the Pope for debts incurred in the matter of Sicily, in which case his Holiness
will remit the twentieth granted to the King of England in aid of the Holy
Land. If [they do] not, let the twentieth be collected without delay. If Rostand
has to take proceedings [to obtain payment] he is to keep silence about any
privileges or indulgences to the Scottish Church, or the question of its independence;

and again,

although the Pope has remitted the twentieth of ecclesiastical benefits in
Scotland granted to the King of England, yet redemptions of crusading vows,
uncertain bequests, and offerings in aid of the Holy Land from whatever cause,
should be collected for the said King's use under the foregoing conditions of
secrecy.[2]

The question of the Empire itself was still unresolved. Any candidate must
first be elected King of the Romans (in effect, of Germany) by the seven
Electors – three archbishops and four princes of the Empire. The Pope's first
candidate, the Count of Holland, died in January 1256. Alfonso of Castile
was favoured by some of the Electors, but the Pope had no desire to see any
king so augment his power. In a year of secret diplomacy Richard of Cornwall
gained three votes, Alfonso had three, and the seventh Elector obligingly
promised his support to both. By the end of January 1257 Richard had won,
at the cost of 28,000 marks (he had been ready to spend more, and was the
only contender who could contemplate such a stake). Henry flew into
ecstasies that recall his excitement when their sister married Frederick II;
he proposed attending the coronation, a wild idea swiftly shot down
(probably by Richard) but typical of Henry's family affection and love of
ceremonial.[3]

He should have been looking elsewhere. In south Wales a revolt against
Geoffrey de Langley's exactions erupted into full-scale rebellion, with
Llywelyn ap Gruffydd, Lord of Gwynedd, summoned to help his coun-
trymen. He began by reclaiming all English-held territory between his own
land and the march with Chester, leaving two coastal castles isolated. Then
he swept through mid-Wales to the Severn; John fitzAlan, the Steward's
cousin, held Montgomery by the skin of his teeth. By Easter 1257 Llywelyn
was back home, Wales was united, and the Marcher lords were clamouring
for a punitive expedition and in no mood to hear Henry's Sicilian dreams.[4]

Yet in March young Edmund was paraded in Apulian robes (modelled
on Byzantine court dress, a delight to Henry), while the Archbishop of
Messina lectured the English clergy on their duty to support the Pope. A
letter from Scotland can hardly have registered while the King was absorbed
in such matters.

It was written on the day Henry first spoke of going to Germany. The King of Scots, with Dunbar at his side, sent news of Margaret and himself (both 'in prosperous condition', and he hoped to 'learn the same of the King and Queen of England and their children'), and desired credence for the letter-bearers, Mr Robert Stuteville and Sir Adam of Morham, charged to report a pressing request from the Comyn earls, with 'other matters to be declared more fully'.[5]

It is the first surviving letter in the light and cheerful style Alexander now adopted to his father-in-law. It masks a statesman-like appraisal of the Scottish situation, his own or that of someone alert to tensions within the Council. Ever since September 1255, when 'matters imputed or to be imputed' were alleged against the Comyns, the new governors had deferred taking action, although Fordun records that

> a great discussion had arisen between the magnates, because the new coun-
> cillors exacted an account of royal goods consumed, and compelled [the former
> councillors] to answer for their acts ... Walter Comyn, Earl of Menteith, and
> his accomplices, frequently summoned before the King and Council on many
> and hard charges, did not compear.[6]

The core of the trouble was that charges were never formulated, and therefore could not be answered. The Doorward and his colleagues preferred to wait until Gamelin lost his case in Rome, but the delay was beginning to strain the Council's unity. Even before the Woodstock visit there had been some approach to the King by his former advisers; now it seems almost as if Alexander were inviting Henry to put pressure on the Council to give justice. It was a risky line, for Henry might respond by calling the case into his own court, incidentally demonstrating his overlordship of Scotland (as his son was to do to King John Balliol); but Henry had too much on his mind to do more than despatch the Earl of Winchester to assess the situation.

Roger de Quincy, the same man who had fled for his life out of Galloway ten years earlier, was now elderly and ineffective. Before he could report, a new storm blew up with the arrival in Scotland of a papal letter addressed to the Abbot of Jedburgh and two archdeacons. It appointed them judges-delegate to examine a letter purporting to have been sent from the Curia in December 1255, in favour of Alan the Doorward and against the Earl of Mar, and addressed to the Bishop of Brechin and the Dean of Dunkeld (Stuteville). The addressees had suspected forgery and returned a copy to Rome; if the judges found the suspicion to be correct, they were to proceed against the forger if he could be found.

The Curia clerks were always alert for forgeries, prepared to count the number of dots on a seal or query minute errors of phraseology. Such care was necessary in an age when written evidence was lightly regarded and when it seemed reasonable to replace a lost document whose tenor was well-remembered, or 'discover' one that fulfilled a known intention. It has been suggested that the 1255 forger was a St Andrews canon, Mr Richard Vairement, formerly a 'Culdee' prebendary and perhaps a member of Queen Marie's entourage at her arrival in 1239. Just how the forgery was aimed at Mar is unclear, but presumably the Doorward still hankered after the earldom. The production had not fooled Bishop Albinus or Stuteville – both, be it noted, of the 'Doorwardite' faction (as the judges-delegate were 'Comynites', though such 'party' labels may be anachronistic).[7]

By the time the judges got to work, Richard of Cornwall had sailed for Germany, Henry was wringing his hands over Wales and Sicily, and a second appalling summer had begun. Coming after the previous year's lost harvest, it brought near-famine:

> There was such rottenness of grain throughout the entire island that flour could scarcely be made into bread nor barley into a potable drink. All spirits sank, especially among the lesser folk and beggars. Thus we saw them fighting like dogs over the carcasses of horses, like pigs devouring scraps put out for pigs, enjoying poisonous plants as if they were healthful herbs. Many indeed, full of the spirit of piety, made great and long distribution to relieve the poor.[8]

Under such conditions it was easier for guerrilla bands to survive in the Welsh mountains than for mounted columns to move against them. A series of Marcher reprisals failed and Henry himself had to move to Chester and take the field, for once with great and justified reluctance. While he waited for his forces to assemble, he amused himself with designing a truly beautiful gold coin, the first English gold since the Conquest, prompted by his discovery of 'a roomful of gold' in the Tower. The coin was overvalued against the silver penny, too valuable for normal use, a convenient means for merchants and papal collectors to export currency. It was an expensive luxury which Richard of Cornwall would never have contemplated; Henry had found Richard's 'Fort Knox', but the idea of a backing for the currency was beyond Henry's comprehension. Meanwhile the terrible Welsh arrows flew from the hillsides, nailing men to their saddles; the longbow was mainly a Welsh weapon at that time, the short-bow a piece of hunting equipment for mounted knights.[9]

In early June Henry learned of Queen Marie's marriage. He felt he should have been consulted, he feared French influence on his flank. When Marie and her husband applied for safe-conducts through England his reply was edgy:

> The King to John, son of the King of Jerusalem and Butler of France. Peter of Savoy has asked for a safe-conduct for John and his consort the Queen of

Scots [*sic*]. Although the King of France sets a bad example in not permitting Englishmen to go through his kingdom to the King's brother in Germany and elsewhere, the King grants the request, provided that John and the Queen of Scotland both swear to do no harm to him or his kingdom, or to the King and Queen of Scotland and their Council. When they reach Dover they are to inform the King, who will send someone with the safe-conduct to receive their oath.

A fortnight later a royal clerk waited at Dover with orders to obtain, before parting with the safe-conduct, an oath that John and Marie would 'neither do nor procure any evil to the King or the King of Scotland in their transit'.[10]

It gave John de Brienne a curious introduction to island politics. Certainly there was no welcome to Court, no offer of royal lodgings; but if the party could travel fast, it might reach Stirling by the end of the summer *colloquium*, at which (or soon afterwards) Alexander re-granted all her dowerlands to his mother.[11]

Henry, back at Woodstock that July, planned another intervention in Scots affairs:

The King, in order to terminate and settle the disputes which have arisen between Alexander King of Scots and certain of his magnates, being about to send the Archbishop of York, the Bishop of Durham, the Earl of Winchester, the Prior of Durham, John Mansel, Gilbert Preston and William Latimer to Scotland for a meeting appointed between the King and his said magnates at Stirling on the fifteenth day after the Assumption [*i.e.* 30 August], promises to ratify whatever his envoys and the King of Scotland shall do for both kings' honour.[12]

Presumably the midsummer *colloquium* had agreed a special meeting, of such importance that the governing group felt the need of external backing. Perhaps charges had at last been prepared against the Comyns; perhaps the Comyns demanded arbitration; perhaps the Council itself was divided over the course to be pursued. It must seem unlikely that the Archbishop made the journey; there had been such prolonged resistance to any intrusion by York that all the monastic chroniclers would have noticed such an event. Possibly only Mansel and the two northern sheriffs attended. Whatever the subject or outcome of the meeting, it was probably then that the Comyns decided they 'dared not expect justice in the assize of the realm'.[13]

Before any English delegates reached Scotland, John Balliol had regained Henry's favour; in mid-August he was

forgiven his transgressions and offences against Alexander King of Scots and Queen Margaret, for which King Henry had caused him to be impleaded. He has made a fine of £500, whereof £100 has been paid and the balance is to be paid before the Nativity of the Blessed Virgin [11 May 1258].

Balliol's deal makes it more likely that the Stirling meeting was to hear charges against the other ex-councillors. As a liegeman of England and Henry's personal representative in 1255, Balliol must of course be judged in England. Matthew Paris, placing his return to favour in 1255 but clearly referring to 1257, writes of John 'prudently making peace by satisfying the King's needs with money'.

On the day Henry despatched his envoys the Pope at last issued mandates for Gamelin, ordering the return of the episcopal property and a guarantee of protection from King Alexander. A copy of the mandate reached the English Chancellor at Chester; it cannot have pleased Henry. The original, if delivered in time, must have affected decisions at Stirling. The Melrose chronicler rolls up the year in one crisp annal:

> Coronation of the King of Germany. The King of England fought against the Welsh and returned defeated to his own place. This year messengers from the King of Scots' tutors accused the Bishop of St Andrews to the Lord Pope, on the King's behalf; after hearing and examining both sides, the Pope with his own mouth pronounced the Bishop innocent of all charges and worthy of the bishopric, and commanded the Bishop of Dunblane and the Abbots of Melrose and Jedburgh to publish the sentence [of excommunication] against the King's councillors throughout the kingdom, at first in general terms and then, if they remained contumacious, by name.

Bishop Clement proceeded through the various admonitions and warnings, but was eventually obliged to excommunicate the entire government individually, 'with striking of bells and extinguishing of candles', in the abbey church of Cambuskenneth beside Stirling. The papal nuncio (Geoffrey de Alatro had recently replaced Rostand Masson) was instructed to go to Scotland and ensure Gamelin's restoration, but in the end he had no need to intervene.[14]

It is a universal instinct to blame the government for the weather. 1257 was a horrible year, and the excommunications were the last straw. The King could not be left at the mercy of men who might prevent him obeying the Pope, so bringing a general interdict upon the country. The interdict on England, in the last years of King John, was well-remembered, when every sacrament from baptism to burial was denied to all. The Council knew its danger, Alexander was as anxious as anyone. He was sixteen that September; at that age Henry had been given control of his lands and his seal by the Pope of the time. Something must be done.

In October Alexander and Margaret went to Kinross, to stay in the small island castle on Loch Leven and doubtless to join in the pursuit of the wild geese which thronged, as they do today, into the flat fields around the loch shores. The fields were barren enough that wretched year without the help of a blanket of greylags and pinkfeet.

Alexander and his Queen, however protected and guarded, were not prisoners. Nobody could prevent them talking with their attendants or with falconers or people struggling to harvest the sodden fields. There was a changing population of knights providing the castle-guard, men whose tenure required them to find a handful of soldiers for a week or a month to augment the garrison, and there was also an eddying crowd of merchants, petitioners and entertainers. It was not difficult to send or receive messages; moreover, the young couple were not merely permitted, they were required to sleep in one bed.

Among those who provided castle-guard at Loch Leven were the lords of Abernethy, Dunmore ('Dundemore') and Lochore. The Queen Mother was at Stirling or at dowerlands nearby, Menteith at his principal castle on the Lake of Menteith. Loch Leven was possibly not the most secure place to house the King; maybe the Doorward had grown over-confident, maybe elements in the Council were turning against him. We have conflicting versions of what happened next; Fordun, having said that the Comyns 'dared not expect justice' (which could be translated 'could not hope for justice') continues:

> having consulted together, [the Comyns] seized the King by night, as he slept, and abducted him before daybreak to Stirling on the morrow of SS. Simon and Jude [29 October]. The Great Seal, which Mr Robert Stuteville carried, they violently removed. In that deception the chief actors were the Earl of Menteith, the Earl of Buchan, William Earl of Mar (a man sufficiently ingenious in evil deeds), John Comyn (skilled in rapine and temerity), Hugh of Abernethy, David of Lochore, Hugh of Barclay, and plenty more satellites of malignancy who, doing nothing by licence but all at will, by right and wrong ruled the people. And thus the last error was worse than the first. Many persecutions and troubles were thus brought out among the nobles of the Scots, because the later royal councillors tried to repay the faults and evils perpetrated by the former ones, whence followed such distresses of the poor and spoliations of churches as have not been seen in Scotia in our time.[15]

This is lavish, given that Fordun was born in the early years of Robert I and lived through the reign of David II. He may have adapted a passage from some earlier record dealing with the Doorward years, or perhaps he was improvising on his regular theme that Comyns were always bad news. Matthew Paris, distant but contemporary, takes another line:

> About the period of those days [autumn 1257], since the King of Scotland, Alexander – from whose youth the greatest benefit was hoped – misgoverned

too unbecomingly, promoting foreigners and exalting them over his native subjects, the inhabitants and natives were indignant and, to prevent him breaking out in worse ways, they placed him and the Queen under custody again; and the Queen they removed and guarded carefully *ne patrissaret* [lest she should return home?] until after the example of the Germans they should have removed all foreigners. And thenceforward the nobles of Scotland held the reins of their kingdom with greater freedom and safety. They upbraided the Queen moreover that she had incited and summoned her father to come upon them as an enemy with his army, and do lamentable destruction.[16]

Matthew, like Fordun, got some things wrong. There was no wholesale removal of foreigners, as there was soon to be in England, and Henry's Border demonstrations had not amounted to damaging invasions; but both were correct that something momentous had happened.

One can hardly construct a convincing scenario in which the King and Queen were carried off kicking under somebody's arm or dragged into a boat past incurious guards; but another script could be suggested.

Suppose, for the sake of argument, that Alexander himself was concerned to break the deadlock, and that he was capable of concerting action with Margaret and even with some anti-Council supporters (including, perhaps, his own mother). Margaret might land with her ladies on some innocent ploy – gathering hazelnuts for Hallowe'en games, or the like – and Alexander at another time would go ashore for his daily ride, accompanied by the Castellan Sir Gilbert of Kinross. He might even instruct Stuteville to leave the seal (not the Great Seal, but the lesser 'Seal of the Minority' then in use), so that he could affix it to some document such as a letter to the Queen Mother. Once ashore, seal and all, he and Sir Gilbert would ride westward, changing horses as dusk fell at some pre-arranged rendezvous, pushing through the night with a trusted guide, reaching Stirling (as Fordun says) before dawn. Margaret would already have made her way into the Queen Mother's care. That makes a convincing fiction, but it is only fiction – apart from two small pointers, and the absence of any resentment or revenge in later years against those whom Fordun alleges to have dragged Alexander out of bed and so forth. The two scraps of evidence are both charters, both undated, both lacking the normal prologue of an explanatory narrative, but dateable between 1257 and 1262. The first grants Sir Gilbert £20 worth of land for his life; the second gives an annual suit of clothes and £2 to one Robert Hod. Robert was drawing his pension in the sheriffdom of Aberdeen in 1266; perhaps he had followed the Earl of Buchan in his younger days. Until these grants are proved to have been made for other signal services, it remains possible that Robert and Sir Gilbert had something to do with that departure from the island castle.

Last but not least, it is worth remembering that to the closing hours of his life King Alexander dearly loved a night-ride; he would hardly have done so if in youth he had experienced a forced journey in enemy hands.[17]

Chapter 9 Notes

1   For Innocent IV see Runciman *SV*, 48 and 69. Envoys' deaths, *Chron.Bower* ii, 90, in Watt, *Biog.*, 210. Pope to Henry III, *CDS I, 2037* (16 Dec., misdated '1255' by Ed.)

2   *CDS I, 2065, 2066* (27 Sept. 1256). The twentieth may have been a concession made at Roxburgh, Sept. 1255 (p.70 above).

3   Young *R of C*, 86–94. Henry to Joanna Q. of Scots on their sister Isabella's betrothal to Frederick II, *CDS I, 1227* (23 Feb. 1235).

4   J.E. Lloyd, *A History of Medieval Wales (1958)*; Degannwy opposite Conway, and Dyserth near Rhyl, were cut off until relieved by Cinque Port ships the next year.

5   Sicily, Powicke 375. Alexander to Henry, *CDS I, 2077* (4 Feb. 1257, Roxburgh).

6   *Fordun*, LI and LII.

7   Pope to A. Jedburgh (Nicholas), Archd. Teviotdale (Mr Nicholas Moffat), and Archd. Dunblane (Mr Duncan, *medicus*), in Watt, *Biog.* 162; and see *ES II*, 589n. Mr Vairement, Watt, *Biog.* 560. E'dom of Mar, p.29 above. For clerical forgeries in general, Stones & Simpson, *Gt. Cause I*, 138.

8   *Chron. Lanercost*, 65.

9   Gold coin, Young, *R of C*, 64 and pl.

10 *CDS I, 2083* (6 June) and *2084* (18 June). Peter of Savoy was Queen Eleanor's maternal uncle. 'K of Germany' = Richard of Cornwall.

11 Re-grant of lands, *APS I*, 1292 list of documents ex-Edinburgh Castle.

12 *CDS I, 2090* (20 July 1257, Woodstock).

13 *Fordun*, LII.

14 *CDS I, 2091, 2092* (12 and 14 Aug.) M. Paris, *Chr. Maj. V*, 507, in *SA* 373. *CDS I, 2093* (memo of *ca.* 16 Aug.) refers to a papal letter on behalf of the Bp. of St. Andrews. *CM* 114. Bp. Clement's proceedings, Watt, *Biog.* 103.

15 LII.

16 M. Paris, *Chr. Maj. V*, 656, in *SA* 376. M.P. here conflates 1255 and 1257 and may even refer to Q. Joanna's return home (p.13 above).

17 Charters (n.d. but 1257x1262) *Hdlist A.III*, nos. 186, 187; payment to R. Hod, 1266, *ER I*, 12.

1258: Changed Days

HENRY WAS slow to realise what had happened in Scotland; his first flurry of activity came in December, when he sent the Earl of Winchester to investigate. He also granted Bolsover Castle to Alan the Doorward, giving him his first English base. The Earl, as Buchan's father-in-law, could surely discover what was afoot in the north.[1]

By mid-January Henry was seriously considering how to rescue the poor kidnapped children. He wrote to the Earl of Lincoln and some seventy northern barons, 'all the marchers of Northumberland, Cumberland, Westmorland and Coupland, of Kermel, Kendal and Gillaund':

> As certain rebels have secretly taken away the King of Scotland from the custody of the council set over him until his lawful age, and detain him against his will to the manifest scandal and disgrace of both kings, [Henry] wishing to give effectual aid commands — and his whole service to join the expedition he is about to send to Scotland to deliver the said king, and to come with a multitude of foot and archers.[2]

The person he blamed for much of the trouble was about to come within range. He wrote next to the barons of the Cinque Ports, the chain of Channel harbours whose ships constituted the nearest thing to an English Royal Navy:

> As Mr Gamelin, Bishop of St Andrews in Scotland, has obtained certain things in the Roman Curia in disinheritance of Alexander, King of Scotland, to the scandal of both kings, [Henry] sends William Bisset to them, to watch for Gamelin's arrival from beyond seas 'or' [*recte* 'towards'?] Scotland, commanding them to arrest the bishop and his party until further orders.[3]

Gamelin's chief offence, in Henry's eyes, was the cancellation of the papal grant of a twentieth from Scottish benefices, and the renewal of Scottish privileges; how these tended towards Alexander's disinheritance is obscure (except that they limited Alexander's power over his realm, power which Henry hoped to keep under his own control). On 13 February Henry addressed Gamelin directly:

> The King to G. Bishop of St Andrews in Scotland, such greeting as he deserves.

Certain of the King's Council have asked him to grant safeconduct through England for the Bishop, although the King understands that he ceases not to compass the damage of the King himself, of the King and Queen of Scotland, and of the King's friends there. If the Bishop will give sufficient security not to do so, and will come to the King; he shall have safe-conduct. William Bisset is sent to Dover to meet him and bring him to the King on these conditions.

On 9 March a safe-conduct to London was issued, with another a week later permitting Gamelin to travel from Wissant in Flanders to London and back, unless Henry decided to allow his progress to Scotland. (The Pope expected Gamelin to be home, and wrote instructing Bishop Clement to remind him of business outstanding).[4]

Clement lay dying in Dunblane and the Scots *colloquium* met at Roxburgh without him. Gamelin may just have arrived for the final sessions; he would find many familiar faces among the company. The new Chancellor was Mr William Wishart; Buchan was again Justiciar, John Comyn Justiciar of Galloway, Aymer Maxwell had replaced David Lindsay as Chamberlain (we are not told if Mary Maxwell resumed her seat in Council). Menteith and Mar were back, of course, the Steward and Robert Meyners kept their places with Strathearn, Hugh Giffard and Gilbert Hay from the previous Council; there had been no clean sweep as in 1255.

A *colloquium* assembled many beyond the Inner Council. Some private business is always done at such gatherings, with friends meeting, minor problems settled, family news exchanged. A score of Comyns and others packed into someone's official lodging on 18 March, Menteith and Buchan with their sisters' husbands the earls of Ross and Mar, Aymer Maxwell, John Comyn with two younger brothers, Hugh of Abernethy, John of Dundemore, David of Lochore and the Barclay brothers. Freskin Murray of Duffus and Reginald le Chen, like Buchan, represented the North-east. Hector of Carrick was sole representative of Galloway (but he was its appointed leader). The two Mowat brothers, back from serving in Henry's Gascon army, completed the company; they called themselves *Mohaut* or *de Monte Alto* from the ancestral home (now Mold) in Fflint, and family ties gave them some insight into Welsh affairs.

They were met for Welsh business. A messenger from Llywelyn of Gwynedd had brought proposals for an alliance.

It will be remembered that Llywelyn had defeated several English attacks the year before, becoming effectual master of all Wales except for parts of Pembroke and some isolated castles. He had united many leading Welshmen, too often divided by local feud. Some had uneasy alliances with Marchers, some were finding that Marcher neighbours preferred their friendship to that of a distant and capricious king. All Wales supported the warbands, but all Wales was starving. Grain was scarce after two bad harvests, all trade-routes with England and Ireland were blocked, and though the invaders could not defeat the guerrilla bands they could and did burn barns and drive off cattle. If England could somehow obtain mountain troops (as King John had done from Galloway) even the guerrilla war might collapse.

Llywelyn made six proposals. Let there be no peace with the King of England or his magnates, nor with Scots hostile to Wales and the Comyns, unless all parties were equally bound and protected by the peace terms. No force, horse or foot, should go from Scotland against the Welsh. If the King of Scotland should compel his lieges to accept truce or peace with England or other adversaries of Wales, they should obtain equal terms for the Welsh. They should try to bring King Alexander into the agreement; and lastly, Welsh merchants should have access to Scottish markets and Scots merchants should be encouraged to trade with Wales.

These headings can scarcely have been compiled without consultation. The aim of the Roxburgh meeting was to get approval from a wider group. They had already been adopted by twenty-six Welsh leaders headed by Llywelyn and his brother Dafydd (formerly his enemy), and including the princes of Powys and Deheubarth – central and southern Wales – and the lords of such castles as Mawddwy, Cedewain and Dryslwyn. All had done homage to Llywelyn and sworn to observe the pact if the Scots would do likewise.

There and then they did so, swearing on a gospel-book held by Gwion of Bangor, who returned to Wales with Alan of Irvine from the Steward's country. One copy of the agreement went with him, the other was stowed in the State archives where it was found in 1292.[5]

The pact was never openly activated; Alexander almost certainly knew of it but the matter remained secret. Hector of Carrick may have brought Gwion to Roxburgh and the Mowats may have been concerned in earlier contacts, but a more highly-placed helper might well have been the Countess of Fife, Llywelyn's daughter Helena (who would marry Mar's son as her second husband, and who lived to at least 1294).

There were no clerical signatories; possibly the Church in Wales was so anglicised as to be distrusted, and in their absence Scots clerics could not be brought in; on the other hand, the thrust of the accord was against military aid to King Henry, and Scottish church lands were exempt from feudal service, owing only the basic 'Home Defence' of *servicium scoticanum*.[6]

The Comyn lords, having made their anti-English pact, remained anxious about their Queen, if Matthew Paris is right. He reports concern lest she *patrissaret*, a word he perhaps invented, meaning either 'might return home' or 'might act like her father'. If she should go home, it would be like the days of Queen Joanna and leave Scotland without hope of an heir; if she acted like her father, she might do anything. (In fact Margaret was probably at Roxburgh, enjoying a new sense of independence, even if shaken by her temerity in defying her father's arrangements). Matthew's other story, that the Scots accused their king of favouring foreigners, might owe more to Henry's resentment of the Brienne marriage and growing baronial anger over Henry's Lusignan and Provençal entourage than to observed fact.[7]

The *colloquium* ended with agreement to convene at Forfar in a month's time, when the Doorward and his associates undertook to answer all allegations. Alan, with David Lindsay and Freskin's cousin Walter Murray immediately crossed the Border, where Henry still had troops on stand-by:

> The King to the barons, knights and lieges in Yorkshire, Northumberland and Cumberland. They know that certain Scottish magnates have long been hostile to him, to the King and Queen of Scotland and to the King's [Henry's] friends there, and are even yet contriving their injury. He is sending Robert Neville and William Latimer to Scotland to oppose their malice, and commands the lieges to be ready to attend them if required for the aid and succour of his friends.

To Neville he wrote:

> Alexander King of Scotland has lately informed [Henry] that he has convened his *parlement* at Stirling [*sic*] three weeks after Easter, and has asked the King to send some prudent and discreet magnates who might redress offences to the King and Queen, and to the King and Queen of Scotland and others the King's friends. But on account of the shortness of the notice, the distance of the place and its inaccessibility, and above all because the King must hold a *colloquium* of his own on divers difficult matters and cannot send the magnates he would choose on the day fixed, he provides that the Abbot of Burgh, the Earl of Winchester and John Balliol shall attend the meeting and induce the King of Scots to arrange a more convenient day on this side the sea [the Firth of Forth],provided that the King's friends are not molested and peace is kept. But if they are attacked and war breaks out in Scotland, he commands Neville and all the knights he can collect in his barony to hurry to their assistance when required by any of them, with William Latimer if possible, without him if necessary, lest from want of aid the King's friends give way to their enemies. He has also written to the Earl of Albemarle. If the adverse party remain quiet, it seems good to the King that Neville and his followers do likewise, keeping in readiness to attend another parliament at Roxburgh three weeks after Easter, when [Henry's] friends have been commanded to meet.[8]

Two days later he reminded Winchester, Albemarle and Strathearn to rendezvous at Chester a week before midsummer to 'finish the Welsh business', unless required to help Neville before then. Robert de Ros, again deprived of Wark 'during the present war and disturbance in Scotland', was promised its return after the emergency, without prejudice to his ongoing lawsuit. The Bishop of Durham was likewise commanded to surrender Norham, without prejudice.[9]

Henry was under papal pressure to conclude peace with France, ending the long series of truces and releasing the French knights Louis had promised for Sicily. In April the English magnates had to be told that the Pope refused to vary his terms over Sicily; the funding of papal debts must continue. A fortnight after Easter a group of leading English barons made a private pact of mutual support. Gloucester, Norfolk and Simon de Montfort, with Peter of Savoy, Norfolk's brother Hugh Bigod, John FitzGeoffrey and Peter de Montfort (head of the English branch) vowed to support each other against all men in the cause of right and well-doing, saving their faith to King and Crown. They could no longer be swept along in Henry's disordered schemes.

Even as they met, Henry found practical help for his Scottish allies. Neville was to let Alan use Norham and Murray Wark, as 'safe retreats', ensuring that the keep and inner bailey of each castle remained in its constable's control. If Norham was not yet available Alan could use Bamburgh.[10]

On 30 April the barons of the pact appeared at Westminster Palace with an armed company. Leaving their swords at the door they confronted Henry and the Lord Edward, and forced them to swear submission to their guidance and consent to their wishes. In return, the barons would do what they could to raise a general Aid for Sicily, provided that the Pope relaxed his demands and Henry undertook reforms. A committee of twenty-four, twelve chosen by Henry and twelve by the barons, should meet in June and decide what was needed. Neither side seemed to appreciate that they stood on the brink of revolution; Henry was more concerned with French negotiations. In what might have been a clumsy attempt to weaken the conspirators he sent Simon, Peter of Savoy and Hugh Bigod to Paris with his own half-brothers Geoffrey and Guy de Lusignan. Simultaneously new proposals went to Rome, with a request for a legate.

Amid these distractions, Henry sent Margaret a present of twelve bucks, promising four more to her *vallet* Adam de Forde who had brought a letter from her. A few days later he received another letter, reassuring if ineffectual:

> Malise Earl of Strathearn has received the King's letter on [1May], directing him to attend the King's daughter Margaret, Queen of Scots, and not to permit her to be taken to any place irksome to her mind, against her will. He assures the King that these commands will receive his close attention.

Earl Malise, whose first wife, the Northumbrian heiress, had died, leaving two daughters, had recently re-married. The girls were fifteen and ten; Adam the Queen's page was their cousin. There is no evidence of any Strathearn contact with the Queen. Henry also asked Neville and Latimer to visit Margaret as often as they could 'for her solace and succour', without neglecting their preparations for the Welsh campaign.[11]

By then Henry had heard from Alexander himself, and began to realise that Scotland was slipping from his grasp:

> [King Henry to King Alexander;] the Scots envoys, Mr Adam of Makarstoun, provost of the 'city' [*recte* of the Culdees] of St Andrews, and Thomas Normanville, have carefully related the matters enjoined on them by the persons sent to the *colloquium* at Edinburgh. In the matters befitting the interests of both Kings' friends, which [Henry] thinks worthy to be toiled for, for several reasons he was unable to send the persons the envoys thought should be appointed, especially since three of them had crossed the sea on important affairs of their own [*sic*]. Since then, he has convened his own *colloquium* at Oxford for a month after Pentecost, when, God willing, he hopes to set out against his Welsh rebels. He therefore asks Alexander to prorogue his *parlement* until September, at a nearer and more convenient place, and that meantime [Henry's] friends in Scotland be protected from any discord or contention. He hopes the result will be to the honour and advantage of all concerned, and asks Alexander to say what he thinks should be done.

He followed this with letters to Latimer and Neville, telling them what he had written to Alexander and asking for some discreet person to deliver the missive and report on its reception; the sheriffs were to attend in Edinburgh on 2 June in case Alexander did not prorogue and so that they could help Henry's friends, if need be, with 'their utmost power'.[12]

The Oxford *parlement* assembled on 11 June; on 17 June the army was to move against Wales. The barons therefore had good reason to bring their armed followers with them. At the last moment, they learned that Henry and Llywelyn had agreed a year's truce. The Marchers were furious, as was Henry's half-brother William de Valence of Pembroke; they wanted the Welsh taught a lesson, not given time to regroup.

While the new committee of twenty-four began work, a large body of fighting men milled about the Oxford meadows. Constitutionalists might be absorbed in discussions, in plans for a permanent elected council with a smaller steering committee, by agendas and forms of procedure, but the bulk of the company was plain bored. They had settled their affairs and left their homes for war, not for a lot of hair-splitting debate. The longer they waited, the more clearly they saw the trouble. King Henry was all right at heart, if a bit simple; he enjoyed a good campaign, even if he did like Art and so forth. The foreign gang had taken advantage of his good nature and confused his mind. As for Sicily, a far distant country of which they knew nothing, that was expensive nonsense.

When they realised that Henry had nominated all four of his half-brothers among his twelve representatives, the barons had a target for their anger. The committee's decisions were hardened and sharpened, the *colloquium* endorsed them, the Lord Edward was induced to accept them, and on 14 July the whole Lusignan clan went into exile overseas.[13]

Henry's unfinished Scottish business was now in his councillors' hands, whether he realised it or not. A delegation rode north in August, passing Scots envoys southbound:

> King Henry having lately sent Simon de Montfort Earl of Leicester, Peter of Savoy and John Mansel Treasurer of York to Scotland with the intention of amending the state of that kingdom and of King Alexander, he greatly wonders at certain things set forth on Alexander's behalf by the Abbot of Dunfermline and William Hay, who brought letters of credence. On the return of his own envoys, with their advice and that of other nobles of his Council Henry will reply to the suggestions, being solicitous for Alexander's honour and advantage.[14]

In early September Alexander came to Roxburgh with part of his feudal levies, having learned that 'his traitors' (as Melrose calls them) had come north with forces of their own supported by some English barons. On 8 September he was in Melrose, visiting his father's grave by the high altar, when he was confronted by the earls of Hereford and Albemarle, and John Balliol. The abbey chronicler, perhaps an eyewitness, had no doubt of their purpose:

> they came on behalf of the King of England as if to calm the people and restore peace, but in reality (as rumour asserted) to seize the King again and carry him off to England; but he, aware of their intentions, appointed a meeting next day at Jedburgh, where a large part of his army was already gathered in the forest.[15]

It was something new for Alexander to muster armies. According to the chronicler he knew that Mansel had joined the Doorward at Norham, having moved from the first group of envoys to the second. Mansel was a professional of a different stamp from the normal run of magnates; if he was in the field, things were serious. Alexander was now seventeen; the Melrose visit was a kind of birthday salute to his father's memory, a moment when he must have longed for some disinterested advice. He was resolved to bring all his troubles to a close.

The army he had led from Edinburgh was primarily the knight-service, scores of individual feudal tenants each with a handful of men, coming to serve for no more than forty days. They could be summoned quickly, but he had not relied on them alone. What was now gathering within Selwood was something else. He had called out the Host, the 'Scottish Service', every man between sixteen and sixty 'coming forth to save his head' as the phrase ran, led by earls, thanes or chiefs and armed with axes, boar-spears or herdsmen's slings according to availability and skill. It was the Scottish equivalent of the Saxon *fyrd*, and it came from every corner of the country.

To the Melrose monk it was a lawless rabble. Some of its components had already been in the Borders at the time of the spring *colloquium*, 'Scots and Galwegians' claiming exemption from Lenten fasting while on military service and feeding themselves on meat, even on Good Friday, much of it good Melrose mutton. Now that the full Host was assembling, greater damage was expected; it was later alleged to have devastated the whole area.

The English earls and Balliol were aware of movement in the woods as they rode down Dere Street to Jedburgh. They rode unchallenged but their horses' ears were never still. Here a solitary figure stood above a ford; at the next rise they smelt wood-smoke and heard steel clink. The forest gleamed dully in the twilight and autumn leaves rustled across the road.

Jedburgh was still fifteen miles inside the Border, but never had its abbey guest-house seemed more welcoming. Abbot Nicholas had news for them, little of it good. There were Galloway men encamped all about, bristling with weapons and uncouth of speech, and there were reliable reports of Argyll men and northerners moving through Clydesdale. The abbey's faithful sons, Elliots, Armstrongs and Kerrs, would guard the abbey's flocks; the Abbot could only trust they found no occasion to settle private quarrels with their English cousins among his tithe-barns.

Alexander had galloped back to Marchmont and sent runners through the forest to hasten the last stragglers forward. It was not yet time to light the beacons, but high time to finish building them. When he came to Jedburgh next morning he wore his mail and rode under his father's lion banner.

He soon made it clear that the English envoys could choose which course they liked; he was prepared for war, ready to talk. He engaged them in painstaking discussions on every point from the Doorward's shortcomings to the finer points in the Laws of the March. When he, or they, seemed half-satisfied on one point his councillors raised another. The Bishop of St Andrews arrived in state, and the Chancellor, and the Chamberlain; the famous Augustinian hospitality was strained to its limit. There was a small royal castle beside the town, but neither it nor the burgh could house all the company, and autumn nights grew chill for tented camps. Whenever messengers passed to Norham they saw more watchfires; the great fleece of Selwood covered a forest of spears.

The conference stretched out, the earls grew anxious, an English *parlement* was about to meet:

Indeed after three weeks the envoys, seeing that the army of Scotland had arrived and was ready to break out against them if they delayed, and that they lacked force to resist, made peace on behalf of the traitors and so returned home.[16]

There must have been some formal arrangement to bring the Doorward and his friends into the King's peace, but it has not survived. What does exist is a letter sent to Scotland in Henry's name. It marks a sharp change in policy:

> The King greets his noble and beloved friends, Gamelin by God's grace Bishop of St Andrews, John of Acre, Mary by the same grace Queen of Scotland and wife of the said John, Alexander Comyn Earl of Buchan, William Earl of Mar, Alexander Steward of Scotland, Alan Doorward, Robert Meyners and Gilbert Hay, councillors of his well-beloved son the illustrious King of Scotland. Because you have undertaken the care of the realm of Scotland, we notify you that we have promised in good faith that when you are in need and we have been asked by you, we shall favourably grant our counsel and help to you in the affairs of the realm of Scotland, so long as you genuinely conduct them with regard to God and justice, and for the profit and honour of our son the King your lord, and of our beloved daughter the Queen of Scotland, your lady, and according to the laws and good custom of that realm. But if all, or any, or one of you fail in any way, and being asked by us to make amends fail to do so within three months of receiving our admonition therein, we shall thenceforward be under no sort of obligation to you. In testimony [etc];
>
> Witness the King, Westminster, 6 November.

To this is attached a schedule, prefaced by a note that letters in the following terms should be obtained from each of the named councillors and if possible from Alexander himself, for enrolment when received (they never were enrolled, so presumably none were returned):

> We, Gamelin [and the others] give greeting in the Lord to all who shall see or hear this document. Since we have the care of the realm of Scotland now in our hands, be it known that we have faithfully promised to conduct the government of the realm with regard for God and justice, and for the profit of our lord the King and our lady the Queen and the welfare of the realm, according to the laws and customs hitherto in force, causing good justice to be given impartially to rich and poor alike. We shall endeavour, as far as we reasonably can, to ensure that love and unity shall always be maintained between our lord the King and our lady the Queen, and we willingly agree that if all, or any, or one of us shall offend in any way in these things, which God forbid, and shall not make amends as we ought, at the request of the King of England within three months of his admonition, he shall thenceforth be under no sort of obligation to us. Further, we and all others of the realm of

Scotland whom we can induce to do so, shall freely render our counsel and aid to the King of England, within the realm of England, when he needs and asks for our help. But if the King does not keep his promises to us, as more fully set out in the letter we have had from him, we do not wish to be committed any longer to him in the matter.[17]

This is what the English Council wanted, not what they received; their envoys spent the winter in Scotland pressing in vain for the letters to be sealed. Their hosts had more to do; whatever else is obscure it is evident that the great rift in Scottish society was closing. Gamelin, Buchan and Mar on one side, the Steward, the Doorward, Meyners and Hay on the other, the Queen Mother and her husband in the centre, made a balanced whole. Someone had applied mature political thought to the composition of the Inner Council. A new era was opening in which all talents could serve the state. There was no need to give binding obligations to foreign powers.

Alexander left them to it and went to Perth that autumn, on his way to hunt at Clunie or Kincardine. As he reached the edge of the Highlands he received two signs that the old order was past. On 10 November Bishop Bondington died at Melrose, where he had been resting after his exertions at the conference; he had been Glasgow's Bishop for a quarter of a century. About the same day died Walter of Menteith, markedly absent from the new Council. Fordun reports him 'poisoned by his wife, as was said', but since the immediate cause of death was a riding accident in which he broke both legs, we may acquit the Countess. They buried him near his only son, in his beautiful little priory of Inchmahome. At least he had seen the dawn of a better day.[18]

Chapter 10 Notes

1   Letters of protection for E. Winchester, *CDS I, 2098* (21 Dec.); Bolsover granted, repairs to be allowed on inspection, *ib. 2099* (24 Dec.).

2   *CDS I, 2103* (17 Jan. 1258, Windsor).

3   *CDS I, 2104* (22 Jan.); the sense requires *ver(sus)* rather than *vel*; I have not seen the original.

4   *CDS I, 2107* (15 Feb.). Pope to Bp. Clement, Watt *Biog.* 212. The business was the provision of an absentee rector to Smailholm (perhaps for help at the Curia). S/cs, *CDS I, 2110* (9 March) and *2112* (16 March).

5   Clement died prob. 19 March, Watt, *Biog.*, 103; *CM* 115. For the Welsh Bond see *CDS I, 2155* (18 March '1259'), *APS I*, JE Lloyd, *History of Med. Wales* (1948); Powicke 381 and 627. Hector of Carrick, p.78 above.

6   *Servicium Scoticanum*, pp.128, 146 below.

7   M. Paris, see Ch.9. Q. Joanna, p.13 above.

8   *CDS I, 2113* (23 March, Westminster), *2114* (25 March). Easter Day was 24 March. 'Inaccessibility' seems slightly more appropriate for Forfar than Stirling. Neville was sheriff of Northumberland, Latimer of Cumberland.

9   Chester rendezvous, *CDS I, 2115* (28 March); de Ros, *ib. 2116* (30 March), *2117* (1

Apl.) Bp. of Durham, *ib. 2118* (2 April).

10 Confederation, Powicke 377; 'retreats', *CDS I, 2121* (5 April).

11 Powicke 377–8; venison, *CDS I, 2124* (4 May), where Adam is called 'de la Stede', but cf. *ib. 2069* and *2071*. Strathearn's letter, *ib. 2125* (6 May, St. Andrews). The Earl's first wife was Marjory de Muschamp, yr. sister of Isabella de Forde (p.44). His second was Mathilda, dau. of Gilbert E. of Orkney and Caithness (who d. 1256). K. Henry to sheriffs, *CDS I, 2128* (16 May, Winchester).

12 Henry to Alexander, *CDS I, 2126* (15 May) and to sheriffs, *ib. 2127* (14 May).

13 For *parlement* and Provisions of Oxford, Powicke 379–384. 'A far distant country', cf. Neville Chamberlain, Prime Minister, BBC radio, 27 Sept. 1938.

14 Envoys appointed, *CDS I, 2131* (4 Aug.); Henry to Alexander, *ib. 2133* (27 Aug.).

15 *CM* 115.

16 *CM* 116.

17 *CDS I, 2139*; full text, Stones, *Docs.*, 35–37.

18 Bp. Bondington (p.74 above) was buried before the high altar of Melrose. Menteith died 6x25, prob. 6x10 Nov., *CM* 116, Fordun LIII, M.Paris, *Chron.Maj.V.*724, in *SA*, 376. Inchmahome (OSA), App. C.

William I, Earl of Pembroke, 'The Old Marshal', in action 1231.
(He died 1233.)

1259: *Household Affairs*

JEDBURGH HAD been a landmark; while the Sheriff of Northumberland and the Treasurer of St Albans spent most of the winter in Scotland, the local authorities were tidying up minor problems revealed by the recent mobilisation. One case survives in fair detail.

There were doubts over the service due from the thirteen merklands of Padevinan (Pettinain) near Lanark, held by Adam de Liberatione. The Sheriff of Lanark assembled a local jury, headed by William Wafrarius ('Warfarer'?) a retired king's sergeant, who had with him William Mutson, Gamel of Hyndford, Richard the seneschal of Carmichael, John Scurry of Pettinain, Thomas Adamson of Carstairs and William Rufus of Ronestrother (Ravenstruther). Decision was complicated by a sublet of part of the land to Sir Thomas Normanville, but eventually they found witnesses who had themselves provided the service in the past. They recorded these names for good measure, and we meet Robert Collan, Robert Scevel, Laurence Lovel, Adam of Forfar, Edward de Liberatione and John Pret.

All those had served, 'taking nothing from the King but their victuals', to make up parties of two archers and a mounted sergeant who issued ('liberated') provisions for royal grooms and hounds when the King came to Lanark Castle. At the end of the talk it emerged that Adam's daughter Isobel should have a charter put away somewhere which she was told to find by next court-day. The ex-sergeant and Gilchrist of Syplaw produced seals for the record, and that was that.

This inquiry gives a glimpse of the underside of the feudal fabric, too often seen only in terms of 'the baronage'. Here are men who made the system work, humping rations about a yard while a clerk kept tally and hounds watched from kennel. A cook banged on a pot and the men dusted themselves down and went to their dinner and a draught of King's ale. The nub is that dinner, they were not serfs or hirelings but men doing an obligement somewhere between feudal service and sergeanty.[1]

More complicated arrangements also needed revision. Reform was in the air; English committees were discussing everything from inequities in administration to royal housekeeping. The French Court was much as Queen Blanche had found it fifty years before, but Louis IX was applying his experiences to evolve simpler ways and planning his *Établissements* to improve administration.

One newcomer to Alexander's Court was likely to take special interest in its procedures. John de Brienne well knew what abuses could arise in complex organisations that evolved piecemeal over many years; it is possible that he commissioned the treatise entitled *The Scottish King's Household*.[2]

As it stands, the manuscript is of around 1305; its editor felt it might reflect arrangements 'in the reign of John Balliol or of Alexander'. It is hard to believe that in John's brief reign anyone had leisure to examine domestic details or that they would omit any reference to events after 1286. The textual blend of tradition ('and be it known that of old time ...') and practical proposals ('There ought to be ...') accord with inspection by an experienced foreign observer; and there was no better time for such analysis than the eve of Alexander's assumption of personal control.

The opening paragraph claims royal authority:

> Whereas our lord the King desires to be assured of the governance of his realm according to the ancient customs and usage of the land, it is thought by some of his realm that he ought to proceed to have a common assembly and personal speech with all the prelates, earls and barons, and show them that he is well willing to govern, and to maintain the estate of Holy Church and of his realm according to the ancient laws and usages at all points. And that they [the prelates and magnates] shall make no purprestures on the burghs and demesne lands in prejudice of the Crown, whereby debate or dispute may arise between them by reason of their offence and he may have a claim against them to their disherison.[3]

The writer next reviews each office of state, their duties and the methods of selecting holders:

> And after this speech and agreement between them, first by the counsel and consent of them and all the baronage there should be appointed good and sufficient ministers to serve the King both within and without [the Household]; firstly the Chancellor, wise, suitable and of good discretion, impartial to rich and poor, as head of his Council.

The Chancellor must know the laws and the proper formulae of writs, and should accompany the King or at his command remain in some central place convenient to the people. He may have as many clerks 'as required in reason'; he must charge the old fees and no more for writs issued, and may issue only 'writs of course' (routine) without royal command under the Privy Seal,

> which shall be carried and kept by one of the wisest and most discreet of the

realm, for if this office is well governed it is the key and safety of the Great Seal and the prevention of all the errors which can arise between the King and his baronage.

Next comes the Chamberlain, to be chosen 'by the great men aforesaid'. He must 'guide and govern the burghs, the demesne lands of the King, and his poor husbandmen in demesne'. He handles wardships and reliefs (succession-duties), and permissions for marriage of heiresses go through his hands. He deals with 'all the realm's issues to the profit of the Crown', makes all bulk purchases (*qil face les achatz en gros*) and 'regulates the King's dwelling by assent of the King himself' according to season and so that the King 'can live by purveyance without ravaging the land' (*saunz ravyne du pays*).

There should be an annual Exchequer Audit, the Chancellor and Chamberlain sitting with appointed auditors at a convenient place for summoning all who handle Crown revenues (the procedure certainly operated by 1263). A Clerk of the Rolls should be appointed to control all charters and muniments, with the Exchequer accounts, so that the King may know 'the fees and ferms due to him in their entirety'.

So much for general administration:

> In the King's Household there ought to be a Steward of fee [a hereditary Steward, as there had been from Malcolm IV's time] or a sufficient knight present for him, to order the Household by counsel of the Chamberlain, to whom all the officers of the Household ought to be heedful; and he shall report the defects of the Household in writing to the Chamberlain when they choose to direct improvements.

The hereditary Constable (whose office existed under David I), or his deputy, guards the King's person and keeps the peace 'for twelve leagues around'. [This is thirty-six miles or fifty kilometres; perhaps twelve miles was meant, although a three-mile 'verge' was usual]. The Constable brings any disturber of the peace to prompt trial in his own court, except for pleas in the King's hand [which the writer defines as treason or breach of the peace within the verge; the Pleas of the Crown were treason, arson, rape and murder]. When the King comes to stay in a castle the Constable takes command of the guard and the King's Porter has the gate-guard:

> And if battle be adjudged between knights, the Constable shall have the guard of the lists, with the Marischal, for the day, and they shall have the fees pertaining as in other realms where knights fight on horseback.[4]
>
> And it be known that the Constable used to have of old time in the King's Household twenty-four sergeants who were called *durwardes*, guarding the King's body and drawing Court rations, so that twelve ate at the first sitting

while twelve kept the Hall door with the ushers, each with the equipment of the twenty-four [ie., with their comrades' weapons as well as their own] until the King had eaten. And after eating, the other twelve kept the door of the King's chamber, outside, until vespers, the whole company mounting guard about the chamber every night at the Constable's command, unless he detached any to guard prisoners. And when the King rode through his realm the twenty-four went before him, on foot, before the Constable, in place of the macers.

The Constable is not to try any burgess who claims burgh privileges ('avouches his cross and his burgh-market') except when the burgess is serving as a member of the Household. All other office-bearers, and any freemen who may be at Court, are to sit with the Constable 'when he holds his court in the King's hall or at the gate'.

The Marischal comes next, his office 'pertains to hall and chamber'. He has charge of seating arrangements for meals, placing the company once the King's table is seated, with the advice of the Steward and Constable; his Valet Marshal controls the second sitting. In wartime the Marischal deals with all offences committed 'under the banner' in summary court [-martial].

The Almoner, with his clerk 'to guard the almonry', may be a hereditary officer or a lay knight or Knight Templar. He has oversight of all royal hospitals and hospices, appointing masters who are good husbandmen and ensuring that 'the King's servants and his poor farm-workers who grow old and cannot help themselves' are received into care. With the Chancellor he must inspect these places annually.

Turning to victualling and supply, 'there ought to be' a Clerk of the Liverance, or Liberation, with two clerks under him, to deal with all provisions and issue to each his due ration. All officers of the Household and 'ushers of the door' concerned with victualling, answer to him, and he accounts to the Exchequer for provisions delivered in kind and outlays on purchases.

Another, 'called of old the Clerk of the Provender', keeps daily account of outgoings and sits by the hall-door checking a list of those authorised to draw rations that day. He has the advice of the marshals and ushers, and his Roll is the only acceptable evidence for expenses incurred by his colleagues of Liverance, Wardrobe and Kitchen.

A treasurer 'called of old Clerk of the Wardrobe', loyal and familiar to the King, shall have the keeping of all the relics, jewels, robes, vestments and 'all manner of furniture' for the hall, chamber and chapel,

> and he shall have the keeping of the spices, wax, and all minor things for the King's body, receiving them in gross from the Chamberlain and accounting to the Exchequer.

The Clerk of the Kitchen supervises the issue of stores to the cooks and the butchering of meat, preventing waste and recording the number of rations issued daily; he also accounts for the disposal of hides and scraps, reporting every night to the Clerk of the Provender. (He has assumed the duties of the *Rannair*, the Divider-of-Food in Celtic palaces who had the delicate task of ensuring that everyone received the cut of meat befitting his status. He has also inherited the duty of allocating tithes of hides and fat, and shares of special delicacies such as whale or porpoise, granted to certain monasteries by earlier kings, though most of these tiresome gifts had been converted into annual payments. Without such arrangements there would still have been lay-brothers from Scone or Dunfermline hovering around the larder and upsetting the cooks).

> Further, be it known that all the ushers of all the offices shall be chosen on the King's behalf from his own people in whom he trusts, and they shall come to the petty accounting with the officers, for the security of his property, although the great officers and many others have been hereditary in the past, for example the Pantler, Butler, Larderer, Baker, Naperer, Chandler, Waterer and such others.

(Here the writer has looked beyond Scotland or used his imagination; William the Lion had a Butler, *Pincerna Regis*, but his small grants to 'Ailif the baker', 'Walkelin my brewer' and 'Ivo the King's cook' suggest these were domestics retiring from service).[5]

Sections on the appointment of judges and sheriffs follow oddly after such domestic details, with the heading *Foraynz Ministres* (those serving outside the Household). 'Justices' [Justiciars] are to be chosen by the magnates and serve in addition to those whose charters empower them to administer justice within their fiefs. There are to be three Justiciars, 'of Lothian', 'of the Sea of Scotland' and 'of Galloway'; no mention of a Justiciar of the North, in post by 1239, and 'of the Sea' is more often entitled 'of Scotia' (the land between Forth and Spey). They handle all cases except 'such as cannot be redressed without the presence of the King himself, by default of the justices or sheriffs'. The Justiciars are to make two circuits, 'on the grass' and 'on the stubble' (spring and autumn); they, not the sheriffs, appoint coroners and are answerable for them. In the course of their eyres they must enquire into the conduct of sheriff and local courts, challenging them at the bar and bringing faults to the King's notice.

Sheriffs are to be 'elected by advice and choice of the *bons gentz* of the county' (*bons gentz* means more than 'good men', it implies superior worth, general trustworthiness, public spirit). They must maintain equal law for poor and rich, and possess property wherein they can be penalised for 'trespass against the King' or failure to render accounts to the Exchequer. Only they, or their duly sworn sergeants, may handle forfeited or disputed goods 'according to the ancient laws and usages of the realm which would be too long to write in this roll' (and which are fully covered by statutes from David I onwards).

Finally it is proposed to clear away a tangle of hereditary posts:

> Further be it known that all who claim to hold office hereditarily from the King, whatever their condition, denizens or *foraynz*, and claim fee or maintenance at the King's expense in his Household, let their right be tried by title-deed if they have one or by a good assize of their peers and the *bons gentz* who best know the facts, so that the King be not deceived nor overcharged, nor they disinherited. And let it be done in full *parlement* and not in the little Council.

The depth of this study and its attention to detail almost equal the Prince Consort's efforts to regulate Queen Victoria's ramshackle Household of the 1840s. Whoever compiled it could be proud of his work. Some points, such as evening meetings of officials, recur in Edward I's Household ordinances (though our author has not seen the need to weigh candle-ends); others, like the appointment of sheriffs from an elected list, appear in the Provisions of Oxford. An instinct for order and a habit of logic suggest French influence; if it is not John de Brienne's survey it may well have been made under his direction.

One would like to be sure which sections contain new proposals and which merely record established practice. What became of the swift-footed *durwardes*, when did macers replace them? Why is there no mention of the Doorward himself, whose duties have been shared between the Constable and Marischal? When Alan of Lundie died in 1275 none of his sons-in-law claimed the office (although one, William de Soulis, was of the line of former *Pincernae Regis* and later served as Justiciar of Lothian).

We catch glimpses of the scheme in operation. There were annual audits; in 1282 the Clerk of the Rolls tackled the herculean task of indexing a century of parchments; in 1291 the Wardrobe held relics and vestments as well as silver cups and a 'gryphon's egg', presumably ostrich, silver-mounted but broken beyond repair.[6]

One medieval Court was much like the next, all slowly evolving from the monarch's dwelling into an administrative centre with a bureaucracy. All, still, travelled up and down their countries, officials and clerks working out of baskets and hurriedly-repacked chests. In every country there were odd fragments of old ways to be accommodated within a modernising framework. A class of professional administrators was developing, men with a degree in law, technically clerics but without ambitions within the Church until the time came to obtain a reward for Crown service. Such men could find employment anywhere, through a network of university friends. Under their influence all Europe might have converged into one indistinguishable superstate; but it did not.

The superstate came into sight in the heyday of papal authority under Innocent III and Innocent IV, but the sheer weight of papal power upon worldly affairs had an unforeseen effect. People began turning instead to half-forgotten notions of nationhood.

There were two Europe-wide languages, Latin and the military slang called *lingua-franca*, spread by returning crusaders as the British Army long afterwards brought words from India – *naker* for a small drum, *karavan* for a mobile command-column (Edward later used both). Other phrases picked up from foreign comrades or camp-followers were added. Again, it seemed everything would vanish into the melting-pot; instead, even at court, vernacular speech revived.

Giraldus had sounded a warning when he reported an old Welshman telling Henry II,

> This nation, o King, may now as in former times be weakened and harassed by your power, but it can never be wholly subdued by the wrath of man unless the wrath of God concur. Nor do I think that any other nation than this of Wales, nor any other language, come what may, shall answer at the Last Day for this corner of the earth.[7]

A resilient counter-current began to flow during the thirteenth century. The heretic Cathars, driven underground in southern France, and the Dominicans sent to preach against them in local dialects, helped feed it. It flowed in Gascony deeper than the dynastic squabbles of magnates; in Sicily it broke surface when settlers of Greek and Arab descent made common cause against the French, using the island speech as shibboleth. In Flanders it held proletarian groups together against exploiting clothmasters who had reduced them to near slavery. In three Alpine cantons it built a league of peasants against the Hohenstaufen emperors. Londoners recalled Saxon laws; even the Oxford barons spoke of 'King and Crown' as if they had some inkling of an ideal beyond their immediate ruler, and their debates would culminate in the assertion that England was a *patria* for which men would die.

The awareness of place, of belonging to a place rather than owning it, is engrained in Celtic minds. Gaelic tradition embraces the idea of communities as building-blocks of society; 'Man alone is no man'. It was a major achievement of the Dalriadic kings to raise their followers' sights above cousinship and the next glen, to accept all other Gaels as members of the King's "family" and then to adjust again to partnership with their ancient enemies the Picts. It was easier for Anglians, led into Lothian by their own jarls (who became earls of Dunbar) and for Danes in Cumbria and the Solway shore who throve in sturdy independence under their Prince of Cumbria until, one fine day, the Prince of the moment became David I, King of Scots. As for Norse settlers, they were of all people the most adaptable; they had scant regard for kings, but set high store by neighbourliness and mutual support.

What bolted the whole Scottish structure together was the Church which, having survived internal disputes, gained papal endorsement in the twelfth century and thereafter had a vested interest in independence. Whatever individual clerics thought of Doorward or Comyn, Church policy upheld the rights which gave it direct access to Rome. They were nationalists ahead of the magnates, who had foreign kin and crusading ideals to distract them from thoughts of *patria*. It was enough for most laymen that they followed a king whose ancestors had led them into battle with honour and whose throne was of unimaginable antiquity. When they met alien intervention they were ready enough to oppose it; a time would come when the richest young man in England would ride north to 'be with his own'.[8]

Through the so-called Dark Ages, when the Roman Empire collapsed and hundreds of petty tyrants scrabbled for loot in the ruins, people cared less for 'liberty' than for safety under some tolerable ruler and defender. The liberty they might find was the one they most dreaded, to be cast on the world's mercy masterless. In the twelfth and thirteenth centuries, when classical authors were again available and men had peace to read them, high ideals returned. The universities, especially the oldest southern ones, cherished their independence; *bons gentz* wanted a hand in government; burghs bought the right to run their own affairs. A time of peace was necessary for men to agree on the value of liberty, and in Scotland Alexander's reign would be remembered as The Time of Peace, although in 1259 few people would have given much for his chances. At the end of the reign a parish priest near Stirling, once on Gamelin's staff, taught his small nephew a couplet:

> *Dico tibi verum libertas optima rerum;*
> *Nunquam servili sub nexo vivito fili.*

('I tell you truly, liberty is best of things; never live, son, under the yoke of slavery'). That priest of Dunipace was a Mr Simon Walens, or Wallace, and his pupil's name was William.[9]

There was a long way to go before William Wallace went to school. Alexander still had many unresolved problems — relations with England, dependent on a solution to Henry's current troubles; some sort of concord or a final showdown with Norway and the Isles. He could not be sure all his councillors agreed on the need, as he saw it, to end the wasteful bickering between factions; some feuds were virtually hobbies, not to be dropped at a word from him. Two things could really unite the country; one, as Jedburgh had shown, was war – *quod absit*; the other was a sign of continuity for his dynasty, which meantime hung on the slender thread of his own life. These were matters in God's hand; his duty was to go up and down his country, meeting his people and hearing their troubles. The only thing that kept bringing him back to Edinburgh that winter was the continued presence of the English envoy Mr William Horton.

There were several things Mr William wanted (sealed letters, and he was not getting those), but only one for Alexander to urge in return. He wanted the abominable Roxburgh document back as promised, and of all things it was lost in his father-in-law's filing system. So much for the wonders of bureaucracy; in Scotland one hove such things into a muniment room and, provided one knew which heap to search, they could be found again. With all the fuss taking place in the south, the English system had collapsed. It was not much to ask; the wretched thing was big enough to stick out of any parchment-basket, and he intended to go on demanding it until they found it. (The search was hopeless; the document had been entrusted to Mansel, and shovelled into some chest among his many charters to his collection of livings and lands).[10]

> In the same year about the Kalends of March returned master William Horton, monk and treasurer of the church of St Alban, from the remotest parts of Scotland. He had long before undertaken the laborious journey ... he asked submissively on behalf of the lord king of the English and the queen and the barons, that the lord king of Scotland and the queen should not omit to come into England to listen and discuss ...a difficult and private matter. And after they had put in the way much opposition and obstruction of difficulties he at last, by persisting in diligent petition, obtained their consent ... provided only that the king of England and the magnates would assure them of the document which before had been faithfully promised to them. And they wrote letters of high commendation of William's unwearied diligence. ...and sent messengers of state, the earl of Buchan, master William the Chancellor, and Sir Alan Doorward, to treat more fully ... And when they had come and spoken with William, who preceded them, they returned leaving no testimony in public concerning the success of their affair.[11]

Chapter 11 Notes

1   *APS I*; *Sel. Cases* no. 53; *CDS I, 2175* ('*ca* 1259').

2   'The Scottish King's Household', M.Bateson, *SHS Misc. III* from MS in Corpus Christi College, Cambridge; *RRS II*, 35 *inf.* cf. Powicke, 291–2 for Henry's Household ; *ib.* 379, 395, for Provisions of Oxford; Louis IX's *Établissements, Joinville* 311 *inf.* (?a late addition to his MS).

3   Purprestures are encroachments, e.g. a building intruding into the highway, or an enclosure on common land.

4 Trial by combat had been abolished under Alexander II (p.16) except on the March. Judicial duel was enforceable in France until 1260; under the Assize of Jerusalem, which still applied in the remnant crusader states, knights accused of homicide must fight the *duellum* on foot (seasoned horses being worth more than murderous knights, in *Outremer*).

5 The Almoner's post may explain the presence of the Templars' Scottish Almoner, p.72. For *Rannair*, cf. *RRS I*, 32 and *RRS II*, 36–7. Grants to baker &c. *RRS II*. The list of hereditary offices omits that of Marischal, already established in the Keith family (Hervé, d.1196, served Malcolm IV and William).

6 *APS I*, 2–11, gives the 1282 archives list and those of 1291/2; for valuables see App.D.

7 Giraldus Cambrensis, *Itinerary through Wales*, Everyman 1908, 205.

8 Bulls of Celestine III, Innocent III and (*Filia Specialis*) Honorius III (20 Dec. 1218). 'With his own', Robert I, when E. of Carrick, 1305.

9 *Dico tibi* (from Fordun) in *Scottish Pageant*, A. Mure MacKenzie, Oliver & Boyd 1952, 170 (my prose trans.) Mr Simon Walens, Watt, *Biog.* 562.

10 Stones, *Docs*, 34, addendum to Declaration.

11 M. Paris, *Chron. Maj.V.*739–40, in *SA*, 377 (here slightly cut). This is our last Scottish report from Matthew, who died soon afterwards. For his career, see R.Vaughan, *Matthew Paris* (Cambridge 1979); *Chronicles of Matthew Paris*, tr. & ed. R.Vaughan (Alan Sutton, 1984); M.R.James, *The Drawings of Matthew Paris*, and F.Wormald, *More Drawings* ... (Walpole Society, 1926 and 1935).

1259–1260: The Troubled Neighbour

ALEXANDER WOULD attain the tenth anniversary of his accession in July 1259, and seven weeks later, celebrate his eighteenth birthday. Whatever the 1255 declaration said, he was taking full powers over his realm. Now was the time for a new Great Seal, for new coinage replacing the childish image which had served until then, and there was one more way to emphasise the change; there could be a second coronation.

Nobody doubted that he had been duly enthroned with all the ancient ceremonies, but something slightly different might be devised. His father had sought a papal blessing and anointing with consecrated oil; it was not part of Scots tradition, but certain foreigners had noted the omission. The Queen, too, might be crowned with him, and for that innovation there was a special reason.

John de Brienne may well have been present in 1246 when Charles of Anjou shocked his mother's Court by protesting that his marriage to Beatrice of Provence was being less splendidly celebrated than that of his brother to her sister, although Charles was the son of a king and a queen and Louis merely the son of a prince. His arrogance was horrifying, but indeed he alone, of all Louis VIII's sons, was 'born in the purple'. The theory belonged to the arcane world of Byzantium and was new to the West, where primogeniture was paramount; but if such ideas were current it would be no bad thing for Scotland's next prince to be born to a crowned queen and an anointed king. It might even restrain his grandfather's pretensions.[1]

That May, John of Dundemore carried a number of proposals into England. Henry's reply was flustered and petulant; he had enough troubles without silly suggestions from that tiresome child in the north, for the Pope had annulled his grant of Sicily, the baronial Council was meddling with Henry's private expenses, and Eleanor de Montfort was impeding affairs of state by her obstinacy:

> The King acknowledges the messages ... about money owed. Because of the peace with France, the Welsh rebellion, and the affair of Sicily, he is involved in great expenses and cannot pay at present though he hopes to do so in whole or in part by Michaelmas. As to the writing the King of Scots wants returned,

Table 7. France

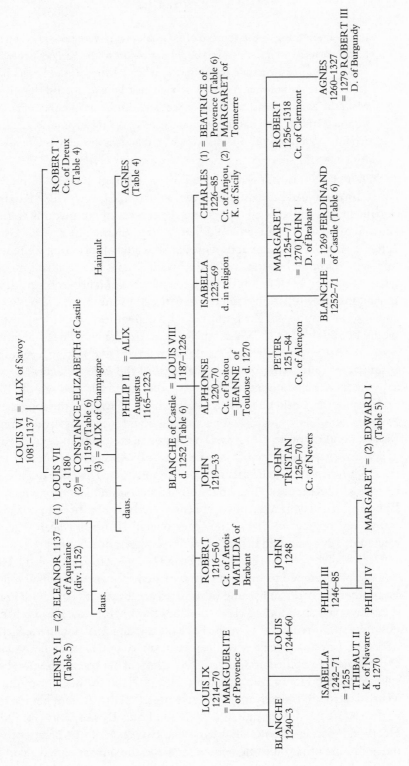

he can do nothing in the absence of his nobles who were present when it was made. As to the request that he should not object to the King of Scots' coronation, he thinks the time is unsuitable; when a better season arrives he will act as befits his honour. As to the request that he will not assist the King of Man, the King informs the King of Scotland that he will neither oppose him in doing justice, nor has he been asked to do so by anyone; if anything is reported to him he will do what is right and honourable between himself and Alexander.[2]

So Margaret must still wait for her dowry, although the 'Aid to marry his eldest daughter' had brought Henry twice the sum expected. The Roxburgh document was still missing, and it and the subject of coronations were best allowed to lapse; Alexander could live without them. The reference to the King of Man is unexplained, though the Steward was planning some sort of military enterprise (he can hardly have invaded Man, but may have mounted guard against raids). The only clue is a letter from Henry to his Justiciar of Ireland that August, telling him to allow the Steward's men to buy 'victuals and other necessities for the purposes of his expedition' on pledges that they would not be shipped to Welsh rebels. Next year he was 'not to permit any Scots to be received in Ireland', and was to arrest 'any seeking leagues with Irishmen or compassing other damage against the King of Scots'; presumably the Steward was hunting pirates or other criminals through the Isles.[3]

Alexander had other problems. Mr Nicholas of Moffat, the long-serving Archdeacon of Teviotdale, had been elected with royal approval to replace Bishop Bondington in Glasgow. The Pope rejected him and provided one of his own chaplains, John of Cheyam (Cheam). Alexander refused to accept the Englishman's fealty and retained the temporalities. The Pope urged Henry to use his influence, but Henry did nothing until spring 1260, by which time Bishop John had won Alexander's approval. Mr Nicholas, he who was 'always quarrelling but never angry' and 'ever liberal' (Lanercost again), was re-elected in 1268 but died before obtaining consecration.[4]

Despite all the pressure for Alexander and Margaret to visit England, Henry was too preoccupied to make any arrangements for them. He had induced his brother Richard, and young Edward, to accept peace terms with France; these involved abandoning claims to lands the English royal house had not possessed in more than fifty years. Richard the diplomat acknowledged the necessity, Edward agreed with deep reluctance, but Eleanor de Montfort could be neither bullied nor cajoled. The claims of her first widowhood were still unsatisfied; Henry had accepted a measly £400 for her out of the vast Marshal estates in Ireland, and now he expected her to give up her last rights in their mother's dowerlands. She had won Louis IX's support and she had Henry in a corner. Eventually there were two texts of the Treaty of Paris, one with, the other omitting her consent, and she only accepted a compromise on the eve of the signing.

Earlier that autumn old Margaret of Kent died. Almost seventy years before, she had been sole heiress of Scotland; King William her father planned to marry her to Otto of Saxony and let them rule in partnership, but the Scots opposed the plan. Queen Ermengarde was pregnant again, but the child was again a girl; then in 1198 Alexander II was born, and in 1209 the Princesses Margaret and Isabella were sent hostage to England. King John kept them in Corfe or Bristol with their older cousin Eleanor of Brittany (Arthur's sister), occasionally remembering to send money for their clothes. There was a half promise of marriage to John's two baby sons, each fourteen years younger than his bride, but it came to nothing. Henry perhaps fancied himself in love with Margaret, but before he was of marriageable age she was snapped up by his Justiciar Hubert de Burgh. When Hubert's inevitable crash came, Margaret saved what she could from the wreckage; in later years she was often at the English court, especially when her long-lost compatriots came south.[5]

Henry had no time to look backwards. He spent Christmas in Paris, sealing the treaty and giving homage to Louis for his remaining lands. The feasting was no less splendid than before, but family harmony was almost wrecked by protocol. The queens of France, Germany and England were naturally seated at the top table, but the Countess of Anjou and Provence was not. It seems grotesque to suggest, as contemporary gossip did, that from that placement came wars in Italy, plots in Byzantium and the nightmare of the Sicilian Vespers, but great events spring from small seeds, and Charles was assured of his wife's support in future moves towards the crown of Sicily.[6]

The festivities lasted into January with the marriage of Count John of Brittany to Beatrix of England. Henry set off for home, but hurried back on learning of the sudden death of Louis' eldest son. His helping to carry the coffin angered his barons who saw it as a public demonstration of his lowered status.

Starting again, he fell ill in Flanders with what was called 'his annual bout of tertian fever', which kept him in St Omer until April. (Recurrent malaria seems improbable; perhaps it was a more dignified name for a feverish cold). Feverish he certainly was, over events in England. Simon de Montfort had returned from Paris and, with Edward, decided that under the Provisions of Oxford a Candlemas *parlement* must meet, with or without the King. Henry forbade the Justiciar to issue the summons, ordered a series of postponements on account of Welsh unrest, and finally organised a highly secret assembly of his trusted friends in lieu of the full meeting. He spent his convalescence hiring knights for his personal service, using funds provided by Louis for the Sicilian campaign (and intended for release under the supervision of Henry's barons). His own expenses he met by pawning the Crown Jewels.[7]

While he was still in Flanders he was visited by Bishop Gamelin, perhaps with news of the Glasgow dispute (for it was then that he wrote at last to Alexander); another visitor was Cecilia Maxwell, one of Margaret's ladies and daughter-in-law of the Chamberlain of Scotland. But Henry was taken up with suspicions of Simon and of Edward; he was convinced that they planned to depose him, with Queen Eleanor's backing.

When he reached London his friends had induced its citizens to close their gates to the Lord Edward. Henry's hand-picked *parlement* summoned Edward to judgment; he refused to be judged by barons who were not his peers, but disclaimed any hostile intent and submitted himself to his father and uncle. Later he rather spoiled this graceful gesture by taking his team to France on a jousting-tour.[8]

Alexander, meanwhile, was visiting Ayrshire with Margaret; they went to Kilwinning Abbey, and presumably to Ayr itself which had already acquired a special characteristic; a thirteenth-century romance says

> *Aroie ...*
> *La u les bieles femes sont,*
> *N'a plus beles en tot le mont*

which neatly prefigures

> Auld Ayr, wham ne'er a toun surpasses
> For handsome men and bonnie lasses.[9]

August found Alexander in the north, probably without Margaret who may not have chosen to ride so far. He stayed in Inverness in his grandfather's 'new castle', on its enormous mound above the river, with the remnants of MacBeth's 'old castle' on the next ridge. A great oaken bridge crossed the Ness under the castle embankment, carrying the road to the north. The little town was packed inside its palisade and the extension of the castle moat, along the riverside from the bridge to St Mary's parish church, with the Blackfriars' house just beyond the north gate. Beyond again were the quays and the shipbuilding grounds, the Longman or *Moine nan Long*, the Plain of the Ships, where twelve years earlier a great ship had been built to carry the Count of St.-Pol to the Crusade.[10]

Next he rode to Durris, and back in September to Selkirk. In October he and Margaret set off on their postponed visit to England, but this time there were secret and elaborate arrangements to be made.

Henry issued the customary safe-conducts in August, again promising no discussion of Scottish business without Alexander's consent, and adding that 'no disturbance or change shall be made in the state of the King of Scotland, his councillors, or his other attendants, during his time in England'. It was symptomatic of the state of England that the Lord Edward, the Archbishop of York, the earls of Gloucester, Norfolk and Hereford and Hugh Bigod the

Justiciar were asked to issue safe-conducts of their own. Brother Robert of Kenleith, once Abbot of Dunfermline and Chancellor of Scotland, came to collect them and Mr Thomas of Kinross, a clerk of John Mansel's, delivered them to him. Mansel, Balliol and the Earl of Winchester were to meet the royal party at Berwick Bridge on 10th October and offer 'escort and entertainment, with all fitting courtesies and honours'.

On 30 September Henry sent a new safe-conduct, repeating that state affairs were not to be discussed and adding that if any of the party 'should happen to fall ill' during the visit, the safe-conduct should extend beyond Candlemas to 'a month after their convalescence'. The same day Henry made oath on his soul by the knight William Latimer that,

> should his daughter the Queen of Scotland become pregnant in England, he would detain neither her nor the child, if one were born there; and should the King its father die, it should be delivered to the magnates of Scotland.

The sheriffs of eight counties from Northumberland to Hertford were commanded to

> meet the King and Queen of Scots on their journey, entertain them in the King's castles and manors with the produce of his forests and parks, and receive them with all due honour and courtesies.

Edward and the magnates renewed their safe-conducts the same day, and again delivered them to Brother Robert.

The escort's task was complicated by the party splitting into two. Alexander had business in Tynedale and Huntingdon, but reached London ahead of the second group. He was met not only by Henry but by Richard of Cornwall, who had returned from Germany a week earlier amid slight mystery. His own horses were not at Dover and he borrowed some from a local priory (and kept them inconveniently long). Wild rumours flew; he was fleeing assassins sent by Manfred, that year's bogeyman since his rout of the Florentines at Montaperti; or he had postponed his Imperial enthronement because the Germans refused to go to Italy so late in the year; or the Pope had asked for postponement. Some dull souls even said he had come home on estate business. In truth Richard was about to abandon his hopes of Empire just when they seemed within his reach; he may have welcomed the prospect of a family gathering with little leisure to question his motives. Sanchia, his beautiful but ailing wife, in the last year of her life, might be thankful the foreign adventure was ending and she need fear no more assaults of sisterly jealousy.[11]

Alexander came with three objects in view, beyond the family reunion and the exercise of his rights over his English lands. He wanted a settlement of Margaret's dowry; he proposed to demand 'the whole land between Tyne and Tweed', the earldom of Northumberland which his ancestors held (and

which his father had resigned by treaty); and he wanted personal confirmation of support against his enemies from Henry and his magnates, 'as promised
in the document brought by Brother William of Horton'. The successor to
Matthew Paris thought 'affairs were completed on either side' but he lacked
Matthew's nose for news. Alexander did not obtain Northumberland, nor
more than a possible 500 marks towards the dowry; and events would show
that the obligation of help was understood to be mutual.

Margaret arrived a few days later, travelling with the Bishop of Whithorn;
her brother Edmund met her at St Albans:

> She was received in formal procession at the hour of vespers, and honourably
> entertained. In the morning she set out for London. And when she arrived,
> there were there at the same time three kings and three queens; and who could
> without admiration think of their splendour and nobility?[12]

It was apparent to the Benedictines of St Albans that their visitor was in
an interesting condition, though hardly (as their scribe recorded) 'very near
her confinement'. Queen Eleanor must have welcomed her with special
delight; at the age of nineteen, and after nine years of marriage, Margaret
was five months pregnant. Her baby would be the first grandchild, for Edward
and his Eleanor were still kept apart.

It must be a matter of astonishment that Alexander was prepared to let his
first child be born abroad. He had gone to some trouble to get Margaret to
her mother, for her condition was not generally known before she set out.
If she wanted to go home, so be it; he could handle any adverse reactions.

How long he had planned to stay is uncertain. The safe-conducts ran to
the following February, but Alexander was needed at home in November.
Before leaving, he extracted a sworn promise from Henry to let Margaret
return forty days after her delivery or at latest by Easter:

> Should the mother die, he promises to return the child, and should the child
> die, to let the mother return freely. Should the King its father die, or other
> unforeseen event occur to him, the King promises that the bishops of St
> Andrews, Aberdeen, Dunblane and Whithorn, the earls of Fife, Buchan,
> Strathearn, Dunbar and Mar, and John Comyn, Alexander the Steward of
> Scotland, Alan Doorward and Hugh of Abernethy, barons, or any four or three
> of them, shall receive and take the child to Scotland, the state of neither country
> being taken in consideration.

Robert Walerand swore this on the King's soul and one of Richard of
Cornwall's knights swore for him. 'For greater security', oaths were made
by Gloucester, Peter of Savoy, Humfrey de Bohun of Hereford, Hugh Bigod
and John Mansel, with Henry promising to obtain the oaths of the Archbishop
of York, the Lord Edward, the earls of Norfolk and Winchester, John Balliol

and Hugh Le Dispenser the Justiciar, all then absent from court.

The list of proposed guardians foreshadows the arrangements of 1286, when representatives of the three ruling groups (not yet the Three Estates) took office in the name of the Maid of Norway. Having thus done what he could to minimise any risk to Margaret and their child, Alexander rode north to face a tiresome problem.[13]

John Comyn had inherited his uncle Walter's lands of Badenoch, the mountainous territory between Braemar and the Great Glen which had been Menteith's inheritance from his mother. John, who had been abroad (possibly on pilgrimage), had returned while the kings were meeting, and continued homeward. There he found that his uncle's widow had rejected several eligible suitors to marry a knight named John Russell, *quidam ignobili Angligena militi*. Russell was not quite the 'certain ignoble English-born knight' indignant rivals considered him; his father had been entrusted by King John with the castellany of Corfe and his mother was of the Norman house of Corbet. Still, he was unacceptable as a Scottish earl and potential elector of future kings; and royal consent had not been sought.

By the time Alexander arrived to challenge the position, John had seized his aunt and her husband and imprisoned them. He found support among the magnates and prepared to charge Isabella with Earl Walter's death by poison. At a Council meeting called to discuss the matter, John put in a claim for the earldom; the Steward's brother Walter promptly counter-claimed in right of his wife, Isabella's niece.

The issue was hardly in doubt. John Comyn could not inherit an earldom his uncle only held by marriage, and his actions had already put him in the wrong. Walter Stewart became Earl of Menteith, the Russells accepted a sum in damages and by way of terce, and left for England. Thence they petitioned the Pope, alleging violent mistreatment and plunder of heritage. In the fulness of time a nuncio was sent to investigate, but summoned the parties to York, in contravention of Scottish privilege. Henry tried to have the case heard in his own court, although as a matrimonial cause it was for ecclesiastical decision. However by then the state of England made the matter impossible to pursue, especially as the Pope upheld Alexander's protest against hearings outwith his realm.[14]

Henry as yet knew nothing of all this; he had more than enough troubles of his own. While he stocked up for Christmas, ordering thirty casks of wine to be sent from Woodstock and Nottingham 'because there is at present the greatest scarcity' at Windsor, and laid out £100 on jewels for Alexander and his retinue, his financial entanglements became ever more frantic. Queen Eleanor, aware that both her daughters were distressed by their father's debts to their respective husbands, swore out a writ to compel payment of the arrears from the earldom of Richmond (granted to John of Brittany on his marriage) and of sums due to Alexander under the corrody agreement. On the long visit during October and November these must have amounted to around £250. Henry borrowed 600 marks (£400) from Florentine merchants and paid 100 marks towards Alexander's arrears, with the balance going to John of Brittany. The loan was covered by an order to Mansel to draw on the revenues of the vacant bishopric of Durham. At the same time Mansel was to refund himself £30, said to have been spent on 'New Year gifts to the King and Queen of Scots on their passing through the bishopric' (in 1251?). Perhaps this was a way to meet the interest on the loan, since the Church frowned on usury.

Henry was increasingly suspicious of his Queen, whom he believed to be plotting against him, or at least aggravating his troubles rather than supporting him through them. He was working hard to free himself of baronial restraint, and looking to the Pope and Louis IX for help. After Christmas at Windsor he betook himself to the Tower of London, concentrating on keeping communications open with France. He made one brief sortie in February to Windsor, where Margaret had given birth to a daughter, and another in April to secure Dover and the road to London. Otherwise he waited impatiently to hear how Mansel was faring in Rome.

Margaret's child was born on 28 February and named for her mother, for her sainted ancestress, perhaps also for the old Princess-Countess. Henry could not organise the sort of lavish celebration he would no doubt have wanted for his first grandchild's arrival, but he did send his personal fisherman to take as many pike and bream as possible from the vivary (fish-farm) of the see of Winchester, for his daughter's churching-feast in early April. The temporalities of Winchester were in his hands since his half-brother Aymer de Lusignan's death in exile.

He had solemnly sworn to send mother and child home by Easter; Easter Sunday came on 24 April, but his complications and worries made such a parting unthinkable. On 9 May he was at Canterbury, awaiting the merce-naries he had hired at St Omer and daily expecting Mansel back from Rome. He did find time to make out safe-conducts for the Earl of Winchester and others going to Scotland, and at the end of the month, in a last flurry of grants, he let Margaret go. His virtue was quickly rewarded by the arrival of Mansel, triumphantly bearing a papal release from all royal oaths sworn under duress to unreasonable subjects.[15]

Chapter 12 Notes

1   There seems no agreed age of majority for kings. Louis IX was declared 'of age' at fifteen; Henry obtained some powers, from Pope Honorius III, in 1223 (his fourteenth year) and declared himself of full age in 1227 (Powicke 42–44). He clearly intended Alexander to remain in pupillage until twenty-one. (pp.68–70). Unction, see p.35 above. Charles of

Anjou, M.Paris, *Chr.Maj.IV*, 546, in Labarge, *St.L.*90.

2   *CDS I, 2157* (14 May 1259).

3   *CDS I, 2163, 2185* (17 Aug. 1259, 29 Apl. 1260).

4   Pope Alexander IV to Henry, *CDS I, 2158* (13 June 1259). Mr N. Moffat, Watt, *Biog.* 399–400; Mr John of Cheam, *ib.* 96. Pope to English bishops, *CDS I, 2194* (21 May 1260; recalling sanctions). Henry to Alexander, *ib. 2182* (6 March, St Omer). *Chron. Lanercost*, 65, says Cheam, though English, was 'hostile to England' because he claimed his see extended to the Rere Cross of Stainmore, to the prejudice of the see of Carlisle; see *ES I*, 140, 396. Rere Cross, see map 1 or 2.

5   Margaret of Kent's executry, *CDS I, 2167* (Michaelmas Term 1259, calling her 'Margery'). Her father's plans for her, *RRS II*, 15; *SA* 315 and 335–6. As hostage, *CDS I, 453* (7 Aug. 1209) and many subsequent refs. Henry and Margaret or her sister Margery, Powicke, 159–160. Brittany, p.33

6   Sisterly conflict, Runciman *SV* 87, qu. Villani. Provence, p.59.

7   Treaty, Beatrix's marriage, Pr. Louis' death, and funds for knights, Labarge, *St.L*, 194–7; Powicke, 257–8. 411.

8   Powicke, 414.

9   Kilwinning (O, Tiron) App.C; *Lay of Fergus*, qu. in R.L.G. Ritchie, *The Normans in Scotland*, (EUP 1954), 306n.; R. Burns, *Tam o' Shanter*, 1s. 15–16.

10 Inverness Castle is shown in an 18th-c. print as a rectangular keep with flat buttresses like Castle Sween or a dumpy Rochester; a moat around the mound continued as the Town Ditch. Ship, M. Paris, *Chr.Maj.V*, 93, in *SA* 295n.

11 S/cs, *CDS I, 2198, 2199, 2202,* (17 Aug.) and *2204* (28 Sept.); revised, *2205* (30 Sept.); oath, *2206* (30 Sept.). To sheriffs, *2207*; to Edward and others, *2208* (all 30 Sept.) For Robert of Kenleith see p.42 above; (?Mr) Thomas, Watt, *Biog.* 306 (son or nephew of Sir Gilbert, p.93 above). For Richard, Young, *R of C*, 104–6.

12 *Flores Historiarum II*, 459–60, in *SA* 378–9.

13 *CDS I, 2229* (16 Nov., Westminster).

14 S/cs for John Comyn, *CDS I, 2196* (1 Aug.) and *2210* (7 Oct.); *ib. 2211* (8 Oct.) Gloucester and others to issue s/cs to John. Menteith case, *Fordun* LIII, Barrow *K&U* 156; earldom, *RRS II*, 469 (7 Dec.1213); *inspeximus, CDS I, 2275, 2276* (20 Sept.1261).

15 Wines, *CDS I, 2225* (13 Nov); a cask held 200–250 gallons. Jewels, *ib. 2227* (14 Nov.); grants and pardons, *ib.2230–2233* (to 20 Nov., the last 'at instigation of Alexr.K.of Scotland'); 600 mks, *ib.2239* (2 Jan.1261); to Mansel, *ib.2241,2242* (29 Jan., at Tower). Powicke 420. Fish, *CDS I, 2248* (25 March, Tower), to be got from Taunton, a liberty of the bishopric, though Farnham was its best-known vivary. S/cs, *ib.2255* (and *2258*, 21 May, for Henry Page, setting out with Margaret Q. of Scotland). Pardons &c at Margaret's request, *ib.2250, 2252, 2253, 2257, 2259* (the last on 25 May). Pope Alexander granted Henry release from his oath on 14 April 'and in later bulls absolved the prelates and magnates from their oaths' (Powicke, 420).

13

1261–1262: Defence Review

ALEXANDER HOVERED about the Borders all spring, awaiting the return of Margaret and the child. He faced some popular resentment, and even rumours that the Queen had deceived him:

> The Scots took it very ill that their queen should have been delivered outside of her own realm; for they had been altogether ignorant when she departed that she was so near to confinement. For she had carefully hidden this from them, and from the king.

The Melrose chronicler, however, merely records the birth of the King of Scots' daughter, in England.[1]

Mother and child arrived home in June, but an archaeological find in May had diverted public interest. Fordun's account is as clear as many an antiquary's of later times. It includes some learned speculation based on literary sources, but that too is typical:

> On 7 May 1261 in the thirteenth year of King Alexander's reign, a magnificent and ancient cross was found at Peebles, in the presence of reliable men – priests, clerks and burgesses. In what year or by whom it had been concealed is quite unknown. It is believed however that during the savage persecution of Maximian in Britain, around the year 296, it might have been hidden by some of the faithful. Soon after, three or four yards away, was found a stone urn containing ashes and bones of a human body as if torn limb from limb. Whose relics these are is not yet known. Some however believe they could be the remains of one whose name is written on the very stone in [*sic*] which that holy cross lay, 'The place of St Nicholas the bishop'. In that place many miracles were and are done by the same cross, and the populace flowed and flow there in crowds, bringing offerings and prayers devoutly to God. Wherefore the King, by the advice of the Bishop of Glasgow, caused a fine church to be built in honour of God and Holy Cross.

The Cross Kirk of Peebles is Alexander's only known religious foundation. Its ruins incorporate a low arched opening through the south wall of the nave, beneath which the miraculous tomb could be seen; cripples seeking a cure at a martyr's grave may have crept through the arch. A stone-vaulted sacristy on the north side of the chancel housed the cross between ceremonial appearances. It was of gold, and small (James IV gave $1^1/_2$ ounces of gold to mend one arm), but there is no full description of it. The grave is a prehistoric short cist which held (if Fordun is right) both a cremation and an inhumation. It is not uncommon to find Christian cemeteries on older sites; chance finds of human bones discouraged building or cultivation, even if the site were not still venerated.

The inscribed stone may survive. A grave-marker of the eighth or ninth century was discovered recently in a garden wall; it bears crosses on both faces, and on one an inscription in archaic letters, NEITANO SACERDOS, 'Neitan the Priest' or 'Bishop'. The name, a form of Nechtan, was long forgotten, and the clerics who tried to read it were not far astray with their 'Nicholas', The attribution to the third century is mistaken, but was easily accepted by men used to hearing martyrologies read in every monastic refectory.[2]

The new church was probably served by a friar, since the burgh already had its parish church of St Andrew. Presently the foundation passed into the care of the Trinitarians, who built a small monastic house nearby. Called 'Red Friars' from their robes, they followed the Augustinian rule and devoted a third of their corporate income to ransoming prisoners from the infidel. By natural extension they became skilled in medical care.

Alexander could spend little time on his new church. The June *colloquium* sent envoys to Norway to renew the offer to buy back the Isles. The decision necessitated a total overhaul of national defence strategy.

Haakon might accept; in which case a force must go to the Isles, take charge, and suppress any resistance. Or he might refuse, and launch a fleet to depress Scottish pretensions. Either way, the existing arrangements would be inadequate.

The Steward in the south and the Earl of Ross in the north had launched punitive raids against the islanders, with limited success; new bases and more ships would be needed if the whole island-chain had to be tackled simultaneously. Moreover, the perceived external threat during two centuries had been from England, with attacks on a relatively narrow frontier using limited and well-known points of access (Solway Sands, Liddesdale, Dere Street, Berwick). A seaborne invasion able to strike anywhere on three sides was something for which defence plans did not exist; the last Danish invasion, in the distant days of Malcolm II, had attacked the east coast only. Modern Norway had fought successful wars against Sweden and Denmark, and sent a contingent to the Crusade as lately as 1251. It was manifestly impossible to cover every landing-place or to hope that local levies could withstand experienced troops in number. In such areas as Caithness it was doubtful if the many inhabitants of Norse ancestry would offer anything but welcome to the invaders.

The only internal wars of recent times had been the risings in Moray and Galloway, both in support of royal pretenders and both put down with severity in the reigns of William and Alexander II. Both consisted mainly of attacks on prosperous areas by hordes of lightly-armed hillmen, some of the best fighters in Europe but ill-equipped against armoured horsemen. It could not be assumed that the present generation of Highlanders and Galwegians would rally to support their fathers' conquerors.

The problem resolved itself into several courses of action. Alexander must ride throughout his kingdom to stimulate personal loyalty; communications must be brought into good order; coastal castles must be overhauled and prepared for siege, and inland castles as reserve bases. Gaps in the coastal chain must be filled by look-out posts so that the passage of Norse ships was quickly reported. And, since manpower must somehow be limited for the invaders and upheld for the defenders, if need be coastal holds must be yielded so that invading garrisons would be tied down and bloodshed kept to a minimum (this touch was likely to receive strong disapproval from the older experts; heavy enemy casualties were a prime consideration, almost as important as capturing leaders and exacting ransom).

There were two traditional chains of command. The sheriffs had the duty of summoning all who owed feudal service, upon orders from the King. This should, in theory, produce a force with some degree of weapon training and roughly standard equipment. A knight's fief, the basic unit, was expected to provide around half a dozen men. There was the knight himself, in armour, with a heavy war-horse and a lighter hack; his squire, either a young aspirant to knighthood or an experienced veteran, also armed and mounted, taking charge of the knight's arms and horse; two or more spearmen or archers on foot, with some protective clothing issued by the knight; and one or more grooms or cooks, not expected to fight unless things went far wrong. The group served together in some castle-guard for a few weeks a year, and might join their overlord's other knights for a local parade or escort, but there was no guarantee that they would co-operate. They were bound to give up to forty days' service a year on demand, within the overlord's territory; if more distant or longer service was required they must be paid. By established custom a knight could escape direct service by paying shield-money, 'scutage', enabling the hire of mercenaries to fill the gap.

The other source of manpower was *servicium scoticanum*, the Host. This in theory was led by the earls as successors to ancient mormaers, and by thanes, holders of pre-feudal estates. Highland levies followed their own chiefs of districts or of kinships (not necessarily the same individuals).

In 1261 there were gaps in the ranks of the earls. Sutherland was a child, the heir of Angus was growing up in de Montfort's English household. The Countess of Carrick, now Buchan's ward, was as yet unmarried. William the

Lion had split Caithness between rivals, giving half to the Earl of Orkney and half to Freskin Murray of Duffus; in practice, the sheriffs would have to summon the Host from these counties.

The Host could be mobilised in part or in whole; at its maximum it included every able-bodied male between sixteen and sixty, 'coming forth to save his head' as the phrase went, armed with whatever weapon he could find and use – boar spear, axe, ox-goad, knife. It is tempting to echo the Duke of Wellington; 'I don't know what they do to the French, but by God they frighten me'.[3]

The oldest surviving Exchequer Rolls are for 1263 to 1266, in an abbreviated seventeenth-century transcript. It is scarcely possible to determine what was done anywhere in 1261–2, but faint outlines are traceable. Everywhere old castles were being refitted with new timber buildings inside the walls, wells cleaned, brewhouses re-equipped. Boats were provided at strategic crossings; weapons were laid in. Some soldiers were hired, mostly crossbowmen with Gascon experience who could act as drill-sergeants and post commanders. Training was essential for the crossbowman, with his complex machine to handle and maintain; his rate of fire was below that of a competent archer, one shot a minute rather than five, but his heavy quarrel could be precisely aimed if he could find a sheltered firing-point such as a bastion. After every shot he had to set his foot in a stirrup and crank up his bow, leaving himself vulnerable; the most successful operators had trainees to load for them.

From Berwick to Cromarty the east coast was well secured by castles royal or private. It was evidently accepted that the north coast might be untenable; an old fort at Durness was manned in 1263, but probably on local initiative. There are vestiges of a defensive chain down the western seaboard; Dun Lagaidh, an ancient fort on Loch Broom, became a sort of motte-and-bailey at some time in the thirteenth century. At Inverie, remote from any mainland support, Buchan seems to have established a castle; in 1265–6 he claimed, as 'Bailie of Inverey', for repairing houses and a drawbridge, building a hall, and keeping eight solders there for six months 'in the time of the coming of the King of Norway'. It must have been a lonely posting; presumably a runner set off by hill-paths past Loch Quoich and Loch Arkaig, carrying reports to Urquhart or Inverlochy.[4]

There were more formidable guardposts. Local tradition claims that Alexander built Eilean Donnain with, or for, the Earl of Ross. It was blown up in the eighteenth century and rebuilt in the twentieth, but the lowest courses of the curtain, too low and too thick to have suffered in the explosion, could be thirteenth-century. Earl William of Ross needed a strong base for his frequent sallies against the Islesmen.

At the head of Loch Linnhe is the massive enceinte of Inverlochy, with its four drum-towers, its two portcullised gates, and its ship-dock under the walls. The Comyns completed it by 1270, on the latest model. Farther south, beyond Ewen of Argyll's strong Dunstaffnage, stands Castle Sween in Knapdale; its ancient walls acquired a new hall-wing in the same period. Its ageing master Dugald MacSween was lord also of southern Knapdale and northern Kintyre; in 1263 he granted these lands, with his hall-house of Skipness, to the new Earl of Menteith. Skipness commands Kilbrannan Sound and looks towards Loch Ranza in Arran, sighting also as far as the Ayrshire coast. The old buildings were quickly engulfed in a courtyard-castle with a portcullis on the seaward face. Skipness lies too far from the shore to guard ships, and offers no safe anchorage, but as a menacing presence it is impressive, and a beacon on its tower would alert the whole Clyde shore.[5]

Walter *Ballach* of Menteith was busy repairing Ayr Castle and fitting out the King's ships in its river-mouth. The King himself was in the north-east, around Elgin. The Sheriff of Elgin laid out £3.10.8d on a new boat with a long cable for the Spey crossing at 'Rothenet' near Orton, where a pious lady had endowed a bridge and hospice; Spey has scant patience with bridges, and a boat was a more practical form of transit. From 'Rothenec', surely the same place, Alexander issued two *quo warranto* writs, devices requiring a sheriff to investigate 'by what right' a named person claimed some privilege. One was to establish the right of the thane of Rothenec to the lands of Meft, by Elgin, with the use of a house in Elgin Castle and a net on the Spey; the other is more curious.

Ewen the thane was readily assured; King William's charter to Ewen's great-grandfather was safely recorded, and he could enjoy his town house and his fishing. The other recipient was Robert Spink, 'the King's crossbowman'. He and his wife occupied Elgin Castle garden and lands nearby (perhaps an orchard outside the town, for there is little space to spare atop the massive castle-mound). Alexander, on his first visit to Elgin, may well have been surprised to find a line of washing in his garden; but Robert knew his rights. His wife's father and grandfather had possessed the ground 'all the days of their lives', keeping the fruit for the King's use and supplying vegetables to the royal kitchens at need. They also kept an area in grass where hawks and falcons could be put out to 'weather' (bathe and perch in fine weather), for which they received an annual supply of oatmeal and a penny a day for each hawk, two pence for a falcon. (This was good money, with a labourer's day-wage at $1^{1}/_{2}$d; the birds were probably newly-taken young stock needing careful handling).[6]

One might picture a royal castle standing empty between royal visits, apart from the castellan's household in one tower and the castle-guard clanking about in another; but in practice things were less tidy. In 1262 the Sheriff of Forfar had to decide the rights of five sisters, daughters of the late gatekeeper of Montrose Castle. Their names were Margaret, Agnes, Swannoch, Christiana and Mariota, and they averred that their father Simon, their grandfather Sweyn, and his father Crane, had all held the office since King William's time, together with the lands of 'Iniancy', for 'nothing else in the world but the duty of gatekeeping'. Their claim was upheld, but we are not told whether they kept the key in turn or entrusted it to the husband of one of them. No wonder the King's Porter assumed temporary charge when the Court arrived.[7]

Such matters are small beer, but they go to show that a general overhaul was in hand. The total outlay must have been considerable, although it is no longer possible to bring out exact figures. The Elgin accounts are fuller than most (the copyist omitted the receipts in kind and money, and the final balance). The boat and cable have been mentioned; there was a 'horse for the King's work', £4.6.8d, and two brewing vats at a shilling each. A thousand planks cost £5, including cartage; 'a buket and rope', perhaps also a windlass, for a well, came to four shillings. But there were larger works:

> To making a new hall at 'Kathenes', with carriage of timbers, and with a double covering of boards, and iron bought, and hire of carpenters to the total completion of the hall with walls of planking, £32.13.4d. To repairing houses in 'Kathenes' and laying down a *garderobe* [latrine], ten shillings. To the King's expenses at 'Kathenes' and Elgin, going to Inverness and returning, £15.10.2¹/₂d., which ought to be deducted from the debt owed by the *patria* as shown in the last account of William, Earl of Mar, Chamberlain.[8]

'Kathenes' has been variously glossed as 'Caithness' or as 'Kettins', a manor near Forfar; but neither could concern the Sheriff of Elgin. Possibly the castle was Keith, standing astride the roads that link Elgin with Aberdeen, Huntly with Cullen. Keith should have been the Sheriff of Banff's responsibility, but his accounts are so summarily transcribed that one cannot judge the extent of his commitments. (The 'debt from the *patria*' is a deficit from former years' dues of the sheriffdom).

Alexander was back at Kinross by the end of August; his movements for the rest of 1261 have not been traced. Perhaps he stayed in central Scotland awaiting news from Norway. He could do little more until he knew Haakon's response; though arms and armour could be mustered, victualling must wait until nearer the time.

The plate-armour beloved of Victorian illustrators was only just coming into use. Manfred of Sicily had twelve hundred German knights in plate at Benevento, his last battle in summer 1266, and they overwhelmed Charles of Anjou's lighter cavalry until a foot soldier spotted the gap between breastplate and backplate when a sword-arm was raised. The new equipment was not universally admired; it was doubly expensive, in itself and because it needed heavier horses (little was done at first to lighten the load of metal, which might amount to 60 lbs, 27kg, for the man, in addition to some protection for his mount). Many people relied on their inherited mailcoats which had changed very little since Hastings. The headgear had become slightly safer, chainmail sleeves covered the forearms and might extend into leather-palmed mitts. The main garment was the hauberk or mailshirt, reaching from neck to knee, with an attached hood of mail which could be pushed back to lie on the shoulders until needed. When it was drawn over the head, a large flap covered chin and neck and was tied under the left ear. Under the hauberk a padded tunic might be worn, and under the hood a leather cap. A horseman's thighs were protected by quilted leggings fastened at the knee by the top strap of a shinguard, either a mail stocking or a metal-studded leather gaiter. Plate shinguards and forearm-guards, like sections of guttering, might be laced over the mail, and small discs of steel were evolving to protect elbows, knees and shoulders. All these were laced in place with thongs passed through the mail-links; tales of ladies arming their knights were anything but romantic, the girls were simply better at threading fiddly strings and tying bows. Their neat fastenings might be hidden under an embroidered armorial surcoat.

The thirteenth century saw changes in head-armour. Foot-soldiers continued to wear 'kettle-hats' rather like British Army 'tin hats'; knights often wore the same until the moment came to don their 'great helm' if they had one. This was a flat-topped steel drum, pierced with eyeslots and much-needed ventilation-holes. It went on over the mail-coif hood, and had a padded leather lining and a pair of strings to fasten it in place at the back; a heavy blow could skew it round and unsight the wearer. Early helms lacked a neckguard and rested directly on the shoulders and coif. They were exhausting to wear and were donned at the last moment. There were those who preferred the old-fashioned open helmet like a half-eggshell with a noseguard.

One result of the introduction of helms was the disappearance of heavy moustaches and their replacement by neat chin-beards, useful as padding for the jaw. Another result was the reintroduction of heraldic crests, last seen in barbaric times; a tuft of heron's feathers or a leather or metal animal-crest was needed for recognition. Efficient moveable visors were not yet invented. Nobody made long speeches, or bellowed anything but the simplest orders, from inside a great helm, and a foam of ostrich-feathers would have caused derision.

All this metalwork took a deal of cleaning. Mail was scoured by shaking it in a barrel, or leather sack, of bran. Plate must be carefully polished with oil and sand; plate and mail alike were greased to prevent rust. Neither was improved by salt spray, and men working afloat adopted the aketon, *hacqueton* or acton. This was a cloth or leather tunic stuffed with raw wool; the Saracens, who invented it, used raw cotton. More elaborate actons called *gambesons*, of padded and embroidered silk, might be worn, or a linen surcoat with heraldic devices; these may possibly, though not certainly, have originated to keep armour cool in *Outremer*.

Having got himself into all this gear with help from squires or ladies, the knight belted on his sword, clambered into the saddle and slung his shield round his neck by its straps called *guiges*. His left hand passed through a loop below the *guige* and he could then take up his reins. Last of all, with his right hand he took his lance.

The lance was the weapon for the initial charge. It might not always be used, it might shatter on impact (there are accounts of considerable damage done with the stump), but a well-organised charge changed the whole course of battle. If the opponents did not instantly flee, the lance was discarded and the sword was drawn. In theory it was only after such gentlemanly encounters that the infantry came into action, (if they escaped being ridden down by terrified horses). The horses might have their own armour, a trapper of decorated cloth covering them from chest to tail, padded or leather-backed. Some even had mail-trappers, but only the strongest horses could carry them at the charge. Both man and horse needed years of training to make good use of their gear.[9]

Other wars, other ways. From the Norse and Saxon 'shield-ring' or from native practice, the Host learned to form flexible blocks of spearmen, able to withstand even a cavalry charge; these were the schiltroms, Scott's 'dark impenetrable wood', ancestors both of the Waterloo squares and the Thin Red Line. They were the answer to that other northern weapon, the devastating downhill charge of yelling swordsmen.[10]

When Alexander and his nobles talked of resistance to a Norse invasion, they must have wondered whether their feudal cavalry would have any part to play, or whether they had best put their trust in the schiltrom and Highland charge. Certainly, if old Haakon saw sense, spearmen and not cavalry would be needed in the Isles. A war in the Isles, or against Norway, would be like nothing the Doorward had seen, no honourable passages of arms, no ransoms, no league-tables of prowess. The experts shook their heads, but the King appeared to be enjoying himself. He had worked the whole thing out from first principles, he had assessed the risks and was playing the odds as their bygone bickerings had taught him to do. Just two points worried him; his father-in-law was getting into deeper waters, and there was no news from Norway.

Chapter 13 Notes

1 *Flor.Hist.* II, 463, in *SA* 379; *CM* 117.
2 *Fordun*, LIV; *PSAS LXX, 192, and LXXX,* 50 *inf.* (building); *ib. 101,* 127 *inf.,* (grave-

marker); *RCAHMS Peebles I.* Trinitarians, App.C. The Bp. was John of Cheam (p.118 above).

3 The Host, Scottish Army, *Servicium scoticanum, RRS II*, 56–7; (statutes in *APS I, Frag.Coll.*, are attrib. to either William or Robert 1).

4 Dun Lagaidh, *Glasgow Archaeological Journal 8*, 178 and *PSAS 119*,122(Scots & English coins of 1180–1250); *PSAS LXXXIII*, 68 *inf.* Inverie, *ER I*, 18 (and xlvi,n, proposed ident. with 'Ulerin' = Blervie); Barrow, *K&U*, 116–17.

5 Eilean Donnain, *Glas.Arch.J.5* (J.G.Dunbar); Inverlochy, Cruden, *Castle*, 58–61; Castle Sween, *RCAHMS Argyll* 7,245–259; Skipness, *RCAHMS Argyll* I, no. 314. (A former seapool might have provided a galley-berth).

6 Meft, *Hdl.A.III*, no.263, *Sel.Cases* no.60, *RRS II*, no.589; Spink, *Hdl.A.III* no.32, *Sel.Cases* no. 57.

7 *Hdl.A.III*, no. 36; *Sel.Cases* no, 56, *APS I*, 100; *CDS I, 2294*; Porter, p.108.

8 *ER I*, 14; (*ib.*10, 'Kathenes' = Kettins, in another context).

9 I am greatly indebted to Claude Blair, *European Armour* (Batsford 1979) esp. chs. 1 & 2, and (horses) pp. 184–5. For the weight, C.McNamee, *Wars of the Bruces* (Tuckwell 1997), 23. The Benevento Panzers, Runciman *SV*, 109–110.

10 Sir Walter Scott, *Marmion*, Canto VI, 34 ('The sullen spearmen still made good/Their dark impenetrable wood'); the technique was developed before Bannockburn (1314) where the units could manoeuvre flexibly (?with arms somehow linked around spear-shafts).

The 'Neitan' stone.

1263: Haakon the Old

NO SCOTTISH source names the envoys to Norway; both Norway and Man recall 'a knight named Missel and an archdeacon'. Mr Godfrey, Archdeacon of Galloway, was probably the cleric; 'Missel' could be a blunder for 'Michael' or 'Frisel' (now Fraser), but the layman might have been Robert Lovel, prominent in Norwegian negotiations of 1281 with Mr Godfrey.[1]

They reached Bergen in July 1261. Their proposals were unwelcome; Haakon said they dealt more in fair words than in good faith. In mid-August they attended the wedding of the Young King, Haakon's only surviving son Magnus, to the Danish princess he had abducted (with her enthusiastic help) from a convent. Missel was said to be overwhelmed by the splendour of the proceedings.

Admitting failure and aware of mounting anxiety in Scotland, the envoys tried to slip away but were hauled back and detained all winter. Haakon *den Gamle*, the Old Man, was a formidable king. He was indeed old for those days (he was born in 1204) and had reigned for upwards of forty years, the posthumous illegitimate son of Haakon III, who had ruled only three years, and whose father Sverre was likewise illegitimate, born in the Faeroes and winning the throne after long wars. Haakon Haakonsson had been tucked away in Bergen choir-school until his twelfth year, when an ambitious kinsman produced him as a figurehead. His only inheritance from his father was a brooch and a finger-ring and his mother underwent an ordeal by hot iron to prove his birth. Jarl Skuli made him a puppet-king and married him to his own daughter, but when after seven years Skuli decided to ditch his protégé and proclaim himself king, he found he had left it too late. The last civil war ended with the jarl's death.

Haakon quickly asserted his place in the world, exchanging embassies with Louis IX, with the Emperor Frederick and with Henry III. Alexander Nevsky sent from Novgorod to offer for the hand of Cristina Haakonsdottir for his son, but in vain; instead she travelled in great state to Castile, to decide which of Alfonso X's brothers she would accept. Haakon told Matthew Paris he had declined the Pope's offer of the Empire, after Frederick's fall; while the 1261 ambassadors were at Bergen they learned that a delegation was voyaging to Tunis, with gifts of rich furs and gyr-falcons for the Emir. Northern merchants had long dreamed of a base in the Mediterranean, something they had not had since Vikings used to winter in the Camargue.

Whatever might come of the Tunis move, a welcome bonus arrived from Greenland, envoys entreating Haakon's protection. As Greenland had been settled by men who rejected Icelandic control, and Iceland had been colonised by rebels against Norwegian royal power, the submission of Greenland was a major event. Haakon had been putting pressure, sometimes violent, on Iceland itself, and next year its Althing also voted to seek Norway's protection. No wonder the Scots offer was scorned.[2]

Alexander III wrote to Henry about the detention of his envoys, and Henry wrote to Haakon in March 1262, but all year he was beset by his own troubles. That autumn he went to France for consultations with Louis; an epidemic swept through his party, John Mansel lay at death's door, Prince Edmund had to be sent home to convalesce. Henry himself was too weak to tackle business until November, when he wrote again to Haakon:

> We have received your letters with the gladness they deserved, and from their contents we are persuaded that you no longer design to lead a host into the kingdom of Scotland or to enter upon any other hostility towards our dearest kinsman the King of Scotland, and also that the messengers of that king detained in your country have not been treated in any manner unworthy of a king, as had been largely declared to us from the serious complaints of certain persons; for which we greatly praise your royal clemency. And moreover, that you have freely and graciously set those messengers at liberty, according to the request of that king, for which we send your Serenity our thanks.

He promised to 'persuade Alexander to repair any injuries done by his subjects to those of King Haakon', and prayed for the continuance of peace and goodwill between Scotland and Norway.[3]

If he wrote to Alexander in the same vein, the letter has not survived; it was scarcely helpful to be scolded about repairing injuries, but at least the envoys were safely home. Henry's admonitions may even have hardened Scots attitudes; that summer the Earl of Ross attacked Skye, with his lieutenant Cormac MacMaghan, 'burning a church and several settlements' and (according to Norwegian sources) inflicting a standard range of atrocities. When these were reported to Bergen, together with 'angry words' from Alexander about bringing all the Isles under his control, Haakon had heard enough. At the 1262 Yule feast he called a general mobilisation for the spring.[4]

A splendid muster of ships assembled around Bergen in early summer. Haakon refitted his own ships, including the great *Cross-sudr*, built in 1253 for the Danish war, her gunwale nine ells above the waterline and her bulwarks as high as most ships' awnings; she had 37 pairs of oars and carried 300 men. He built himself a new flagship with gilded dragon-heads at bow and stern, and many others which he gave to his chief supporters. In May he sent two men with Orkney connections west-over-sea to engage pilots; after Earl Magnus of Orkney spoke with them, he left immediately for Norway to offer his service, and was rewarded with one of the new ships.

Dugald MacRuaraidh, *regulus* of the North Isles, was at last sent home to organise ships and stores, leaving his son as a hostage. He was to summon his brother Alan back from Ireland, where he led a mercenary war-band, and to advise his son-in-law Aedh O'Connor what was afoot. Aedh *na nGall*, 'Hugh of the Strangers', was considered pro-English by his people, but when all the Anglo-Irish were taken up with English affairs, it was time for native leaders to draw together.[5]

Haakon did not spare English feelings. Norway had recently built some deep-bellied cogs ('round ships'), but a few seasoned merchantmen would carry useful stores. He commandeered several English ships, among them one great ship of Yarmouth who was to take her revenge in due time. Magnus the Young King volunteered to lead the armada, but the Old Man would have none of that; he installed his son as regent, cleared all outstanding business, and set sail in early July. It was later than he had intended, but against that the expedition was the best prepared there had ever been. He made Shetland in two days; after waiting to mid-month for stragglers he moved to Orkney and lay off Kirkwall with around forty ships. More were following, and the Shetland and Orkney men seemed keen to join.

That first swift passage helped hide a major flaw in the great design. Haakon the Old – the boy from nowhere who regained his throne, the man who defeated the Danes and made peace with the Swedes, who sent embassies across the known world – Haakon had never sailed the western sea and knew of Atlantic storms only from saga-tales.

He kept St Olaf's feast on 29 July in Kirkwall cathedral before shifting his anchorage to South Ronaldsay at the southern outlet of Scapa Flow. Here they lay another eleven days while Earl Magnus swept Caithness for stores. Haakon wanted to divide the fleet and send half down the eastern coasts, but that idea was voted down in council. Not even the Old Man could gainsay a Ship-thing in plenary session; it was the first sign that all was not well.

The second sign came on Sunday 2 August, when the sun was darkened. The eclipse, seen across Europe, was annular in Orkney, and brave efforts were made to assert that it predicted victory; but it was generally taken to be unchancy.

On 10 August they got a fair easterly and by nightfall were off Cape Wrath and bearing away for Lewis. The same kindly wind brought a last squadron of eight ships from Norway, led by Andrew Nicholasson, a veteran crusader and diplomat. Delayed by trouble completing their stores, they were in dread of missing the action entirely. After sighting Sule Skerry (probably following the flight of gannets) they stood south-east and landed near Durness, attacking a 'castle' and raiding twenty farms before continuing to Stornoway.

There they found above a hundred ships, at anchor or drawn up ashore. Far from missing the action, Andrew and his squadron were heroes who had struck the first blow, and they enjoyed a week's feasting while local leaders came to Haakon. The Islesmen differed widely in their response; some joined gladly, some offered stores, others had to be harried into contributing at all (it was the same for Prince Charles Edward in 1745). Eventually Haakon led his fleet across the Minch, inside Skye to Kyleakin, ('Haakon's Narrows'), where the King of Man awaited him with another fleet and where they were welcomed by those who had suffered the Scots raids.

Through the Sound of Sleat and round Ardnamurchan they entered the Sound of Mull, where castles watched their passage – Mingary and Ardtornish to port, Dunara, Aros and Duart to starboard. All to starboard was Ewen of Argyll's, all to port was Dugald's, and Dugald himself came out to urge Haakon to hurry on. The Old Man was not to be bustled by sub-kings; he wanted to daunt the Scots before he conquered them.

In Oban bay lay still more ships, but there were notable absentees – nobody yet from Islay, no sign of Ewen. Even without them, the fleets totalled over 200 keels. Haakon sent fifty ahead under Magnus of Man and Dugald, to gather provisions down the coasts. The main fleet followed, to an anchorage inside Gigha off the west shore of Kintyre.

Angus Mor, and his kinsman Murchadh, now appeared, having seen that there really was a Norwegian expedition this time. Cistercian Saddell sent to plead for its flocks; Saddell was Somerled's own foundation and his resting-place, and with so many of his kinsmen in the muster, peace was soon granted. One of the royal chaplains, a Dominican, took ill and died, and the monks conveyed his body for burial in their church. Here, too, appeared an Irish ship, with an invitation to come and throw the English out of Ireland – a tempting idea, but one that must wait until this Scottish affair was settled.

Angus and Murchadh had both been compelled to give hostages to the Scots. Murchadh's son was at Forfar, young Angus with his nurse and a maid in Ayr. (This is the same Angus Òg who fought at Bannockburn fifty-one years later).[6]

At last one more ship came out of Loch Tarbert, bringing Ewen of Argyll, but not to join the muster. He came only to offer his services as a mediator between his two masters. Haakon was bitterly disappointed; he had dismissed suggestions that Ewen would fail him, attributing them to cousinly jealousy. He kept Ewen with him until wind and tide served for the perilous passage round the Mull of Kintyre.

Just east of it lay the small castle of Dunaverty; after signalling the fleet's approach it surrendered without a fight; Haakon installed Guthorm

Bakkakolf and his crew as garrison. By now it was September, and old hands
began talking of equinoctial gales.

In an easy passage they fetched Lamlash, an ideal anchorage on the east
side of Arran. If anyone cared to scramble about the shores they might find
old Viking runes in a cave on the island that closes the bay. Watchers in
Ayrshire saw the bright windvanes flash as the ships swung at anchor.

Ewen and the bishops of Orkney and Shetland were sent to find King
Alexander and announce King Haakon's peace terms. Alexander had moved
to Ayr after spending the summer at Forfar, ready to turn whichever way
was needed. He was very willing to discuss terms, and did so at considerable
length. Haakon demanded formal renewal of the 1098 agreement, with an
admission that every island off the Scottish coast was fully part of Norway.
The first meeting left no doubt that Bute, Arran and the Cumbraes could be
crossed off that list for a start. As to more distant islands, Alexander required
guarantees that raiding or sheltering criminals would cease and that Haakon
would keep due order in future. Delegates, with Dominican interpreters,
were ferried back and forth.

Ewen claimed to be trying to dissuade the Scots from war. Alexander was
entirely reasonable and wholly immovable. The Norwegian captains
reminded Haakon that time was not on his side. He lost patience, and
summoned the little Scots king to meet him face to face, at the head of
whatever army he possessed. Alexander chose to regard this as a challenge,
and said he could not think of single combat against a man so much his senior.
Haakon sent ships to attack Bute.

Bute was the Steward's island. It had a magnificent castle, but to everyone's
surprise the castle surrendered at once; tiresomely it needed a bigger garrison
than Dunaverty. Haakon decided the Scots had no stomach for a fight, but
then his envoys came to say the enemy had gathered angrily around the
meeting-tent and Ewen had advised them to go while they still could.
Haakon, 'greatly exasperated', sent another squadron up the Clyde.

He planned to panic these craven Scots into splitting their forces and
rushing them from one danger-point to another. The sixty-strong squadron
passed northward, disappearing into one of the fiords under the distant hills
(the Norwegian narrative correctly interprets Loch Long as 'Shipfiord'). King
Magnus, King Dugald and his brother Alan, and the Islaymen were all fretting
for action; with them went a stiffening of Norwegians headed by Vigleif
Priestsson and Ivar Holm. They left ten ships to hold the crossing, and hauled
the rest over the low neck of land (another Tarbet) to reach Loch Lomond.[7]

The main fleet got under way and swept majestically towards Ayr. There
were some Scots ships in the river, but these were ignored; they might come
in handy for carrying loot. Late on Saturday 29 September, on a flood-tide
and southerly breeze, the fleet entered the channel inside the Cumbrae isles.

Here they anchored for the night. The equinox had passed, the doom-merchants were proved wrong, the spring-tide covered Southannan Sands and the moon shone bright, just past the full. It was time to dish up the evening meal, rig the awnings and settle into fur-lined sleeping bags.

Largs and Fairlie are, in the words of the pilot-books, 'very shoal ... much exposed to winds from North to West, and from South'. Ballochmartin Bay on Great Cumbrae is 'much the best anchorage, fairly well inshore in about four fathoms', but it could not give sea-room to over a hundred ships. Anyway Haakon wanted the Scots to feel the full menace of his presence. He chose the mainland side of the channel; the ships anchored up and down the passage, from the Gogo Water to Brigurd Spit. There they lay all Sunday.[8]

Late that afternoon a breeze sprang up from the north-east. By dusk it was backing northerly and freshening, with stinging showers. At tide-turn around midnight, with the ebb plucking at the hulls, a wind whooped out of the north-west. Through the cloudwrack the moon showed a fleet beginning to pitch in the short seas. Some ships bucked so wildly that their men axed down their masts to save splitting the keelsons. In normal conditions a galley's mast could be unstepped and walked down to lie fore-and-aft, but things were not normal that night; besides, there were plenty spare masts in the store-ships.

At the height of the uproar the Yarmouth ship hove her anchor out of the ground and set off through the crowded anchorage. She found Haakon's flagship (already in trouble after parting half a dozen walrus-hide cables), rubbed along its side, fouled its rigging with her high anchor-spit, and was with difficulty fended away. She blundered down to ground on the southern end of Cumbrae, where her crew prudently abandoned her; on the next flood she came off masterless and floundered through the fleet to strand herself at the Kelburn Water foot.

She did one good turn, leaving her anchor and tackle in the flagship's fore-end; by no mean feat of seamanship they got it laid out and lay to it until morning. At dawn the King landed on Great Cumbrae to hear Mass and pray for deliverance from witchcraft; that storm was no accident. All down the sands lay stranded ships and spars. By the next high water, around noon, a gale from south-west was strengthening with every gust.

There were a good many men ashore by then, from wrecked ships or swept overboard. Chilled and hungry they drew together to beat off attacks from the woods, where local volunteers had gathered with slings and bows. The men on the beach defended themselves with spars, spent enemy arrows, beach cobbles and whatever came to hand.

As the tide came in it rolled wreckage up the beach and packed the survivors into a narrowing strip of shingle where the arrows fell more densely among them. Towards sunset the ebb left long sands gleaming, the fleet far out of hail, the stream-beds too narrow for any boat. The stranded hulls settled, the men crouching behind them, dashing out to salvage an axe or a spear. It was indeed a 'tide of battle'.

In a brief lull near dusk some boats did land reinforcements, but could not get out again. They spent the night wakeful among the hulls, hearing people scrunching over the shingle to carry off gear they sorely needed. The south-west gale flung spindrift at them.

On Tuesday morning the wind moderated. Haakon landed to direct salvage, but from the ships the main Scots army was seen coming down the steep glen above Kelburn, and the Old Man was forced by his companions to embark again. He left around a thousand men ashore, some two hundred and fifty under Agmund Kredikants on a ridge above the shore. Andrew Nicholasson, seeing armour glint in the woods above, ran up to warn Agmund.

Six hundred Scots, 'some on Spanish horses', charged down the spur with foot-soldiers loping at their stirrups. They swept Agmund's men back until a rabble went streaming downhill. A few, whose names the saga faithfully records, broke for the boats and capsized one in an ugly panic. The main body rallied to Andrew and Agmund and fought doggedly around a stranded ship. The Scots horsemen could not readily manoeuvre on the shingle; one young man, Piers Currie, charged alone and was cut down. He is the only named Scots casualty.[9]

The gale strengthened again from south-west, the dry ground narrowed, the Scots smelt victory. Then a boat packed with men and steered by Eilif of Naustadal, and another under Erling of Bjarkey, shot yelling through the spume; their unhoped-for coming put new heart into the Norwegians. Much later they trudged down the sands to be taken off as the wind dropped at sunset.

Next day the weather was quieter; boats came in to collect the dead for burial on Cumbrae. The day after that the Loch Long ships rejoined, laden with plunder but without some ships lost in the storm, and without Ivar Holm, dead of sickness and buried on Bute.

Friday, 5 October, was 'a fine day'. Under rainwashed skies the most damaged hulks were burnt, and when that sorry work was over the fleet slipped away to its old Arran anchorage. The Scots were still on guard, fearing renewed attacks, but the Norsemen were patching, re-rigging, stripping damaged craft to repair others, re-distributing crews and stores.

While they worked an Irish ship brought details of the chiefs' invitation. Haakon and Alan MacRuaraidh were tempted but were voted down. It was time to go home.

On the night of 9 October they left Arran, collecting Guthorm and his men as they passed inside Sanda to round the Mull. Next day they stood across to Islay, where Angus found them meat, meal and cheese equivalent to 360 cattle – little more than a day's ration for the former fleet. The Manxmen had gone, the Islesmen were going, there were fewer mouths to feed and little zest for feasting.

Another gale with heavy mist caught them before they reached Mull and sent them into Oban, the flagship with a split sail. King Dugald was still in company when they got to Tobermory, where Haakon rewarded the faithful, giving Ewen's lands to Dugald, Bute to young Rory Alansson, Arran to Murchadh. The saga admits these were empty gifts, although the charters were to be seen in the Scots royal archives twenty years later.

Then it was on to Kyleakin and a night's shelter under Rona before they staggered out to the Minch and had to run for 'the west fiord of Skye', Loch Snizort and its many coves. They are next reported off Durness on 21 October, becalmed, landing in 'Gjafiord' where they lost seven men to an ambush. On 29 October the flagship passed Longhope; on All Saints' Day Haakon worshipped in St Magnus' Cathedral. Shortly afterwards he fell ill.

His chaplains read him the lives of saints, but he soon tired of that fare and called for the sagas of the kings his ancestors. On 15 December his speech failed; he signed to the poets to continue reading. About that midnight they reached the end of his grandfather King Sverre's saga, and a little later, having nothing more to interest him, King Haakon died.

Those who had remained with him buried him in the cathedral until they could convey him home in spring. Ships had already reached Norway with tales of the expedition. In a quiet spell of weather around Yule somebody crossed to Caithness and rode south with the news that the last great Viking voyage was over.

Chapter 14 Notes

1   ES II, 601; Watt, Biog.224 (and 583); p.212 below.
2   I have assembled material on the 1263 campaign over many years and cannot now attribute every detail to its source. Johnston, Chron.Man, and Dasent, Hacon, offer contemporary accounts. Magnus Magnusson's recent Haakon the Old –Haakon Who? (Largs Hist.Soc.1982), has been invaluable.
3   CDS I, 2289 (Alexander to Henry, 12 Feb.1262); ib.2295 (Henry to Alexander, 23 March). Henry's illness, Powicke 430. Henry to Haakon (15 Nov., Reims), Fergusson 82–3 and CDS I, 2320.
4   Skye raid and reactions, Haakon's Saga in ES II, 605, where Cormac is 'Kjarnak Machamalson'; in Highland Papers II,6, 'Genealogie of the surname of MacKenzie' (17th.-c.) he is 'Kenneth Matthewsson, heritour of Kintail'. MacMaghan=Matheson.
5   For Dugald and kinsmen, p.2 and Ch.1. Aedh was son of Felim, King of Connacht (d.1265).
6   These castles are in RCAHMS Argyll 3. Murchadh was possibly Angus's brother-in-law and one of the Lamont-MacSween group (p.5). Saddell Abbey, O.Cist., RCAHMS Argyll 1, no. 296. Hostages, ER I, 8 (Murchadh's son, 24 weeks at Forfar, £1.1.0d. Angus with

nurse and maid, 26 weeks at Ayr, £3.19.10d).

7 For Tarbet/Tarbert, a portage, pp.4, 11.

8 Tides calculated as p.11, n.1. Where the Saga omits wind direction(which is seldom), I follow the normal equinoctial weather-pattern. Anchorages, *Clyde Cruising Club Sailing Directions* and *Admiralty West Coast Pilot.*

9 *Archaeologica Scotica II*, 363 *inf.*, collates many traditions and gives a sketch map showing the Scots moving up Glengarnock, 'lying at Camphill', and down to Kelburn about the line of the present A760 road.

Longships and a 'round ship' resembling the Yarmouth ship

15

1264: A Wider Realm

THE GOING of the Norse fleet could not be taken as retreat. For all the Scots knew, it might be retiring into winter quarters, to descend again refreshed; a prolonged and messy skirmish on the tideline could not seal the fate of nations.

As time passed, and the fleet's limping progress was reported, hopes rose a little. Some ravaged districts may well have felt aggrieved by the lack of organised resistance. Many observers, like Haakon himself on his deathbed, felt that Norway had been smitten by 'the immediate power of God'; others (like Haakon during the battle) attributed the storm to witchcraft. Along the coasts there were those who had ways of raising storms, ways their descendants would continue to practise, nor were they left to operate on their own.

Sir John of Wemyss, too ill to join his kinsman the Earl of Fife in the general muster, dreamed that he saw St Margaret 'in glorious apparel of gold', hand in hand with Malcolm III and attended by their three crowned sons. She told him they were going to a place called Largs, to defend Scotland against invasion. He got himself to Dunfermline, prayed at her shrine, and was healed. As he recounted his dream to the Prior, news of the battle arrived.[1]

Haakon's death was reported to Alexander in the third week of January. The Court had kept Christmas at Linlithgow, in brief respite from revictualling castles. After the festivities the Queen withdrew to her manor of Jedburgh, where on St Agnes' Day, 21 January, she gave birth to a son.

> Whence in all the bounds of Scotland redoubled praises resounded to God; because in the same day by one messenger came news of the death of the King of Norway who had plagued the King and kingdom, and by another the King was told of his son's birth.[2]

Bishop Gamelin christened the baby Alexander. Soon afterwards the King rode into the south-west with an army. Seizing the advantage given by Magnus Haakonsson's accession (which must at least delay a second onslaught), he had the Isle of Man in his sights. It might be the toughest target, but it would also be the most influential. He could only hope Henry III would not intervene, but he had no intention of forewarning him; anyway, Henry was in no position to handle external troubles.

It was a heady moment for a young man, to be setting out to lead an overseas expedition, very different from last year's trot through the hills to Largs. In the context of the times it would have been entirely appropriate to use the occasion to enhance his reputation, to rival his wife's brother as a useful fighting-man; his world was geared to judge achievement by prowess in battle. His commanders yearned to see him lead them into a spectacular triumph; instead, he resolved to achieve his aim with a minimum of bloodshed. Despite the speed of his march, he made sure his plans were known in Man:

> As soon as the news [of Haakon's death] was brought to King Alexander, swiftly assembling an army he prepared to sail to the Isle of Man. On hearing this, the King of Man sought a safe-conduct to come to the presence. Alexander neither turned back nor drew rein but, having sent the safe-conduct, rapidly led his army onward to Dumfries. The sub-king, hurrying there, became the King of Scotland's man, doing homage for his little kingdom [*regniculo*], to hold it in perpetuity with the proviso that if the King of Norway, whoever that might be, should attack Man, he and his should have refuge in Scotland for all time coming. And he should provide to the King of Scots, at need, ten war-galleys [*galeas piratas*], five of twenty-four oars and five of twelve. This business completed, the earls of Buchan and Mar, and Alan the Doorward, at the King's command with due haste went to the Western Isles and slew those traitors whose exhortations had brought the King of Norway into Scotland the year before, and put others to flight; having hanged the principals, they returned with very much booty.[3]

That, at least, is what Fordun felt should have happened. Magnus of Man indeed made terms early in 1264, and his ships may have served in the Isles expedition which was perhaps lacking longships. Menteith had spent £60 'making the King's ships' and another seven marks 'cutting and making two hundred oars' in 1263, but there is no telling how many ships he had in all, and although he employed four watchmen he seems to have enlisted no crews.[4]

The expedition presumably relied mainly on ships assembled for the Man voyage. Its purpose was to bring the Isles under Scots mastery, or at least under such influence that a new Norwegian fleet would receive no support. Wholesale executions and plunderings were no means to that end. Angus of Islay, and Murchadh, both of whom had some mainland possessions and could therefore have been accused of disloyalty, continued to flourish to the end of their natural lives; as for 'booty', no medieval army left empty-handed. Victualled and armed they might be, but only the professional knights and sergeants expected to be paid something eventually; the rank and file took what they could find.

The Chronicle of Man asserts that Ewen of Argyll 'finally declared for King Alexander by ravaging the Isle of Mull'. Ewen always got a bad press in Man, where his viceroyalty was never accepted. Mull was his own; if he fined those who had helped Haakon he did so to keep the earls out and show he was still in charge.

Elsewhere men paid dearly for wavering. The laird of the Cumbraes, Gilaverianus, had to surrender his son as hostage for the payment of sixty cattle. His name might be a corrupt form of Gill'Adamhnain, suggesting that he could have been of Somerled's kin. He must have done more than simply succour shipwrecked seamen, for if that were all the Church would have befriended him; possibly he had offered Haakon his allegiance.

He was not alone. In Ross, Sutherland and Caithness, cattle were driven off and hostages taken until fines were paid. Calculations were based on a statute of 1220, during the Moray rising, which set penalties both for absence and for desertion from the army. These ranged from fines of six cows and a heifer for a thane, down to one cow and a sheep for a 'rustic', the livestock to be shared between the King and the offender's overlord (unless the overlord was found to have connived at the absence, in which case all was the King's). A fragment of an earlier law set similar penalties for killing or wounding a fellow-soldier. The 1264 fines were mostly for failure to serve at all; they were levied on the Bishop of Ross and the earls, who were expected to deal with their subordinates. In 1263 the Sheriff of Inverness shipped 540 head of cattle to Leith and held twenty-one Caithness hostages with two from Skye. Next year he sent another 200 cattle south, kept the Caithness hostages for six months, and entertained the Chamberlain 'coming to set the King's lands at farm', presumably lands forfeited by offenders. Cormac MacMaghan was active in taking cattle; it may have been he who, as 'lawman of the Isles' was reportedly killed by King Dugald of the Nordreys in Caithness later in 1264. Dugald had no plans to submit; 'he saved himself in ships and they took no hold of him'.

Ross had been unable to muster all his men; he was fined a hundred and twenty cows, a penalty suspended by royal command. To the Sheriff's annoyance Cormac got twenty cattle from the Ross drove on the order of Buchan and the Doorward, empowered by letters patent 'at the time of the coming of the King of Norway'.[5]

Mar cannot have found his Chamberlain's duties easy to fulfil while he cruised the western seaways; his staff coped valiantly. Their returns for the 1264 Audit show the range of business they handled. No comparable statement survives for a peacetime year, but some present items must be inflated by special circumstances, not merely wages and weapons, but wine (not all as 'garrison comforts', some for use in cleansing wounds). 'Expenses of hospitality', too, must have been inflated by meetings and consultations.

Plate I *Henry III, tomb-effigy in Westminster Abbey*

Plate II *Site of the Battle of Largs. The Cumbrae Channel, Southannan sands drying out at half-tide.*

Plate III *Entrance to Dirleton Castle*

Plate IV *Kinross (Loch Leven) Castle*

Plate V *First Privy Seal (of the minority);*
'Be ye wise as serpents and gentle as doves.'

Plate VI *The adult Great Seal.*
A standard 'enthroned King' (the full beard seems unlikely); the horseman's
mount is the first to be fully caparisoned and to show the tressure fleury
bordering the lion rampant.

Plate VII *Silver penny of the early series (some have less well-drawn heads).*

Plate VIII *Silver penny of the 1280 coinage.*

Plate IX *Cambuskenneth Abbey, detached Bell-tower.*

Plate X
Inverlochy Castle,
Fort William.

The Audit was held before Gamelin of St Andrews and Richard of Dunkeld, sitting with the abbots of Dunfermline, Lindores, Holyrood, Scone and Coupar, Robert de Meyners and John de Cambrun, and clerks of the *capella* and *curia* (sample page overleaf).[6]

The figures presented are almost meaningless today, requiring to be multi-plied almost a thousandfold. One must also bear in mind that the calculations were done on an abacus, with the totals noted in Roman figures – a fruitful source of error as can be seen in the total of income, written as *m.*^{v}*cccxiii lib.xvii.sh.i d.* (whereas the true figure was *m.*^{v}*ccccxiii lib. xiii sh. i d*; the Chamberlain's clerks had achieved a miraculous near-balance). One need only try writing Roman numerals in haste to discover the difficulties.

The item of £16 'for the King's play' sits oddly among armours and wages, but may reflect long evenings awaiting news. Various table-games were played; cards had not yet been invented.

It is interesting to have confirmation of Matthew Paris's guess at the amount of Queen Marie's terce, '4,000 marks and more'; on the 1264 figures her income should have been around 4,060 marks.[7]

Queen Margaret, by contrast, had never had more than a tenth of her promised dowry, so that her clerk had to apply to the Chamberlain's office for funds. Early in 1263 her husband reminded her father of the obligation, and received a querulous response. Henry had been ill; his Treasurer had died, leaving no record of what might still be due, people had searched ledgers in vain. When he acquired a new Treasurer he would discover how much had been handed over directly, how much given to Scots agents in Rome or to Italian merchants on Alexander's behalf, how much (if anything) remained outstanding; he would do all he would wish Alexander to do for him in a like case. As to other matters in Alexander's and Margaret's letters, he really could not answer at the moment but had told his people to do what they could.[8]

Another petulant letter summoned Edward home from Gascony. There was renewed trouble in Wales, where Llywelyn's attempts to obtain a lasting peace were being ingeniously thwarted by Marchers eager to attack. Across England the baronage was increasingly taking power, and Henry was not getting the hoped-for backing from the new Pope. Alexander IV had died in 1261 and James Pantaleone, Patriarch of Jerusalem, had been elected. A shoemaker's son from Troyes, the first French Pope and a skilled adminis-trator, he had taken the regnal name of Urban IV. All his energies were directed towards a new Crusade; he had Louis IX's wholehearted support. Only the necessity of settling the matter of Sicily could induce Louis to endorse his brother Charles's acceptance of that throne. Henry had hoped Urban would prefer Edmund and ease the terms, but John Mansel was speedily informed that the question was closed.[9]

Chamberlain's Account 1264
Sample page

	£	s	d
By fermes of bailliaries on both sides of the Sea of Scotland	2896	18	3
By fermes of burghs in the same	675	18	2
By general receipts, fines and reliefs	1808	5	0
By arrears from last account	32	11	7

Total income: £5313.17.1d *[recte £5413.13.1d]*

	£	s	d
To saddles and horses for the King's work	719	0	2
To *gemellis* [sets of horse-harness] reckoned to this day	11	4	0
Fees of sergeants for 3 terms to Michaelmas 1264 [=18 mths]	85	5	0
In gifts of the lord King	122	3	6
Messengers of the lord King	150	2	9
Knights' fees [salaries of knights hired]	180	17	8
178 tuns of wine, summer 1263, with £10 to Luc of Gisors for armours supplied to the King	449	16	8
67 tuns and 1 pipe of wine, summer 1264	373	16	8
To the lord King's play, to date of account	16	2	9
To Alexander the Queen's clerk for her expenses, for which he will answer	795	16	6½
Expenses of hospitality	2224	8	0
Whereof paid by Chamberlain	1624	16	3½
Balance due to *patria* by King [*recte, £599.1.8½*]	589	11	8½
Purchases of silk, cloth, furs, trimmings and ornaments, and other small outlays, 1263	410	8	1
[as above] 1264	469	9	8
To arrears to the King's sergeants	48	15	0
Total expended	£5467	13	9

And he overspent £153. 15. 8d [*sic*] whereof they allow him £100 to be received of the Earl of Dunbar and 2 marks from the profits from the burgh of Aberdeen 'etc'

[A sum of £21. 15. 6d is needed to balance]. Also he overspent £30.13.6d in food for 200 sergeants he took with him to the Isles, by precept, summer 1264: Total excess 62. 3. 6 [*recte, £16.19.2d cr.*]

By midsummer 1263 Simon de Montfort was in England and rallying his forces. He claimed that Urban approved the Provisions of Oxford (from which the last Pope had released both Henry and his barons). In July Simon seized the Cinque Ports, the citizens of London rioted, and Henry took refuge in the Tower. Edward raided the Temple and removed as much money as he could to Windsor where his wife and a body of foreign mercenaries were installed. Queen Eleanor, trying to join them, was forced to land when her boat was stoned on its way upriver; she found sanctuary in St Paul's. Edmund, meanwhile, took Dover Castle, but both brothers were ordered to cease resistance when Henry made peace with Simon, yielding the Tower to the Earl's nominee. The feudal army was to meet at Worcester and march against Wales, but Simon diverted it to London 'to remove the foreigners resisting the royal will at Windsor'. Every sheriff in England was given a new colleague, a sort of baronial commissar to watch his every move, and everywhere private scores were settled.[10]

For men in outlying districts it was hard to tell what was afoot. Robert Neville wrote from Northumberland to Walter of Merton (whom he believed still to be Chancellor; he had just lost the post); Neville was hearing alarming rumours that 'the kings of Denmark and Norway' were in the outermost isles of Scotland, whither bound was not yet known, but Neville feared the worst. He was newly appointed 'captain of the shires beyond Trent' and custodian of York; Bamburgh needed urgent repairs; where was he to turn for funds?[11]

In September, as the Norse fleet reached the Clyde, Henry and Eleanor crossed to Boulogne where Simon joined them. Louis had called a *conseil de famille* intended to scold Simon into good behaviour. Eleanor remained in France when Henry returned home; Edward made good use of Simon's absence to detach some of his followers, young men who had been his own jousting companions, among them his cousin Henry of Almain. He seized Windsor again and brought his father there, calling on such barons as he could trust to join him. Papal messengers, *en route* for Scotland to bid Gamelin preach the Crusade, prudently stayed in Paris.[12]

In January 1264 both Henry and Simon were summoned to Amiens, to hear their overlord Louis' adjudication of their dispute. Simon broke his leg in a riding accident, and returned to Kenilworth; Henry went ahead to receive an award wholly in his favour. Louis ruled that no anointed king could accept direction from his subjects without forfeiting his duty to God who made him king. As soon as Simon learned the verdict he activated a secret pact with Llywelyn; Richard of Cornwall, always well-informed, moved to cover the March. When Henry returned, delighted with Louis' support and equally delighted with the news of a grandson in Scotland at last, he found his brother calling out the knight-service of England against his brother-in-law the Earl.

Worse, Edward's swift moves bewildered Henry and he leapt to the conclusion that, as he had often feared, Edward was in league with Simon. His suspicions were reinforced by Edward's ex-Montfortian followers.[13]

Far to the northward, King Haakon's body had been conveyed to Norway and his son Magnus had been enthroned. Magnus's first ambassadors reached Scotland after the Manx submission and before the Isles force sailed; they were coldly received, for they were empowered only to offer the cession of Bute, Arran and the Cumbraes in return for confirmation of Norwegian rule over all the other Isles.

The bearers of these ingenuous proposals were Bishop Henry of Orkney and Askatin, Chancellor of Norway, a career diplomat. According to Norwegian sources they were treated to a rare display of anger by the King of Scots, who 'threatened imprisonment or worse' and claimed that more than a third of Scotland had been burned and harried; far from granting concessions Alexander was considering a demand for reparations and had not forgotten his own envoys' detention. The embassy hastily withdrew, 'regretting' the lack of progress.

Later that summer the Bishop returned with two Franciscans, Maurice and Sigurd; they were accorded a slightly kinder reception but brought no new proposals. They took back Alexander's request for 'good messengers', plenipotentiaries with negotiating powers, and were followed by two Scottish Dominicans, Malise of Strathearn and Simon de la Fontagne, who returned through England that November.[14]

It suited Alexander well to delay any settlement. With each month that passed he improved his position in the Isles; by suspending heavy penalties, supporting local law-givers, opening Scottish markets to the Islesmen, he was gradually drawing them towards himself. Some would never accept his friendship; one 'Manus the King of Norway's son', perhaps a son of King Dugald, was still under arms in Ardnamurchan in the 1270's.[15]

There was another way to influence the Islesmen. They were devout people, and it was always hard to provide enough parish clergy for all the small communities. Even ahead of Mar and the Doorward, a pair of Gaelic-speaking Dominicans set off, perhaps from the Inverness priory, to walk through one island after another, finding people who had long lacked any pastoral care. As they left one island the air was full of demons 'howling and wailing' as they fled before the Blackfriars.[16]

The Devil lost the Isles but he was busy in England. The Lord of Annandale, after attending his King at Dumfries, rode south to fulfil his obligations to Henry. He came late, but made amends by bringing John Comyn with him and collecting John Balliol en route. He had need of any goodwill he could gather, being already under suspicion of Montfortian leanings, but rode on with Henry from Nottingham southward.

It had come to war. Each side formally defied the other, each created new knights among their supporters. On a fine May morning the royal army was drawn up on a Sussex Down under a great red samite banner of Henry's own designing, a mighty dragon with jewelled eyes. Here was to be a truly chivalrous encounter, a fair field of arms. Earl Simon had travelled to Lewes by cart but got himself to horse on the day. For Edward and his friends it was the end of rehearsal; the curtain was rising.

Edward instantly swept away the citizen-army of London; they escaped through a marsh in which Edward's horsemen floundered, leaving a gap through which Simon promptly turned the flank of the royal line and rolled it up. By nightfall, Henry was in sanctuary in the Cluniac Priory of Lewes, Edward, less comfortably, in the Franciscan house; Richard, King of the Romans and Earl of Cornwall, had been chased into a windmill and captured. Bruce, Balliol and Comyn were likewise prisoners; Balliol made an instant deal and was on his way home before night. Next day Edward arranged a truce and offered Henry of Almain and himself as hostages for its observance (his choice of refuge is revealing; the Greyfriars were among Simon's most fervent supporters).[17]

Henry was escorted to London and lodged in St Paul's Augustinian Priory. He emerged from his initial deep shock into something near euphoria. It took about a month, during which he was cut off from all his friends (busy ransoming themselves or fortifying their castles). Only in July did Henry understand that Edward's life might be in danger if the Queen launched a rescue-party from France; until then he had dealt only with minor business, answering a letter from Norway, making a belated gift to the man who brought him news of Margaret's son.

To Magnus of Norway he wrote of his sorrow at learning of Haakon's death 'for whom he grieves as for his special friend'. As to other matters in the letter brought by Mr Adam of Stavanger,

> namely that certain Norwegian merchants came to the late King of Norway in the past winter and told him on Henry's behalf that Norwegian merchants who suffered losses in England would be reimbursed if the same were done for English merchants in Norway, but that nothing had been done to give effect to this; one reason is that during the late disturbance in England some English ships were arrested in Norway to be used in the war against Alexander King of Scots, King Henry's son-in-law, which seemed harmful to both. But wishing to continue the peace begun with the late King, Henry wills that traders may go and come freely between Norway and England for a year from next Michaelmas, provided that peace is made between Norway and Scotland in the meantime.[18]

Clearly those who now controlled Henry's actions had little thought of supporting Alexander, who was at Melrose that July and who may well have interviewed the Franciscans who brought the house's chronicler a Montfortian view of Lewes. Continuing royalist support in the North of England might owe something to Scottish influence perhaps, although the chief exception, William de Vesci of Alnwick, was unwavering despite messages from Alexander and attempted pressure from Henry.

It mattered more to Alexander that Annandale was still detained. Bruce was as rich a prize as anyone could hope for, and his ransom was not easily negotiated. His wife and his sons went to England that autumn, vainly trying to arrange it, but in the end it was probably the old man's intransigence that set him free. Long afterwards his eldest grandson was sent south for his education and as hostage for the last instalment of the Lewes ransom. John Comyn faced greater difficulties and had to turn to moneylenders to release himself. Such troubles, whether seen as mere annoyances or as deep and lasting disgrace, did little to endear King Henry to former friends in Scotland.[19]

Chapter 15 Notes

1   Numerous traditions of storm-raising survive (e.g. against ships of the Spanish Armada). Vision of St Margaret, *Bower*, ii, 97–8; *Wyntoun* ii, 250–6.

2   *Fordun*, LVI.

3   *Fordun* (as last), shortened. *Galeas piratas* is his name for Viking longships. Barrow, *K&U*, 119 amends Fordun's figures to ten ships of 24 oars and five of 12 (a side, understood).

4   *ER I*, 5–6, Sheriff of Ayr's accounts. Either the storm prevented these ships joining battle at Largs, or they were simply outclassed.

5   Angus Mor lived to at least 1296. Ewen, *Chron.Man* in *ESII*, 635. Gilaverianus, *ER I*, 5. The statute, 2 Alex.II,27, of Feb.1220, is in *APS I* with a fragment of *Leges Inter Brittos et Scotos* from the 14th-century Berne MS, omitted from *Regiam Majestatem*.

6   *ER I*,13 and 19 (Sheriff of Inverness's accounts).

7   *Ib.*,10–11; the first Earl of Haddington, who preserved these accounts by transcribing them in the seventeenth century, writes 'etc' when his source is illegible or when he considers the entry of minor interest (*ib.*, xxxvi). A tun = ca.250 gallons, a pipe = ca.110 gallons. The 'debt to the *patria*' is a refund due to the Sheriff from the Chamberlain. Queen Marie's terce, p.38 above.

8   *CDS I, 2328* (13 March, Westminster; misdated '1262' by Ed.). There is no other suggestion of outlays on Alexander's behalf by the English Treasury.

9   Powicke, 430; Runciman *SV*, 69, 81–2.

10 Powicke, 435 – 440.

11 *CDS I, 2351* ('Aug.or Sept.1263'; Merton was ousted on 16 July).

12 Powicke, 442–3; papal messengers, Watt, *Biog.*212–13.

13 Powicke, 453–7.

14 Haakon's funeral, *ES II*,645. Envoys, Lustig (Ch.16 below). OP envoys, *ER I*, 19 (Sher.Inverness, £2.7.7d for their expenses), and *CDS I, 2373* (s/c, 17 Nov.1264). Fr.Malise was a first cousin of his namesake the Earl of Strathearn.

15 *ES II*, 647–9. 'Manus', p.189 below.

16 *Innes Review* 13, 108–9 (Note by Fr.Anthony Ross O.P.). The demons were *incubi*, afflicting young women.

17 Powicke, 459–460. Balliol, *CDS I, 2354* (14 May, Lewes) Letters of Conduct to go to his lands and remain there, with retinue, horses and arms.

18 *CDS I, 2336* (6 May '1263', St.Paul's) grant of lands of Robert de Clerebek lately dead, to Walter Cofton Q.Margaret's *vallet*, promised 10 mks worth of land when he brought news of her son's birth. (The date must be 1264, unless she bore an unrecorded child between Margaret, 1261, and Alexander, Jan 1264). Walter was in her service from 1251. To Norway, *CDS I, 2355* (28 June 1264, St.Paul's). A free-trade treaty had been made with Norway in 1217. For problems besetting foreign ships off England, p.160 below.

19 De Vesci's mother was a daughter of William the Lion. Robert Bruce *le Noble* m.1st Isabella de Clare, sister of Earl Richard of Gloucester, whose son Gilbert had grievances over delays in granting him his father's title and lands and joined Montfort. S/cs for Isabella and her third son Bernard, *CDS I, 2356* (8 July 1264) and *ib.2358* (9 Aug.) for Robert jr. to arrange Robert sr.'s release. *Ib.2370*, obligation by John Comyn to Luke de Batencourt, citizen of London, for £ 324.6.2d.

Henry III going to Gascony in 1243.

1265–1266: Peace in Prospect

THE SCOTS *colloquium* in March 1265 received English envoys bringing letters endorsed by the baronial Council but bearing signs of Henry's anxious dictation. One was formal:

> When peace was lately made between the King and his barons, the King granted Edward his eldest son and Henry son of the King of Germany, his nephew, as hostages with their own assent; now a *forma* has been arranged by the prelates and barons to secure the peace and liberate the hostages. The King sends the Prior of Durham, David of Offinton, Robert de l'Isle and Mr Robert Trillawe, commanding [Alexander] by the faith and homage wherein he is bound (while wishing to save him trouble and expense) to send envoys with full powers. And this, as he loves his own and his kingdom's tranquillity and the liberation of the hostages, he must not omit to do.

The second is a fervent entreaty:

> Henry knows by Alexander's frequent letters that he is concerned for the tranquillity of this kingdom and for Edward's liberation and feels the ties of blood and affinity and the need for mutual help in view of the nearness of the two countries. He earnestly begs that duly empowered lieges be sent, lest the prince's deliverance be delayed, and he hopes that Alexander can induce his magnates and others to aid the English if another disturbance occurs, and will urge those not yet committed to do so.

The envoys were to 'urge these matters verbally in every way'; they were told that Alexander had been 'commanded' to give them safe-conducts and Margaret to use her influence on their behalf, while informing Henry frequently of her own condition which he trusted was pleasant and prosperous.[1]

The peace formula had been patched together through months of reluctant compromise. Its conditions included one that Henry and Edward must ensure the adherence to it of Ireland, Gascony, the King of Scotland and 'other lands subject to the King of England', and another that Edward must swear to uphold the corporate government, bring in no aliens, and remain within England over the next three years, on pain of papal sanctions and disinheritance. The two hostages were released on 11 March but Edward's steps were dogged by an escort of young Montforts. Henry of Almain was allowed to leave for France, in the hope that he could dissuade Queen Eleanor from intervention. She had already sold to Louis the lands granted to England under the Treaty of Paris, and was reported to be raising men and ships.[2]

Throughout 1264 a papal legate had waited at Boulogne, refused entry by the Montfort party; it was even alleged that his letters of credence had been thrown in the Channel. He was the Cardinal of Sabina, Guy Foulquois, an eminent lawyer who had taken Holy Orders as a middle-aged widower. He could only send letters of lofty rebuke and logical analysis into England, and in December returned to Rome for a conclave following Urban IV's death. In February he was himself enthroned as Clement IV, and lost no time in despatching another legate with the fullest possible powers.[3]

That spring Alexander and his councillors considered some kind of expedition, either to rescue Henry or to reinforce de Montfort; opinions were deeply divided. In the country at large Earl Simon was acquiring a near-mystical aura of single-minded faith and honour, while it was hard to decide if Henry's trouble was simplicity or duplicity. Many nobles and Alexander himself had feudal obligations within England which, strictly speaking, were to Henry in person and owed by individuals.

The English embassy was soon followed by another from Norway, led by Askatin the Chancellor and the Bishop of Hamar, who came via Lynn and York so as to consult Henry (or Simon) or at least exchange letters with them. They brought no new proposals and although they received a slightly more cordial welcome they found no sign of softening on Alexander's part. On their return they may have been accompanied by a Cistercian of Melrose, Reginald of Roxburgh (to whom the Melrose chronicler attributes the final success of negotiations).[4]

The Norwegian delegation was still at Perth when a new storm arose in England. In April young Gloucester quarrelled publicly with Simon. In May, a tiny force led by Surrey and the ex-Lord of Pembroke William de Valence landed in south-western Wales. Simon moved from London to Gloucester and thence to Hereford, raising the western levies to help keep the peace. He took Henry and Edward with him as visible proof that his actions were in the King's name. On 31 May Edward rode out with his usual escort, started a discussion about horses in which everyone changed mounts, picked the fastest and vanished at the gallop. He was next discovered in Ludlow with Gloucester, and Roger Mortimer, a prominent Marcher; within days they held the Severn valley from Worcester to Shrewsbury, cutting Simon off from his Midland allies.[5]

Henry, in Hereford, poured out condemnations of Edward's faithless desertion, mixed with appeals for armed help. By July the administration had virtually collapsed, Henry was near total breakdown and Simon must have felt the reins slipping. His countess removed her household from Kenilworth to Dover, leaving her brother Richard a prisoner with young Edmund, Sanchia's son, for company. Simon had his own eldest son, Henry, with him; young Simon held Kent and Sussex; Guy, not yet knighted, was with the western army. Amaury the clerk was already in France, and the boy Richard and Eleanor the only daughter were with their mother.[6]

Earl Simon himself, with the King in tow, was trying to establish a base in the Marches, making a treaty with Llywelyn (which that experienced Welshman regarded with scepticism), planning to deprive Mortimer and Gloucester of their castles along the Usk, lastly and belatedly hunting for a way to cross the Severn and join up with young Simon. Contacts were almost cut between the armies; young Simon marched towards Kenilworth, pausing to sack Winchester in passing, while his father hoped he was forming one arm of a pincer-movement against Edward. Reaching Kenilworth on the evening of 31 July he dismissed his men 'to find baths' in the town, and himself prepared to stay in the priory rather than the castle. Edward changed his plans for him by a forced march from Worcester; Simon got inside the castle walls but most of his company were killed or captured.

Edward was back in Worcester when Earl Simon at last found an unguarded ford near Kempsey. His army marched eastward through the night of 3 August, expecting to meet young Simon at any moment. At dawn they halted for food at the Benedictine abbey of Evesham; the army could have carried on but Henry was on the point of collapse.

Simon went up the abbey-tower after breakfast and had a grandstand view of Edward's army advancing in immaculate order. 'They learned that from me,' he said; and a little later, seeing Mortimer come from the other side, 'Let us commend our souls to God, for our bodies are theirs.'[7]

The armoured knights wearily formed a shield-ring around the King. It was the end of an era, and there was something symbolic in the reversion to ancient warfare. As at Hastings, the ring could not hold for ever; Edward's tournament-trained companions broke through. Among them was Roger Leyburn, Edward's steward who left him after a quarrel over accounts, then became Simon's right-hand man, then returned to Edward. It was he who recognised the voice whimpering from inside a helm, and threw himself over his King. Henry, slightly wounded, was quavering that he was an old man, too old for war, loyal subjects must not hurt him. As Roger led him to safety Simon and his son were being hacked to death and Guy taken prisoner. A man who had followed Simon to Lewes now dismembered his body so that tokens could be sent to distant towns in proof of his death.[8]

Henry needed three weeks' convalescence at Gloucester before he could move to Marlborough and rouse himself to former interests (adorning the chapel, improving the fishponds). Edward stormed north to regain his city of Chester while Leyburn dealt with the Cinque Ports. In the first flush of victory Edward was ready to be generous, but as Henry recovered he was in no mood to show mercy. Young Simon came to treat for the surrender of Kenilworth, bringing his uncle Richard to make terms, but nobody could make anything easy for any Montfort. 'A state of peace', proclaimed on 16 September, revoked 'all letters, charters, writings and grants of land' made since Lewes; measures against rebels were progressively stiffened until anyone alleged to have been 'an accomplice of the late Earl of Leicester' was forfeit, his lands to be given away as the King chose. The possibilities for private revenge were boundless.[9]

Within weeks, reaction set in. The ordinary people of England recalled Simon's virtues and magnified them. Comparisons were drawn with St Thomas Becket, that other opponent of royal power. Miracles were reported from Evesham field, from Simon's grave in the abbey, from his mutilated hands and bloodstained scraps of cloth:

> Earl Simon sought Thomas, Simon waged the cause of Thomas, with Thomas he wore away false laws by martyrdom. Thomas, sun of the east, Simon, star of the west, each pious man fought for justice.

It was remembered that in 1261 he had exiled himself, saying he would 'rather die without a country than desert the truth'. Not for the last time, in ridding themselves of a nuisance the victors made a martyr.[10]

No Scottish army had marched south, but Evesham and its aftermath touched many Scots. Guy Balliol of the Inverkeillor family, 'by race a Scot, fighting for the justice of England', had carried the Earl's banner and died with him, refusing quarter. Henry Hastings, David of Huntingdon's grandson whose cousins were earls of Atholl, had been knighted by Simon and held Kenilworth for his widow; Gilbert de Umphraville, the posthumous son of the Earl of Angus, had been Simon's ward from infancy and reached his majority in summer 1265. He and Hastings cannot have known much about Scotland unless they accompanied the Earl on one of his embassies. Many others were to find themselves involved in lawsuits arising from those sweeping forfeitures.[11]

There is a faint possibility that some technical help was exchanged. Leyburn had on his staff a 'Master Peter the engineer', in charge of siegeworks, whose assistant was Imbert de Montferrand. Imbert is recorded as a knight at Henry's court, to whom Mansel wrote about fortifying a house; but at Roxburgh in 1263 a man with the unusual name of Imbert was constructing 'engines'. The sheriff-castellan, accounting for hides of cattle, reported that 'W. the cook had nine and Imbertus seven for the machines, and W. the *ballistarius* [crossbowman or catapult-gunner] had two'. In 1288 a 'Master Imbert' reported on repairs needed at Jedburgh after a storm. These may be three different men, but it is curious that they were all military engineers.[12]

The Earl and Countess of Buchan went to England in October 1265 on family business arising from the death, in 1264, of her father the Earl of Winchester; his title lapsed and his estates were divided among heiresses (who litigated over them for years). They set out after the autumn *parlement* at Scone, where on 10 October King Alexander granted the Dominicans of Perth an annual five chalders of corn and ten of malt from royal farms, and £ 7.16.0d. and a wey of wax from the burgh. This probably reflects the service given by interpreters and envoys to Norway, especially since Perth is the most likely Dominican house for Father Malise of Strathearn to have joined. The Order had been settled in Perth by Alexander II, on the North Inch where an old royal motte had been swept away by a spate in 1210.[13]

That November King Magnus of Man died, leaving a childless widow (Ewen's daughter Mary of Argyll), and a natural son named Godred, of whom little was heard for some years. A succession of Bailiffs, both Manx and Scots, was appointed to administer the island, among them Alan 'fitz Count', Thomas of Atholl's son. The native justiciars remained in office.[14]

Ottobuono dei Fieschi, the new Legate, had at last been allowed into England. He was a member of the great Genoese family that had produced Pope Innocent IV; on his mother's side he was related to Savoy and so to Queen Eleanor. He had been concerned in the negotiations to make Edmund King of Sicily and had supported Richard of Cornwall in the Curia and Charles of Anjou in Genoa. Now Cardinal-deacon of St. Adrian, he crossed to Dover with the Queen to be met by the Lord Edward, who had come to accept surrender of the castle from Eleanor de Montfort, to take her servants into his protection, and to smooth her passage to France before his mother's arrival.

Ottobuono brought an impressive staff which included the Archdeacon of Liège, Tedaldo Visconti, and a chaplain named Benedetto Gaetani. There were thus three future Popes in the delegation; Tedaldo became Gregory X, Ottobuono himself was briefly Adrian V in the 'year of the four Popes', Benedetto was Boniface VIII. None of them forgot how Edward guarded them from hostile English crowds during their mission.

The Legate's task was enormous. He was to restore peace, examine the conduct of the English bishops (Henry was accusing eight of them of abetting Earl Simon), and preach a general Crusade against the infidel as well as local campaigns against rebels 'from Norway to Gascony, from Germany and Denmark to Ireland'. He could make little headway at first. Edward was dealing with former companions; he had no wish to sow dragons' teeth over the land he might soon come to rule; but Henry wanted vengeance. He and his remaining supporters shook their heads over Edward's impatience and frivolity, his sudden departures, his friendship (still) with undesirable elements. They could not accept that he alone could influence Gloucester and Mortimer, nor that he was within sight of bringing his cousin Simon to terms.[15]

The stumbling-block was Kenilworth. Whatever young Simon might say, Hastings was the castellan and had sworn never to surrender except to the Countess in person. Simon slipped off to the Fens and rallied some surviving supporters; Edward brought a feudal levy against him and allowed some rebels to give sureties for their appearance in the spring. Simon was taken to London and lodged with the Templars; if he would abjure the realm and swear to do no harm to King or country, he could draw a pension from the revenues of Leicester, now held by Edmund. While in the Temple Simon smelt treachery and fled to France, where his brother Guy managed to join him from Windsor. The remaining rebels, greatly heartened, vanished into Sherwood or the Peak, or back to the safety of the Fens.

In summer 1266 Edmund opened the siege of Kenilworth. In June Henry, Edward, and the Legate joined him; in July Richard of Cornwall vainly tried to negotiate a surrender. Kenilworth had been fortified by every King of England since the Conquest; it stood at the centre of a hundred acres of lakes and moats, its walls out of range of all but the heaviest siege-engines. Edward, doubtless cursing himself for failing to include Kenilworth in the Dover settlement, even brought flat-boats from Chester, a feat of ingenuity and exertion that deserved better success. The defence held until December when Ottobuono got them honourable terms; if they had done nothing else, they gave Edward valuable lessons in castle-planning.[16]

Long before the sick and starving men dragged themselves out of battered Kenilworth another campaign had reached successful peace. In April 1266 Askatin returned, with Andrew Nicholasson of Largs fame, empowered to negotiate terms and seal a treaty. Settlement was reached on 4 May, reported to Norway, and formally sealed in the Perth convent on 2 July. As the oldest surviving Scottish state treaty with a foreign power other than England, the Treaty of Perth would merit analysis even if it were otherwise unremarkable.[17]

It opens in regular form with an invocation to the Holy Trinity and a statement of place, date and parties. Then follow concessions and considerations.

King Magnus of Norway cedes Man and all other islands in the west and south of *Magni Haff*, the Great Sea, with the patronage of their bishopric, to King Alexander and his heirs, saving the rights of the church of Nidaros [the archbishopric of Trondheim], and excepting the islands of Orkney and *Yhetlandie*. The men of the ceded islands are henceforth to be subject to the laws and customs of Scotland, but are not to be punished for past offences and are to be free to emigrate in peace if they so desire. For this 'concession and resignation and quitclaim', Alexander will pay 100 marks every 1 July to the Bishop of Orkney or another appointed Norwegian official, and a further four thousand marks over the next four years. These terms are sworn on the soul of King Magnus and their own souls by Askatin and Andrew, and on the soul of King Alexander and their own souls by Adam Earl of Carrick and Robert de Meyners the Chamberlain. Observance of the terms is to be under papal jurisdiction, with personal excommunication and national interdict for any breach, together with a penalty of ten thousand marks.

Three concluding clauses lay down that (a) all previous offences are to be forgiven; (b) criminal refugees are not to be received unless and until they have passed a year in good behaviour, 'and for treason they shall never be received'; and (c),

> If, *quod absit*, either Norwegians or Scots shall suffer shipwreck or collision, they shall freely and quietly both have and sell or take away their wrecked or damaged ships and all their goods and gear, whether salvaged by themselves or others, without any challenge except for dereliction [a counterclaim by the other ship in a collision, or pilotage error perhaps]. Anyone infringing this clause will be treated as a robber and peace-breaker.

The copy sent to Norway was sealed by Alexander, with Bishop Gamelin and Bishop John of Glasgow, the Earls of Buchan, Dunbar, Mar and Carrick, and Robert de Meyners. On 10 August in Bergen the other copy was sealed by King Magnus and the bishops of Bergen and Stavanger, Gunter de Mel, Kynsitus Jonsson, Finn Guntersson, Andrew and Askatin. It was returned to Scotland with a mandate instructing the islanders to give homage to Alexander. Previous Norwegian trade-agreements had all been in the form of letters patent; these were with England in 1217, Lübeck in 1250, Greifswald in 1262 and the series of accords 1262–1264, by which the community of Iceland placed itself under the protection of Norway.

It was a generous and sensible end to a long dispute. The phrase that opens the payments clause is no mere formula; Alexander, *veritatis zelator et pacis et concordiae amator*, the zealot for truth and lover of peace and concord, offers to buy the peace he has already won by the sword. Anyone who rejected his rule was free to go elsewhere, as long before Norsemen had left the Isles for Iceland to evade Harald Fairhair's rule. The vexed question of wreck and salvage is solved in passing. Improved trade and rising prosperity are to reward both countries.

No such happy solution had yet been found with England, where foreign ships were liable to be plundered to the keel if they so much as sought a lee in heavy weather. Alexander dealt with many such cases; in 1252 for example, Robert le Stater, burgess of Berwick, lost one of his ships at Mablethorpe in

Lincolnshire. She was cast ashore, and next year Robert obtained an English writ to let him recover the hulk and her gear and cargo. After seven months the Sheriff of Lincoln reported a valuation by local assessors totalling four marks (£2.13.4d). Robert had spent as much on the cable alone, and valued the rest of the gear at 40 marks. The Sheriff admitted that much was *distracta* before his assessors got there. Next January a new panel, made up of neighbouring seamen who loved not Mablethorpe, reported:

> A jury of the men of Grimsby, Boston and Kalsworth find that Robert of Wells had the mast and yard, worth £2; the township of Mablethorpe had the hull and fittings and some small gear, £6, part of the sail, 4 marks, an anchor, two great cables and five ropes, with the side of a small boat, £4.6.0d. William the reeve's son of Mablethorpe had two entire anchors and another broken, and many ropes, £4. The township of Trusethorpe had a linen cloth and nine chests, £1.1.0d. Alan Raven had a certain bundle, they know not its value. The Sheriff shall levy the value of goods from those that hold them, and must enquire about any more chattels recoverable.[18]

At least future traders between Norway and Scotland could hope for better fortune. Like the rest of the Treaty, the arrangements rested upon mutual understanding of realities, not on delusions of grandeur; there were no lofty phrases to hurt national pride, only the praise for a just settlement.

There were those who did resent the Treaty, especially the payments:

> Much as this agreement pleased some, it displeased many more. For in the course of many ages, before the Scots came into Britain, they lived in those isles, and until that fatal contention between the sons of Malcolm Canmor against Donald [Bàn] their uncle, when, the realm being totally divided, Magnus Olafsson King of the Norwegians invaded the isles with power and brought them under his rule, the Scots had possessed them continuously with no interruption attempted.[19]

Fordun does not identify the objectors; some may have been dogged guardians of tradition, others Islesmen who suddenly found themselves facing demands from Scots officials after a lifetime of happily chasing Norwegian tax-gatherers back to their boats. Alexander had not committed himself to irrecoverable expense; if Ewen of Argyll had felt able to bid 300 marks a year for a part of the Isles, the whole could well yield more than the total promised to Norway.[20]

One new name among the Scots signatories deserves a word or two. Adam of Kilconquhar, a kinsman of the Earl of Buchan, was now Earl of Carrick by marriage with Earl Neil's heiress. He did not enjoy it for long, for within a couple of years he went to the Crusade and did not return.

With the Treaty, a new era opened which later generations would recall wistfully as 'The Time of Peace'. In England, however, there was as yet no peace. After a meeting at Bury St Edmunds in February 1267, when the *parlement* laid plans to clear the last resisting groups, Edward rode north on one of his sudden sweeps, to subdue two northern leaders still offering a focus for disruption. He struck first at William de Vesci, correctly judging that Roger de Vipont would not long hold out in Appleby if Alnwick fell. Fordun, holding up his hands in horror at 'villages burnt, towns sacked, churches despoiled, nowhere peace or safety', records that Edward 'swiftly gained Alnwick by stealth'; historians can be ill to please. Sending de Vesci south to make his peace with Henry, the Prince allowed himself a rare breathing-space.

He rode on for some fifty miles, in brisk March weather, through country he had only seen once in a rainy summer. The Tweed valley was greening as he came to Roxburgh for a few days with his sister. It was probably the first break since his return from Gascony, apart from some uneasy weeks after Lewes; his wife was far away with two small girls (one dangerously frail) and awaiting the birth of another child. To find himself in a family home where he need keep up few pretences must have come as a shock.[21]

It was fortunate that maps were not readily available, or the shock might have been worse. The domains his great-grandfather had held and his grand-father and father had claimed had included more than half France. Since the Treaty of Paris Louis had repossessed Normandy, Brittany, Maine, Anjou, Poitou and Guienne, with the half of Toulouse that had once lain under Angevin rule. Queen Eleanor had recently sold the last French footholds to raise her ineffective army; Wales was in turmoil, Ireland, as usual, uncertain, England itself had almost slipped away. While he had been hauling himself and his father's realm out of disaster, Margaret's little red-headed husband had quietly doubled his own territories by means of one insignificant skirmish and a deal of patient diplomacy. Diplomacy and legal agreements were always interesting to Edward; he was sure to ask about Perth and get Alexander's opinion of Norwegian negotiators, in the intervals of playing with the two small children and reminding Margaret of their own childhood.

It was all too short an interlude; news came of more trouble in London; he rode away promising to return soon and bring Edmund. Once things were quieter, Alexander must bring Margaret to see her father, who would be better soon when summer came; and one day he really must see more of Scotland, he had not appreciated its prosperity.[22]

Chapter 16 Notes

1   *CDS I, 2377 -8–9* (5 March 1265, Westminster).
2   Powicke, 488–490; *forma* adopted 8 March, Edward and Henry of Almain released 11 March.

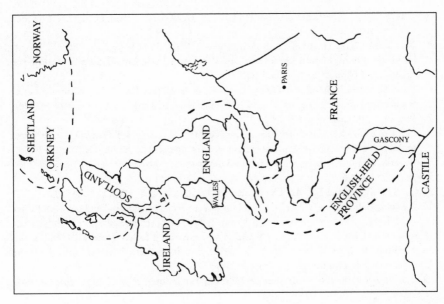

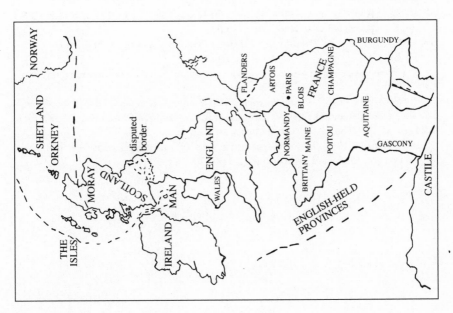

Map IV English and
Scottish territories,
*c.*1170 and *c.*1270

3 Guy Fulquois (Clement IV), Runciman *SV* 97,99–100. Urban IV died 2 October. Ottobuono, p.205 below.

4 R.I..Lustig, 'The Treaty of Perth reconsidered', *SHR*, 58 (1979).

5 Powicke, 496–9; Pembroke, taken from Valence (a Lusignan), had been entrusted to E.Gilbert of Gloucester. *Fordun*, LVIII.

6 Powicke (as n.5); Montfort family, Labarge, *S de M* and *Bar.Hsehd.*; Montfort, p.33; Richard of Cornwall, Young, *R of C*, 130. (Sanchia died 1261; Edmund was 14 in 1265).

7 Powicke, 502; Labarge, *S de M*.

8 *CM* 132; Powicke, 500–2. Leyburn, Powicke 435–6,443,502–4. E.Simon's head was sent to Wigmore, where Mortimer's wife held the castle. The trunk was buried by the Benedictines at Evesham; Edward would never visit the town thereafter, Powicke 720.

9 Powicke, 503–6.

10 *CM* 131–4; Labarge *S de M*. The quotation is from the contemporary *Song of Lewes*.

11 *Fordun* LVIII; Balliols, *CM* 107,133 (Henry of Inverkeillor and his daughter were buried in Melrose, hence the chronicler's interest). Gilbert E. of Angus to be sent with his nurse to Simon, *CDS I, 1687* (1245–6); Simon was rumoured to have paid £10,000 for this wardship. *Ib.2399*(30 May 1266), John Balliol to have 300 of the 600 mks due from Gilbert to E.Simon for seizin of his heritage.

12 Imbert, *ER I*, 30 and 44; Imbert de Montferrand, Young, *R of C*, 115; with Leyburn, Labarge, *Bar, Hsehd.*, 149.

13 S/c for Buchan, *CDS I.,2385* (5 Oct.1265,Windsor); litigation, cf.*CDS II,91*. Blackfriars grant, *Hdlist A.III* no. 57. Fr.Malise O.P., p.144 above.

14 K. Magnus died 24 Nov. 1265, *Chron.Man.* in *ES II*, 653. Mary (Man & Isles, p.2) married three more times, all childless. Bailiffs of Man, *Chron.Lanercost* 64 (muddled annal '1256'). Alan, p.47 above.

15 Ottobuono, Powicke, 526; Edward's rescue of the delegation from a mob, *ib.527*, Young, *R of C* 138.

16 The young Montforts and allies, Powicke, 518–26, *R of C* 131–4. Kenilworth, Powicke, 531–2,539 (at times 'artillery duels' occurred, incoming missiles struck by defensive bombardment).

17 Lustig (n.4 above); text, *APS I*. Mandate for Isles homage, in 1282 archives list, *APS I*, 2–11. I am greatly indebted to Lustig's study.

18 *CDS I, 1915,1938,1950* (March 1253–Jan.1254); numerous others in *CDS I*.

19 *Fordun*, LVII.

20 For Ewen in 1249, Ch.1 above. The payments continued, Robert I confirming the Treaty 1312.

21 *Fordun*, LVIII. English events, Powicke, 544; Young, *R of C*, 137. Edward's children in 1267 were Berengaria (b.1264, d.young), and Eleanor,b.1265. John(d.1272) was born later in 1267. The Scots royal children were then six and three.

22 *CDS II,86* (1276–7), belated payment for exps. of a messenger with news of London insurrection to Edward 'in Scotland' (cf.Powicke, 543–4).

A Knight; see pp. 131–2

1200–1300: A Century of Skills and Visions

IN THE SUMMER of 1267 John of Brienne came from France with King Louis' proposals for making peace with the Montforts. Henry insisted that Simon must stand trial; if he submitted to judgment it might be possible to let him sell his lands to the royal family, and take abroad whatever remained after meeting any deduction for injuries. It was apparent that there would be little left to take, so Simon and Guy preferred to seek their fortune under Charles of Anjou.[1]

Ottobuono turned his attention to his other task, preaching the Crusade. Henry had never forgotten his vow, but what *Outremer* needed was a trained army under competent leadership; the Pope tactfully suggested letting Edmund deputise for his father. He granted Henry a tenth of clerical incomes for three years, firstly to meet his obligations to Rome, next to clear the Queen's wartime debts, lastly to help Henry's own tangled finances. Much of the expected windfall was committed long before the clergy gave anything; treasures gathered to adorn St. Edward's new shrine, even the Crown Jewels, were pledged in the Legate's hands. Unfortunately Clement IV overlooked the 1251 ruling and included Scotland in the grant. Alexander (himself a creditor) refused to allow payment and appealed to Rome.[2]

Ottobuono summoned a Legatine Council to meet in London in April 1268, at a time of *parlement*:

> All the bishops of Scotland were cited to compear ... he ordered the Scots clergy to send two abbots or priors for the whole realm. The bishops in General Council appointed Richard, Bishop of Dunkeld, and Robert, Bishop of Dunblane, lest in their absence statutes might be made to their prejudice or harm. The rest of the clergy sent the Abbot of Dunfermline and the Prior of Lindores. The Legate made some new statutes, especially about secular and regular priests, which the Scottish bishops utterly refused to adopt.

The delegates were carefully chosen. Abbot Simon, only a year in office, represented the senior Benedictine house, a daughter of Canterbury. Thomas of Lindores was the oldest serving Prior and a former papal judge-delegate. Robert de Prebenda of Dunblane, an Englishman who had made his career in Scotland, was an old friend of Gamelin. Richard of Dunkeld had been both Chamberlain and Chancellor. Both bishops were graduates, of Bologna, Paris or Oxford. They set out with Alexander's permission to deliver 700 marks already collected, to show they were obeying papal orders as far as possible.[3]

The King spent April at Berwick, Gamelin beside him for advice and swift reaction. Gamelin did not attempt to attend the conference; his health was failing, and unwelcome friction might have arisen over his status *vis-à-vis* York.

Besides, he had an immediate diocesan problem. In the valley of Wedale (now traversed by the Galashiels-Edinburgh road) lay the ancient sanctuary of Our Lady of Stow. Kelso and Melrose both had grazing rights in the surrounding royal forest, St Andrews possessed the manor beside the sanctuary. Despite 1194 rulings on Melrose's boundaries, in spring 1268 the Abbot, in person, led a mounted raid into episcopal territory.

Quarrels between herdsmen are among the world's oldest, but the spectacle of a Cistercian abbot leading a posse of choir-monks is not one to fit readily into standard perceptions of the religious life. Still the Abbot himself was untypical, for he was Robert of Kenleith, last encountered collecting safe-conducts in England, formerly Chancellor of Scotland and Abbot of Dunfermline. He was a jealous guardian of his community's rights, had already obtained writs for the Sheriff to examine a prejudicial diversion of Gala Water, and was supported by the exceptional privileges of his Order; Cistercians answered only to the Pope and to the annual convocation of abbots at Cîteaux. So he rode out; but Gamelin, the Borderer, knew all about moss-troopers. He had the Abbot and his troop excommunicated at the next General Council.[4]

It might not be too far-fetched to see such incidents as symptoms of the growing split between monastic and other clerics. Until the twelfth century monasteries held a virtual monopoly of learning. Every house educated its own novices for their place in the cloister, though not every Order kept schools for the laity. The oldest Scottish foundations looked back to Irish traditions, carried through Europe before St Benedict sat down to frame his Rule; others claimed the influence of Lindisfarne or Bede's Jarrow. David I brought representatives of many newer Orders; as well as learned Benedictines he fetched monks from Tiron in Brittany who urged the use of skills learned in the world, so that Kelso had excellent master-masons and a namely peal of bells when such things were rare. He settled Cistercians in desolate places where they developed sheep-farming from convents bare of all adornment but music; and many more.

Each Order began as a fellowship vowed to poverty, chastity and obedience; each in turn, loaded with gifts from the faithful, sank a little below perfection; each produced reforming offshoots. It was left to Alexander II to introduce two new groups, which in time became keenly resented by parish and monastic clergy alike.[5]

Dominic Guzman, a Castilian canon regular, born in 1170, joined a papal mission to the heretics of Languedoc in 1206. He and the mission's director, Bishop Diego, abandoned the confrontational approach and tried to persuade their main opponents by reasoned argument, a formidable task against intellectual Cathars unhampered by orthodoxy. The Pope launched a savage war against the Albigensian Cathars, with Simon de Montfort (the Earl's father) as leader, but Dominic continued his work and in 1216 established his Order of Preachers. Its members were highly educated and encouraged to learn vernacular languages. In the year of their papal approval they sent a small party to preach in Paris, and in 1221, just before St Dominic's death, others travelled to Oxford.

Francesco Bernardone entered religion by another path, 'dropping out' from the life of a rich young man to work among the poor of Italy. He and eleven companions were authorised to preach in 1210; by 1217 the Franciscan Order had grown so large that it had to organise in provinces. In 1224 it too sent missionaries into England. In 1229, when Alexander II and Henry III met at York, both Dominicans and Franciscans accompanied the King of England. Shortly afterwards Alexander established their first Scottish houses.[6]

Already in Scotland there were both choir-schools attached to cathedrals, and burgh schools concentrating on 'business studies' such as arithmetic and neat handwriting; the schools of Perth, under a graduate master, were directed from Dunfermline, those of Roxburgh came under Kelso's guidance. The Gaelic title *ferleiginn* ('man of reading') was conferred on headmasters in St Andrews and Inverness.

There was as yet no university in Scotland, but students readily found their way to Salerno, Bologna, Toledo, Paris or Salamanca. Bologna, with traditions stemming from Imperial Rome, was the centre for law; Salerno, oldest of all, not only preserved Greek medical texts but permitted anatomical dissection (Christianity and Islam both disapproved, but did not yet forbid it; both got round the problem by using the bodies of criminals, and infidels to either faith). Arab practitioners, whose skills surpassed anything known elsewhere, came to Salerno and later to Montpellier (then in Aragon), where a group of Muslim doctors obtained protection from a local bishop and attracted Jewish physicians and Albigensian survivors to join them in scientific research. At Toledo in the previous century an enlightened bishop had established a School of Translators with skills in Hebrew, Arabic and Greek, whence came a flow of Arabic texts which had preserved lost Classical Greek material. (Salerno also recovered texts, some through Arabic and some direct from Greek originals). Not only was a store of long-lost knowledge released, but also it became essential to examine the sources critically rather than accepting them at face-value. Earlier scholars had dreamed of gathering the world's learning into one encyclopaedic net to rout chaos and harmonise the whole creation; some new texts opened avenues of thought leading into new spheres (some troublous); others were not all they were claimed to be.[7]

Early in the century a Scots student reached Toledo and plunged into the new pool of learning. His name was Michael Scot, by tradition from Balwearie in Fife. He was interested in everything – science, medicine, music, mathematics. He seized upon the innovation of what we still call 'Arabic' numerals, and as quickly realised the value of algebra and the Indian concept of zero (all liberating his mathematical mind from the bonds of counting-frame and Roman numerals). He was a practical physician, with sound views on diet and clothing for hot countries (he may have accompanied the Emperor Frederick II to Palestine in 1229), and gives tantalising glimpses of his own early life, as when he advocates a student learning to play 'a lyre, which if they play it well, pays their way everywhere in Christendom ... as is clear from the experience of anyone who goes from door to door playing it'. In later life he was court physician to the Emperor, a post not without its dangers. Invited to calculate the length of Frederick's life, Michael admitted that he feared the Emperor would only outlive his own unworthy existence by a fortnight. Having thus taken out life-insurance he continued his studies, discovering that his own death would follow a blow on the head from a pebble (whose weight he calculated). He took to wearing a metal skullcap, but while hearing Mass bare-headed he was struck by a chip of stone falling from a church vault. He took the chip home, weighed it, put his affairs in order, and died within days.[8]

Michael's work was accomplished in Europe, whereas many lesser men returned home with their learning. Watt's *Biographical Dictionary* lists some seventy-five graduates in the twelfth century, some four hundred and eighteen in the thirteenth (excluding possible duplications); twenty-two of these were *physicus* or *medicus*, including Alexander II's doctor, Ness de Ramsay of Banff. In 1268, seven of the eleven Scots bishops were graduates. The vision of the country as a hive of learning, with 'lads o' pairts' setting out in thirsty pursuit of knowledge, is beguiling but misleading; many scholars were sustained by the income from livings in their family's gift, to which they were presented long before they could enter the priesthood (if they ever bothered to do so). Their parishes meanwhile were served by vicars, some zealous and learned, others with as much latinity as they could pick up as altar-boys. They existed on pitiful stipends, 'at least ten marks if the resources of the church suffice' (though this is better than England, where the minimum was five marks). Few attained the level set at Oxford in 1222, of being able 'at least to pronounce the words of the canon of the Mass and the baptismal formula, and have an intelligent notion of what they mean'. Few could preach a sermon (indeed this was one of the attractions of the Franciscans and Dominicans; they could, and did).[9]

Some with a little learning made dangerous use of it. The priest of Inverkeithing was caught instructing young girls to dance round a phallic symbol during Easter week,

> himself capering like an actor, with songs, inciting all who watched to join in obscenity with shameless words ...

until proceedings were brought to a close by a scandalised burgess, who knifed the offender in his own churchyard. Predictably this was noted by the Lanercost Franciscan, whose cold eye also fell elsewhere; under the year 1268 he reports

> a sickness called *Lungessouth* went about the herds, and certain vile men, cloistered in dress but not in spirit, taught the fools of the country to make fire by friction of wood, and set up Priapic images to make the beasts pass under them, which a layman did before the hall-porch of the Cistercians at Fenton [Barns] ... The lord of the place claimed innocence because this was done without his knowledge, adding, 'Besides, until this month of June my cattle were well while others sickened and fell, but now mine are dying by two and three so that few are left for the summer work'.[10]

Such reversion to ancient ways could be found throughout Europe. Men of education were drawn away from country districts, and the parish teinds, which should have paid the priest's stipend and the upkeep of the chancel, instead supported the laird's younger son at Bologna. It was fortunate that many Scots parishes had stout little Romanesque churches with thick walls and a barrel-vault; the chancel was the priest's responsibility, the nave and churchyard were the congregation's. Unless there was a rich patron, or the priest had private means, the building might not receive much maintenance though it was the centre of the community. Vividly painted all over the inside, and with its carved doorway picked out in red and yellow on the outside, it could be a lively and cheerful place. There were no pews; a stone bench along the wall served for the old and weak who could not stand throughout a service.[11]

Those whose parish church was the nave of a monastery or cathedral had something other churches lacked; they had choirs, or at least could hear the singing from beyond the screen. The music was based on the great Gregorian chant, but the basic pattern was elaborating. At least two musicians who had studied at Paris and knew the work of the choirmasters of Nôtre Dame, Mâitres Pérotin and Léonin, returned to Scotland; they were David de Bernham, Precentor of Glasgow and later Bishop of St Andrews, and the musical theorist Simon Tailler whose treatises are all now lost, but who is known to have stayed with his fellow-Dominican Bishop Clement in Dunblane.

The choirmasters had at most one large book to be shared by all who could stand around it, with symbols only beginning to show the length of notes; and one helpful instrument, a tiny organ of some two octaves, portable and played with one hand while the other worked its bellows. For church festivals tuned sets of bells, struck with hammers, might chime and a harp or viol might be admitted, but wind instruments (apart from the *orgue portatif*) were barred for heathen associations. The chant was now adorned by an upper 'discant' and still-higher *broderies*, sometimes using secular airs, the whole developing into three- or four-part motets. Brother Adam, a Cistercian of Melrose, composed many motets in honour of the Virgin which were sung by the community at their evening recreation; it was this music that Alexander II had greatly enjoyed. Perhaps the supreme example of the new-found skills is the 'Reading Round' (*Sumer is ycumen in*) with its miraculous harmonies, mathematically true yet simple enough to be enjoyed by children; and Reading was closely linked with the small priory on the Isle of May.[12]

All the new ideas stemming from rediscovered writings produced a surge of original thought throughout the West. It would be tedious to list names and dates, but one should recall, among the Dominicans, St. Albert *Magnus* the scientist, and St Thomas Aquinas; among Franciscans, Ramon Lull, St John Bonaventure, Roger Bacon and Duns Scotus (John of Duns near Kelso). New impulses in art brought not only architectural innovations but a new approach to painting, moving from the icon tradition towards perspective and landscape (Cimabue, Duccio, Giotto). Piere Cardenal, last of the Provençal troubadours, died in 1274, but Rutebeuf launched the Parisian tradition of anti-establishment satirical songs which has never ceased; the aged Sieur de Joinville dictated his vivid (and honest) memories of his Crusade, and the century was crowned by the genius of Dante Alighieri. Perhaps we have more names only because their works survive; yet consider that there are other landmarks, farther afield. Alexander Nevsky, Prince of Novogrod, Vladimir and Kiev, died in 1263; Ghengis Khan had died in 1237, Kubilai his grandson ruled in China until 1293, Marco Polo crossed Asia and returned by sea to the Arabian Gulf. Rukn-ad-Din Baibars, Mameluk Sultan in Egypt, overwhelmed the last fragments of the Crusader states; more must be said of him. Remember also that in 1252 the Great Buddha of Kamakura was completed, a technical achievement far beyond the capabilities of any European craftsmen (and one that owed nothing to the 'New Learning'). Lastly, to come down to earth and nearer home, there was Thomas Learmonth, of Ercildoune or Earlston, one of the Earl of Dunbar's knights; and Hugo Giffard of Yester, who died in 1267 after a long career of royal service, leaving a remarkable reputation as practitioner of black arts, alchemist, builder of a sinister vault (Bo Ha') which survives and is in fact the vaulted undercroft of a tower, dug into a motte-mound; here he is alleged to have kept a demon-servant (possibly a Moor or other foreigner), and here he may have conducted scientific experiments like many a Scots laird of later times.[13]

Away from courts and cathedrals, minstrels sang and peasants danced, and we can only guess at their music. In both Gaelic and French custom, the heroic epics were chanted to a musical accompaniment, and the best practitioners travelled with their own accompanists who might, where the tale required it, take part in snatches of dialogue. Teams of performers, acrobats, singers and jugglers, travelled the countryside from fair to wedding-feast. They might with luck be summoned to perform in the local castle, where also the young men of the household danced, vying against each other in high leaps and tricky footwork while the ladies sat and admired. Ladies did not dance, except in private among themselves.

No doubt some visiting entertainers found good welcome at Haddington in early summer 1267, when Queen Margaret's brothers arrived to visit her. There was no protocol for English state visits to Scotland – most such visitations had not been of a social nature – and Edward and Edmund came informally. At a guess, they would be escorted from Berwick by the Earl of Dunbar, up the coast to his red castle above its harbour. It was an easy route (Edward did not forget it). From Dunbar they would turn up the Lothian Tyne, in the lee of Traprain Law, to Margaret's manor among its orchards. Edward's great pleasure was hunting – in that he rivalled his grandfather King John – and there could be little hunting in May; just as well perhaps, for he liked to ride down his stag and kill with the sword, and if he had come later he might have been taken to Kincardine and encountered some of the big royals coming into its hunting-park. The entertainment offered can only have been a matter of riding up into the Lammermuirs for alfresco meals, playing with the two children (who made firm friends with their young uncles, and often wrote to them later), and generally enjoying a break from the pressures of home.[14]

The princes were on the brink of a momentous decision; they were about to take the Cross. It would be a risky thing to leave England together, abandoning their father to his own increasingly erratic devices. If they went, they must stay until something was accomplished; too many groups had drifted home in defeat or after petty squabbles. Someone must take command of the growing band of volunteers, including many potential troublemakers. Shared service in a noble cause might heal the scars of Evesham, but if certain hotheads went on their own they might instead join the Montforts and launch a different 'crusade', against Gascony or even against England.

They could hardly discuss it at home. Even Edward's Eleanor, with her family background, would rate the Crusade above all other considerations. Henry must be dissuaded, the journey alone would kill him (and the Pope agreed). Edward was not jealous of his young brother with the crooked back, but he could not contemplate letting Edmund reap all the glory. And if only he could persuade Alexander to come too, with a sizeable body of his knights, that would make a noble addition to Edward's army. Failing that, he might at least get the funding the Pope had granted, which Alexander so tiresomely withheld.

Alexander was not to be persuaded; but others were preparing to go, and some who had gone earlier had worthwhile advice to give. Some of Dunbar's people, for instance, had followed their old earl to Marseille, gone on to Egypt and disaster, and returned to tell the tale. Among them might have been Thomas Learmonth – though if he had travelled to southern France he probably spent his time talking to troubadours. He was now an admired poet, but he had a tiresome knack of uttering strange thoughts. Perhaps he was kept in the background during the visit.

No surviving poetry can be safely attributed to him; a *Tristan* long claimed as his is now thought to be the work of a twelfth-century Breton namesake. The long narrative *Ballad of True Thomas* is thick with later accretions, but a shadowy original glints through it. Up on Eildon, under a thorn-tree, Thomas met a lady on a grey horse – a Border gypsy or a Celtic goddess – who drew him into an enchanted country. He came back at last to the life of a country laird until, one winter night, his servants reported a pair of roe deer acting strangely outside; he walked out of a feast to meet them (they were reported to be white, but that must have been the snow on their backs) and was never seen again. He sleeps in Eildon, or in any number of other hills, coming out to buy horses against the day when his armies break from their spell. Haunting couplets survive in the *Ballad*:

> They rade on, and further on,
> They forded rivers abune the knee,
> They saw neither the sun nor the moon
> But they heard the roaring of the sea...

His lady's parting gift was an apple which gave him 'the tongue that cannot lie', an uneasy gift indeed.[15]

Edward had one last matter to arrange before he went home. He had in his party a young squire for whose safety he was concerned. The boy is nowhere named, but easily imagined; a large, brave, bone-headed youth, who simply could not grasp that his moment of glory was not to be talked about. It was his dagger that had finally despatched Earl Simon, and so he told anyone who would listen. Edward's feelings about his uncle were deeply ambivalent; he had formerly admired him, even loved him; he would never visit Evesham. He was reasonably sure that someone would eventually kill the squire, probably in circumstances of the utmost embarrassment for his master; to take him on Crusade would offer a hundred opportunities. The perfect solution was to ask Margaret to take the boy into her household, and to tell the young man that he was there as Edward's own deputy, to protect her.[16]

With that weight off his mind he rode homeward. The brothers took the Cross together at midsummer, when the Legate preached in Northampton. Henry was already making plans for Alexander and Margaret to visit him at York; he may have hoped Ottobuono could persuade Alexander to join the expedition, but in the end arrangements took too long and the Legate left England before the State Visit could begin. By then all Europe knew that a Crusade was desperately needed; on 18 May the Sultan Baibars captured Antioch, and was poised to swallow the last Christian footholds on the coast of *Outremer*.[17]

Chapter 17 Notes

1   Powicke, 535–6; Labarge, *St.L.*, 202.

2   Powicke, 558–562; *Fordun* LIX. See pp.25, 86 above.

3   *Fordun* LIX; delegates, Watt, *Fasti Ecclesiae Scotticanae Medii Aevi*, (second draft, Scottish Record Soc., 1969), and *ib.*, *Biog.* 280 and 456. Pr. Thomas was judge-del. in *Reading Abbey vs. Adam*, (*Sel. Cases* no. 58).

4   Alexander at Berwick, *Hdlist A. III* nos. 67 (13Apl.) and 68 (16 Apl.). Easter was 8 Apl., the Legate's Council 23–25 Apl. Stow, *RRS I*, 246; 1194 dispute, *RRS II*, 289; *CM* 44. Manor and raid, Watt, *Biog.* 214, Abbot Robert, pp.42 and 121 above.

5   Royal and other foundations, App.C; Barrow, *K&U*, 77–82.

6   SS. Dominic and Francis, *Penguin Dict. of Saints*, ed. D. Attwater (1965). Scottish houses, App. C.

7   Burgh schools, *RRS II*, 373 (1195); masters, Watt, *Biog.* 446, 530; 'ferleyn', *ib.* 187, 531. Universities, F. Heer, *The Medieval World*, Mentor, 1963; Watt, *Biog.* Introd. and *passim*.

8   Anatomical dissection, condemned by both Muslim and Christian orthodox theologians, was not formally banned until 1305. For M. Scot see Lynn Thorndike, *Michael Scot*, Amsterdam 1940, and Watt, *Biog.* 490.

9   Vicars' stipends, *St.Sc.Ch.* 11 (*ca.* 1226); standards, *ib.lxxvi*, where the abysmal level of Scottish clerical education may be exaggerated.

10 *Chron.Lanercost*, 85 and 109. *St.Sc.Ch.* 26(*post* 1237), listing offenders for general excommunication four times yearly begins with 'All fortune-tellers, male and female witches, incendiaries …' perhaps meaning raisers of need-fire, an essential part of pagan Beltane ritual. *Lungessouth* is probably Husk (Scots lungsocht), a parasitic bronchitis characterised by coughing and wasting.

11 R. Fawcett, *Scottish Medieval Churches*, HMSO, 1985; *St.Sc.Ch.*, 10.

12 John Purser, *Scotland's Music*, Mainstream, 1992, is invaluable (esp.pp.49–56). Adam of Lennox, *CM* 121.

13 This 'lucky-dip' of selected medieval names is drawn from many sources including the *Penguin Dict. of Saints* (n6 above) and general works. For Giffard, pp.72, 96 above; Bo Ha', S. Cruden, *Sc.Cas.*, 104.

14 The princes' visit, *Fordun* LVIII (telescoping Roxburgh and Haddington and placing the episode after they took the Cross; but there was scant time for it after midsummer). Powicke, 686–8, for Edward's 'passion for the chase'. Kincardine Castle, near Fettercairn, now ruinous, still has deer park embankments 4.5m wide at base. Letters by Pr. Alexander and Pss. Margaret are in *NMssS,I.*

15 Sir Walter Scott, in *Minstrelsy of the Scottish Border*, provided a 'standard' text of *True Thomas* (an anglicised version is in *The Oxford Book of English Verse*; other fragments are known). A white deer (usually a doe) is a death-symbol in Celtic tradition. For Thomas's gift in operation, see p.228 below.

16 *Chron.Lanercost* 81 (misdated '1266'), and see p.192 below.

17 Northampton (24 June) and Legate's departure (July), Powicke, 562. Arrangements for York, *CDS I, 2482, 2483* (14 June); s/cs, *ib. 2486* (2 Aug.). For Baibars, and *Outremer* (the general term for the Crusading lands, lit. 'Oversea') see next chapter.

A Saracen herding Crusader prisoners towards 'Babilonia' (Cairo). The scene illustrates the first battle of Mansourah, 1221, and continues at p.194.

1268–1270: Easterly Winds

THE YORK VISIT of September 1268 was a low-key affair with few political undertones. Annandale, the Doorward and John Balliol were all present, and each took home some grant or grace. Alan was exempted from tallage on his Derbyshire estate (this was a tax levied from the royal demesne, a stop-gap until the English *parlement* allowed the first general taxation of laymen since 1237). Bruce obtained leave to sell some forfeited lands back to their former owners. Balliol redeemed corners of Hastings lands which interlocked with his (or rather Devorguilla's, for they had been assigned long before to the Chester heiresses). He had scant enjoyment of these gains, for he died within a month; Henry ordered his officials to deliver her heritage to the widow, 'of special grace'.[1]

Margaret had her own requests; for her elderly treasurer, the Northumbrian William Swinburne, she obtained lifelong freedom from jury-service, and freedom from attendance on sheriffs for as long as he remained in her service. (Such obligations carried penalties for absence, very burdensome to Englishmen working abroad). It was proper for her to arrange favours for a senior member of her household, but she backed other petitioners too. It was probably she who won a writ to investigate the plundering of merchants by 'evildoers near Whitby'. The victims were Hugh Bone Broc and his partners of Douai, and Thomas of Carlisle, John le Flemeng, and their partners of Newcastle; their ships had carried 'divers wares from Flanders to Scotland for profit'. The Bone Broc or Bonebrok family, John, Hugh and Philip, are later called 'the Queen of Scotland's merchants' when given leave to shelter in English ports and to export Scottish goods overland through England at need, despite a general ban on Anglo-Flemish trade.[2]

Exactly what is meant by 'the Queen's merchants' is unclear. It was every queen's duty to help her country's trade. Her household was a magnet wherever she travelled, sellers of fine textiles and imported delicacies brought her their best samples, and long sessions of admiring rich silks and tasting exotic sweetmeats gave perfect opportunities to gather news. How was trade with Spain now, and what was the word from the Baltic fur-markets? Had the Fair of Champagne been as successful as ever? An intelligent woman could learn things about distant places that her husband's envoys might never report.

Margaret was now in her prime, 'a woman of great beauty, chastity and humility – qualities that seldom meet in one soul'. She had a happy relationship with her husband (surprisingly so, considering the traumas of their early days): and she exercised great influence over her father and brother. Her life was, however, shadowed by a deep private grief; it is impossible that she was never pregnant between 1264 and 1272, her twenties, but there is no record of a live birth. In that respect her contemporaries could rate her a failure in her primary duty.[3]

She was beloved, she was accessible, she learned of distant wonders. The 'gryphon's-egg goblets' and silver-mounted 'cups of nut' on her table were visible proof of the travellers' tales, though some tales were a little garbled. Joinville, interrupting his narrative of campaigning in Egypt, considers the Nile:

> Now this river is different from all other rivers, for the further they flow, the more little brooks fall into them ... but this river comes all in one channel into Egypt and then throws out seven branches that spread through the land ... Before the river enters Egypt, people who are accustomed to do so spread nets in the river at night; when morning comes they find in their nets such goods as are sold by weight, ginger, rhubarb, wood of aloes, cinnamon. And it is said that these come from the earthly paradise, for the wind blows down the trees in paradise as it does in our own land, and it is the dry wood of paradise that the merchants sell us.[4]

The scope of trade was enormous. Goods from India and beyond came through Egypt to meet Venetian ships in Alexandria, where also caravans from 'the South' brought Sudanese gold. Other caravans came up to Tunis and Algiers from Timbuktu and the Niger kingdoms, which in turn had links with Great Zimbabwe and Kilwa. Barcelona was developing its *entrepôt* commerce to outflank the Muslim kingdoms of southern Spain, founding its *Consulado do Mar*, launching marine insurance. Genoese merchant houses had depots along the Black Sea coasts, hampered but not abolished by Mongol disruption; when the storms of these invasions slackened the merchants travelled into the Mongol Empire, to Sarai on the Volga where they met the northern arm of the Silk Road. Along that road, duly impressed by its security, its chain of official rest-houses, its horses waiting saddled to carry the Great Khan's commands, went envoys from popes and kings, even some private venturers. The brothers Maffeo and Niccolo Polo took that route, returned with letters, and set out again with Maffeo's teenage son Marco, in the 1260s (Marco would return eventually in a Chinese ship to the Persian Gulf). Few people still believed the earth was flat; some seriously doubted if Jerusalem was really the centre of the world, despite the map-makers' insistence. They did believe the Equator was a ring of fire, beyond which God did not wish men to go; it was living near the flames that blackened African skins. Only at the end of the century, when the last crusading footholds were lost and Mediterranean trade was crumbling, was there a fresh impetus to explore. Three Genoese merchants, Teodosio Doria and the brothers Vivaldi, equipped a couple of their redundant galleys and sent them off around Africa; but they did not return.[5]

At York they talked of matters nearer home. Henry was obsessed with the Crusade, chiefly with problems of funding it. Queen Eleanor kept a shrewd eye on the activities of her brother-in-law Charles. He and Beatrice had at last attained the coronation she so desired. She had entered Rome in a blue-velvet-lined chariot, but had not long enjoyed her new status, for she died in 1267. Charles no longer needed her driving ambition; he had greater plans than Sicily, nothing less than the replacement of the Greek Empire with an Angevin empire of the Mediterranean. There were a few hindrances still to clear up; one fell into his hands in August 1268.

The last lawful heir of Frederick II was his grandson Conradin, reared in the safety of Bavaria among his mother's people. Early in 1268 and aged sixteen he led a small army into Italy where he found considerable support, patriotic, anti-Angevin or emotional; the golden boy and his gallant band contrasted vividly with Charles's grim materialism. They met at Tagliacozzo in the Abruzzi, where Conradin came close to victory, but not close enough; within weeks he was hunted down, given a show-trial, and publicly beheaded in Naples. The Neapolitans never forgot him, and laid part of the blame for his death upon the Pope. When Clement IV died a month to the day after the execution, all could see the Finger of God.[6]

Clement had been a good friend to Charles, yet his death gave the King of Sicily new advantages. He could easily ensure there would be no speedy papal election; Clement's French cardinals opposed any Italian, their colleagues wanted no more Frenchmen. Louis IX, appalled at Conradin's brutal death and shaken by hints of Charles's ambitions, now tried to divert him into better ways with a conclusive onslaught on the infidel. He could not even carry France with him; Joinville was among those who stood firm:

> Much was I pressed by the King of France and the King of Navarre to take the Cross. To this I replied that while I was overseas in the service of God and of the King, the sergeants of the King of France and of the King of Navarre had ruined and impoverished my people, so that to all time I and they would be the poorer for it. And I told them that if I wished to do what was pleasing to God I should remain here, to help and defend my people; and if I put my body in danger in the pilgrimage of the Cross, while seeing clearly that this would be to the hurt and danger of my people, I should move God to anger, Who gave His body to save His people.

I held that all those who advised the King to go on this expedition committed mortal sin; for at the point at which France then was, all the kingdom was at good peace with itself and with its neighbours, while ever since he departed the state of the kingdom has done nothing but go from bad to worse.

Great was the sin of those who advised the King to go, seeing how weak he was of his body, for he could bear neither to be drawn in a chariot nor to ride. So great was his weakness that he suffered me to carry him in my arms from the mansion of the Count of Auxerre, where I took leave of him, to the abbey of the Franciscans. And yet, weak as he was, if he remained in France he might have lived longer, and done much good, and many good works.[7]

Joinville was not alone. Richard of Cornwall, bringing his new wife Beatrice of Falkenberg to England, met his son Henry and the Lord Edward going to concert plans with King Louis; he refused to support or to join them. The young men duly met Louis, received funds from him, and promised to join him at Aigues Mortes by 15 August 1270. Edward expected to lead a noble company, including his brother and cousin, his father's half-brother William de Valence, the Earls of Surrey and Gloucester, John de Vesci, Roger Leyburn and many more. Gaston de Béarn, whose daughter had just married Henry of Almain, would join them in Gascony. All that was needed now was more money.[8]

Some volunteers had not waited for the great expedition. Earl Adam of Carrick was already in Acre; the Earl of Atholl set off in April 1270, followed by three Mowbray brothers from Scotland and by Devorguilla's second son Alexander, whose wife was a Savoy kinswoman of Queen Eleanor. The wives were not being left; headed by Edward's Eleanor, sometimes taking small children, they set out with enthusiasm.

These details illustrate some of the troubles that beset the crusading movement. There were always those who rushed ahead, impatient of planners, and others who went *en famille* as if to a festival. What the grim remnants of the eastern states needed was a disciplined army, seasoned and strongly led, able to stand the climate and resist the pull of conflicting interests. The last strongholds of *Outremer* squabbled continually, Hauteville lords of Antioch against Ibelins of Beirut and Jaffa, Templars against Hospitallers, Venetians against Genoa or Amalfi. While the Sultan was steadily mopping up the outer ring of castles, the High Court of Jerusalem met in Acre to determine the disputed right to the throne of a city none of them could visit. The Military Orders all had their private pacts with individual emirs and Italian traders; they had sunk vast sums in castle-building, men and horses were acclimatised, they were the true professionals. The last thing they needed was a swarm of disorderly amateurs, arriving full of ignorant zeal, setting about the first Arab they saw regardless of whether he carried a Templar safe-conduct or was delivering stores to a Teutonic Knights' castle. The wretched incomers were nothing but trouble, succumbing to fevers brought on by ignorance, demanding rescue from the consequences of their own head-strong actions.

In every Crusade there were misfits seeking an outlet for violence, greedy adventurers dreaming of quick wealth (most people thought every Saracen rode into battle loaded with jewels), others escaping from domestic discord, some exiled for unpardonable crimes. There were aged men hoping for a last-minute remission of sins, and young men fired with zeal, burning to die in the best of causes. Many had only the vaguest ideas of what they would find to do, or expected to see the golden towers of the Heavenly Jerusalem rising above the landing-place. Edward did his best to learn the problems ahead of him; he would find all these and more awaiting him.[9]

There were many elements to study. Louis had been greatly heartened, at the outset of his first expedition, to receive envoys from a Mongol general:

> While the King was sojourning in Cyprus, the great king of the Tartars sent messengers with many good and gracious words ... he signified that he was ready to help the King conquer the Holy Land and deliver Jerusalem from the hands of the Saracens. The King received the envoys in very friendly fashion, and sent other envoys in return, who remained away two years ... two brothers of the Order of Preachers, who knew the Saracen language, and could show the Tartars what they ought to believe.
>
> The Tartars come, being there created, from a great plain of sand where no good thing would grow ... They put raw meat between their saddles and the lappets of their clothing, and when the blood is well pressed out, they eat it quite raw ...
>
> With the King's envoys returned others from the great king of the Tartars ... saying; 'a good thing is peace; where peace reigns those that go about on four feet eat the grass of peace and those that go on two feet fill the earth ... thou canst not have peace save thou have it with us. For Prester John rose up against us, and such and such kings' (and he named a great many) 'and we have put them all to the sword. So we admonish thee to send us year by year of thy gold and silver, and thus keep us to be thy friend' ...
>
> And you must know that it repented the King sorely that he had ever sent envoys to the great King of the Tartars.[10]

Despite his disappointment Louis sent again to investigate rumours that the 'Tartars' (as he called the Mongols) were about to convert. He learned that at best they were heretical Nestorians, at worst shamanists with a tinge of Buddhism. The Great Khan was indeed willing to eradicate the Muslims, and intended to do so, but he insisted that the chief of the Frankish tribe, with his priest whom he called 'pope', must come and pay homage. In Runciman's words, 'the Mongols did not recognise that independent states could exist'.[11]

The Mongol empire extended from the Caucasus to China, where a younger brother of the Great Khan, named Kubilai, was steadily conquering the remnants of the Southern Song Empire. In 1257 a Mongol army sacked Alamut, the Persian headquarters of the Ismaili sect called Assassins (literally, 'hashish-eaters'). Louis, disillusioned with Mongols, switched his hopes to the Ismailis whose leader, the Old Man of the Mountain, was offering him an alliance; he had already sent useful intelligence about Mongol movements. Louis' envoy was shown ancient Christian apocryphal writings in the library of Masyaf, the Lebanon castle which replaced Alamut as the Old Man's base. The sect was hostile to orthodox Islam, ready to oppose the Mongols and well-disposed to Christians; Masyaf paid tribute to the Hospitallers of Krak. They seemed promising allies; their private practices need not concern the French, and they frightened the opposition above all else. They had even frightened the great Saladin in former times.

The Assassins had a magic potion which they gave their novices, admitting them to an Earthly Paradise; from this garden the young men were snatched away, to be told that they could return for life by doing the Old Man's will. If they died fulfilling it, they would go straight to Paradise itself. Primed by further doses they killed anyone the Old Man might direct; in 1192 they knifed Conrad of Montferrat on a street-corner in Tyre; in 1270 they were hired by the Sultan to eliminate Philip de Montfort. (In 1272 they had a rare failure, when the Lord Edward brained his attacker with a three-legged stool; but he was ill from the stab-wound for months).[12]

In 1258 the Mongols overran Baghdad and killed the last Caliph. In 1260 the lords of *Outremer* sought help from the Sultan, whose army included a commander named Baibars. The troubles of *Outremer* centred on Baibars for as long as he lived, and it is time to discover more about him.

The Mameluk guards of the Sultans of Egypt were recruited afresh in each generation, originally from Turkish and Circassian children given as tribute, latterly (when the Mongols interrupted the supply) by purchase. As they had no family ties and were wholly dependent on their masters they were considered totally trustworthy, a *corps d'élite*. Though the flow of recruits lessened, the rule held that no Egyptian child, not even a Mameluk's son, might join. The slave-markets were well supplied by the results of Mongol raids, the trade often handled by Italian merchants. Around 1225 a Mameluk emir nicknamed *al Bundukdar*, 'the Crossbowman', saw a boy in the Homs market. He had already been rejected by the local Emir as too coarse for domestic service, but he was a sturdy youngster, brown-skinned and blue-eyed, a Kipchak Turk from somewhere between the Don and the Volga. The Mameluk bought him and gave him the name of *Rukn-ad-Din*, Supporter of God. By the time he was old enough to join the Guard he had acquired the byename of Baibars, 'the Panther'.

His abilities were recognised in 1244 when he led an army to Gaza which overwhelmed a Christian force with allies from Homs and Damascus at La Forbie (Herbiya). In 1250 he took command at Mansourah when the initial charge of French cavalry killed his general, and destroyed Louis' whole Crusade by trapping the horsemen in the narrow alleys of the town. In 1260 he was at Acre with his Sultan, Saif ad-Din Qutuz, being feasted by its Christian garrison which had invited them to confront the Mongols (who had taken Damascus and Sidon, sent columns against Gaza, and were demanding the surrender of Egypt). Baibars pointed out to Qutuz that Acre itself could easily be taken while they were there, but the Sultan preferred to tackle the job in hand. At Ain Jalud, Goliath's Well, in Galilee, they did just that, inflicting their worst defeat on the Mongol army; but Qutuz sealed his own fate by refusing Baibars the reward he asked, the governorship of Aleppo. On the return to Egypt, during a hunt, Baibars killed Qutuz and rode into Cairo as its new Sultan.

Saif ad-Din was not the first Sultan to be killed by his guards. The last descendant of Saladin was murdered before the eyes of Louis and his fellow-prisoners after Mansourah; Baibars was present, but not among those who waved bloody swords at the captives, demanding rewards for killing their enemy. In the first years of his reign he was content with minor raids, taking Nazareth in 1263, Caesarea, Haifa and Arsuf in 1264. In 1266 he won Safed from the Templars, gaining mastery of all Galilee, while sending an army against Armenia. In 1268 it was the turn of Jaffa and the Templar strong-hold of Beaufort; that May he descended upon Antioch. The ancient city had endured the longest siege of the First Crusade, its capture the greatest triumph until the Christians reached Jerusalem itself. Its garrison in 1268 was too small to man the vast perimeter; it fell in four days. The massacre was appalling, the loot incalculable, the slave-market hit rock bottom. The Templars immediately abandoned all their northern inland castles, and two isolated enclaves remained to the Franks in Syria.[13]

This was the background of disaster against which the Crusade assembled. Mercifully for the English princes, their father's zeal was diverted to the fulfil-ment of his longest-cherished project.

In summer 1269 the rebuilding of Westminster Abbey reached the point where the new shrine of St Edward the Confessor could be erected. Henry had taken over the project from the abbey monks back in 1220, planning works, having the shrine designed by his own goldsmith, assembling jewels (which had frequently to be sold or pawned as time passed). The Abbot brought Italian craftsmen to lay a mosaic pavement beneath the shrine; Henry had already had new tombs made for the bones of his Saxon predecessors around the sanctuary. In a last-minute scramble the altar had to be finished in gilded wood with painted 'jewels' (doubtless intended to be replaced, though it never was). On the Saint's feast-day, 13 October, Henry with Edward and Edmund, and Richard of Cornwall, carried the relics amid splendid ceremonial to their new resting-place.

Margaret and Alexander were present, having come, in Henry's words, for 'solace and recreation and to attend the feast'. For Henry it was the culmination of his life's work. He had meant the ceremonies to be even greater, with a second coronation followed by a coronation-banquet; the date was close to the fifty-second anniversary of his accession, and circumstances had prevented any fiftieth commemoration. Great preparations were undertaken by all those with traditional duties at coronations; on the eve, it became apparent that there would be a confrontation between the citizens of London and Winchester, both claiming the right to carry wine at the feast. The whole 'coronation' was hastily cancelled. The Londoners, who had spent a great deal on robes and cups, and who had suffered considerably for their support of Earl Simon, attended the service out of reverence for their Saxon saint, but went home straight afterwards. They were not the only ones offended; Boniface of Savoy, the old Archbishop of Canterbury, was too frail to attend, and the Archbishop of York thought fit to have his cross carried at the head of the clergy procession. The other bishops promptly staged a sit-down-strike, remaining in their stalls throughout the service.[14]

It was Margaret's last meeting with her family. Edward was to sail in June next year, first to Gascony and thence to Aigues Mortes, Louis' crusade-base near Marseilles. Even in October there were signs of trouble; Gloucester absented himself to stir up trouble in Wales. He declined Edward's offer to arbitrate, and made it clear that he would not be going on any Crusade. Gaston of Béarn also failed to turn out, while Edmund had to wait at home and raise his own funds, Edward having taken all that had been collected for their joint expedition.[15]

Long before Edward reached Aigues Mortes a fearful disaster overwhelmed the movement. Charles of Sicily, unwilling to waste time on his brother's idealistic notions, persuaded Louis that the Emir of Tunis was ready to embrace Christianity. A North African base would be invaluable; it could be supplied direct from Sicily, it would remain of practical value long after the Crusade had succeeded (indeed it would, for Charles); a landing at Tunis would force Baibars to march west, lifting the pressure on Acre. Louis could not resist his youngest brother pleading so excellent a cause.

The French fleet left Aigues Mortes on 1 July 1270 and reached Tunis after seventeen days. Far from welcoming it, the Emir strengthened his walls and kept the force on open ground outside. Sickness broke out in the summer heat; on 3 August a young French prince died (he was John Tristan, born at Damietta in 1250 while his father was a prisoner). His brother Philip, the heir of France, lay at death's door; hundreds succumbed to fever and dysentery, nobles and soldiery alike, among them the Earl of Atholl and many Perthshire men. Early on 25 August, as Charles was sailing in, Louis himself ended his life.

Edward only left England on 20 August, learning of Louis' death at Aigues Mortes. He got to Tunis in November as the survivors were packing up to re-embark. Charles, who had accepted a handsome indemnity from the Emir, invited Edward to pass the winter with him in Sicily while the new King of France escorted his father's body homeward. It was a dreadful end to an expedition of such high, if ill-directed, hope.[16]

Chapter 18 Notes

1 Alan, *CDS I, 2492, 2493* (24 Sept.). Consent to Bruce's assignation of lands and rents forfeited by Robert of Hilton, Walter Fauconberg (married to a Cumberland Bruce), and John de Meaux, worth in all £1063. 6. 8d and returned to them for £1000 in rents &c., *ib. 2489* (15 Sept.). Balliol redeems 10 librates in five named areas, *ib. 2488* (same day). Devorguilla to have heritage, *ib. 2501* (21 Oct.). Chester heiresses, p.7.

2 Swinburne, *CDS I, 2493, 2495* (24 Sept., 'at instigation of Q. Margaret'). Merchants, *ib. 2496* (– Sept.). John le Flemeng already had compensation for part of his house, removed for the moat of Newcastle, *ib. 2430* (1267). Bone Brocs also *ib. 2615–6–7* (July 1271). For Q. Margaret and merchants see *ib. 2020,2257,2656.*

3 *Chron. Lanercost,* 97, and see p.192 below for the younger son, David, b. 1273.

4 *Joinville,* 182.

5 Routes &c, I. Cameron, *Lodestone and Evening Star,* Hodder & Stoughton, 1965; M. Collis, *Marco Polo,* Faber 1950; G. Jackson, *The Making of Medieval Spain,* Thames & Hudson, 1972; E.H.Byrne, *Genoese Shipping in the 12th–13th Centuries,* Cambridge Mass., 1930 (names, charters, cargoes).

6 Runciman, *SV,* 92–112, 118–135. Conradin (1251–68) was the son of Conrad K. of Jerusalem, p.62 above, and Elizabeth of Bavaria. Pope Clement died 29 Nov.

7 *Joinville,* 320.

8 Young, *R of C,* 141; Powicke, 576–7. Louis gave Edward 70,000 *livres Tournois,* 25,000 of which were to be passed to Gaston de Béarn. Beatrice of Falkenberg was reputedly a great beauty; a statuette in the Burrell Collection may be a portrait. (Richard had made his own Crusade in 1241).

9 Runciman, *Crs. III, passim*; see A. Throop, *Criticism of the Crusade,* Amsterdam, 1940, and Bedier & Aubry, *Chansons de Croisade,* Paris, 1909 (contemp. comment and protest songs, with tunes).

10 *Joinville,* 168, 253–9; Runciman, *Crs. III,* 260. The opening contact came from the Mongol governor of Mosul.

11 Runciman, *Crs. III,* 280, 293–8, for embassies.

12 Runciman, *Crs. III, passim.*

13 Runciman, *op. cit*; *bundukdar* was also used = 'Venetian'. *Baibars,* given as = 'Panther', is not in any dictionary available to me. And see *Crs. III,* 226, 310–14, 317 *inf.,* 324–5; *Joinville,* 221–3.

14 Powicke, 570–6; S/cs, *CDS I, 2542* (6 Sept.).

15 Powicke, 577–581; Young, *R of C,* 146–7.

16 *Joinville,* 320–4; Labarge, *St. L,* 238–244; Runciman, *Crs. III,* 291–2.

1270–1273: Kingship and Law

KINGSHIP AS a political institution reached a peak in thirteenth-century Europe. It rested on ancient foundations, buttressed by the Church, adorned with the gleam of chivalry, but retaining the sense that a king was the person-ification of his people rather than their figurehead. In long-established kingdoms such as France and Scotland, personal contact with the head of state was not a privilege for the few but a kind of tribal bonding-right. Belief in the kinship of king and people was not entirely fictional; the feudal lords who carried out the king's orders might descend from the hireling swordsmen of some bygone chief, but the king was a *nativus*, as much bound to the soil as any serf.

It followed that the king would give the sort of help one was entitled to expect from a kinsman who embodied justice. Ailred's picture of David I 'sitting at the hall-door wherever he lodged' to receive petitions is matched by Joinville's of Louis IX holding open court in the public gardens of Paris. Twelfth-century philosophers, including John of Salisbury, wrote that in the last resort it was no sin but a duty to kill an unjust king.[1]

Earlier Scottish kings did not assert laws, rather they chaired a committee of elders who interpreted customary rules to meet the need of the hour. From David I onward these interpretations were committed to writing with the formula *Statuit dominus Rex*, 'The King laid down that ... '; these statutes incorporated archaic principles, as that an unsatisfactory judgment must be appealed instantly, before the aggrieved party 'turned his toes where his heels had been'. Central to all Scots law was the criterion of contract, the main-spring of pre-Christian Irish laws believed to have had St Patrick's endorsement. Every case, civil or criminal, rested on a question of contract made or broken, between men, between man and woman, subject and ruler, man and God; every breach incurred penalties graded according to the status of both parties as well as the gravity of the offence. Intention was a degree of performance, assistance (in modern terms, 'art and part') was proportional. William the Lion's statute on 'Homicide committed in revenge' states:

> If a man accused of theft dies of the Ordeal, or if justice is done to him according to the law of the land, or he is killed in possession [of stolen goods], and if his

friends avenge his death by killing the person who brought him to justice, the King shall have full right against such persons as being in the fullest sense breakers of the King's peace, and no mercy or remission shall be given them except by consent of the family of the man so slain. And if the King, unaware of the dead man's kin, should grant protection to his killers, nevertheless the family will be entitled to exact vengeance.[2]

Law-courts, even those staffed by graduate professionals, still preferred oral to written evidence, understandably, given the blithe resorts to forgery and the problems of testing a document that few witnesses could read. The matters brought to court ranged over every aspect of life, not forgetting road-traffic offences:

Anyone riding through a village and trampling a pedestrian in front of him shall pay *cro* and *galnes*, but if the horse backs and kills someone behind him only the fourth part of the horse's value is payable, to the relatives of the deceased or to the sheriff. For it has been ordained that 'every horseman must keep the forefeet of his horse from doing harm, but people who stand behind a horse should beware'.[3]

Feudal tenure added its share of complications, as did the growth of hunting-forests under William the Lion, necessitating a whole new body of forest laws covering tree-felling, admission to grazings, and the pursuit of game:

If a freeman with hunting-rights over his own land looses his greyhound and it chases a beast into the King's forest, he may follow as far as he can cast his leash or his horn, and if the hound takes the beast within that distance he may carry off the prey, but if he go far into the forest he shall forfeit the hound and pay eight cows. A greyhound found running loose shall be impounded by the forester and sent to the King or to the Justiciar of the Forest. If a mastiff be found with a broken chain its owner is quit, but if it lacks a chain he shall find six guarantors [for his court appearance], whatever his standing may be. Any earl, bishop or baron coming to the King may pass through a forest and take one or two beasts, and if the forester be not present let him sound his horn, that it be not said to be furtively done. Likewise returning let him do the same.[4]

Scots forest law was less draconian than English versions, but all hunting rights were assumed to be the King's unless he granted them to a subject (his Highland kindred considered themselves to have family rights to 'a salmon from the river, a stag from the hill, a stick from the wood', as they still do, and a wise king did not push into awkward corners). A case brought before Alexander II shows the range of a royal grant and casts more light on conventual life at Melrose. David I gave rights in Eskdale to Robert Avenel, who gave the ground to the abbey, reserving the hunting. His grandson Roger fell out with the monks over the extent of rights reserved. The King and his Council ruled that Roger might take stags and hinds, boars and sows, he-goats and she-goats (so feral goats were around), and protect the nests of hawks and falcons. The monks must not 'maliciously interfere' with eyries or trees where hawks nested, until after the breeding-season. Charges of trespass must not be brought against persons looking for strayed cattle or sheep, or engaged in other lawful pursuits by day or night; if taken in any offence they must be handed over to monastic officials. Roger could employ foresters to protect the birds; the monks must not 'hunt with packs or nets, bring visitors to the hunt, or set snares except to trap wolves'. Roger's activities must be without fraud or evil intent, and without damage to the monks' crops; the monks could erect sheds and buildings.[5]

There were efforts to protect salmon stocks and to prevent the blockage of waterways by weirs or nets. William the Lion forbade fishing from vespers on Saturday until first light on Monday; a statute entitled *Defensio Aquarum* (with penalties of imprisonment, suggesting a later revision) sets a close season for salmon from 15 August to 11 November and forbids taking *salmonunculi* (smolts) in weirs or milldams from April to June. Similar arrangements were made in 1269 for Northumberland and 1279 for Cumberland, with local conservators and a ban on small-mesh nets 'as in past times'.[6]

No Scot will be surprised to learn of a dispute over peat-cutting. In 1262 a case in Peebles Sheriff Court went to the King for verdict. The burgesses accused Robert Cruik of having

> cut and broken peats and prevented them being brought home, and he has impounded a horse worth four shillings and a load of heather worth one penny. They further declare that the said Robert has built his house on common land and ploughed the common pasture of Peebles.

Cruik was in deep trouble; not only had he damaged peats laboriously cast and dried, he had impounded a horse (when at most he was entitled to sue its owner if the animal strayed on to his ground); he had stopped someone bringing in thatching material; finally he had committed purpresture on land granted to the burgh by royal charter. It sounds as if he might have been a stranger cozened into buying a non-existent building-plot by some smart operator. Again we meet the jurors; Archibald and Clement of 'Hopkelioc', Roger and Michael of Kidston, Alexander of Winkston, Richard the farmer and Roger the gardener, Archibald of Hundleshope, Adam of Stobo, Thomas the smith, Richard Godardsson, Gauri Pluchan, William and Walter, shepherds, John Modi, Robert Gladhoc, Cokin the smith and Adam Hacksmall.[7]

Such were the good-ganging pleas of the nascent Time of Peace. Alexander had other concerns; early in 1270 his envoys sought a re-grant of Huntingdon. How it had been lost is not stated; presumably it was involved in the general forfeitures after Evesham, either through administrative error (the Hastings family had extensive holdings within the Honour), or because Henry felt Alexander had failed to help him. The state of England made all decisions difficult, and there was little point in harrying the muddled old man; the matter was left in abeyance.[8]

Later that year Henry suddenly offered to pay two thousand marks of Margaret's dowry (a change from 1265, when he had questioned if there was anything due). Unfortunately payment depended on Llywelyn giving 4000 marks under a peace-treaty which the Welshman repudiated; so nothing reached Scotland. Soon afterwards Henry fell seriously ill, still talking of joining his sons in *Outremer* even as he wrote imploring Edward to come home. By next spring, convalescing, he abandoned all thoughts of his vow, left financial business to his Council, and accepted £10 a month 'in parcels of pennies' to distribute as he chose.[9]

Overseas news continued bad, and at home the effects of the long papal interregnum were piling up. No bishops could be enthroned without a Pope's endorsement; Albinus of Brechin and John of Glasgow were dead, their chosen successors waited in vain. Nicholas of Moffat, re-elected to Glasgow, died unconsecrated. He was replaced by Mr William Wishart, for whom the delay proved fortunate; before he could be installed a greater prospect opened.

At the end of April 1271 Bishop Gamelin ended his life at his manor of Inchmurdo where he 'had lain long in sickness'. Wishart, who had served the diocese well as its senior archdeacon, was elected to replace him, and a Mr Robert Wishart, Archdeacon of Lothian, was chosen for Glasgow. When Robert of Ross died later that year and Matthew or Macchabeus, succentor of Fortrose cathedral, was elected, five of the eleven Scottish sees had bishops-elect.[10]

It must have been soon after Gamelin's death that Scotland learned of a distant tragedy. The survivors of the Tunis *débâcle* were moving slowly through Italy, bearing King Louis' bones and escorted by Charles. In March at Viterbo they found the cardinals still deadlocked over a successor to Clement IV. The new young King of France, Philip III, and his uncle, spent some time trying to find a compromise candidate, in line with Louis' known wishes. With them was Henry of Almain, despatched by Edward to stiffen the English government during King Henry's illness (Edward himself was going to Acre). Guy de Montfort was now Charles's deputy in Tuscany, and came with Simon his brother to report on his administration. Henry of Almain had Edward's instructions to bring the Montforts back into peace, if he could, but he had no chance to exercise his diplomacy. On 13 March an armed gang, headed by Guy and Simon, rushed into the church where Henry was praying after Mass and stabbed him before the altar, wounding a priest who tried to shield him. The sacrilege, in the near-presence of two kings and of the great dead, shocked all who heard of it.[11]

Edward reached Acre on 9 May, too late for memorable deeds. Baibars had just taken the great Hospitaller castle of Krak, after a five-week struggle gate by gate and tower by tower, sending the surviving knights under safe-conduct to Tripoli in tribute to their courage. Over the next year Edward's company was whittled down by sickness and warfare – Roger Leyburn among them – while he mourned the cousin he thought he had sent to safety. His grief and anger over Henry's murder preoccupied him for years as he sought revenge, and punishment for the killers.[12]

In Scotland Alexander still had to deal with unrest in the Isles and western seaboard. King Dugald, the leader of anti-Scots resistance, had died in 1268; it may have been a son of his, reputed 'son of the King of Norway', who led rebellion in Ardnamurchan, an area claimed by Dugald's MacRuaraidh cousins (but settlers of Norse descent may also have resisted assimilation). Islaymen were used to put down the rising; tradition claims their leader was Angus Mor's youngest son Iain 'Sprangach', but as his next brother had been with a nurse seven years earlier, tradition may be confused.[13]

Trouble of another kind arose in Ayrshire, and brought Alexander to Dumfries that August. News had come of Earl Adam of Carrick's death in *Outremer* (he had gone out ahead of the main body, despite Melrose's note of his death at the end of a page of 'war news'). Countess Marjory, his young widow with a baby daughter, faced the possibility of a second arranged marriage, and took her own steps. Her mourning did not preclude all normal activities; out hunting, she met her neighbour Robert Bruce. This was Robert *le Jeon*, Annandale's son, always overshadowed by his heroic father; Annandale himself was on Crusade, having gone out with Prince Edmund. 'Young' Robert, then around thirty, was temporarily his own master in 1271; Marjory was a few years younger. Fordun (calling her 'Martha' and making her Earl Adam's daughter) is a trifle prim:

> When they had saluted each other with kisses, in the fashion of courtiers, she begged him to stay and hunt and stroll about; seeing him somewhat reluctant she drew him back with her own hand, if it may be said, and led him, not very willing, to her castle of Turnberry. There for fifteen days he dallied, with his followers, and secretly married the Countess, unbeknown to friends and well-wishers, and without any leave from the King. When this came to King Alexander's ears he seized Turnberry castle and all her lands, and took recognisances of all her goods; but by the intervention of friends' prayers, and payment of a sum of money, Robert obtained the King's goodwill and all the domain. From which marriage, by Divine providence, he begot a son, the future saviour, champion and king of the battered Scots race, as the course of history will show ...[14]

The reaction of Robert *le Noble*, when he returned, is not recorded. He had made no match for his eldest son, but soon after he got home he himself married the widow of his crusading companion Adam of Jesmond, adding wide Cumberland estates to his Scottish and English possessions. He was sixty when he went to the Crusade, and had another quarter-century before him. His grandsons were to prove better chips of the old block than their downtrodden father ever was.[15]

In September 1271 the cardinals at last agreed; Tedaldo Visconti, Archdeacon of Liège, was leading the Flanders contingent in Acre when he learned that the choice had fallen upon him. Taking time only to send two friars with the Polos to Kubilai Khan, and to preach a farewell sermon on the text *If I forget thee, O Jerusalem*, he left for Rome and enthronement as Gregory X. He immediately called for reports on current opinions of the crusading movement and planned a General Council to discuss all the views and criticisms. As returns came in, there was little to encourage him.[16]

The winter of his accession was bitter; Melrose calls it 'severe and cold'. There had been great floods in the Borders; Devorguilla's eldest son, Hugh, died, and the Northumberland escheators wrote off two of his four mills on the Tyne, 'totally swept away by the water'. A dry spring and broken summer brought 'great drought on land and unfruitfulness in the sea, in Scotland, England and France, and a murrain of man and beast, and stormy weather' with houses blown down and buildings struck by lightning, 'especially the church of Arbroath'. With bad news from *Outremer* came sorrows at home; Edward's eldest son John, aged five, died in his great-uncle's care in August. In December Richard himself suffered a stroke which left him dumb and half-paralysed; he continued indomitably attending to business, but died in April 1272, in his sixty-fourth year. His reputation was founded on diplomacy and financial shrewdness, but a few contemporaries would remember him as a young soldier strolling unarmed over a bridge in Gascony to set up terms for his brother's army to withdraw before superior French forces. His death left affairs of state to Queen Eleanor and the officials, for Henry had virtually ceased to reign.[17]

In January 1272 Alexander was dealing with a tiresomeness in Northumberland, where a dispute over grazing rights between an English manor and one of his North Tynedale holdings had been inflated in the English Council as 'intrusion by the King of Scots' bailiffs and servants'. The ground was shared common; Alexander, agreeing to a perambulation, hoped the inspectors would be equally drawn from his lands and the others, had ordered his people to assist, and enclosed a letter of consent from his chief bailiff William Swinburne, the heritable tenant involved. It was a small thing, but he wanted no friction.[18]

Even more did he want his bishoprics filled; administering all those vacant sees laid burdens on his staff. In April yet another vacancy was caused by the sudden death of Richard of Dunkeld. There were rumours of poison, Lanercost alleging that the culprit confessed to selling his potion far and wide, with a 'full phial left yet in the kingdom'. (For good measure the chronicler links the poison with the Queen's death, three years later). He also claimed that

> because in that kingdom the goods of a vacant bishopric devolve to the King, [Richard] and another named Robert de la Provendie, Bishop of Dublin [sic, for Dunblane], gave away all their goods when death approached, making a virtue of necessity so that they left scarcely anything to satiate the royal greed.[19]

The unwary reader or listener might be led to think such things befell only in Scotland, whereas there were few, if any, kingdoms where temporalities did not escheat to the Crown. The Dunkeld election gave Mr Robert Stuteville his chance at last; he hastened to join the queue at the Curia. The Wisharts were before him; Lanercost is discreet about Mr Robert (who was probably still around when that section of the chronicle was penned), but he lets himself go on the older man. William, he says, was elected to St Andrews 'as through the eye of the needle', obtaining a dispensation for consecration 'by the grace and piety of King Edward. How he carried out his office, it happens that for good reason I shall not trouble to set down'. (Some journalistic techniques are of long standing). He reports Pope Gregory 'swearing by St Peter that if he had known he would have to deal with such allegations he would never have sought to be Pope', and proceeds to the tale of the new bishop's first pastoral visit to an outlying parish. It had a poor vicar (poor in pocket and morals alike), who had been censured for his domestic arrangements. He was suspended on the eve of the visit, and went weeping to his woman whom he blamed for his misfortunes. She replied briskly, 'You leave this bishop to me'. Next day she crossed his path as he arrived, laden with poultry and eggs which she let fall as she curtsied. Wishart kindly asked her name and her errand, to which she answered guilelessly,

> 'Please your Honour, I'm the priest's wench and I'm begging round the neighbours for the makings of a decent meal for this new bishop that's coming, to make a show for my poor man's sake.'
> Stricken in conscience and captivated, he took his way to the church, and meeting the Vicar bade him prepare to celebrate Mass; he answered that he could not, for he was suspended, but he was absolved with outstretched hand. Mass completed, the Bishop hurried from the place as if silenced.

The chronicler does not add, as he might have done, that Mr Wishart held twenty-two benefices at his election, not does he attempt to untangle the numerous young Wisharts obtaining Church advancement in the next generation. Certainly he omits to mention that Bishop William completed the nave and west front of the largest cathedral in Scotland.[20]

On 16 November 1272 Henry III died, frail and confused, in his palace of Westminster. He had ruled, or others had ruled in his name, longer than any English monarch until George III; Fordun gives him a handsome obituary:

> *Vir grandaevus Henricus, rex Anglie pacificacissimus*, [*sic*] the very old Henry, most pacific King of England, having ruled his realm through fifty-six years with the highest peace and justice, migrated to Christ.

He was buried in the grave from which the Confessor's body had been removed. The funeral was over before the news could reach Scotland, and Margaret, loving daughter though she was, could not go to her mother because she was expecting a child.[21]

Nine years after Prince Alexander, the son born on 20 March 1273 was named David. In April his father went on pilgrimage to St Cuthbert's tomb at Durham, to give thanks to his own birth-saint and to pray for the child and his mother. Margaret was unwell, mourning her father, fretting over her brothers, slow to recover from her 'time of peril' (as her mother-in-law had described her own pregnancy). In early summer the Queen's household moved to Kinclaven, a large castle twelve miles upstream from Perth. It overlooks the junction of the Ericht with the Tay, and stands within embankments protecting it from spates:

> Margaret Queen of Scotland, weighed down with this and that, deeply saddened by her father's death and anxious about her brothers' return, one evening after supper went to walk on the banks of the Tay for solace, the air being serene; her knights and handmaidens with her, and her confessor who told me about it. Among the rest was a squire who, as I have said, had been commended to her by her brother. As they sat on a ridge of the bank he went down to wash his hands, muddy from playing. As he half-lay there, one of the girls, incited by the Queen, ran and gave him a push into the water. Delighted and treating it as a joke, he said 'What care I? I can swim better than anyone.' As he splashed about with everyone applauding, suddenly he felt the current sucking him down, and began shouting for help. The only person to respond was his little servant-boy, who was playing nearby and who ran up and jumped in; in a moment both sank before the eyes of all. So the enemy of Simon, Satan's satellite, who claimed to have been the means of sending that knight to perdition, perished miserably; and the married woman, not a little seduced by family affection, had the taint of a secret love publicly exposed through her grief.

This is too much. The squire, boastful and hearty, may never have been a favourite with Margaret but he was a token of Edward's kindliness. She must have blamed herself for allowing the childish romp, for letting it get out of hand, above all for that fatal push. She would scarcely be consoled to know that, far from hurrying back to take up his responsibilities, Edward was 'saying farewell to his youth' by competing in one last tournament in France.[22]

Chapter 19 Notes

1   Barrow, *K&U*, 23 *inf.* and (Ailred) 41. Labarge, *St L*, 25–8, 174; *Joinville*, 149–151; John of Salisbury (d. 1180), qu. in G.Leff, *Medieval Thought from St Augustine to Ockham*, (Penguin, 1958),126.

2   Appeals, *QA* 13, 'Falsing of Dooms'; Irish laws, J. Cameron, *Celtic Law*, Hodge, 1937. Revenge-killing, *Reg. Maj.* IV, 17 (Ass.Wm.15). The distinction between wrongs against the State, pardonable by the King, and a wrong against kinsmen, continued in later laws of assythment (abolished in 1976). See *Reg.Maj.*II.56, 'Restitution of Felons', the King may remit penalties but must not infringe others' rights.

3   *Reg. Maj.* IV. 24 *Cro* and *galnes* are blood-fines, assessed in cattle.

4   *APS I*, Ass.Wm., 10.

5   *Sel.Cases* no.31; *APS I*, 408; *NMssS I*, XLIX. The eyries provided young birds to train for falconry.

6   *Defensio Aquarum,APS I,Fragmenta Collecta*. English 'byelaws', *CDS I, 2538* and *CDS II,146*.

7   *Sel. Cases*, no. 59; jurors, *CDS I, 2313* (6 Nov.1262); horse, see *QA* 48. The range of Peebles jurors' occupations is noteworthy (they must all be freemen).

8   *Fordun LXI*; Barrow, *K&U*, 156.

9   *CDS I, 2580* (2 Nov.1270, endorsed 'Cancelled as he received nothing'). Powicke, 582; Young, *R of C*, 148.

10   Watt, *Fasti Ecc. Scot. Medii Aevi*, (2nd draft, Sc.Record Soc.1969) and *Biog.* 7, 214, 385, 400, 585, 591. Mr Robert, called William's *nepos*, was either his son or a son of John Wishart of Conveth (p.72 above). See Watt, 583 *inf.*

11   Runciman, *SV*, 162–3; Young, *R of C*, 150–1; Powicke, 608–9.

12   Runciman, *Crs.III*, 333–4.

13   A. & A. MacDonald, *Clan Donald* II, 146–7 (Inverness, 1896), translating the byename as 'the Bold' (not in my four Gaelic dictionaries; perhaps misreading of *sreangach*, 'stringy, lean', since Gael. byenames are commonly uncomplimentary). *Celtic Review* X, no. 38(1915) gives traditions of expeditions 'to oust the Norsemen, ca. 1270'.

14   *Fordun LX*. The daughter prob. married Sir Thomas Randolph (son of Thomas s.Ranulf, a confidential clerk of Alexander II), and became the mother of Robert I's Earl of Moray; (Barrow, 'Problems').

15   Robert *le Noble*, 5th of Annandale (1210–1295) married as his second wife Christian of Ireby (d.c.1305) widow of (1) Thomas Lascelles and (2) Adam of Gesmuth/Jesmond.

16   Runciman, *Crs.III*, 338–9; text, Psalm 137,5.

17   Weather, *CM* 123, *Chron.Lanercost* 86, *Chron.Pluscarden* VI, xxviii('1272'). Hugh Balliol, *CDS I, 2600* (10 Apl.1271). Prince John, and Richard, Young, *R of C*, 152. For Richard's truce at Taillebourg, 1242, Powicke 199–200.

18   *CDS I, 2627* (7 Jan.1272,Kinross); the disputed common lay between the manors of Langley and Staworth.

19   *Chron.Lanercost*, 97 ('1275'; Robert de Prebenda died 1284). The chronicler is working

up to a general denunciation of Alexander. (p.222 below).

21 *Chron.Lanercost*, 84, 92–3; Watt, *Biog.* 590–5; *ib.*583 *inf.* for James, Robert (Bp. Glasgow), Thomas, and William (2). St Andrews Cathedral, Cruden, *Churches*, 92 *inf.*

21 *Chron.Lanercost*, 90–1; Runciman, *Crs.III*, 338; Powicke, 603. *Fordun* LXI('1273'); the funeral was 20 Nov., Powicke, 588–9.

22 Alexander at Durham, *CDS II,1* (22 Apl., misdated '1272'); to Q. Eleanor about amercements by English foresters of his Cumberland tenants. Kinclaven, Cruden, *Castle*,30. The drowning, *Chron.Lanercost*,96,*CM* 141; (and see p.174 above). Edward's 'farewell', (July),Powicke, 613.

See p.175. 'Chorasmii' (Turcomans) and Saracens rout the Crusader army, even the Templar standard bearer (at right, with furled banner).

1273–1275: The New Broom

EDWARD'S ACCESSION proceeded smoothly; the administrators who had kept England running while the old King drifted away, were issuing letters in the new King's name while they sent him news of Henry's death. He came slowly homeward, visiting Paris to give homage to Philip III for (among others) the lands newly fallen to him, under the Treaty of Paris, with the childless death of Alphonse of Poitou and his wife. There, too, he consulted with London merchants and took them to meet the Countess of Flanders at Montreuil, where he settled a long dispute and re-opened the cross-Channel wool trade; while in Gascony he launched detailed surveys of rights and dues, as well as refurbishing the Castile alliance.[1]

The Countess of Flanders was a formidable old lady. Her father had been proclaimed Emperor of Byzantium by the leaders of the 1206 Crusade (Baldwin, the late co-Emperor, had been her cousin); she had outlived two husbands and two sons, and her remaining interest was her youngest son Guy. For him and for herself she claimed an English pension which Henry denied (or was unable to pay), and she then began arresting his merchants. From 1270 the wool trade to Flanders required the purchase of special licences, which damaged the fortunes of English flockmasters more than Flemish weavers; the Exchequer lost export duties, and Cinque Port ships were authorised to intercept Flemings at sea — an order they gladly interpreted in the widest possible sense.[2]

In November 1273 the English chancery issued a writ for the barons and bailiffs of Winchelsea to investigate the case of three Aberdeen merchants, Thomas Ker, John of Aberdeen and Walter de la Bothe, attacked off Yarmouth,

> while on a voyage to St Omer with wool and other goods. John Adrian of Winchelsea took 56¹/₂ sacks of wool, 5¹/₂ dacres of hides, 150 salmon, 200 oak boards, a trussel of deerhides, lambskins and much other merchandise which he still detains at Winchelsea, besides beating and mistreating the merchants and their servants so that some lives were despaired of. They have sworn on the Gospels that the goods belong to themselves and to other Aberdeen merchants and that they were shipped there, and no subject of the

Countess of Flanders is concerned. The King orders restitution without delay, with freedom to take the goods anywhere except Flanders.

A second writ went to the bailiff of St Augustine of Canterbury's abbey at 'Garesendene', where Henry Kenteys held twenty-two sacks of wool and other goods taken from the same three merchants 'at sea off Garesendene'. The luckless voyagers got no satisfaction until after the coronation, when a terse letter 'at the King of Scots' instigation' informed the Keeper of the Cinque Ports that he personally was in contempt because the goods had not been recovered.[3]

There were other troubles afloat. In April 1272 a Lincoln jury considered the case of Adam, son of Richard of Bedford, captured 'in the company of sea-robbers' and beheaded in Scotland, at the north end of Berwick bridge. He was held to have committed no felony in England, so his widow received his estate – a house worth three shillings and four pence and waste land worth £1, with 'a cellar which was his, and the solar above, which was not'.[4]

Two larger executries ground their way through English courts. The vast estates of the late Earl of Winchester had still to be apportioned between his heiresses (he was thrice married, but had no son). His last wife was Eleanor Ferrers, daughter of a former Earl of Derby who had taken Winchester's oldest daughter (by Devorguilla's half-sister) as his second wife. Eleanor had been married off to Roger Leyburn in her widowhood, part of his reward for saving King Henry at Evesham; the Derby family was then in deep disgrace and could not protest at the disparagement. Leyburn died at Acre, leaving Eleanor to sue and be sued by a step-mother who was also her step-daughter, and by two other daughters of de Quincy's first marriage, the Countess of Buchan and Lady de la Zouche. The Leyburn heirs claimed lands that should have formed Eleanor's terce; Devorguilla joined the debate as did the heiresses of Winchester's brother Robert de Quincy. All the ladies travelled to Scotland in pursuit of their rights, leaving attorneys to continue their English campaigns; all could be trusted to oppose every settlement. Eleanor's own death in 1274 merely produced more counter-claims.

Devorguilla was the principal executrix of her husband, a business only marginally less complicated since it involved John's brother Eustace (dead on Crusade, leaving a litigious widow), and John's son Hugh who had died soon after him. Both Hugh and his next brother Alexander married kinswomen of King Henry, who had kept up pressure for prompt settlements. Alexander Balliol was at Acre when Hugh died, and hurried home with a letter from Edward seeking remission of succession-duty (it was granted, but did not prevent Edward, when King, pursuing him for the debt). In parts of England inheritance was divided by lot, elsewhere by apportionment; it all made prime entertainment for the older ladies while severely overloading the courts.[5]

At last it became known that Edward was coming back; the Mayor of London met him in Paris to discuss coronation plans, and sped back to attempt a cleansing of the city. There would be a fortnight's feasting for all comers; Westminster Palace was redecorated, with temporary halls and kitchens erected wherever there was room, and huge quantities of food were assembled. Edward landed at Dover on 2 August, entered London on 18 August, and next day was crowned.[6]

Both his sisters were there with their husbands. Fordun believed they brought the children:

> The King of Scocia with his queen and children made a special effort to attend … with many lords.[7]

Possibly they brought the Prince of Scotland, then aged ten, but it must seem probable that Margaret and the baby David remained with their grandmother. Queen Marie was still active, though her visits to France appeared to have ceased (it was a weary journey). She had a hand in the choice of a 'governor' for her elder grandson, for the appointment went to a kinsman of her own. His name was William de St.-Clair, a veritable Norman unlike many 'Norman barons' brought into England and Scotland by earlier kings. Possibly he came in Marie's marriage-train, to join cousins established in Scotland for a century. He became Sheriff of Haddington, Linlithgow and Edinburgh in the year of the Prince's birth, and in 1279 was given the barony of Roslin.[8]

The Lanercost chronicler says nothing of children at the coronation (and he had an informant in Queen Margaret's household):

> There came together the great ones of the land, with innumerable people, to show their magnificence in many ways because of the favour of the new king. But the lord King Alexander of Scotland, who was there with his wife and a company of nobles, exceeded all others in the greatness of his bounty and gifts.[9]

Alexander may well have ridden south bracing himself for demands of homage and the re-opening of old disputes, but nothing marred the great occasion. Edward had begun a careful examination of all his rights and obligations, and only when that was complete would he move to fulfil them. While Alexander was with him, he ordered a report on

> whether Alexander King of Scotland and his men of Penrith and Salkeld were wont to have common pasture in the park of Plumpton enclosed by King Henry, and if so by what metes and bounds; and if they have *husbote* and *heybote* in the King's forest of Inglewood, or *estover* in the same, and at what time and of what kind.[10]

Later that autumn the Barons of the Exchequer were ordered to 'certify the balance due to the King of Scots of the £5000 [*recte* 5000 marks, £3333.6.8d], granted at the marriage of Margaret the King's sister, that the King may do right concerning it'. In November £175 was paid for Alexander's normal corrody in attending the coronation, but no trace remains of any further dowry payment; conceivably, the sum had been reached in slow instalments over the years.[11]

Edward was struggling to sort out the tangled finances of his kingdom, a task made worse by the load of debt he had brought home with him. Endless disputes raged over the affairs of those who had died in *Outremer*, those who hoped to recover forfeited estates for loyal service at Acre, those who had only funded their Crusade by pledging lands dubiously acquired during the 'disturbance' (as the Montfort era was officially known). There were also Crown debts from those years:

> The King commands the Barons of the Exchequer to allow the executors of Eustace Balliol, formerly Sheriff of Cumberland and Keeper of Carlisle Castle, £200 against his debts, besides £304.14.11d for the keeping and munition of the castle during the war and disturbance in the kingdom, and in knights' and sergeants' pay, namely two knights at two shillings daily, a sergeant with a barded horse one shilling, two esquires at sixpence each, nine crossbowmen on foot at threepence, thirtysix archers on foot at twopence, from the close of King Henry's forty-seventh year to the feast of St Lucy in the forty-ninth year [October 1264 to 13 December 1266], one year and seventy days; and for the expenses of Hugh and Guy Balliol and other knights, divers sergeants with barded horses, foot crossbowmen and archers, at different times coming in aid of the munition of the castle; and for fifteen archers on foot for twenty-five days after St Lucy's, while Eustace came to Court to deliver the castle; of all which he rendered account to the late King's Wardrobe, as attested by Eustace's rolls long ago transmitted by the late King to the Exchequer. And after allowance of the £200 they are to enrol the £304.14.11d, unless allowance and enrolment have already been made by the late King's writs to Eustace or his executors.[12]

These outlays were for a castle which had not stood siege nor suffered assault; the cost of manning others may be imagined. Many years of peace would be needed to heal the scars.

Alexander could feel reasonably satisfied. Edward was buckling down to work in a sensible way, bringing order where chaos had long flourished. When he got to the matter of Huntingdon he would no doubt settle it fairly, there was no point in pressing the matter. It had been a curious experience to attend an English coronation, stirring memories of a different ceremonial a quarter of a century before.

All the rulers of Europe, including of course Edward and Alexander, were invited to the Pope's General Council opening at Lyons on 7 May. Only King James of Aragon turned up; Pope Gregory was deeply hurt by his friend Edward's absence. (He had even planned his coronation to clash with the opening ceremony, and though the coronation was delayed, the new King was too busy to return across France). The Council ended in July, giving the English bishops just time to hurry home. The bishops of Argyll, Glasgow, Ross and St Andrews were also present (Macchabeus of Ross took ill and died at Lyons). The main aim of the Council was to promote Christian unity and proclaim a new Crusade; it declared the reunion of the Greek and Latin Churches, and announced the Crusade, but both acts were largely illusory. Some new canons were added to Church Law, another Crusade tax was imposed (a tenth of clerical incomes for the next six years). A ban on arms sales to Saracens and a command that no Christian ship should enter a Muslim port merely raised a few eyebrows in Genoa, Venice, Pisa, Amalfi and Barcelona.[13]

Alexander wrote next to Edward to inform him that he had consented to a widowed heiress marrying a Northumbrian knight; he was then in the Highlands, on a hunting trip, and had no councillors to witness the letter. The kingdom's business went quietly forward; the Countess of Buchan accepted her share of the Quincy lands, including the manor of Southoe near Eynesbury, with its 'garden, vineyards and fishpond', but could not travel to give her homage because she was pregnant. Both Alexander and Margaret wrote to obtain a delay for her.[14]

One subject the royal ladies must have canvassed when they gathered in London was the choice of a bridegroom for young Margaret. The Princess was fourteen; by that age Queen Eleanor and her eldest daughter had both been married several years. But even when they put their heads together it was difficult to find a bridegroom. The royal houses of France, England and Sicily were far too closely related; the Spanish kingdoms offered no obvious candidate, Hungary was dreadfully far away and Russia was worse. (Besides, as far as they could recollect, there was no hopeful name there). The new Emperor, Rudolf of Hapsburg, was already married. Charles of Anjou was snapping up bridegrooms for his many daughters wherever his ambitions could be advanced. There were Irish dynasties older even than the Scots one, but to consider them would incur Edward's opposition; besides, they were allied with Alexander's uneasy subjects in the Isles.

Queen Margaret was in no hurry to send her daughter into exile. Later, perhaps, a Scots earl's son might be considered, or Alexander could confer an earldom on a native suitor; he had Gowrie, the Garioch, and Moray dormant in his hands. Time would tell; she wanted Margaret with her.

In February 1275 the Queen was in Fife when she became seriously ill.

There were rumours of poison. The trouble, whatever it was, quickly proved fatal:

> This year died Margaret, Queen of Scotland and sister of the King of England, a woman of great beauty, chastity and humility ... When she was taken ill many abbots and bishops came to visit her, to all of whom she refused entry to her room; nor, after receiving the sacraments from her confessor, did she allow conversation with anyone until her soul's departure, unless perchance her husband happened to be there. She left three children, Alexander and David and a daughter Margaret, who all after a short interval followed their mother, for the sins, as is believed, of the father.

Thus Lanercost; Fordun says only that she died on 26 February in Cupar castle and was buried beside King David in Dunfermline. By sad coincidence the same year saw the death of her sister Beatrix.[15]

Margaret was almost thirty-five, and had been Queen of Scots for over twenty-three years. Her gentle and loving influence over her brother endured for some years more. Henry III had maintained a chaplaincy for her in St Margaret's church in Westminster, which Edward renewed immediately after his coronation. In May 1275 he ordered the restoration to Alexander of 'all lands taken into the King's hands on account of the death of Margaret the King's sister, to be held saving the rights of the King and others'. Apart from Sowerby, which Alexander gave her, there is no record of any English lands assigned to her.[16]

Alexander, a widower at thirty-four, mourned her for ten years (if we discount Lanercost's insinuations). The record is silent on his movements that spring; May found him at Berwick, in August he was in Elgin. From there he went quickly to Roxburgh, on news of trouble in the Isle of Man.

It began over the election of a new bishop. Richard, the St Andrews canon, died in March. The Cistercians of Furness in Lancashire had held the right of election to Sodor and Man since the days of Olaf Bitling; Alexander, not wanting the choice vested in English hands, changed the procedure:

> The abbot of Furness went to the King of Scotland and claimed his right ... the King received him with courtesy and deceived him with false promises, but with guile and treachery positively commanded the clergy and people of Man, on pain of grave peril, not to dare to receive anyone elected by the abbot and convent of Furness. The clergy and people of Man agreed upon the election of a bishop and unitedly appointed Master Gilbert, Abbot of Rushen; but the King, contrary to canon law, annulled this election and intruded a Master Mark, brother of the Bailiff of Man, and immediately sent him with letters from himself and letters extorted from the clergy and people, with their seals, to his metropolitan the Archbishop of Trondhjem in Norway, to be consecrated.

At that time Godfrey, the son (but not legitimate) of Magnus the former King of Man, landed in Man with some ships. … Some rejoiced and received him, some turned about and were aggrieved; but he soon subdued all to himself in fear and affection, and in the end they all universally and unanimously appointed him their prince. So he came to the fortress and took it, for the keepers had fled …

But when the King of Scotland learned that the people had conspired with Godfrey … he was very angry, and caused more than ninety ships to be collected, with a great army, from Galloway and the islands. The leaders were John de Vescy, a great baron in England; John Cumin, Justiciar of Galloway; Alan fitzCount, Alexander fitzJohn of Argyll, and Alan fitzRother … The Manxmen, unarmed and naked, could not resist the slingers, ballistaries, archers and armed men, and fled with Godfrey their king. And the others pursuing them cut them down and slew both man and beast, sparing not for sex or place. Godfrey with his wife and some followers escaped to Wales. The enemy despoiled Rushen abbey and the monks, and sent them away almost naked. Then perished miserably all the nobles and captains, and also the rest of the people whose number no one knows. And thus was the land destroyed and despoiled, and the armies retired, returning to their ships.

That was the view from Furness. Lanercost has another angle, and a date:

On 7 October the fleet of the King of Scotland entered the port of Reynaldway [Ronaldsway]. At once Sir John de Vesci and the King's nobles with their army went up into St Michael's Isle, the Manxmen being ready for battle with Godred Magnusson whom shortly before they had made their king. The magnates and captains of the King of Scotland offered the bond of peace to Godred and the people of Man, offering them the peace of God and of the King of Scotland if they would desist from their most stupid presumption and surrender their king and nobles. Godred and his perverse advisers not agreeing to the proposals of peace, next day before sunrise, when yet darkness covered the earth and the hearts of foolish men were darkened, a battle was made and the wretched Manxmen fell miserably, turning their backs.[17]

The list of leaders is informative. John de Vesci, newly home from Crusade, was William the Lion's grandson and held his mother's dowerlands in Scotland while his elder brother had the ancestral estate of Alnwick. Both brothers had been fervent Montfortians; John, having made his peace, is unlikely to have served Alexander without Edward's approval (he was at the English Court in June 1275). 'Alan fitzCount' is Thomas of Atholl's son, of 'Dunaverdin' notoriety; Alexander 'fitzJohn' is Ewen of Argyll's son, 'Alan fitzRother' can only be Alan MacRuaraidh his cousin. The impressive fleet is explained by the presence of these island lords. It would suit Edward well to have Man under Scots control rather than available for piratical support of Welsh rebels or attacks on supply ships to Ireland, (where the Vesci family had considerable interest, as lords of Kildare).

It was after this belated 'conquest' that the Prince of Scotland was designated Lord of Man.[18]

One Argyll ship missed the expedition. In July she put into Bristol for stores and trade, and met a hostile reception:

> [Alexander] has learned that men of a baron of his, Alexander *de Ergadia*, touching at Bristol, have been arrested on suspicion of piracy. As proof that they are his liegemen he names Master Alan the steersman, and Gilfolan Kerd [*Ceard*, craftsman] ; he does not know the other men's names as yet. He begs King Edward to cause the bailiffs of Bristol to permit them freely to depart to Scotland with their goods.[19]

She was still detained that autumn, when her release is one of a list of requests, annotated with Edward's decisions. The ship's cargo is there valued at 160 marks; her release is granted 'as it seems right'. Other items reveal a gradual hardening in Edward's attitude; Alexander asks for the wardship of Henry Hastings' lands within the earldom of Huntingdon, as freely as his predecessors held them by their charters; 'let him show them'. He seeks a decision on the manor of Whitley (in Cumberland, according to an earlier entry; the editor confuses it with a Nottinghamshire namesake), in dispute since 1262; 'let him show the same'. He asks about a hundred acres or more of his land, taken into the hunting-park of Plumpton, and the enclosure of land at Morton where the men of his Cumberland manors had common with their 'swine all year, in wood or plain or lawn, except in the fence-month'; 'it appears to have been enclosed of old, as the King had the right to take animals of the King of Scotland found in the lawns' (forest clearings). A reference to the £5 daily allowance on visits to the English Court draws the response, 'He comes not at the King's mandate but to do his devoir'. For all these petitions Alexander (routinely) asks justice, grace and favour, and concludes with three requests for his subjects. Firstly there is the Argyll ship; then he seeks the release of a Leith burgess, arrested at Hull for a debt owed by John Comyn to two York merchants; ('Let him be delivered, as seems just'). Lastly he seeks confirmation of King Henry's charter of trading-rights to the burgesses of Berwick; 'the King will do what is fitting'.

It was not an entirely satisfactory outcome, and it boded ill.[20]

Chapter 20 Notes

1   Powicke, 589,593–4,613–14. Alphonse was King Louis' third brother, married to Jeanne of Toulouse. They both died on the way back from Tunis. France, p.117.

2   Young, *R of C*, 137; Powicke, 616 (settlement).

3   *CDS II*, *9,10* (10 Nov.1273); *ib.20* (28 Aug.1274). A sack of wool held 24 stone (approx.

152 kg.), a dacre contained 10–12 hides; a trussel is a bundle. 'Garesendene', identified in CDS index as 'in Kent', may be Gorleston, which had a house of Austin Friars (OS Monastic Britain map, Southern sheet).

4 CDS I, 2646 (inquiry after 17 Apl.1272); the 'robbers' were presumably captured at sea and brought ashore to judgment.

5 Quincy inheritance, CDS I, 2360 (1264) and passim to 1280; p.47. Eleanor Ferrars' father, E.William, died 1247; her brother E.Robert lost everything after Evesham (Powicke 524–6). Balliol inheritance, CDS I, 2505 &c. Eustace Balliol's widow Helwisa Levington was herself an heiress (CDS I, 2665 inf.) Alexander Balliol, CDS I, 2644 (16 March 1272) and ib. II, 118 (Easter Term 1278).

6 Powicke, 616–17.

7 Fordun LXI.

8 St.-Clair, p.33 under Dreux-Coucy; and Barrow, 'Problems', 102 (also The Scottish Peerage, 'Earldom of Orkney'). William as Sheriff, ER I, 32–3; Roslin and Inverleith granted, Hdlist A.III, nos.127(14 Sept.1279) and 131 (8 Apl.1280).

9 Chron.Lanercost, 96.

10 CDS II, 17 (27 Aug.1274,Windsor); husbote is timber for house repairs, heybote is fencing-wood, estover for repairing tools.

11 CDS II, 25, 33.

12 CDS II, 31 (25 Oct.1274); a 'bard' is horse-armour (padding &c). Note CDS I, 2035, for report on ruinous state of Carlisle at Nov.1255.

13 Powicke, 615, Runciman, Crs.III, 341, SV 180–5. Lyons was an Imperial city, not French.

14 NMssS I,63; Hdlist A.III, no.91; CDS II, 23 (23 Sept.1274). Christiana, widow of Walter Lindsay, married Walter Percy of Keldale (n18 below). Southoe and other lands, CDS II, 36 (3 Dec.1275); homage deferred, ib.40 (5 Feb.1275).

15 Chron.Lanercost, 97 (see p.177 above); Fordun, LXI. Margaret and Beatrix, 'ladies of greatly renowned and very beauteous youth', Flores Historiarum, in SA, 382 n4. 'Poison', p.191 above.

16 CDS II, 22 (14 Sept.1274) and ib.44 (3 May 1275). The chaplain's annual fee was £3. St. Margaret's, Westminster, is ded. to St.Margaret/Marina of Antioch, presumably the Queen's patroness.

17 See App.A. Annals of Furness in SA, 381–3; Chron.Lanercost, 98.

18 John de Vesci at Westminster warranted payment of Walter Percy's fine of 80 mks for marrying without leave (CDS II, 52, 14 June 1275). His nephew-heir's widow held one-third of Sprouston in terce, June 1297, and lands at Crail from her mother, a Beaumont (CDS II, 863,865). For the other leaders see Man & Isles, p.2; Alan, p.48 above. 'Lord of Man', Hdlist A.III, no. 171 (conf.grant of two Manx churches to Whithorn, undated).

19 CDS II, 55 (15 Aug.1275, Elgin).

20 Whitley ('Weteley', 'Wheteley') near Alston, CDS I, 2307 (13 June 1262). Alexander to Edward, CDS II, 63 (Michaelmas Term 1275). Leith is not among the burghs shown in App.B. (Its charter is much later, despite this reference to a 'burgess').

1275–1280: Keeping the Peace

EDWARD FACED a struggle to restore his distressed and debt-laden kingdom. He must establish respect for the law, ensure that Crown revenues were fairly assessed and duly rendered, sort out the confusion of forfeitures and claims arising from the troublous years. He had often been irked, sometimes infuriated, by muddle and waste; now he must put all that to rights. Even in his wild youth he had a reputation for clear judgment; he was increasingly called to arbitrate in disputes, and was earning a European reputation as upholder and interpreter of laws. The Montreuil agreement was a shining example.

In its aftermath he tackled the evasion of export duties. His first plan, to restrict outward trade to a handful of supervised ports, quickly foundered; his new inventions, a national Customs Service and the crime of smuggling, were unmanageable while little boats sailed from moonlit creeks. He complained that sea-robbers received shelter in Scotland; Alexander assured him that he would see justice done according to the laws of his realm. Another request, to levy an Aid in Tynedale as in the rest of England, was parried because Alexander must consult his Council; he was spending Christmas quietly with his Brechin kinsmen, the next *colloquium* two months away.[1]

One subject was not discussed. Edward had grown up in the certainty that Wales and Ireland were his own (he had, after all, held them since boyhood), and that Scotland, though it had a king, was rightfully subject to England. Ancient records told of Scots homage, of boat-loads of sub-kings on the Dee at Chester; within the last century, William of Scotland had knelt to Henry II. Edward remembered Alexander being amusingly pert at York, but now that he had grown into a likeable fellow he must soon regularise his position. Tales of a Saxon king of Wessex might have small relevance to an Angevin monarch four hundred years later, Richard Coeur-de-Lion might have annulled the Treaty of Falaise in return for a handsome subsidy for his Crusade, but Edward was so sure he knew the facts that it was only when he entered himself as a competitor for the vacant Scots throne, in 1291, that he called for a search of monastic chronicles. Alexander was careful not to stimulate his interest.[2]

A new Legate entered Scotland. Boiamond de Vicci came to arrange a revaluation of church property for the latest crusade-tax. The Scots clergy sent outraged protests to the Curia, claiming that they had always enjoyed one tax-free year in seven (Fordun says 'seven years were reckoned as six', which gives the opposite sense). Alexander always resisted the export of funds, whether in barrels of pennies or as credits; he could hardly resist Boiamond, but he could support delaying tactics; 'Bagimond's Roll' took years to complete.[3]

There were more private worries. The child David, for whom Alexander had made pilgrimage to St Cuthbert, remained delicate. He had no personal governor and perhaps needed constant nursing; he lived with his grandmother, or later in Lindores Abbey, a sheltered spot on the south side of the Tay estuary. In 1276 Queen Marie undertook a pilgrimage to Canterbury; she first planned to set out in February, but was persuaded to await better weather and eventually went in autumn. Possibly, if her son's appeals to St Cuthbert had been less than wholly successful, she was going to see what St Thomas could do. Having gone so far, she carried on to France in midwinter, perhaps to present her prayers to the friendly saints of her childhood. Very probably she was also considering brides for her elder grandson, if not for her son.[4]

Such were the interlocking relationships of European royalty that almost any alliance would require a dispensation for consanguinuity, and 1276 was the worst possible year for such a thing. Gregory X died in January; Peter of Tarentaise, a Dominican from Burgundy, enthroned as Innocent V, followed him in June. Ottobuono, so effective in England after Evesham, was soon elected; he had been a cardinal-deacon since 1252 but was not a priest. Arrangements were in hand for his ordination, and enthronement as Adrian IV, when he fell ill and died in August. In September the learned Portuguese John Peter Juliano became John XXI; next May he was killed when his bedroom ceiling collapsed. Not until November did the cardinals decide on their senior member, John Caetan Orsini, who took the regnal name of Nicholas III.[5]

Among many victims of these uncertainties was Llywelyn of Wales. He was growing old, he wanted a fair peace, he lacked an heir. Long ago his pact with Earl Simon had included his betrothal to Simon's daughter Eleanor, then aged twelve; Llywelyn still considered himself bound to her. In winter 1275 her brother Amaury tried to bring her to Wales, but they were captured at sea; Eleanor became a hostage in the Queen's household, Amaury, despite his status as a papal chaplain, was held in Corfe until 1282. Llywelyn continued to offer homage at the traditional place, the Fords of Montgomery; Edward insisted on Windsor or Winchester. There matters rested until 1277.[6]

In Scotland the summer of 1276 passed with only a flutter over a Berwick ship plundered at Sutton (near Mablethorpe of evil memory). Alexander and Edward each bought horses in the other's country; soon after, Alexander wrote with news of his children and enquiries for their cousins, adding as an apparent afterthought that his envoys had verbal messages to deliver. The envoys were the Bishop of Brechin (Mr. William Comyn O.P.), Randolph the Chamberlain, and Thomas de Carnoto (Charteris), a royal clerk. Such an embassy was not going just to ask after Edward's family: they were concerned with a freak of nature. The Tweed had carved itself a new outlet opposite Berwick quays; a few acres of silt were hardly matter for dispute, and Alexander viewed the subject lightly. He was to find that Edward was outraged:

> The Bishop of Durham has shown the King that the straight course of Tweed is the March, and all land and water on this side has been, beyond the memory of man, in Norhamshire within his kingdom and the bishop's liberty; yet the King of Scotland's justices and bailiffs, with a multitude of the men of Berwick, have crossed at Tweedmouth and held courts and outlawries on land once covered by the waves, as if it were part of Scotland. Some burgesses lately imprisoned a servant of the Bishop at Berwick, to the prejudice of the Crown and bishopric. The King, having admonished the King of Scotland to rectify these matters, commands the Sheriff of Northumberland, if amends are not made, to arrest all Scots passing through or staying in his bailliary until satisfaction is given.[7]

Alexander was answering angry remonstrances for months. He sought only to maintain his frontier 'on the floodmark to the south', and sent envoys to treat 'according to the laws, usages and customs hitherto in use', insisting that 'neither now nor at any time will I do anything to injure the eminence of your majesty'. In July 1277, when English envoys appeared the day after two bishops and an earl had gone south, he hinted gently that things were getting overheated:

> From letters and verbal explanation [Alexander] learns that some have given [Edward] to understand that matters are on a different footing. Let him not be anxious or moved, nor give credence to sinister reports; the King is and ever has been ready to preserve the King of England's rights and liberties unsullied as his own, as Edward has promised to do for him.[8]

Disregarding the sting in the tail, the letter conveys a sense that Edward could have been laughed out of his anger, in days gone by. But Edward had other matters in view.

In March 1278 he informed his Chancellor:

> Our beloved brother and vassal the illustrious King of Scotland has, by a solemn embassy, offered and yielded the homage he owes us without any condition whatsoever; and we have appointed him a day at London for the performing

of it at Michaelmas next, when you shall be present, God willing.[9]

Three weeks later, having sent the latest Scots envoys home with safe-conducts for Alexander, Edward informed the Bishop of Durham that he had received the Bishop of St Andrews and Sir William Soulis, and

> expressed his will about the excesses and outrages by Scotsmen on this side of Tweed, always held to be the March. If the King of Scots and his men keep to their side of the river, the Bishop should endeavour to maintain peace.

No formal reply came from Scotland until May and then, most unusually, it was accompanied by a letter from the last envoys themselves. Wishart and Soulis had shown the safe-conducts to the Council:

> The King of Scots earnestly desires to come to the King and do his pleasure within reason; but it would greatly satisfy the people of his realm to have the usual safe-conduct of English magnates, or at least a letter from the King stating that [Alexander's] coming should not hereafter injure him or his heirs. They humbly beseech King Edward to send such a letter to the bearer, along with the safe-conducts issued by the English chancery which they return under the Bishop's seal, granting, *si placeat*, that the King of Scots shall go where he pleases in England, and that his escort may be the Archbishops of Canterbury and York and the Earls of Gloucester, Warenne and Lincoln, whom he desires to have.[10]

A startling detail hid within this document; one wonders if Edward and his Council noticed it. To satisfy, not the king, but the *people* of Scotland? How and why could that arise? It is, perhaps, the first note of a theme that was to become the *leitmotiv* of the Wars of Independence; the supremacy of the Community of the Realm. Edward did at least realise he had somehow overstepped the mark, and sent new safe-conducts in the traditional form, (at the same time forbidding profiteering in foodstuffs during the visit, though he added warily that the ban was not to form a precedent). His mind was not on Scotland, for he had invaded Wales and imposed terms on Llywelyn; he accepted the Prince's homage at Rhuddlan, and they proceeded in a glow of harmony to Worcester and the long-delayed wedding. It took place on 13 October, St Edward's day, with all the splendour Edward could devise. The Welsh wars were over, the Montfort feud forgotten; the only thing that could have added to the triumph was Alexander's presence, but he was delayed by his own *colloquium*.[11]

He left Roxburgh immediately afterwards, with the Earl of Carrick, and at Berwick met Carrick's cousin Gloucester and the Earls of Lincoln and Warenne. For whatever reason (to discount any idea of delay, to demonstrate the potential speed of a Scottish invasion, simply because he disliked slow journeyings), they raced through England at twice the normal pace.

Using Roman roads wherever possible (the only surfaces on which horses could get out of a cautious trot for any distance), they followed Ermine Street through York to Lincoln, Fosse Way to beyond Leicester. The baggage-carts were left creeping towards London, the bishops were excused attendance and made their dignified progress towards the Michaelmas *parlement*. Alexander and the earls clattered into Tewkesbury on 16 October.

Alexander immediately offered his homage; he was ready to kneel with the dust on his cloak if Edward pleased. Edward had no intention of accepting such an important submission in any hole-and-corner way. Next day at Coberley, the first halt down the Cirencester road, he issued letters patent acknowledging the offer and deferring the ceremony to London, without prejudice to the King of Scots or his heirs. Alexander was perfectly content, he knew what had to be done and he too wanted plenty of witnesses.

The kings arrived together in Westminster by 27 October, on which day Edward wrote to his northern sheriffs acquitting Alexander of attendance at their assizes 'because he is with the King'. This was a stop-gap; for years the sheriffs had put Alexander's name first on their lists of absentees, and each time he had been relieved of penalty 'by special grace'. Between Tewkesbury and London someone had reminded Edward of his father's charter to Alexander II, granting the Cumberland manors

> free of all scot, geld, aids of sheriffs and their servants, hideage, carucage, danegeld, horngeld, hostings, wapentakes, scutages, lestages, stallages, shires, hundreds, wards, warthpenny, averpenny, hundredspenny, borghalpenny, tithingpenny; and works of castles, bridges, park enclosings, and all *kareio*, *summagio*, *navigio*, building of palaces and so forth.

Edward could hardly take his stand on legal rights without admitting the force of Henry's charters.[12]

The homage ceremony took place next day. There is a narrative in the Close Roll, and another in the Dunfermline records, a fourteenth-century transcript of an eyewitness account (probably dictated by the Abbot). The first is unambiguous:

> 'I, Alexander King of Scotland, become the liegeman of Edward King of England against all men'. And the King of England received the homage of the King of Scotland, reserving the right and claim of the kings of England for the realm of Scotland when they wish to discuss the matter. And the King of Scotland straightway offered his fealty and asked that he might swear by the mouth of Robert Bruce, Earl of Carrick. And the King of England allowed it as a special grace, for that occasion. Then Robert was asked by the King of Scotland to do this, and thereupon (the King of Scotland having given him power to swear 'on the soul of the King of Scotland'), he swore fealty to the

King of England in the name of, and on behalf of, the King of Scotland, in the following words:– 'I, Robert Earl of Carrick, by virtue of the power given me by my lord the King of Scotland, in the presence of the King of England and the prelates and magnates [etc] do thus swear fealty to Edward, King of England; I, Alexander, King of Scotland, will keep true faith with Edward, King of England, and with his heirs, the kings of England, in matters of life and limb and of earthly honour, and will faithfully perform the services due for the lands and tenements that I hold of the King of England'. And the King of Scotland confirmed and ratified the fealty thus sworn and undertaken by Robert in his name and on his behalf.

The Dunfermline witness heard something more. He heard Alexander swear in words he had used at York in 1251:

'I become your man for lands which I hold of you in the realm of England for which I owe you homage, reserving my kingdom'. Then the Bishop of Norwich said, 'And let it be reserved to the King of England, if he should have right to your homage for the kingdom'. The King answered him publicly at once, saying, 'Nobody but God Himself has the right to homage for my realm of Scotland, and I hold it of nobody but God Himself'. Then Robert Bruce, Earl of Carrick, swore fealty for the King of Scotland on the King's soul, in the following words; 'So may God help me, and these Holy Gospels, my lord the King of Scotland here will be faithful to you in matters of life and limb and of earthly honour, and will keep your counsels secret'. Then the King of Scotland added, according to the form of homage which he had done above, 'for the lands that I hold of you in the realm of England'. And the King of Scotland agreed to perform the proper and customary services to the King of England for the lands for which he had done homage, reserving his kingdom.[13]

It was the Dunfermline version which reached the Curia; in 1299 Boniface VIII would remind Edward:

When also the King [Alexander] appeared in person to offer you the usual fealty for the lands of Tynedale and Penrith, he publicly declared by word of mouth, in the presence of many, in the very act of offering this fealty, that he offered it only for those lands situated in England, and not as king of Scotland for the realm of Scotland; nay, he openly declared that for that realm he ought not in any manner to offer or swear fealty to you, as being entirely free from subjection to you, and you received the fealty of this nature offered to you.

Whatever his records might state eventually, for the moment Edward had suffered public defeat. Even to admit the use of a deputy for the oath was to accord Alexander the status of an independent monarch. The celebrated Angevin temper needed a tight rein (Edward's family prided themselves on

stupendous rages, attributed to their descent from a daughter of the Devil).
The decencies, however, were observed; the kings feasted each other; Edward
rewarded Alexander's musicians:

> To Master Elyas the King of Scotland's harper, £5; to two of the King of
> Scotland's trumpeters, £2; to four minstrels of the King of Scotland, £2.13.4d;
> to two minstrels of the King of Scotland, £1.16.8d.[14]

Alexander's homeward journey took him to Barnard Castle, to condole
with Devorguilla; his namesake her son had recently died, after surviving all
the perils of the Crusade. She was left now with her youngest son, John (not
the shining light of the family), and a handful of married daughters. Still
formidably in control of all her vast estates, the old lady was growing slightly
strange in her ways. Her main interests were her late husband's hostel for
poor scholars at Oxford, and her new abbey rising on the Solway shore. She
intended to be buried there, with John's heart on her breast; embalmed
within an ivory and silver casket, it was placed before her at every meal and
served with a helping from every dish (the platters were later taken to the
hall door and given to beggars, in return for their prayers). With her in the
castle was her natural brother Thomas, Pretender of Galloway and prisoner
for forty-three years, with his wife and family. There were few reasons now
to detain the old man, but Devorguilla and some Scots lords remained nervous
about Galloway reactions to his release.[15]

Once home, Alexander kept up a steady defence of his newly re-granted
rights. Edward might order his northern assize judges to observe the charters,
specifically to admit the Steward of Scotland as their colleague on the bench,
but Cumberland and Northumberland continually raised difficulties. An old
dispute over four ploughlands on the March was resuscitated by Kirkham
Priory. A more serious situation arose when Carlisle Assize ruled that the
silver and lead mines at Alston had been unjustly taken out of English jurisdiction at some date between 1247 and 1278. The mines were said to 'harbour
many evildoers'; two English judges went there in January 1279. They found
the mines closed 'although there is ore enough to last to the end of time',
because of hindrances by the Vieuxpont family to whom the King of Scots
had granted the manor. 'The King of England should have every ninth disc
dug, each disc to be as much as a man can lift', and the fifteenth penny of
all ore sold; he should find at his own expense ' a man called *drivere* who
knows how to separate silver from lead'. At their first report Edward ordered
restoration to Alexander, but on careful examination he found the old charter
omitted any reference to the mines, which should therefore have remained
with the English Crown. A final decision, reinstating the Vieuxponts in the
manor but retaining the mining rights, was only reached after intervention
by the Prince of Scotland.[16]

A native source of silver was highly desirable (strange that it had not been missed), but Alston could hardly be back in production for the 1279 English re-coinage. Some new ore was always needed; normal wear reduced the thickness of coins, and there were those who did not scruple to pare a sliver off the edge of a worn penny. Moreover the only way to obtain small change was to cut a coin into quarters, along the lines conveniently provided by the cross on the reverse; again, a chip might not be missed. In 1279 Edward was introducing a marginal devaluation, coining 243 pennies instead of 240 from the Troy pound (12 oz.) of silver with 8% copper for strength.

A new Scottish coinage followed next year. The procedure was the same in both countries; a weight of silver was rolled into a long baton and sliced into discs, which were laid individually on a miniature anvil, the pile, bearing the king's-head design, and struck with a steel punch, the trussel, bearing the cross-and-border reverse. The Scots 'pound' was of 15 ounces and yielded 300 pennies. From 1250 in both countries the reverse had borne a cross extending to the rim, in the pious hope that the faithful would not mutilate a sacred symbol. It is worth noting that there would be no appreciable change in the value of the Scots coin until the reign of Robert I, when 315 pennies were coined instead of 300 – a curious fact in view of the troubles intervening.

The 1280 coinage brought a new portrait-head, and one welcome innovation, the minting of halfpennies and farthings (King John had introduced farthings in his Irish coinage). There was no central Mint; dies were issued to mintmasters in burghs from Ayr to Inverness, simplifying the recall of old money and issue of the new.[17]

Edward's interest, aroused by the Tweedmouth debate, led to long reviews of March law. In 1280 an appeal reached him from Henry Scot, a Cumbrian who bought a mare at Carlisle Fair only to have her claimed by John of 'Wyncheles' as stolen property. John invoked the March laws and asserted that Henry must find surety of whatever John estimated in damages 'up to £1000', or undergo judgment as if legally convicted. As 'judgment' still meant *duellum* on the March, Henry was appalled. Edward called for a full explanation; unfortunately the Sheriff of Cumberland's report survives only in a damaged form, so that we cannot tell how accurately he stated the procedures. There is a clearer text from 1249, compiled by the sheriffs of Northumberland, Berwick, Edinburgh and Roxburgh and twelve knights from either side:

> They said that if any Scots thief have stolen in England oxen or cows or anything else, and brought them into Scotland, he whose thing it is may search for it and appear in [the court of] whatever fief he finds it, and reclaim it by the oath of six loyal men and himself the seventh, lest perchance he in whose hand it

is should say it is his own, and so war might arise on the March. They said that if anyone claims horse or ox or cow or pig in the realm of England or Scotland [the possessor] shall have all the allowable delays [amounting to two months] and on the last legal day, to avoid *duellum* and realising the thing is not his own, he shall bring it to the March, and if it be a horse it shall be as well shod as on the day he claimed it; and he shall tell the other party that on examination he finds the horse is not his own, and shall drive it into the Tweed [or Solway], and if it cross the midline the defendant is quit of the charge. And if it drown, he shall compensate the other according to the custom of the March, and so for ox, cow, pig and other things, except that there is no mention of bundles.[18]

The Carlisle document states that the victim of robbery must proclaim his loss within a day and a night 'at Brunscathe on the English side or Rocheland on the Scottish', and then has forty days to find the thief and obtain a writ from the sheriff, requiring him to take pledges from the accused to appear for trial. Such archaic proceedings did not appeal to Edward. Fortunately the people most likely to deal with his queries were all experienced; Buchan, by far the longest-serving officer of the Crown, was still Justiciar, Thomas Randolph was Chamberlain, and the Chancellor was William Fraser, now Bishop of St Andrews. (The country had lost a hardworking servant with the death, in May 1279, of Bishop Wishart, the famous laugh silenced at last).[19]

In May 1280 King Magnus Haakonsson died; within weeks his young son's advisers sent ambassadors to ask Alexander for his daughter's hand in marriage. King Eirik was twelve and Margaret nineteen, but it was a royal marriage and a reinforcement of the Treaty of Perth. Margaret's opinion is not recorded; Lanercost says bluntly that 'the girl's mind was greatly against it ... it was arranged by her father alone'. Around the same time Margaret writes to her Uncle Edward in high spirits, saying she is 'healthy and happy, by God's mercy' and hoping he will keep her informed of his own health; she ends with *milles saluz*, forgetting to date the letter, but it does not read like the outpouring of a heartbroken young woman. She might even be relieved to have her future settled; everyone was trying to arrange her brother's marriage, and if she stayed at home she might have to give place to some haughty foreign princess, or accept an elderly husband who disapproved of gaiety and modern ways.

All was proceeding smoothly when a shadow fell. Young David, by then aged nine, quietly died in Lindores. His death brought 'great lamentation of the Scots, above all of the King ... the beginning of sorrows to come'. It was an ill omen for Margaret's marriage, about to be confirmed.[20]

Chapter 21 Notes

1 Customs, smuggling; N.Williams, *Contraband Cargoes*, Longmans Green, 1959. Robbers, *CDS II, 59* (24 Oct.1275,Stirling); Tynedale, *ib.62* (29 Dec., Brechin).

2 Texts in *SA*, 74–77(945–975 AD), 258–263 (Henry II and William, 1174–6 AD), 308–9 (Richard I, 1189 AD). The 1291 researches, Stones & Simpson, *Gt.Cause, I,* 138 *inf.* and *II*, 296 *inf.*

3 Legate's Council, Perth, from 19 Aug. 1275, *Fordun* LXII (see Powicke, 726–7, for the English tax, and *Fordun* LXV, accusing Edward of diverting proceeds for his Welsh wars).

4 The Durham pilgrimage, p.192 above; S/c to Canterbury, *CDS II, 67* (24 Feb.1276) and *ib.80* (14 Sept.); 'overseas and return', *ib.84* (26 Dec.)

5 'Year of the Four Popes', Runciman *SV*, 190–3; Nicholas III died 20 Aug.1280.

6 Powicke, 646 inf.; the pact, p.149 above. Montfort, p.33.

7 Berwick ship, *CDS II, 74* (11 May); horses from London, *ib. 78* (16 June) and from Stirling Fair, *ib.79* (14 Aug.). Envoys, *ib. 96* (there misdated 18 Aug. '1277', corr.in Watt, *Biog.* 108, q.v.for Bp.Comyn, brother of Adam, Earl of Carrick). Edward to sheriff, *CDS II, 82* (26 Oct.).

8 *CDS II, 90, 91, 93* (April-July 1277).

9 *Fergusson*, 166.

10 S/cs, *CDS II, 107–8–9,112–5*; Alexander to Edward, *ib.119* (24 May, Yester); Wishart and Soulis to Edward, *ib.120* (n.d., ca.24 May).

11 Community of the Realm, Barrow, *Bruce* (discussion and many refs.). *CDS II, 121–2–3–4* (June 1278); prices, *ib.126* (15 Sept.). Wales, Powicke, 648–651.

12 Coberley decl., *CDS II, 128* (17 Oct.); quittance from summons, *ib.130* (27 Oct.,Westminster); Henry III's grant to Alexander II, in Treaty of York, *CDS I, 1358* (25 Sept.1237).

13 Full text, Stones, *Docs.*, 38–41; *ES II*, 675–6n; *Fergusson*, 166–171; Barrow, *K&U*, 156–7; *Fordun*, LXI; *Chron.Pluscarden*, VII, xxix, noting that Edward 'actually though not right-fully' kept Huntingdon (p.187 above).

14 Stones, *Docs.* 82(27 June 1299). See Barrow, *Bruce*, 85; Stones & Simpson, *Gt. Cause, I*, 91 and 154. Largesse to musicians, *CDS II, 131* (29 Oct.).

15 Alexander Balliol died *ante* 13 Nov.1276 (*CDS II, 135*). 'Sweetheart' Abbey (New Abbey), *Sc.Abbeys* 73; R.Fawcett, *Scottish Medieval Churches* (HMSO 1985), 47; and App.C. The heart (from Wyntoun), A.M.MacKenzie, *Scottish Pageant*, 48–9. Devorguilla, married 1233, died 28 Jan.1290. Thomas, pp.47 above, 227 below.

16 Kirkham plea re lands in Carham (temp.William the Lion), *CDS II, 144*, referred to, *ib. I, 1699* (Dec.1246); Stones, *Docs,*. 27–8. Alston, *CDS II, 146–7, 160, 205*. Manor (not mines) granted ca.1205 to Ivo de Vetere Ponte (Vieuxpont, Vipont), *RRS II*, no.432. (Miners, p.68 above).

17 Stewart, *Sc.Coin.* 1–2,18,20–24; Mints, App.B, p.246; coinage, App.E, p.256.

18 *CDS II, 183* (Sept.1280); 'Wyncheles' might represent 'Whinshiels' or similar. *Leges Marchiarum* agreed 14 April 1249, *APS I* in Appendix ii to *Acta A.II.*

19 Watt, *Biog.*593–4.

20 Marriage negotiations, Ch.22; *Chron.Lanercost* 104–5; Margaret to K.Edward, (in French), *CDS II, 185*. Lindores, App.C; David's death (buried in Dunfermline), *Fordun* LXIII.

1281–1285: Three Weddings

WITHIN THE space of four years, between *colloquia*, councils, and private contacts, three state marriages were arranged. The wedding of the Princess was the first and remains the best-documented; alone of the three, its contract can be seen in Edinburgh.

It includes a careful statement of Margaret's rights to the Scottish throne; there follow financial details. Alexander dowered his only daughter with the huge sum of 14,000 marks, of which a quarter went with her to Norway and the rest would be paid in three annual instalments. On the bridegroom's behalf Queen Ingibiorg and her advisers promised a marriage-gift (*dos*) of 400 marks' worth of land and a terce of 1400 marks, in land or money as Margaret might choose. A 'fitting castle' would be prepared for her; her coronation would form part of the wedding-service. Eirik himself should confirm the arrangements when he reached the age of fourteen; if he died sooner, the terms would still be observed, under pain of £100,000 to be paid at Berwick. If he refused to confirm he must repay the 100 marks paid yearly under the Treaty of Perth, and cede Orkney to become a fief of Scotland under Norway. If Margaret withdrew her consent before Eirik could confirm, Scotland would pay £100,000 and cede the Isle of Man to be a fief held under Scotland.[1]

These are enormous figures for the time, tenfold heavier than the penalties under the Treaty of Perth. However bedecked with feudal trappings, the agreement implies a sound business approach, a family deal between the heads of two trading nations whose mercantile wealth can support their proposals. Most Norwegians and many Scots were actively engaged in trade, as shipowners if not as active traders. Scottish trade with Scandinavia had risen greatly since Perth and to compensate for difficulties in reaching France or the Low Countries during the Anglo-Flemish quarrel. There were even Scots established in Italy; in 1270 Bernard *le Scot* and his partners (Reginald de Manasteco, William Gayneben, Ancelin Villanus and others unnamed), 'merchants of Piacenza', had English safe-conducts as did Albert Scot and his partners 'of the Scotti of Piacenza' in 1279.[2]

The marriage-contract was sealed at Roxburgh on 25 July 1281, Robert Lovel and Godfrey, Archdeacon of Galloway, swearing as proxies for the

King and the Princess. The witnesses were the Earls of Dunbar, Mar, Angus, Menteith and Fife, the Steward and John Comyn, William Soulis, William of Brechin and Dunbar's son Patrick; Buchan and Strathearn swore by procurators. The Norwegian negotiators were the Bishop of Orkney and Bjarne Erlingsson of Bjarkey (whose father was at Largs), Mr Bernard the Chancellor, and Brother Maurice OFM, a negotiator at Perth. Six Norwegians remained in Scotland as hostages until King Eirik ratified the agreement or King Alexander gave them leave to go; they are named as Vivenus brother of Sir Bernard, Jon Finnsson, Isak Gautsson, Andreas Petersson, Elanus Arnfinnsson and Audun de Sindone. Alexander pledged the Isle of Man and £100,000 for their safety.[3]

Preparations for Margaret's voyage were well advanced. She sailed from Leith on Monday 11 August, with the Earl and Countess of Menteith, the Abbot of Balmerino and Sir Bernard Mowat among her company. The presence of Walter *Ballach* again suggests he was the 'high admiral', although the title was not in use. No doubt the Princess was given a splendid farewell, but one sound most modern readers would expect was not heard; no pipe band countermarched along Leith quay, for the great Highland bagpipe had not been invented. The national instrument was the small harp.

It must seem then that the little ships left to the music of a string-orchestra and the blare of royal trumpets. The convoy reached Bergen in four days, to be received with 'demonstrations of great joy'. Events moved fast; the wedding and Margaret's coronation took place on 31 August in the Mariakirke. No Norwegian Matthew Paris records the occasion, but we do have one rare treasure, the words and music of a wedding-hymn. A single melodic line was written out with some indications of phrasing. Time-signatures were not in use, but the verse directs singers towards triple (or waltz) rhythms. At some points it has the flavour of a lullaby.

Verse is notoriously difficult to translate; the first stanza may give some inkling of the whole:

> *Ex te lux oritur o dulcis Scotia*
> *Qua vere noscitur fulgens Norwagia*
> *Que cum transvehitur trahis suspiria*
> *Tui subtrahitur quod regis filia*

('From you has risen, o gentle Scotland, a light which gleaming Norway truly acknowledges, at whose transit you sigh deeply because your king's daughter is taken from you').

The writer continues with pious hopes that the bride will be as loveable as Rachel, as pleasing to her king as Esther, as fertile as Leah, as steadfast as Susanna, and that the couple will grow together into happy old age – conventional wishes, tragic in hindsight.[4]

There is no record of the trousseau, but when Isabella Bruce became Eirik's second queen in 1293 her luggage included:

> A robe of *bruneto* scarlet with a tunic, sleeveless supertunic, hood and cape; a robe of murrey scarlet with two supertunics, one close, the other open, and a furred hood and cape; another of white *camelia* trimmed with sindon; all the rest furred with miniver, except a mantle of *bluet*, furred with great vair.

There were three beds, 'couches *de carda*', with sheets and pillows, one bed with red hangings and two with green and yellow; a coverlet of 'bloody scarlet furred with miniver' and a cover of cloth-of-gold with the arms of France, another of red cloth-of-gold stamped with golden coins, a third of *perse* and miniver. There were two lengths of red samite and two of cloth-of-gold, four pieces of arras and 'a silk cloth to make a cushion'; twenty-four silver plates, twenty-four saltcellars, twelve cups, four pitchers and a thurible for incense. All this was packed into three pairs of coffers for the clothes and a pair for candles, three leather sacks, three bundles, two leather-covered baskets for the silver, and in one last parcel 'two small crowns, one greater than the other'.[5]

The Daughter of Scotland can hardly have had less. The Lanercost chronicler, catching echoes of Turgot's hyperbole over St Margaret, says,

> such favour she had with the king and all his, that she improved their customs, taught them French and English, and instituted better ways of dressing and eating.

Margaret's charm and beauty passed into Norwegian folklore as 'she who made our King a man'. Lanercost recorded also that the expedition 'endured great danger of life' on the outward voyage; it certainly made a fast passage, possibly with more wind than the passengers liked. Fordun says nothing of that, but reports that Mowat, the Abbot, and many more, drowned on the way home, though the Menteiths arrived safely. That there was a wreck is certain, presumably coastal, since objects (if not people) were rescued; Mr Thomas de Carnoto, labouring to index the archives next year, made up a file 'Of the Norwegian Marriage' which contained some documents *obfuscata* by water, and 'a transcript of things found after the shipwreck of the envoys'.[6]

No court correspondent at the feast, but a nameless balladeer may have saved us a deck-level view of the voyage. *Sir Patrick Spens* opens at Dunfermline (not Stirling or Edinburgh, as a later singer might have claimed), and proceeds briskly:

> They heysed their sails on a Monday morn
> Wi aa the speed they may,
> And they hae landit in Noroway

Upon the Wodensday.

(Well, it rhymes, and 'Thursday' would not). Sadly, there is trouble along the quayside:

> They hadna been a week, a week,
> A week but barely ane,
> When that the men of Noroway
> Began tae speak and maen,
> 'Thir Scottismen drink aa oor king's gowd,
> 'And eke oor queenis fee.'
> 'Ye lee, ye lee, ye leear lude, ·
> 'Fu lude I hear ye lee!
> 'I brocht as much good gowd to Noroway
> 'As feed my men and me,
> 'And eke as mickle siller money
> 'As aa your queenis fee!

They set sail, with an Ancient Mariner prophesying doom:

> 'Now ever alack, my maister dear,
> 'I fear a deidly storm;'

and sure enough,

> The luft grew dark and the wind grew lude,
> And gurly grew the sea.

At home the ladies 'wi their fans intil their hand' and the girls 'with the gowd kaims in their hair' wait in vain, for

> Hauf oure, hauf oure tae Aberdour
> Tis forty fadom deep;
> And there lies gude Sir Patrick Spens
> Wi the Scots lords at his feet.

(It has been argued that Sir Patrick went either to bring the Maid of Norway home, or to fetch Margaret of Denmark/Norway to be James III's bride, but neither of these voyages ended in shipwreck; a bit of revision over seven centuries may be allowed).[7]

Before he could learn of disasters, Alexander had turned to his son's future. By December a marriage had been arranged with the Count of Flanders' daughter. Her name was Margheritain in Flemish (everyone seemed to be Margaret in those days), and she was approaching her tenth birthday. Alexander set out 'the custom of Scotland' for Count Guy, as he had for the Norwegians, and sent Simon Fraser to swear it on the King's soul, while bishops and earls swore to uphold it and the Pope was asked to enforce observance. As it included a clause protecting the prior claim of 'the King's son by a second marriage', it appears that Alexander was facing his own duty.[8]

In July 1282 the Prince of Scotland sought his uncle's help for Mr Adam of Kirkcudbright, a *medicus* formerly in Bruce service and rewarded with the livings of Great Dalton near Kirkcudbright and Conington on the Bruce lands in Huntingdon. Mr Adam was being hounded to take up his parochial duties in England, but he had 'already restored me from the gates of death, contrary to the opinion of other physicians'. His presence in Scotland 'cannot be dispensed with, without irreparable damage to my health'. Edward immediately gave Mr Adam leave to remain, and ordered the harassment to stop.[9]

In August a splendid company brought young Margherita in to Roxburgh, where on Sunday 15 November the marriage took place

> With many knights and ladies of Flanders, with great joy and applause, where many bishops of Scotland, abbots, earls, barons and other nobles assembled for the space of fifteen days, celebrating the nuptials honourably before returning home. But alas, after such joy followed huge grief.[10]

The first blow fell from Norway; Margaret bore a daughter, named after herself, and within a few days died, on 9 April 1283. When Eirik's messengers came to King Alexander,

> They were kindly received, and by advice of his lords the embassy returned with honour to the King of the Norwegians, with vast and diverse gifts.

Anxiety about the Prince's health redoubled. The winter after his sister's death he passed at Cupar, where their mother had died, and there contracted a 'slow ague':

> In which for a time his mind endured alienation; coming to himself on Thursday evening [20 January 1284] he foretold that next day at sunrise the sun of Scotland would set; and of Edward King of England he said, 'My uncle will go to three battles; two he will win and in the third he will be defeated'. This I had from those who were with him, one a knight his *magister*, the other the rector of the church his priest.

Next day was the young man's birthday:

> On the second feast of St Agnes, Alexander son of the King was taken from this world, just twenty years old, the joy of his rising changed into the grief of his death; if he had lived, he would have been the light of his country and the joy of his family.[11]

They buried him in Dunfermline, and soon four Flemish knights came to escort the little princess home,

About which the King and his Council treated long, and at last consented that the lady should return home without pledging her fealty to the lord King for her dower [*recte* terce]. Which was then done, and with munificence they were sent home.

Had she been older, she might have remained a year and a day in her husband's country, until all hopes of pregnancy were past, but she was so young, and the Prince had been so ill, that it is unlikely that the marriage had been consummated. The next *colloquium*, at Scone on 5 February, referred to the possibility only to dismiss it.[12]

February meetings cannot always be well-attended, but that *colloquium* was crowded with men from all over Scotland, united in sorrowful anxiety:

They issued a declaration on the succession, not in their King's name but in their own, drawing on the statements to Norway and Flanders. The succession of a monarch's grandchild was already established; they need look no farther than Malcolm IV. King William had wanted to make his daughter his heiress, before Alexander II's birth, and though his nobles had opposed his wishes their descendants were prepared to face the possibility of a queen-regnant (a company of countesses helped to keep Pictish traditions alive). The 1281 letter to Norway had been unequivocal; if Alexander left no lawful son or grandson, his daughter or her eldest child would inherit the Scots throne, her daughters also inheriting 'everything they can under Norwegian law'. Norway had had no queen-regnant in recent times, but its laws strongly guarded women's rights. The Flanders statement was equally precise; if a King of Scots' son predeceased his father, leaving a son, that child was heir to the throne. If a king's son left daughters by a first marriage and sons by a second, the eldest son was the heir, with the eldest daughter of the first marriage following if the male line failed. If a king's son had no son, the eldest daughter was the heiress unless the king himself had a son by a second marriage. The *colloquium* endorsed these rulings:

Be it known that, the Most High having been pleased to take from the way of flesh our lord Alexander, the firstborn son of our lord King Alexander, there is no immediate progeny of the King left alive; we oblige ourselves the more strictly by these presents to our said lord King and his heirs, direct or by mediation of his body, who by right should be admitted to the succession and whom we will hold in faith and fidelity as they hold us, promising that if our King has neither son, daughter, sons or daughters legitimately of his body or of the body of his said son Alexander on the last day of ending his life, we shall all receive our illustrious child Margaret, daughter of the daughter of our said lord King, Margaret of good memory, sometime Queen of Norway, by the illustrious lord Eirik King of Norway; and as she descends with full legitimacy we [*shall receive*] her as our lady and right heir of our said lord King, in the whole realm and in the Isle of Man and all the other isles pertaining to the realm, and also Tynedale and Penrith with all other [   ] rights and liberties which look or should look to the King of Scotland, and [*?defend*] her against all living or [   ] may be, we shall maintain, sustain and defend [*her*] with all our men and with all our powers. We promise moreover faithfully to hold both faith and fidelity with our lord King and his posterity, and with the executors of his will [   ] he will do, and to two of them and even to one of them; and we most strictly bind ourselves and our heirs to this, and every one of us is singularly obliged as aforesaid, whatever may happen when the King dies and some bailiffs [   ] whoever may be rebels and not wish to carry out his last wishes [   ] as he may dispose in his life; and we and our heirs and each one of us and our bailiffs [   ] debtors and rebels more strictly [   ] with our power together with [*the King's*] executors or any one of them, to help them deal with all and singular debts to the said King and enable them to put down rebellions. Submitting ourselves and our heirs, and each one of us and his heirs, to the jurisdiction of the venerable father bishops [*here all eleven sees are named*] for that time being, that they or one or more of them shall compel and coerce us and our heirs to observe this agreement. In witness whereof we cause our seals to be attached.

The signatories are many; it would be hard to find anyone of note unrepresented. All thirteen earls are followed by Robert Bruce *pater* (Annandale), James the Steward, John Balliol, John Comyn, William Soulis, Ingram de Guignes (Queen Marie's nephew, long-established in Scotland), William Murray of Bothwell, Alexander Balliol of Cavers, Reginald le Chen *pater*, William de St.-Clair, Richard Siward, William of Brechin, Nicholas Hay, Henry Graham, Ingram Balliol of Redcastle, and Alan fitzCount; Reginald le Chen *filius*, John Lindsay, Patrick Graham, Herbert Maxwell and Simon Fraser; and three principal Islesmen, Ewen's son Alexander of Argyll, Angus Mor of Islay and Alan 'brother of Roderick'. All these are designated barons of the kingdom of Scotland.[13]

It was a fine roll-call; but great anxiety remained. Their 'illustrious child' was toddling about some Norwegian palace, liable at any moment to succumb to one of the innumerable ills of childhood; not a man of that gathering but had followed some infant's coffin to the grave. In the King's time of grief it was probably to the Queen Mother that the nobles turned, and through her that steps were taken to find a new Queen.

In April Alexander wrote to Edward, in an effort to acknowledge his sympathy:

To the exalted prince Lord Edward, by the grace of God the illustrious King of the English, Lord of Ireland and Duke of Aquitaine, and his most beloved brother, Alexander his friend, and by the same grace King of Scots, sends greeting and every good wish, with true affection and the desire to do what pleases him. Although faithful friends know not fickleness in their affection, and after our long experience we ought with good reason to praise the faithfulness of your excellency for the many kindnesses that we have received, yet at present, because after the grievous and unbearable trials and tribulations which we have suffered and do suffer, from the death of our dear son your beloved nephew, you have offered no small solace for our desolation by sending Brother John of St Germains to say that though death by his decree has thus borne away your kindred in these parts, we are united perpetually, God willing, by the tie of indissoluble affection:- we are bound to thank your dear highness, beyond what is due for other courtesies and acts of benevolence, in that you have regard to our kinship, and we would recall, if we may, to your recollection, that in the providence of God much good may yet come to pass through your kinswoman, the daughter of your niece, the daughter too of our beloved, the late Queen of Norway of happy memory, who is now our heir apparent, who [*two or three illegible words*] indissoluble bond created between you and us, as men who are firm and constant, should never be broken, as we firmly believe, except by death. Hence it is that we particularly ask your beloved majesty to be kind enough to give credence without question to what the monk Andrew, Abbot of Coupar, [has to say to you on our behalf?] and to send us by the same messenger trustworthy [news concerning?] your own [state?]. [Wishing prosperity to your excellency] for many years to come. [Witness myself at] Edinburgh, 20 April, in the thirty-fifth year of our reign.[14]

It might almost seem as if, in the midst of his mourning, thoughts of another Anglo-Scottish marriage had come to Alexander. Not until 1287 would Edward seek a general dispensation for his children to marry within the prohibited degrees; only in 1290 would he betrothe the infant Edward of Caernarvon to the Maid of Norway – a move often presented as illustrating his resolve to dominate Scotland. Alexander well knew that if his grand-daughter came to the throne she would need English goodwill. That apart, the Abbot may also have been charged to acquaint Edward with other matters in progress.

In the tenth year after the Queen's death, King Alexander chose ambassadors from among his trusted advisers, his Chancellor Thomas de Charteris (Carnoto), Patrick Graham, William St.-Clair and John Soulis, knights, to find him a bride born of a noble race; who without delay went to France after Candlemas.[15]

Further progress was halted by the death of Queen Marie. Her tomb stood ready at Newbattle, where she had sought the community's prayers in her 'time of peril' before Alexander's birth. She must have been in her sixties; the date of her death is not recorded but it was probably in June, when

Alexander is found at Haddington. Almost certainly, she had done the realm a last service by finding him a bride from among her own kindred, named Joleta (Yolande, Iolanthe, Violetta), the youngest daughter of the Count of Dreux and nineteen at her next birthday.[16]

That marriage-contract has not survived. In autumn 1285 the bride's elder brother escorted her through England to Jedburgh, part of her dowerland. Fordun's account is darkened by after-knowledge:

> The lord King Alexander on St Calixtus' day [14 October] married Yolent, daughter of the Count of Dreux, to celebrate which nuptials there came together very many nobles of France and of Scotia, with an unnumbered crowd of either sex. Which things being done, the French returned home rejoicing and laden with gifts, except for a few who remained with the Queen.

By the time Bower revised Fordun's text an omen had been added. There had been a masque at the feast, armed men dancing behind musicians. They were followed, says Bower, by a single gliding figure at whose appearance the music died, the dancers stood, the watchers were appalled. Later commentators have seen this as an early version of the Dance of Death, a gruesome choice for such an occasion, and one made familiar by Dürer long afterwards. The Lanercost writer (who might have pounced upon the story) omits it but has plenty to report:

> This year at All Saints, Alexander King of Scotland took a second wife, by name Yoleta, daughter of the Count of Dreux, who to grief and almost perpetual loss condemned the whole province as shall be shown.
>
> In December under the sign of Capricorn, terrible thunders were heard and lightnings seen, which in the opinion of the wise foretold the fall of princes … When truly these and more warnings could not achieve the instruction of [the King's] soul, God punished him. He was in the habit of sparing neither for time nor tempest, nor dangers of waters nor rocky cliffs, but by night as by day he would go, sometimes changing his dress, often with only one companion, to visit, not honestly, matrons and nuns, virgins and widows.[17]

The good friar was nearer the scene than we are, but it does seem odd that, if the King were indeed in the habit of imitating his revered grandfather, not a single natural child of his appeared among the 1291 competitors (some of whom had scanty grounds for their ambition). True, he had lived ten years without Margaret; he was in the prime of life; many contemporaries would not have been shocked, let alone surprised, if he had taken mistresses. Yet nobody else supports the friar's hints; it must seem that Queen Joleta had no living rival to fear.[18]

Chapter 22 Notes

1   The Revd. John Beveridge in *PSAS LXXIII*, 68 *inf.*, summarised the Norwegian marriage-treaty, the Scottish text of which was returned to the Register House in Edinburgh from the Public Record Office in London in 1937. Text in *APS I*, (calendared in *CDS II*, *197*). For the succession rules, see p.219. 14,000 mks equal £9,333.6.8d.; 400 mks equal £266.13.4d. A modern equivalent requires multiplication by around 600. Dowerlands (GWS Barrow, *SHR LXIX*, 120 *inf.*), included Rothiemay, Belhelvie, Bathgate and Ratho, plus Menmuir if necessary to equal 700 mks. p.a.

2   Treaty of Perth, p.159 above. The Piacenza merchants, *CDS I*, *2560* (20 May 1270) and *CDS I*, *167* (15 Nov.1279). See also Byrne, *Genoese Shipping* (cited p.184), for merchants Ogerius and Johanninus Scotus (1250, 1253).

3   For Lovel, and Mr Godfrey, p.135 above. Earl William of Mar had been succeeded by his son Donald. I have traced no further ref. to the 'hostages'.

4   The hymn (words and music), is in Uppsala University Library, MS. Uppsalensis C233. I have followed Dr Warwick Edwards's edition (reproduced in Purser, *Sc.Music*, 59–61 and 280). Beveridge (n1 above) gives a transcription in 4/4 time. I offer a prose version of v.1.

5   *CDS II*, *675* (25 Sept.1293). Isabella was the eldest sister of the future King Robert I. *Bruneto* is red/brown, *murrey* is mulberry, *bluet* in Mod.French means a Bluetit, *Parus caeruleus*; *perse* was a rich Provençal cloth dyed in imitation of 'Persian ultramarine' (derived from lapis lazuli). *Scarlet*, p.35 above, was a fine cloth, *camelia* a very fine woollen (cf. 'Cashmere') of goat- or camel-wool, 'drycleaned' by expert shearing of its long nap. *Sindon* was satin, *samite* a heavier satin from Greece. *Miniver* is ermine, *great vair* is grey or white Hungarian squirrel. The weight of the silver items amounted to £50 sterling. Now see B.E. Crawford, *SHR LXIX*, 183–4.

6   *Chron.Lanercost*, 104–5; *ES II*, 680. *Fordun*, LXIV (calling bridegroom 'Hangow'); Archive list, *APS I.* 2–11.

7   There are many versions of *Sir Patrick Spens* (e.g. an anglicised text in *The Oxford Book of English Verse*). Purser, *Sc.Music*, 62 gives a traditional tune.

8   The Flanders marriage, Barrow, *K&U*,154–5; *Fordun* LXIII; s/c, *CDS II*, *221* (11 Aug.1282, Rhuddlan). Flanders, briefly, p.59.

9   Pr.Alexander to K.Edward, (3 July 1282, Scone), *ES II*, 682; agreed, *CDS II*, *222* (15 Aug.1282,Rhuddlan). Mr Adam, Watt, *Biog.*, 306–8.

10 *Fordun*, LXIII.

11 *Fordun, loc.cit.* Q.Margaret died at Tönsberg and was buried in Christ's Kirk, Bergen, where a fine modern memorial marks the grave of the Maid of Norway and both her parents. Prince Alexander's death, *Chron.Lanercost*, 111; *Fordun, loc.cit.*

12 *CDS II*, *247* (undated appl.for s/c by Raoul Flemeng, *chevaler*, going to Scotland to escort the Count's daughter home). For *dos*, dower, and terce, p.45 above. The decision not to require her fealty left re-marriage negotiations uncomplicated; her Scots terce included the manor of Linlithgow and 1300 mks from the revenues of Berwick (being paid in 1294; *Hdlist [A.III.&] John*, no.372. 16 May 1294). Margharitain later married René II of Gueldres, and died in 1331.

13 *APS I*; gaps in the source are shown by square brackets. James the Steward succ.his father in 1283. For Ingram/Enguerrand de Guignes see Coucy, p.33, and Barrow, *Bruce*, 19, (and *CDS II*, *241*); for the last three signatories see Man & Isles, p.2.

14 Stones, *Docs*, 42–43 (and calendared, *CDS II*, *250*), Gaps in the damaged original supplied by Stones from related texts. Edward's own letter has not survived; but compare his desolation at the death of Eleanor of Castile, when he retreated into a religious house for a

month (Stones & Simpson, *Gt.Cause*, I,7).

15 *Fordun*, LXVI; the envoys presumably left after a Candlemas *colloquium*.

16 Queen Marie married in 1239 and was then of childbearing age; her kinship with Joleta, see Coucy and Dreux, p.33

17 S/c, *CDS II, 273* (19 August 1283); *ib.274* (10 Sept.) shows Devorguilla setting out for Scotland. *Fordun*, LXVII; *Bower, Fergusson* 179–180. *Chron.Lanercost*, 114 (continued, p.228 below).

18 For the thirteen Competitors of 1291, Stones & Simpson, *Gt.Cause*, I,13, and fig.4; Barrow, *Bruce*, 52 inf.

18 March 1286: A Great and Bitter Day

ONE OF THE DIFFICULTIES confronting the student of the Middle Ages is the lack of authentic portraits. All those carved heads, worked with such vigour, must be modelled upon observation, but most are nameless. There are images of Louis IX that strongly resemble each other; we see him clean-shaven and earnest before his first Crusade, bearded and grave after it. Henry Torel's effigy of Henry III, placed in Westminster Abbey in 1291, must surely be based on studies from life; no carver set to produce 'the figure of a king' would invent that fretful brow, that petulant underlip.

It is not a question of inability; this is the time of Duccio, when painting was moving from icon towards realism. The stone carvers led the painters, and had worked lively vignettes into their capitals long before scenes of daily life appeared in book decoration, though Matthew Paris completed his pages with sketches that verge on strip-cartoons, and there is the odd marginal cari-cature.[1]

For Alexander himself we can be sure only of the coins; some early ones are not helpful, one does suggest a portrait (Plate VI). The final issue (Plate VIII) is, unusually, three-quarter-face with a rather large nose, a firm chin, and a conspicuous crease in the cheek – a laughter-line? It is the face of an active and cheerful man in early middle age. As for his colouring, tradition persists that red hair goes with the blood-royal of the old pre-Stewart line (an equally strong tradition claims it as a mark of bastardy, which might perhaps be blamed upon William the Lion); and there was John of England's 'red fox-cub' remark about Alexander II.[2]

It is easier to picture the state of Scotland in the 1280s than to visualise its ruler. In its Time of Peace the country flourished. Trade was strong; one later chronicler, after detailing a hotchpotch of improbable 'export controls', continues:

> When these statutes had been in force for a time, the country so flourished in fruitfulness and abundance of all wealth, in crafts and metals and moneys and all other advantages of good government, that numberless ships and merchants poured in from all parts of the world, hearing of the King's justice and wisdom, and said they saw in the country better and greater things than they had heard

from afar. Accordingly the country became so wealthy that Lombards came from the borders of Italy, bringing untold gold and silver and precious stones, and made the King an offer to build a city on their own account, on Queensferry hill or on an island near Cramond, if the King would see that they got the due and needful privileges and liberties. This would have been accorded them had not death, which snatches all things away, so soon carried off the King from this world ...

Whether or not Cramond Island was indeed poised to become a Free Port, matters were certainly prosperous; but one community, important in all medieval countries, is not traceable in Scots sources. We are rightly proud of our record as the only western country never to have persecuted Jews; it is possible that some refugees from the Angevin atrocities in England made their way north, but if so they probably moved on under the constant menace of English intervention. If they were here they must have got safely away before 1296, or they would have shared the fate of the Flemings who died defending their Red Hall in Berwick.[3]

One shipmaster who sought royal help did so in unusual circumstances. An undated missive in Spanish, 'much blackened and defaced', survives among English Chancery documents:

John, the King of Castile's man, shipmaster, to King Alexander; he kisses the King's hands and feet, and narrates that his ship sailed from Bordeaux for London but was driven by tempest to *Incha Guala*, where they found a good harbour; Alan Rhadric's men came with sealed letters bidding them move to a better port where he would take care of their goods as his own. When they went there, he took all the goods ashore and left only two men on board; 'at prim saon' [high tide?] the cables parted and the ship was cast ashore, and broke up. Alan kept all that had been placed in safety; 'and Lord, for the great mercy in you, make Alan and his men come before you and tell you these things in our presence; and Lord, do me justice in your court.'

He adds a list of 'articles in the ship'; eight tuns of wine, three hundred dozen [*sic*] of *Korduan* [Cordoba leather?], eight hundred quintals of *aln de Douay* [ells of Douai?] wool dyed crimson, twenty quintals of raisins, thirteen quintals of dates, a bale of silk cloth; 'and twenty-six axes and staves, twenty crossbows, ten *ankers*, and shields, purpoints, iron hats and lances to arm thirty men, and the ship was as well found as any, each man had two robes, there were twenty silk banners wherewith we received Alan, and we had ten marks sterling and seven hundred *livres Tournois*, and a hundred shillings *Burgeleys* [of Burgos?] for spending.'[4]

Sadly, there is no sequel to this pathetic story. Among so many foreign traders there was bound to be the odd rotten apple. One John Mazun, merchant of Bordeaux, caused more than his fair share of trouble. He first appeared in 1283 at a Household Accounting Day, demanding payment for wines but producing no invoices. The clerk on duty consulted other merchants present and was advised to withhold payment until the paperwork was in order. Mazun got King Edward to write on his behalf; Alexander replied at some length, explaining that payment would follow as soon as Mazun followed normal procedures. In August 1284 officials of the Bordeaux commune appealed to Edward because Mazun faced bankruptcy; Mazun himself wrote that the King of Scots had told him to come and be paid, but when he went, the Scots cheated him of 200 marks, 'injured him in many ways too long to detail', and finally imprisoned him, snatching away the King's letter of obligation. From jail, he implored Edward's help.

By April 1286 he was back in London, being made to swear he would not harm any Scotsmen anywhere in Edward's dominions; he then returned to Scotland, with results revealed in 1288. By then his account had been inflated to £2040, to cover the value of a ship and her cargo of wine and corn. These he had lost because, in an attempt either to evade duties or dodge creditors, he had tried to run his cargo illicitly and land near Queensferry. (How he thought he could pass unobserved by all the Forth harbours is unexplained). Naturally he was intercepted, some of his men were hanged as disturbers of the peace and others imprisoned (including Mazun, again); most of the cargo was seized by his Scots creditors. The case rolled on in increasing confusion, but it served a purpose, for it was one of those King John Balliol was compelled to answer in person, as an ordinary tenant of England; a step on that unfortunate man's road to disaster. The case is often cited as an example of incompetent royal accounting, especially in 'poor countries such as Scotland'. It might be better taken as proof that every age has its chancers.[5]

The winter of 1285–1286 was bitter and stormy, and there was talk of the End of the World approaching. On 18 March the Council met in Edinburgh Castle, on a day when snowladen winds howled round the Rock. The meeting was chiefly to discuss King Edward's demand that old Thomas 'of Galloway' should be released; he was being sent up to Norham within days. John Balliol was keen to get rid of him; Devorguilla was probably at Buittle in Galloway, supervising the abbey-building and unaware of her son's plans. She, like Buchan and Bruce, had not forgotten the Galloway troubles.[6]

The two elder statesmen had strong influence in the Council, and the debate ended without a decision, closed only by the need to let people get to their lodgings before dark. Some councillors were absent because of the weather; young Patrick of Dunbar deputised for his father, who was seventy-three.

Down at Dunbar, as snow-showers drove in from the sea, the Earl was entertaining English friends and half-listening to Thomas of Earlston, who was off on one of his doomladen speeches:

> Woe worth the morrow, for it will be a day of disaster and woe, a very great and bitter day in the kingdom; before noon such a wind shall blow as has never been heard of for many years, and the blast of it shall humble lofty hearts and level the high places of the hills.

Thomas was getting old; the weather was terrible, but no worse than many a winter they had seen. They fell to discussing the End of the World stories; these broke out from time to time, under the influence of vehement sermons by friars, or as a result of some learned recalculation of numbers in Scripture. One could not believe all one heard, but it was shocking weather for March, and thank goodness they were not catching their deaths of cold up there in Edinburgh.[7]

Within Edinburgh Castle the meeting was over and dinner was served. It was not a feast; for one thing they were in the middle of Lent, for another the Queen and her ladies were absent. The big silver covered-cup, the silver boat and the crystal goblets, were stowed away until Easter, and the ivory horns had not summoned the diners. But it was a cheerful meal; Alexander, recommending a dish of eels to one councillor, bade him 'Eat hearty, for you know this is Judgment Day'. The guest replied that in that case they would all rise well-fed.

Dinner was usually served around noon, a light buffet-meal serving as breakfast and an informal supper after dark. They ate late that day, thanks to the long meeting, but it was over before twilight. When they went down to the courtyard they found four of the King's horses standing saddled under cloaks; he was going to Queensferry and nothing would deter him. They all tried, but he was adamant; next day was the Queen's birthday, he had promised to be there, he could not disappoint her. (Perhaps, remembering Margaret's troubled pregnancies, he was anxious not to let anything distress Joleta). He and his small party clattered away down the long ridge into the gathering dusk.[8]

It was a foul evening, far worse than anyone had realised inside the thick walls:

> In that very day, when he was coming to judgment however little he knew it, a tempest so heavy fell upon us that to me and many other mortals it was seen to flay the weatherbeaten face opposed to the north wind, rains, and snows.

They rode into the teeth of it. Night had fallen when they reached the south side of the ferry and began looking for the ferryman. He had not expected to be called out in such weather, and told the King it would be downright dangerous to cross; on being asked if he was scared to go with Alexander (who was clearly going, if he had to take the boat out himself), he replied,

> 'Be it far from me, lord; it well beseems me to share the fate of thy father's son'.

The use of the familiar *tu* is noteworthy, and one wonders what link had existed with Alexander II.

> He came therefore in profound darkness to the burgh of Inverkeithing, with only three squires; there the master of his saltworks, a married man of the town, knew him by his voice;
>
> 'Lord', he said, 'what art thou doing here in such weather and such darkness? How often have I told thee that these night journeys do thee no good? Stay with us, we can give you decent hospitality and all you need until morning-light'.
>
> He answered, laughing:
>
> 'No need to trouble you; just find me two local men to go on foot and guide us'.
>
> So, when they had gone some two miles, they lost the way in the gloom, except that the horses kept to worn paths by instinct. When they were thus separated, and he at a distance, the squires found the right road, and – to cut it short – he fell from his horse and bade farewell to his kingdom in the sleep of Sisera. To whom it befell in proof of Solomon's proverb, 'Woe to him that is alone, who has none to help him if he falls'.[9]

The others struggled on to Kinghorn, expecting to find the King there before them; he was always outriding his company, he knew the ground from childhood. One by one they blundered in half-frozen, snow on their cloaks, the horses exhausted. There was no point in trying to look for him in the dark and that storm; he must have found shelter. The wind dropped by dawn; they made up search-parties of the Queen's guards and local men, and soon found him, and his horse. They lay on the foreshore below what is still called the King's Craig, a little to the westward of Kinghorn.

The common report was that he had galloped over the cliff and broken his neck, but nobody would ride at a gallop in those conditions. One late account may even incorporate scraps of first-hand reporting, though it starts in a muddle, asserting that he was trying to cross from Fife to Lothian, but was prevented 'by an exceeding great storm':

> So he changed his mind, and straightway flew on horseback to Kinghorn, where for the time he occupied a manor. On the seashore to the westward, however, on a sandy road, his horse by chance suddenly sank his forelegs into

the sand, in the darkness, and stumbled; and when pricked by a spur he tried to rise, he fell again more heavily and crushed the King under him. So, for want of due watch and ward on the part of his companions, this most noble King died of a broken neck, and lies entombed at Dunfermline before the high altar.

That writer sat down to his task about 1461, after a long overseas career entering the peace of Pluscarden (by then a Benedictine house, refounded from Dunfermline). In compiling a chronicle for the new establishment he drew on older sources, and may even have had sight of some infirmarian's notes of a pensioner's childhood memories, of tagging after his elders as they beachcombed and found that trampled sand, that big horse, and all the horror of the grown-ups.

We have no better guide. No other commentators bother with details, they are in haste to launch into eulogy. But it must seem possible that Alexander, who knew the place well, recalled some way down the cliff into shelter and called to the others, the wind sweeping his voice away even as he turned his horse's head out of the blizzard. The rector of the parish would be brought to escort the body, once freed from the dead horse; that rector was a Mr Baldred Bisset, who would have a part in national affairs.[10]

Back at Dunbar they teased old Thomas. The day was calm, the inland hills white; True Thomas had been wrong for once:

> Nevertheless, while they were at dinner, lo suddenly a messenger came from the north in hot haste and knocked at the gate; and when he had formally related the King's death the night before, they all wondered and were stupéfied as though fallen into a trance. Therefore let princes, prelates and magnates remember how little we can count upon this earthly life, how unstable it is, how piteous its end, how wretched its dissolution, how terrible is death; for the hour thereof is most uncertain, and all the past is as nought and like unto the wind.[11]

The King's death was a shattering blow to the whole community, not least to one who gets scant sympathy from Lanercost:

> He did not choose to be detained by intemperate weather nor by persuasion to rest, but took his way to Queensferry for the sake of visiting his newly-wed, Yoleta [sic] by name, she who brought the whole province into sorrow and perpetual doom. She ... would have taken the veil before the betrothal, but with the facility of a female heart and the ambition of reigning had looked back.

He does not think it necessary to underline the point that Alexander virtually caused his own death by rushing to his wife, and in Lent too. Some southern chroniclers were quick to develop the theme of the hot-blooded king who put base desires before his country's welfare (some do suggest he was anxious to procreate a child, but that was already done). Alexander had to deal with a girl younger than his lost daughter, far from home in a strange country and in an early stage of pregnancy. If Margaret's pregnancies had been difficult, this one was vital for the whole country's sake; nothing must be allowed to trouble Joleta.

The Franciscan, having satisfactorily laid blame equally on the Queen and on Alexander himself (for 'impeding the liberties of St Cuthbert's bishopric [Durham] already for three years', a reference probably to the Tweedmouth dispute), reports the funeral briefly:

> He lies in Dunfermline, alone in the southern part near the presbytery. There we saw a multitude weeping as much for his sudden death as for the destitution of the realm; only those cheeks were not wet who had, during his life, clung more closely to his friendship and favour.[12]

Others are more generous:

> He was beloved of God and men, and endeavoured to keep the nations of his land always at peace; and none of his predecessors was able to hold the kingdom with so great peace and so great rejoicing.

Fordun goes farther:

> How grievous and harmful that death was to Scotia the tribulations of the following times will make clear. He reigned thirty-six years. All the days of this King's life the Church of Christ flourished, priests were honoured with due reverence, vice withered, intrigue was absent, injustice ceased, virtue increased, truth flourished, justice reigned. He was called a king with reason and on account of the merit of his probity, because he ruled himself and his people aright, giving everybody his own, and if at any time he had some rebels he repressed their madness with such strict discipline that they would put a rope around their own necks ready for hanging, and would submit to his rule. Wherefore near and far, not only friends but also enemies and above all the English held him in equal fear and love. And all those times in which he lived in the earth were under firm peace and tranquillity, and the joy of secure liberty.
>
> O truly unhappy Scotia, who hast lost such and so great a ruler and director [*dux et auriga*] and what is unhappier, no legitimate children to succeed him ! Therefore from that death arises a spring of mourning and sorrow for one whose laudable life brought thee such and so many increases of prosperity.[13]

In his emotion Fordun has forgotten all the early years, therein reflecting the national mood. Nobody looked back to old troubles, or if they did, it was only to recall the King's share in surmounting them. At least two subjects left material tributes. A northern landholder, Simon, Thane of Aberchirder, endowed the chapel of St Menimius on the banks of the Deveron, and its chaplain Christinus and his successors, with multures and lands, 'and all buildings built or to be built within the cemetery, and common grazing with my own stock for twenty cows and a bull, for the soul of Alexander of good memory, illustrious King of Scots, and his heirs, and my father's soul and my own, and all Christian souls'. In Elgin, Hugh Heroc, burgess, with consent of Margaret his wife, founded two chaplaincies for the King's soul and the souls of his own kindred and the bishops of Moray, one at the altar of St Nicholas in the cathedral and the other at the altar of the Holy Cross in the parish church. His choice curiously reflects the dedication and associations of the King's only known religious foundation, far to the southward at Peebles.[14]

Chapter 23 Notes

1   Louis IX, Labarge, *St.L*, frontispiece and Pl.14, and Muller-Weiner, *Castles of the Crusaders*,(Thames & Hudson,1966), Pl.160; Henry III, see pl.1; Bernham (from his Pontifical), Purser, *Sc.Music*, Pl.15. See p.57.

2   'Fox-cub', p.1 above. Neither the Seal of the Minority with its characterless image (pl. V) nor the Great Seal showing an enthroned and heavily-bearded ruler on one face and a speeding horseman on the other (pl. VI) convey much sense of portraiture.

3   *Chron.Pluscarden*, VII, xxxiii; *Bower*, ii, 131;during the Roman Occupation of Britain the Cramond rivermouth was a port. For the Jews in Scotland see A.Levy, *Origins of the Scottish Jewry*, (Glasgow, 1959); Berwick, Barrow, *Bruce*, 99.

4   *CDS II, 288* (n.d., 'Spanish, much blackened and defaced'). Incha Guala =Innse Gall, the Outer Hebrides; for Alan, see Man & Isles, p.2. 'Anker' may be a misreading of *adarga*, 'a heartshaped shield of Moorish origin, used in Spain 13 x 18th century' (Blair, *Medieval Armour*, 183; Batsford, 1979). Purpoints were padded tunics.

5   For Mazun, *Sel.Cases* no. 71, and *CDS II,252* and *passim* to *685–688*; Barrow, *Bruce*, 78–82. Mazun claimed for 365 casks of wine at (variously) £2 or £2.4.-d. (£780 or £803) while acknowledging payments of £627 to account, before inflating his bill to cover the ship episode. (*CDS, II, 688*, his executors agree he had received all bar £100, which his creditors had intercepted).

6   Thomas 'of Galloway', pp.47, 210 above. Barrow, *Bruce*, 156, for his eventual release in 1296, aged 88.

7   Sir Thomas Learmonth of Ercildoun ('True Thomas') p.173 above. For this episode, *Chron.Pluscarden* VII, xxxiv. 'End of the World', *Chron.Lanercost*, 115.

8   Barrow,*Bruce*, 3–4; (Also Skene, 'Traditionary accounts of the death ...', *PSAS XX*, 177–185). Goblets etc., App. D, pp.253–4.

9   *Chron.Lanercost*, 115–17. The hospitable burgess was Alexander Le Saucier of Forfar. Texts. *Judges*, IV, 17–21(inapt) and *Ecclesiastes* IV, 10. I owe the information about the Queen's birthday to the late Mr.A.G. Williamson (Dumfries), who traced it in a Breton source.

10 *Chron.Pluscarden*, VIII,xxxii. and *ib*., preface. Mr.Baldred Bis(s)et, (Watt, *Biog*.49–51) was in Scotland from Oct. 1285, returning to take up a lectureship at Bologna, 1289. For his later career see Barrow, *Bruce, passim*.

11 *Chron.Pluscarden*, VIII, xxxiv.

12 *Chron.Lanercost*, 116;cf.*ES II*,688, *inf.* for a range of foreign comments.

13 Skene, *Chron. of the Picts & Scots*, 303, in *ES II*, 688;*Fordun*, LXVII (*Auriga* = charioteer).

14 *Moray Reg.*, p283, no. 221; Peebles, p.126 above.

EPILOGUE

Aftermath

ONE SLIP of a horse's hoof on a stormy night had ended a reign of thirty-six years. Queen Joleta, who had fallen asleep thinking of birthdays, awoke to find herself a rich widow. The Earl of Buchan – Constable as well as Justiciar – was probably the first magnate to reach her and take charge of the distraught household. Bishop William Fraser and the young Earl of Fife, both homeward-bound by way of the ferry, could be intercepted to join him.

The first necessity was the Queen's safety and well-being. She moved to Stirling as quickly as possible; it is likely that most of the Inner Council were aware of her condition, whether or not it was generally known. Alexander's body was escorted to Dunfermline and buried before the high altar on 29 March. The Bishops of St Andrews and Glasgow despatched two Dominicans to carry the news to King Edward in Gascony.[1]

The next step was to call a *colloquium* to take measures for government. It was arranged to meet at Scone a fortnight after Easter (14 April that year), giving time for people to assemble from all over Scotland. There is a hint that Joleta planned a small Easter feast, to celebrate the great festival of hope, to bring some slight relief in her mourning, perhaps to allow her to spread her own good news ahead of the Council meeting. It was important that people should know she was carrying a child before hard-and-fast commitments were made elsewhere. A list of provisions was seen and translated in Stirling some fifty years ago; it summarised victuals and delicacies ordered (which included oranges, fresh or candied), and was perhaps a leaf from a Household clerk's book. It was endorsed with a note that 'Bishop William' (of St Andrews) and 'the Lord of Roslin' (Joleta's kinsman William de St.-Clair) had visited the Queen and forbidden any entertainment. They were right, it was too soon, but one feels some sympathy for the young woman.

Here it should be noted that we should not picture a court draped in black. It is difficult and expensive to get a lasting black from vegetable dyes, and accordingly great ladies more often mourned in 'humble' dress of russet or undyed woollen; Eleanor de Montfort did so for Simon.[2]

The Scone *colloquium* swore homage to the Maid of Norway, their 'illustrious child', and proceeded to form an interim government. Buchan, Dunbar and Bruce of Annandale could remember the last time that had been

necessary. There was no confusion, no fear of anarchy or external intervention; decisions were evidently guided by the arrangements of 1260, before
the birth of the late Queen of Norway. The meeting elected six *custodes*
(usually translated 'Guardians'), to conduct affairs until the little Queen could
come to be enthroned. (Obviously, if Queen Joleta bore a child, the meeting
would reconvene and nominate the same or new *custodes*).

They chose Buchan (Justiciar and Constable), and Fife whose duty it would
be to enthrone the future monarch. William Fraser of St Andrews and Robert
Wishart of Glasgow represented the clergy; John Comyn and James the
Steward represented the magnates. Between them they covered East and
West, North and South, young and old. Buchan had been Alexander's choice
in 1260, with Fife's grandfather and the fathers of John Comyn and the
Steward. As Professor Barrow has said, 'Constitutionally impeccable, the
election was also politically prudent'.

The Guardians equipped themselves with a new Great Seal; on one side
it bore the royal arms, with the legend *Sigillum Deputatum Regimini Regni*
('the seal appointed for the government of the realm'), and on the other the
figure of St Andrew, with *Andrea Scotis Dux esto Compatriotes* ('Andrew be
thou Leader of the compatriot Scots').[3]

All summer there was a curious lack of reaction from Edward, busy with
the problems of Gascony. The first hint of trouble came from within Scotland;
in May the earls and the Steward alerted the Host to 'uphold the peace and
tranquillity of the realm'. The cause lay in the south-west. Annandale and
Carrick his son, possibly angered by exclusion from the Guardianship, always
aware of their standing and determined to depress any Balliol pretensions,
took possession of the royal castles of Wigtown and Dumfries. For good
measure they also seized Buittle, Balliol's *caput* near Dalbeattie. That they
were able to take Buittle suggests that Devorguilla had returned south; even
in old age she would scarcely tolerate such impertinence from mere fourth-
and fifth-generation immigrants. (She may have been persuaded to come
home by her son; more probably she had returned to discover what he meant
by letting old Thomas go free to stir trouble in her territory).

Whatever the extent of the crisis, it subsided without serious trouble; in
September the Bruces, with the Steward and others, were making a pact at
Turnberry with the Earl of Ulster and Gloucester's brother for a campaign
in Connacht. By then an embassy had gone to seek Edward's advice and
protection, both for Scotland and for the late King's lands in Cumberland.
The envoys returned in November, to find that the nation's hopes and prayers
had not been fulfilled; the Queen had borne a son, but he had not survived.[4]

Local tradition claims he was buried in Cambuskenneth, not with his father
in Dunfermline. The birth must have taken place before mid-November at
latest, more probably during October. Unhappily for Joleta's memory, the

only reporter is again the misogynist Franciscan:

> Yet she, with female cunning, lied that she was pregnant, so as to give courage
> to the wavering patriots and to gain popularity with the people. But the cunning
> of woman always comes to a miserable end; while she habituated the country
> to her deceits from the day of the King's death to the Purification [2 February
> 1287], nor would she admit honest matrons to discern her condition, she kept
> deluding the populace about her pregnancy. She had a new font made, of
> white marble; she procured an actor's son to be ascribed as hers, and when at
> the time of birth (as she had announced it), people came to Stirling, in which
> place the lady dwelt, as many as for such a birth exulted in the liberty of the
> dance, by the prudence of William [sic] Earl of Buchan she was caught out at
> that castle's gate in her deceits, to the confusion of all present, and all who
> later heard of it execrated her. So she left the country in disgrace, she who had
> been brought at such expense to be married to the King. This I would say for
> the faith of women, for whose sake in other matters I would add another
> example …

He has overdone it again. Most women could count on their fingers
enough to work out that a birth near the Purification could not be of
Alexander's begetting; there are few signs of any 'wavering patriots' in need
of encouragement; if the Queen did use her condition to hearten doubters
it was scarcely blameworthy. She may have ordered a font, she may have
found a potential wet-nurse, but how Buchan could 'catch her out at the
gate', literally or metaphorically, is not explained. The mistake over his name
could be a copyist's error, dropping a reference to Bishop Fraser; more impor-
tantly, the Exchequer was still remitting her terce in 1288, which would
hardly have been the case if she had been 'caught out' in deception.

Joleta eventually returned to France; the Candlemas date might mark her
departure. There she married the widower Artus II of Brittany, son of Beatrix
of England, and bore him six children. One wonders what she told them
about her brief time in a distant country.[5]

She faded quickly from the nation's memory; not so Alexander. His reign
had materially altered the state of his country in an age of change. With his
counsellors he had fused the ancient consultative processes of Celtic kingdoms
into those of a feudal state, to produce a mature and balanced system of
government. The concept of a Community of the Realm was given time to
form, not the mutual bonding of kinship-groups nor the personal loyalty
between lord and vassal, but something more than either. The Guardians
inherited a strong and self-confident country which could resist future stresses.
The *colloquium* which elected them was not itself elected – the idea of universal
suffrage had scarcely occurred to anyone, anywhere – but behind the leaders
and their immediate backers stood a nation in the process of finding itself.

That discovery might have taken longer but for two external stimuli.

The first of these had happened already. It was the revolt against Charles of Anjou that erupted in Sicily at Easter 1282, sparked by one French sergeant's insult to one Sicilian woman, and spread to engulf all Charles's plans and dreams. It was partly fomented from outside by exiles and alarmed Byzantines, but its fighters were the Sicilian peasantry and their local leaders. The second stimulus would soon be supplied by Edward, out of his assumption that he was divinely appointed to steer a backward province into obedient harmony with the rest of his possessions.

Alexander's lifelong insistence on consultation with his advisers may have misled both Henry and Edward into thinking him inept and his administration ineffective. They took their barons' advice only in time of crisis, and then only if they had failed to impose their own will. They were the heirs of a Conqueror, whose initial success had been seen by his contemporaries as 'The judgment of God at Hastings', and who applied the old Norse doctrine of 'swordland' as a man's personal property to his new-won kingdom. Saxon notions of elective kingship were swept aside to be replaced by a monarchy which was the sole fount of law. As strongly as St Louis, Henry and his son believed in the Divine Right of Kings; it was their duty not merely to enforce the law but to formulate it. No other method of government could be tolerated; the laws of Wales or Galloway were swept aside as 'too barbarous to be considered Law at all'.[6]

The upheavals of the next forty years, from the death of the Maid of Norway to the accession of Carrick's son as Robert I and at last to the Treaty of Edinburgh-Northampton, cannot be covered here. Terrible and tragic events, moments of glory, years of despair, lay ahead but by their end the Community of the Realm was a reality transcending the lives of individual kings and spearmen; it was Alexander's lasting bequest to his people. Amid all the chroniclers' fine phrases, one anonymous vernacular poet has left his King a fitting epitaph:[7]

> Quhen Alessandre oure King was deid
> That Scotland held in love and lé,
> Awa was sonse of ale and breid,
> Of wine and wax, of gamyn and glé;
> Oure gold was changèd into leid,
> The frute was faln fra everie tree.
> Christ, born into virginité
> Succour Scotland and remede,
> That stad is in perplexité!

Epilogue. Notes

1 Envoys to Edward I; Barrow, *Bruce*, 23n.

2 This document, then in the possession of a relative of the historian Sir William Fraser, and translated by a local schoolmaster, has not been traced since (as far as I can ascertain). I know of it only by the kindness of the late Mr A.G.Williamson (Dumfries). For William de St.-Clair see p.197 above, and Dreux-Coucy, p.33. Mourning dress, Labarge, *Bar.Hsehold*, 133.

3 Barrow, *Bruce*, 21–2.

4 Barrow, *Bruce*, 24–26. Devorguilla had intended remaining two years in Scotland (hoping to die near New Abbey?). For the 'crisis', *ER I*, 35, reference in Dumfries Sheriff's accounts to lands affected by 'the war moved after the King's death'. Turnberry Band, Barrow *loc.cit.* The August envoys to Gascony were the Bishop of Brechin (Mr William Comyn of Kilconquhar), the Abbot of Jedburgh (John Morel), and Geoffrey Mowbray.

5 *Chron.Lanercost*, 117–18. The child must have been conceived between late October 1285 and early February 1286, assuming Lenten abstinence was observed. Payment of terce, *ER I*, 39. Brittany, p.33.

6 Runciman, *SV*, *passim*, especially 236 *inf.*; for Edward, Stones & Simpson, *Gt.Cause*; 'barbarous laws', Barrow, *Bruce*, 192–3. (Cf. Powicke, 681 *inf.*, on Edward's problems with Welsh laws).

7 A vernacular *cantus* of unrecorded authorship, preserved in Wyntoun's *Originale Cronykil* (1425). The second line can be interpreted as 'He who held Scotland. .' or 'He whom Scotland held …'. *Lé* = loyalty; *sonse* = abundance; *gamyn and glé* = sport/gaming and mirth; gold into lead is the antithesis of the alchemist's ambition. The sixth line, missing from most versions, is said to have been recovered by the late Dr W.Douglas Simpson. I have not traced his source.

BIBLIOGRAPHY

APS I	*Acts of the Parliaments of Scotland*, vol. I, ed. Thomson and Innes; Edinburgh, 1844-75.
Barrow, *A-N Era*	*The Anglo-Norman Era in Scottish History*, G.W.S. Barrow; Clarendon, 1980.
Barrow, *Bruce*	*Robert Bruce*, G.W.S. Barrow; Edinburgh U.P., 2nd ed., 1976.
Barrow, *K & U*	*Kingship and Unity*, (New Hist. of Scotland, vol. 2), G.W.S. Barrow; Arnold, 1981.
Barrow, 'Problems'	'Some Problems in 12th- and 13th-c. Scottish History', G.W.S. Barrow, Trans. Sc. Geneal. Soc., XXV, no.4 (1978).
BL	*Ancient Laws and Customs of the Burghs of Scotland*, ed. C. Innes; Sc. Burgh Recs. Soc., vol. II, 1868.
CDS	*Calendar of State Documents relating to Scotland*; Vol. I, to Henry III, Vol. II, Edward I; J.S. Bain; Edinburgh, 1881, 1884.
Chron. Bower	*Johannis de Fordun Scotichronicon cum Supplementis et Continuatione Walteri Boweri*, ed. W. Goodall; Edinburgh, 1759.
Chron. Lanercost	*Chronicon de Lanercost*, ed. J. Stevenson; Bannatyne & Maitland Clubs, 1839.
Chron. Man	*The Chronicle of Man*, ed. Munch & Gross; The Manx Society, 1874.
Chron. Pluscarden	*Liber Pluscardensis*, ed. F.J.H. Skene; Edinburgh, 1877.
CM	*The Chronicle of Melrose*, facsimile edn., ed. A. O. & M.O. Anderson; Humphries, 1936.
Cruden, *Castle*	*The Scottish Castle*, Stewart Cruden; Nelson, 1960.
Cruden, *Churches*	*Scottish Medieval Churches*, Stewart Cruden; John Donald, 1986.
Dasent, *Hacon*	*The Saga of Hacon* (Icelandic Sagas iv), ed. G.W. Dasent; Rolls Series, 1894.
ER	*The Exchequer Rolls of Scotland*, ed. J. Stuart & G. Burnett; Vol I, Edinburgh, 1878.
ES	*Early Sources of Scottish History*, ed. A.O. Anderson; 2 vols., revised ed., Paul Watkins, 1990.
Fergusson	*Alexander the Third*, James Fergusson of Kilkerran; Maclehose, 1937.
Fordun	*Chronica Gentis Scotorum*, John Fordun, ed. W.F. Skene; 4 vols., Edmonston & Douglas, 1871-2. (The *Annales*, material collected for Bk. V onwards, are mainly used here, cited by section numbers).

Hdlist A.II	*Handlist of the Acts of Alexander II*, compiled by J.M. Scoular; Edin. University, 1959.
Hdlist A. III	*Handlist of the Acts of Alexander III, the Guardians, and John*, compiled by G.G. Simpson; Edin. U., 1960.
Joinville	*Chronicle of the Crusade of St. Louis*, by John, Lord of Joinville; ed. F. Marzials in *Memoirs of the Crusade*, Everyman, 1908.
Johnston	*The Norwegian account of Haco's expedition———-with a literal English version*, Revd. J. Johnston; Edinburgh 1882.
Labarge, *Bar. Hsehd.*	*A Baronial Household in the 13th Century*, Margaret W. Labarge; Eyre & Spottiswoode, 1965.
Labarge, *St. L*	*Saint Louis*, M.W. Labarge; E & S, 1968.
Labarge, *S. de M.*	*Simon de Montfort*, M.W. Labarge; E & S, 1962.
Moore, *Lands*	*Lands of the Scottish Kings in England*, Margaret F. Moore; Allen & Unwin, 1915.
Moray Reg.	*Registrum Episcopatum Moraviensis*, Bannatyne Club, 1837.
M. Paris, *Chr. Maj.*	*Chronica Majora*, Matthew Paris OSB, ed. H.R. Luard; Rolls Series no. 57.
NMssS.	*National Manuscripts of Scotland*, (facsimiles and trs.); HMSO, Pt. I, 1867, Pt. II, 1870.
Norris, *Costume*	*Costume and Fashion*, Hubert Norris; 2 vols., Dent, 1940.
Powicke	*Henry III and the Lord Edward*, F.M. Powicke; Clarendon, 1965.
PSAS	*Proceedings of the Society of Antiquaries of Scotland* (series).
Purser, *Sc. Music*	*Scotland's Music*; John Purser; Mainstream, 1992.
QA	*Quoniam Attachiamenta*; printed with *Regiam Maj.*, *q.v.*
RCAHMS, *Argyll*	Royal Commission on the Ancient and Historic Monuments of Scotland, *Argyll* 1–7; HMSO, 1971–1992
RCAHMS, *Peebles*	*Peeblesshire*; 2 vols., HMSO, 1967
RCAHMS, *Roxburgh*	*Roxburghshire*; 2 vols., HMSO, 1956
Regiam Maj.	*Regiam Majestatem et Quoniam Attachiamenta*, ed. Rt. Hon. Lord Cooper; Stair Society, 1947.
RRS I	*Regesta Regum Scottorum, Vol. I*, to Malcolm IV, ed. G.W.S. Barrow; Edin. U.P., 1960.
RRS II	*RRS Vol. II*, William the Lion; ed. G.W.S. Barrow; Edin. U.P., 1971.
Runciman, *Crs.*	*A History of the Crusades*, Stephen Runciman; 3 vols., Penguin, 1965.
Runciman, *SV*	*The Sicilian Vespers*, S. Runciman; Penguin, 1960.
SA	*Scottish Annals from English Chroniclers*, ed. A. O. Anderson; Dutt, 1908.
Sc. Abbeys	*Scottish Abbeys*, S. Cruden; HMSO, 1960.
Sc. Cas.	*Scottish Castles*, W.D. Simpson; HMSO, 1959.
Sc. Stud.	*Scottish Studies*, Journal of the School of Scottish Studies, Edinburgh University. (series)

Sel. Cases   *Select Scottish Cases of the 13th Century*, the Rt. Hon. Ld.
                              Cooper; Hodge, 1944.

SHR   *Scottish Historical Review* (series).

SHS   *Scottish Historical Society* (series).

St.Sc.Ch.   *Statutes of the Scottish Church*, D. Patrick; *SHS* 1907.

Stewart, *Sc.Coin.*   *The Scottish Coinage*, I.H. Stewart; Spink, 1955.

Stones, *Docs.*   *Anglo-Scottish Relations 1174-1328, Some Selected*
                              Documents, E.L.G. Stones; Nelson, 1965.

Stones & Simpson,   *Edward I and the Throne of Scotland, the Great Cause*, E.L.G.
   Gt.Cause   Stones & G.G. Simpson; 2 vols., Glasgow UP, 1978.

Watt, *Biog.*   *Biographical Dictionary of Scottish Graduates to AD 1410*,
                              D.E.R. Watt; Clarendon, 1977.

Wyntoun   *The Orygynale Cronykil of Scotland* (to 1408), ed.D.Laing,
                              Historians of Scotland, ii,iii,ix (1872-1879).

Young, *R. of C.*   *Richard of Cornwall*, N. Denholm Young; Blackwell, 1947.

APPENDIX A: THE KING'S YEAR

Compiled from Hdlist A. III and other sources.

★ Starred entries are based on doubtful evidence (possibly spurious charters).

1249
9 July: Accession (Alexander II died)
13 July: Scone – enthronement
4 Sept: 8th birthday

1250
1–3 June: Edinburgh
19 June: Dunfermline
3 Dec: Scone

1251
4 March: Crail
25 April: Haddington
29–30 April: Roxburgh
20 May: Kinghorn
31 May: Scone
26 July: Scone
19 Aug: Kincardine
20 Oct: Edinburgh
Dec: to England
24–31 Dec: York
26 Dec: 1st marriage, to Margaret of
England

1252
Jan: Return to Scotland
21 April: Linlithgow
23 April: Edinburgh
8 June: Newbattle

1253
17 Sept: Stirling
12 Nov: Roxburgh
17 Dec: Stirling
19 & 27 Dec: St Andrews

1254
4 Feb: Edinburgh
★12 May: Edinburgh

1255
Aug: Edinburgh
Sept: Roxburgh
7 Sept: Wark
20 Sept: Roxburgh

1256
14 Jan: Holyrood
★ 10 May: Kinghorn ?
July: to England
15 Aug: Woodstock
25–9 Aug: London
Sept: Huntingdon and return to
Scotland
Earldom of Huntingdon granted

1257
4 Feb: Roxburgh
By June: Queen Mother re-married
10 June: Edinburgh
24 June: Stirling
29 Aug: Stirling
Oct: Kinross
29 Oct: Stirling

1258
Ca. 18 March: Roxburgh
Ca. 15 April: Stirling
2 June: Edinburgh
20 Aug: Holyrood
8 Sept: Melrose
9 Sept: Jedburgh
16 Oct: Perth

1259
[No record]

1260
21 May: Kilwinning

18 Aug: Inverness
28 Aug: Durris
21 Sept: Selkirk
Oct: to England
29 Oct: London
Nov: return to Scotland (Queen
Margaret remains in England)
12 Dec: Traquair

1261
28 Feb: Pss. Margaret b. at Windsor,
May, Q. and Pss. return to Scotland
May: Peebles ?
19 June: Edinburgh
13 Aug: 'Rothenec' (Spey)
29 Aug: Kinross
4 Sept: 20th birthday

1262
★ ?12 Feb: Newbattle
24 Feb: Traquair
21 March: Montrose
★ ?31 March: Scone
10 April: Stirling
10 & 13 May: Traquair
7 Oct: Lanark
21 Dec: Forfar

1263
6 Feb: Selkirk
14 Feb: Edinburgh
19 March: Scone
3 May: Roxburgh
21 June: Melrose
?July: Forfar
5 Aug: solar eclipse
?Sept: Ayr
29 Sept x 3 Oct: Battle of Largs
2–3 Oct: Largs
25 Dec: Linlithgow

1264
2 *colloquia* in Edinburgh during year.
?Jan: Jedburgh
21 Jan.: Pr. Alexander b. at Jedburgh.
?Feb: Jedburgh
March: Dumfries
10 April: Newbattle
21 July: Melrose

7 Aug: Machan, nr. Larkhall
Nov: Edinburgh
9 Dec: Selkirk
12 Dec: Traquair

1265
14 March: Lindores
19 March: Perth
31 March: Scone
10 Oct: Scone

1266
4 March: Stirling
★ ?March: Melrose
14 April: Scone
19 May: Roxburgh
20 May: Edinburgh
2 July: Perth; Treaty of Perth signed

1267
★ ?12 Feb: Scone
March: Roxburgh
Pr. Edward at Roxburgh, 'Lent'
    (during March)
1 May: Jedburgh
1 June: Scone
3 Aug: Cadzow
14 Aug: Aboyne

1268
13 & 16 April: Berwick
May: Haddington
Princes Edward and Edmund at
    Haddington during May
★ ?31 Aug: Balmerino
28 Nov: Elgin

1269
6–7 Jan: Kelso
Sept: to England
13 Oct: London; dedication of St.
    Edward's shrine, Westminster
    Abbey

1270
28 March: Scone
21 June: Haddington
28 Aug: Dumfries

1271
23–5 April: Kinclaven
★ ?28 June: Selkirk ?
4 Sept: 30th birthday
3 Oct: Newbattle

1272
7 Jan: Kinross
26 Jan: Haddington
1 July: Kintore
16 Nov: Henry III of England d.

1273
15 March: Scone
20 March: Prince David born (at   ?)
5 April: Kelso
22 April: Durham
15 Oct: Scone
2 Dec: Kintore

1274
20 March: Roxburgh
1 Aug: Haddington
To England
19 Aug: Westminster; coronation of
    Edward I
23 Sept: 'Loch Cumberay'

1275
★ ?Feb: Cupar; Dunfermline (26 Feb:
    Q. Margaret d. at Cupar, Fife;
    buried in Dunfermline)
20 May: Berwick
18 June: Edinburgh
15 Aug: Elgin
12 Sept: Roxburgh
24 Oct: Stirling
14 Nov: Roxburgh
29 Dec: Brechin

1276
20 Jan: Stirling
16 June: Selkirk
18 Aug: Scone
8 Sept: Stirling

1277
27 Jan: Kincardine
10 March: Cupar, Fife

15 & 18 April: Forfar
20 April: Kincardine
18 May: Haddington
5 June: Roxburgh
2 Dec: Traquair

1278
20 Feb: Scone
24 May: Yester
3 Sept: Traquair
2 Oct: Roxburgh
To England
16 Oct: Tewkesbury
28 Oct: Westminster; homage to
    Edward I for English lands
Nov: Return to Scotland

1279
26 March: Edinburgh
29 March: Traquair
10 April: Edinburgh
6 May: Haddington
25 May: Selkirk
19 July: Dumfries
28 July: Durris
5 Sept: Stirling
10 Sept: Edinburgh
14 Sept: Traquair
12 Nov: Coupar Angus
1 Dec: Dunfermline

1280
1 April: Scone
8 April: Haddington
4 July: Berwick
7 Aug: Perth
?14 Aug: Perth; Church General
    Council (perhaps at time of a
    parliament)

1281
?June: Lindores; Dunfermline (Prince
    David d., Lindores, June; buried in
    Dunfermline)
25 July: Roxburgh
11 Aug: ?Leith (Pss. Margaret sailed to
    Norway)
4 Sept: 40th birthday

1282
1 July: Scone
12 July: Kinross
23 Aug: Durris
4 Oct: Newbattle
11 Nov: Roxburgh; Prince Alexander
   m. Margaret of Flanders
25 Dec: Dunkeld

1283
20 Feb: Scone
28 March: Scone
(–) March: Pss. Margaret of Norway b.
9 April: Q. Margaret of Norway d.
7 June: Stirling

1284
10 Jan: St. Andrews
?Jan: Cupar, Fife; Dunfermline (Pr.
   Alexander d. 21 Jan., Cupar; buried
   in Dunfermline)
5 Feb: Scone
20 April: Edinburgh
18 May: Dundee
25 May: Forfar
17 June: Scone
(–) June: Marie, Q. Mother, d.; buried
   at Newbattle

26 June: Haddington
27–28 June: Edinburgh
1 July: Stirling
11 July: Dundee
12 July: Kinross

1285
29 March: Kintore
1 April: Aboyne
★ ?10 April: Scone
30 April: Scone
24 May: Glenluce
17 June: Dundee
26 June: Largo
10 Aug: 'Tuly Mac Argentuly'
?14 Oct/?1 Nov: Jedburgh (2nd
   marriage to Joleta de Dreux)
25 Oct: Edinburgh
13 & 15 Nov: Scone

1286
18 March: Edinburgh
18 x 19 March: d. near Kinghorn
(–) buried Dunfermline

APPENDIX B: BURGHS ESTABLISHED BEFORE 1286

Aberdeen	David I	by 1153	Mint, Alex. III
Auldearn	David I	by 1153	Moved to Nairn q.v.
Ayr	William(prob.)	?c. 1205	Mint, Alex. III
Banff	David I (prob.)	by 1153	
Berwick	David I	c.1124	Mint, D.I, W., A. II, A.III.
Crail	David, or Ctss. Ada		Confirmed, Malcolm IV
Cullen	David, or William		
Dingwall	Alexander II	1227	
Dumfries	William	c.1185	
Dumbarton	Alexander II	1222	?Mint A.III('Dun—')
Dundee	Earl David, or Wm.	1180–1202	
Dunfermline	David I	by 1153	
Edinburgh	David I	by 1153	Mint, David I., Alex. III
Elgin	David I	?1134	
Forfar	David I, or Wm.	by 1214	Mint, Alex. III
Forres	David I	by 1153	Mint, Alex. III
Haddington	David I	by 1153	?Mint, David I
Inverkeithing	Malcolm IV	1161–4	
Inverness	David I	by 1153	Mint, Alex. III
Inverurie	Earl David	by 1191	
Irvine	Alexander II	by 1249	
Jedburgh	David I or Malcolm IV	by 1165	Mint, Malcolm IV
Kinghorn	?Ctss. Ada, or A. III	by 1286	Mint, Alex. III
Kintore	David I, or Wm.	by 1214	
Lanark	David I (prob.)	by 1153	Mint, Alex. III
Linlithgow	David I	by 1153	
Montrose('Salorch')	David I	by 1153	Mint, Alex. III
Nairn	William	by 1195	Replacing Auldearn q.v.
Peebles	David I	by 1153	
Perth	David I	by 1153	Mint, Wm., Alex. III
Perth 'New Burgh'	William	1178–95	
Renfrew	David I (prob.)	by 1153	
Rosemarkie	Alexr. (II or III)	by 1286	
Roxburgh	David I	by 1153	Mint, David I to Alex. III
Rutherglen	David I	by 1153	
Stirling	David I	by 1153	Mint, Wm., Alex III
Glasgow	Bishop	1175–8	
St Andrews	Bishop	1153–62	

Canongate	Holyrood Abbey	by 1200
(Edinburgh)		
Cromarty	unknown	
Fyvie	unknown	

Sources: *BL I; RRS I & II; Hdlists.A.III; PSAS XXX;* Stewart, *Coinage.*

APPENDIX C: RELIGIOUS FOUNDATIONS

Abbreviations:-

A Abbey (with date when raised from Priory, where appropriate)
P Priory
G Remains in care of Historic Scotland
C Part or whole still in use for public worship
d Remains of considerable interest
e Replacing a Culdee or other early foundation

Order/Name	Dedication	Founder	Dates/Remarks
Benedictine			
Aberdeen		?	A by 1231, ceased by 1300
Coldingham	S. Cuthbert	Edgar, Alex. I or David I	P by 1139; C,d
Dunfermline	Holy Trinity	St Margaret	P 1070, A 1128; C,G,d (from Canterbury)
Iona	S. Columba	Reginald of Islay	A by 1203; C,d,e
Isle of May	S. Aethernan	David I	P 1142–7
Urquhart (nr. Elgin)	Holy Trinity	David I	P, ca. 1136
Cluniac			
Crossraguel		Duncan of Carrick	Oratory 1214, A by 1286. G,d
Paisley	SS. James, Milburga & Mirinus	Walter I Steward (originally at Renfrew)	P 1163–5, A 1219; C,d
Tironensian			
Arbroath	S. Thomas of Canterbury	William the Lion	A, 1178. G,d
Fyvie	Our Lady & All Saints	?Reginald le Chen	P or Cell @ 1285
Kelso	Our Lady & S. John	David I (originally at Selkirk, 1113)	A 1128; G,d
Kilwinning	S. Vinin (Finnian)	Hugh de Morville	P by 1162; G,d
Lesmahagow	S. Machutus	David I	P 1144
Lindores	Our Lady & S. Andrew	David Earl of Huntingdon	A 1191
Cistercian			
Balmerino	Our Lady & S. Edward	Q. Ermengarde & Alexander II	A 1227; Nat. Trust Scot.
Coupar Angus	Our Lady	Malcolm IV	A ca. 1162
Culross	Our Lady & S. Serf	Earl of Fife	A by 1217; G,d
Deer	Our Lady	Earl of Buchan	A by 1219; G,e
Dundrennan	Our Lady	David I & Fergus of Galloway	A 1142; G,d
Glenluce	Our Lady	Roland of Galloway	A 1190–2; G

Kinloss	Our Lady	David I	A 1150; d
Melrose	Our Lady	David I	A 1136; G,d
New Abbey (Sweetheart)	Our Lady	Devorguilla	A 1273; G,d
Newbattle	Our Lady	David I & E. Henry	A 1140 (now college)
Saddell	Our Lady	Somerled &/or Reginald (from Mellifont)	A 1160–1207; G,d

Valliscaulian

Ardchattan	Our Lady & S. John Bapt.	Duncan of Argyll	P ca.1230; G(& private house)
Beauly	S. John Baptist	John Bisset	P 1223–30; G,d
Pluscarden	S. Andrew	Alexander II	P ca.1230 (now OSB,1948)

Augustinian Canons

Abernethy		Hugh of A., &/or Bp. of Dunblane	P ca. 1272; d,e (Round Tower of 11th cent.)
Blantyre		Alexander II	P by 1249
Cambuskenneth	Our Lady	David I	A 1140–7; G,d (from Arrouaise)
Canonbie		?Turgis de Rosdale	P ca. 1168
Holyrood	Holy Cross	David I	A 1128; G,d
Inchaffray	S. John Evang.	E. of Strathearn	P 1200, A 1220; e
Inchcolm	S. Columba	Alexander I	P 1123, A 1235; G,d,e
Inchmahome		E. of Menteith	P 1238; G,d
Jedburgh	Our Lady	David I	P ca.1138, A 1154; G,d (from Beauvais)
Loch Leven	S. Serf	Bp. of St. Andrews	P 1152; e
Monymusk	Our Lady	Earl of Mar	P by 1200; e
Pittenweem	SS. Fillan & Aethernan		P by 1200 (later OSB ex-I. of May) e
Restenneth	S. Peter	David I or Malcolm IV	P by 1160; G,d,e
St Andrews	S. Andrew	Bishop	P 1144; G,d
St Mary's Isle	Our Lady	— of Galloway	P by 1200
Scone	Holy Trinity	Alexander I	P ca.1120, A 1164; e

Premonstratensian (White) Canons

Dryburgh	Our Lady	Hugh de Morville	A 1150; G,d
Fearn	Our Lady	Earl of Ross	A (Old Fearn) 1220–7; New Fearn 1238
Holywood (Dercongal)	S. John Bapt.	Alan of Galloway	A by 1225 (e ?)
Soulseat	Our Lady	— of Galloway	A by 1175
Tongland		Alan of Galloway	A 1218
Whithorn		Bishop	P ca.1175; C, G, d, e

Gilbertine (Double houses of men and women)

| Dalmilling | | Walter Steward | 1221–38, failed |

Trinitarians ('Red Friars')

Aberdeen		K. William or Q. Ermengarde	1181–1211
Berwick (& S. Edward's Hosp.)		?William the Lion	by 1214
Dunbar (& Maison Dieu Hosp.)		Ctss. of Dunbar	1240–8
Fail(ford, Ayr)		?Andrew Bruce	by 1250

Houston (& Grace of God Hosp.) (East Lothian)		Christian de Mowbray ca. 1270	
Scotlandwell (& 2 hosps.)		Bishop of St Andrews	1250–55
Peebles	Holy Cross	Alexander III	(to the Order by 1300); G

Dominicans; Order of Preachers ('Black Friars')

Aberdeen	S. John Bapt.	Alexander II	1230–49
Ayr	S. Katherine	Alexander II	ca. 1242
Berwick	S. Peter Martyr of Milan	Alexander II	by 1240
Edinburgh	Assumption of Our Lady	Alexander II	ca. 1244
Elgin	S. James	Alexander II	ca. 1234
Glasgow	S. John Evang.	Bp. and Chapter	by 1246
Inverness	S. Bartholomew	Alexander II	by 1240
Montrose	Nativity of Our Lady	Alan Doorward	before 1275
Perth	S. Andrew	Alexander II	1231
St Andrews	Assumpt. & Coron.of Our Lady	Bp. of St Andrews	?1274
Stirling	SS. Laurence & Kentigern	Alexander II	1238
Wigtown	Annunciation of Our Lady	Devorguilla	1267–87

Franciscans, Friars Minor ('Greyfriars')

Berwick		Alexander II	1231
Dumfries		(Alan of G. or) Devorguilla	1234–66
Dundee		Devorguilla	before 1289
Haddington		?Q. Marie	by 1242
Inverkeithing		Philip de Mowbray	ca. 1268
Roxburgh	S. Peter	Alexander II	1232–4

Carmelites ('White Friars')

Aberdeen	Our Lady of Mt. Carmel	?Reginald le Chen	by 1273
Berwick	Our Lady of Mt. Carmel	John Gray	1270
Tullilum (Perth)	Our Lady of Mt. Carmel	Bp. of Dunkeld	1262

Friars of the Sack

Berwick	?	?	1267; Order suppressed 1274.

Knights Templar

Balantrodoch (Temple)		(prob.) David I	by 1175
Maryculter		Walter Bisset	1221–36

Knights Hospitaller (S. John of Jerusalem)

Torphichen		David I	by 1153; G,d

Houses for Women Religious

Benedictine

Lincluden		Uchtred of Galloway	1164–74; G

Cistercian

Abbey St. Bathans	Our Lady & S. Bothan	Ctss. of Dunbar	13th cent. (?e)
Berwick	Our Lady & S. Leonard	David I	P by 1153
Coldstream	Our Lady	E. of Dunbar	P by 1166
Eccles	Our Lady	E. or Ctss. of Dunbar	P by 1156
Elcho	Our Lady	Marjory or David Lindsay	P by 1241
Haddington	Our Lady	Ctss. Ada de Warenne	P by 1159
Manuel	Our Lady	Malcolm IV	P by 1164
North Berwick	Our Lady	E. of Fife	P ca. 1150

Augustinian Canonesses

Iona	Our Lady	Reginald of Islay	P by 1208; G,d
Perth	S. Leonard	?	P before 1292

Also many hospitals and hospices for pilgrims, lepers, travellers, sick people, aged and poor men and women, some conducted by Orders and others established by burghs or individual piety; (partial list in *MRHS*).

Sources: *Medieval Religious Houses, Scotland*, I.B. Cowan & D.E. Easson, 2nd edn., (Longmans Green, 1976); *Scottish Abbeys*, and individual Guidebooks (HMSO) where available; and see Cruden, *Churches*.

APPENDIX D: TREASURES OF SCOTLAND

Apart from the Stone of Destiny (p.18), the fate of the Scottish regalia is unknown. There are two lists of valuables found at Edinburgh, and some notes of objects collected elsewhere. The first list is in *APS I* (pp.5-6 of main text), at the end of the long *Indenture of Muniments captured in the Treasury of Edinburgh and deposited by order of the King of England at Berwick, 1291*. The indenture is witnessed by the abbots of Dunfermline and Holyrood and by four laymen (including William of Dumfries, Thomas de Carnoto's colleague in cataloguing the archives in 1282). The indenture ends with:-

A schedule of the King of Scotland's armour handed over to Ingram de Umphraville;
A roll of the ancient statutes of the kingdom of Scotland;
Moreover:-
3 crystal cups [ciphi]
3 cups *de nuce*[1]
1 silver cup
1 silver-gilt censer
2 glass goblets [godecta]
3 ivory horns [see List II and n.12]
Aaron's Rod[2]
A baton wherewith Eustace de Vesci gave seisin of the earldom of Northumberland to King Alexander [II] when he was at Norham besieging the castle [in 1215]
22 serpents' tongues set in silver[3]
A *clavis* of St.Mahuscy[4]
A silver cup
2 crystal cups ['*costelli*' for *costrelli*]
4 boxes [*cophini*] with various relics
A box with a silver cross, containing part of the True Cross
2 *tam'elli* bound with silver[5]
2 old rolls of the Queen's wardrobe
All these were found in a certain chest [*cista*] in the Dormitory of the Holy Cross,[6] and replaced there by the said Abbots and other under their seals.

And in the Treasury of Edinburgh Castle were found the following precious things:-
2 copes nobly embroidered
a chasuble nobly embroidered
another not [embroidered]
a tunic and dalmatic of red samite
2 stoles
2 embroidered *favones* [covers] with an amice and an embroidered alb
a towel and an embroidered [altar-] frontal
2 *filatoria burellata* partly gilt[7]
a pair of shoulder-pieces and cuffs with [?a box of] embroidered corporals [linen cloths for use at the altar]
a cope of green samite

2 copes of purple samite and one of red samite
a tunic and dalmatic of *baudekyn*[8]
an embroidered amice
3 *baudekyns*[8] [see n. 22?]
Several small things wrapped in a linen cloth[9]
a complete old vestment lacking a chasuble
a shrine of gilded silver wherein reposes the cross called *La Blak Rode*
an ivory comb
3 hand – towels [*manutergia*]
and a ship for incense.
[I am deeply grateful to Mrs. M. O. Anderson for help with this list].

List II, of June 1296, was printed in full by Joseph Hunter, 'King Edward's spolia-
tions in Scotland', *Archaeological Journal XIII* (1856), 247 – 9, from P.R.O. Exchequer,
Accts. Various (E 101), 354/9 m.l(e); calendared in *CDS II, 840*.
Found in the Castle of Edinburgh
In a coffer marked +;
First a handsome box [*forcerium pulchrum*] containing an armorial shrine, damaged[10]
a gilded morse [clasp or brooch]
a cross of tin
a shrine with gryphons
2 cloths of *arista* [hair-cloth, worn as penance; *CDS II*, 'Arras']
an alb with the arms of the King of England
a stole and a maniple
Item,
a shrine with the arms of the King of Scotland, covered in red sindon
a gilded crozier which belonged to the Bishop of Ross[11]
a nut with a foot and cover of silver decorated with gilding
a crystal cup with a gilt foot
a cup entirely of crystal, silver-mounted
3 ivory horns harnessed with silk and silver[12]
a buffalo horn [*cornu de bugle*][13]
2 small cups of *tammari*, silver-mounted [see [5]]
a small silver-gilt cup with mazer [maple-wood] foot
a nut with silver-gilt foot, broken
a crystal cup with silver-gilt foot, broken.
In a coffer marked L;
2 crystal cups bound with silver
a mazer [maple-wood bowl] with silver foot and cover, with gilding
a cup of gryphon's-egg[14], with totally broken silver mount
a crystal cup with silver-gilt foot
a cup with a *mugetto* cover[15] and silver-gilt foot
a *mugetto* pitcher with silver-gilt mounting
a mazer without a foot, of little value
a silver ship of £9 weight[16]
a pair of silver basins, £6 in weight
a pair of silver basins, £5. 17. 6d weight
In a coffer marked N;
a great silver-gilt cup with foot and cover, £4. 2. 6d

a silver-gilt cup with foot and cover, £2. 18. 9d
a silver-gilt cup with foot and cover, £2. 6. 8d
a silver-gilt cup with foot and cover, £2. 9. 9d
a silver-gilt cup with foot and cover, £1. 18. 6d
a silver cup with foot and cover, £2. 12. 11d
a silver-gilt cup with foot, lacking a cover, £1. 15. 3d
a silver cup with foot and cover, £2. 11. 5d
a silver cup with foot and cover, 14/9d
a silver cup with foot, lacking a cover, £1. 18. 4d
a white cup[17] of silver with foot, no cover, 19/7d
a silver-gilt cup with foot, no cover, £1. 3. 0d
a cup plated with silver, £1. 3. 6d
a silver pitcher with cover, £2. 1. 4d
a water-pitcher, white[17] £1. 6. 0d
a *lavatorium*,[18] white, silver, £1. 2. 0d
a water-pitcher, white, silver, £1. 0. 8d
[All in N, and the last three items of L above, are marked 'Entered in the book';
   those in N are also marked 'Later restored to the Wardrobe'].

On the back of the last membrane is a note that all these 'jewels' were sent from
Berwick to London on 17 September 1296 in three coffers, with one big and two
small coffers of documents and a coffer of relics, and
   19 buffalo-horns and a griffin horn, which were found in a priory near Forfar,[19]
      and a bundle with various things which belonged to the Bishop of St Andrews,[20]
      and a large silver alms-dish.[21]
Hunter (*loc.cit.*) adds, from a 1303 inventory of King Edward's treasures, together
with a hamper and a red coffer containing documents of fealty and homage from
Scottish magnates, and others 'touching the realm and dominion of Scotland',
   A pyx with the impression of the seal of the King of Scotland
   2 *pallia* for hanging in church, covered in green baudekyn[22]
   A wooden cup wrapped in a linen cloth sealed with sundry seals.[23]
The indenture of 1292, listing the documents to be returned to King John
Balliol (*APS I*, p. 10), adds
   In an old trunk [*maletta*] which Sir Ralph Basset [then keeper of Edinburgh Castle]
      brought with him with the aforesaid two coffers, two large *papiri*.[24]
Finally, *CDS II, 1434* (12 Aug. 1303) reports the finding, in Brechin castle, of
   A silver cup with foot and cover, made after the manner of a chalice, and
   2 forks, silver-gilt, with crystal handles.[25]

Notes

1   'of nut'; probably coconut. Such cups were not exceptionally rare; an 'Indian nut' with
    silver mountings belonged to the Master of Sherborne Hospital (Labarge, *Bar. Hsehd.* 123).
2   Probably a rod with entwined snake; sometimes a cross-&-snake.
3   Fossil sharks' teeth (M.O.A. cites Larousse, *Dict.Universel*, 1872, s.v. *Glossopetre*, 'in Malta
    believed to be the teeth of *grands serpents* turned to stone by St. Paul').
4   Mahuscy = S. Machutus, of Lesmahagow etc. *Clavis* = key, but might possibly be an error
    for *clava* = staff, (i.e. the saint's staff, Gaelic *bachul*?)
5   M.O.A. suggests *tamborelli*, little drums (Du Cange, *taborellus*, 'used in Church processions

1391'); but cf. *Tammari*, List II, where a (foreign ?) wood seems likely. Hunter says 'tamarisk'; perhaps tamarind would be better ?

6   For this 'Dormitory' cf. p.48 *supra*.

7   M.O.A. gives *f.* = *phylacteria* and *burell* = a course russet cloth, and suggests bags with gilt fittings for carrying relics on the person.

8   Baudekyn was an oriental brocade, woven with figures which were re-embroidered. The word becomes *baldacchino*, a canopy over an altar or throne.

9   These were presumably relics, dust/bones from a saint's tomb or cloths which had touched a tomb, collected by pilgrims. With the next four items, which includes St. Margaret's famous 'Black Rood' (another relic of the True Cross), may they have been specially associated with her ? (See p.26).

10 With the two shrines below, and the 'tin cross', this may account for the '4 boxes with relics' of List I. Shrines were often used for the taking of oaths, and selected to fit the occasion.

11 Robert of Fyvie, Bp. of Ross, died in 1292 and his elected successor was transferred to Caithness before consecration. Mr Thomas of Dundee was elected to Ross in 1295, (and presumably had not been invested at 1296). Watt, *Fasti*. (See p.174, n.3).

12 The 'harness' suggests these were carried, and perhaps blown rather than used as drinking-horns. 'Ivory' could be used for walrus or narwhal tusks as well as for elephant tusks. If elephant, they would be very heavy even if bored out. (Now see Purser, *Sc. Music*, 63 and Pl. IX).

13 This, and the nineteen from Forfar (n.19 below), are more probably the horns of Highland cattle, used as drinking horns; perhaps their size (3 ft. long is not uncommon) mystified the English clerks.

14 Almost certainly an ostrich-egg. Margaret of Kent owned a 'gryphon's egg' cup (*CDS I,1163*).

15 *Mughetto* = Lily of the valley in modern Italian. A foreign wood is probably meant. Almug (red sandalwood) suggests itself.

16 The weights are calculated in terms of the equivalent value of the silver used. The 'ship for incense' of List I ?

17 Possibly pewter ? or refined silver ?

18 L. = a basin or a pitcher (often in the form of an animal) used for hand-washing at table.

19 The priory is probably Restenneth. For the horns, see n. 13 above; might the 'griffin's horn' be a feral goat's ? or a narwhal tusk ?

20 Bp. William Fraser was in exile in France, where he died next year.

21 This addendum is also in Stones, *Docs.*, 75(to which I owe the reference to Hunter), where the date of dispatch to London is given.

22 *Pallia* = 'palls' but also hangings; see n.8. above.

23 There is no indication of why this cup was so carefully treated; cf.n.9 above.

24 Either papyrus or paper; in either case a great rarity.

25 Forks for use at table are said to have been introduced into England by Queen Eleanor of Provence.

APPENDIX E: THE COINAGE OF ALEXANDER III

Nicholas Holmes

Throughout most of Alexander III's reign, the only coins in circulation were silver pennies, which were frequently cut into halves and quarters to facilitate smaller transactions. It was not until 1280 that Scotland's first round halfpennies and farthings were struck.

The earliest pennies attributed to Alexander's reign are a small group similar to those of his father, Alexander II, and belonging to the period 1249–50. They show the king's head in profile to left or right, with a sceptre, and on the reverse a short double, or voided, cross with a six-pointed star in each angle. It is probable that all these pennies were minted at Berwick.

In 1250, after just a year of Alexander's reign, a major recoinage commenced. Some three years earlier the reverse design of English pennies had been changed from a short to a long voided cross, extending to the edge of the coin, in an attempt to discourage the practice of clipping silver from the edges of coins for private profit. This change was copied in Scotland in 1250, and for the first time an attempt was made to recall earlier coins for melting down and conversion into new pennies. In order to achieve this, it was necessary to open mints all over Scotland, so that people could take their old coins and exchange them for new ones. Consequently, a total of sixteen mints were involved in the early stages of production of the new coinage – the highest number ever operating at one time in Scotland. The identity of some of these mints has still not definitely been established, and most of them operated for only a short period, with the majority of the coins emanating from the major mints at Berwick, Perth, Roxburgh and Edinburgh. (See App. B, p.246).

The standard type of the 1250 coinage has a profile bust to left or right, with a sceptre, on the obverse, with the king's name and title around, and on the reverse a long voided cross, with six-pointed stars in the angles, surrounded by the names of the mint and moneyer, usually abbreviated. Within this general description, eight major types have been distinguished, largely as a result of the study of some 1800 examples from a hoard found in Brussels in 1908. This hoard was buried around the year 1265, and although there are some types of Alexander's voided-cross coinage which post-date the hoard, it appears that the number of coins struck between 1265 and 1280 must have been very small.

In 1280 a second major recoinage was instigated. In the previous year a major change to the design of the English coinage had been introduced, with a single long cross replacing the voided cross on the reverse. The advantage of the voided cross had lain in providing guidelines for the accurate halving and quartering of pennies, which appears to have been an officially accepted practice. Edward I's new coinage provided for the minting of round halfpennies and farthings, however, thus removing much of the necessity for cutting up pennies. The fact that Alexander III felt obliged to introduce the same measures into the Scottish coinage reflected the inevitable economic involvement of Scotland and England, which existed despite frequent crises between the two countries.

Alexander's second recoinage again involved the opening of a large number of different mints for a short period, but unfortunately the names of these are not recorded on the coins of this issue. It is generally accepted that the output of different mints was distinguished by the combination of mullets of five and six points, and stars of seven points, which appeared in the angles of the reverse cross. Between 1280 and 1286 very large numbers of pennies, and smaller quantities of halfpennies and farthings, were struck. The traditional Scottish profile bust was retained on the obverse, with the legend ALEXANDER DEI GRA, and the words REX SCOTORVM appeared on the reverse. Because of the large number of coin hoards buried during the troubled times of the late 13th and early 14th centuries, the pennies of the 1280 coinage have survived in considerable numbers, and are today the commonest Scottish medieval coins.

Further Reading

Stewart, I.H. 'The Brussels Hoard: Mr.Baldwin's Arrangement of the Scottish Coins', *British Numismatic Journal* 29 (1958–9), 91–7.

Stewart, I.H. *The Scottish Coinage*, revised edition, London (1967).

Stewart, I.H. 'Scottish Mints', in *Mints, Dies and Currency: Essays in Memory of Albert Baldwin*, ed. R.A.G. Carson; London (1971), especially pp.202–5.

Stewart, I.H. & 'Classification of the Single-Cross Sterlings of Alexander III;
  North, J.J.   *British Numismatic Journal* 60 (1990), 37–64.

Author's Note

The Lesser Seal's legend (Plate V) has its last word, *columbae*, 'doves', set to the left of the King's head. While a reader would concentrate on the document's contents, one unable to tackle clerkly script might manage to decipher letters enough to believe that St Columba's power was invoked. Might this have influenced the 1286 Seal's design (p. 235)?   MC

INDEX